HURRICANES
OVER
TOBRUK

THE PIVOTAL ROLE OF THE HURRICANE IN THE
DEFENCE OF TOBRUK, JANUARY – JUNE 1941

BRIAN CULL
WITH DON MINTERNE

GRUB STREET · LONDON

Published by
Grub Street
The Basement
10 Chivalry Road
London SW11 1HT

British Library Cataloguing in Publication Data
Cull, Brian
  Hurricanes over Tobruk
  1. Tobruk, Battles of, 1941-1942 2. World War, 1939-1945 –
  Libya – Tobruk – Aerial operations
  I. Title II. Minterne, Don
  940.5'423

ISBN 1-902304-11-X

Typeset by Pearl Graphics, Hemel Hempstead
Printed and bound in Great Britain by
Biddles Ltd, Guildford and King's Lynn

BRIAN CULL is the author of the following Grub Street titles:

AIR WAR FOR YUGOSLAVIA, GREECE AND CRETE 1940-41 with
  Christopher Shores and Nicola Malizia
MALTA: THE HURRICANE YEARS 1940-41 with Christopher Shores and
  Nicola Malizia
MALTA: THE SPITFIRE YEAR 1942 with Christopher Shores and
  Nicola Malizia
BLOODY SHAMBLES Volume 1 with Christopher Shores and Yasuho Izawa
BLOODY SHAMBLES Volume 2 with Christopher Shores and Yasuho Izawa
SPITFIRES OVER ISRAEL with Shlomo Aloni and David Nicolle
TWELVE DAYS IN MAY with Bruce Lander and Heinrich Weiss
WINGS OVER SUEZ with David Nicolle and Shlomo Aloni
249 AT WAR
THE DESERT HAWKS with Leo Nomis

CONTENTS

DEDICATION

This book is dedicated to the memory of, and as a tribute to, those who fell during the siege of Tobruk from all the warring nations and from all the services, including 5954436 Private Alexander Donald Macgregor of the 9th Battalion, The Durham Light Infantry – a first cousin I never knew – who was posted Missing, Presumed Killed in Action 27 June 1942. He has no known grave. His grieving twin sister was reputed to have died soon afterwards from a broken heart.

Brian Cull

One of the defenders of Tobruk composed a poignant and fitting epitaph for those left behind:

> There's a quiet spot even in Tobruk,
> There's a piece of hallowed ground, even there.
> Towards that spot our spirits look,
> And we spare a thought for those who lie forever there.
>
> Though we had to leave them behind
> When we at last returned to base,
> They are forever present in our mind
> And in our hearts they hold their place.
>
> We know their loved ones far away
> Will bravely bear their losses,
> For we have made the enemy pay
> For those rows of wooden crosses.
>
> So when the strife is o'er and done
> And to this land we say goodbye,
> 'Tis to those graves 'neath Libyan sun
> That our farewell thoughts will fly.

ACKNOWLEDGEMENTS

First and foremost, my sincere thanks to my wife Val for bearing with me during the long hours over the many months this book was under preparation. Her contribution to this, as with my earlier books, extends far beyond simply supplying copious cups of coffee and snacks plus the occasional tot of Scotch to keep me going under the constant pressure of trying to meet the deadline for completion, but to assisting with research, typing, editing and proof reading.

Much of the original material relating to 73 Squadron included in *Hurricanes over Tobruk* had been collected earlier by Don Minterne when researching for his *History of 73 Squadron, Part 2*, since that squadron played a vital role in the defence of Tobruk during the month of April 1941, the main focal point of this account. Don had interviewed and corresponded with several of the survivors of the siege and had obtained copies of important and relevant logbooks and diaries, together with accounts of those dark days. For access to this material, and many of the photographs used within, I herewith acknowledge his generosity.

My gratitude is extended to Mrs Nancy Rankin and her family for their permission to allow me to use extensive quotes from the journal of her late husband, Captain Kenneth Rankin; the journal was published under the title *Top Hats in Tobruk*, and is highly recommended; also to my long-standing Australian friend and fellow researcher/writer Russell Guest, who kindly supplied a copy of Sqn Ldr John Jackson's diary for the period covered by this account; and to Peter Moulding, a former pilot of 6 Squadron, for permission to quote from his book *Six Squadron* and for the entertaining meeting with him and his charming wife. Thanks is recorded for the assistance received from many others including old friend and eminent aviation historian Christopher Shores, particularly for permission to use quotes and photographs from his *Fighters over the Desert*, while much information and many photographs relating to the French pilots involved in the struggle for Tobruk were supplied by Christian-Jacques Ehrengardt, Vital Ferry, Bernard Baeza and Joss Leclercq, the latter two also providing translations of French-language material. Paul Sortehaug provided invaluable information, as did Heinrich Weiss, while Dennis Newton supplied photographs. Much of the Italian information came via the wonderfully generous Nico Malizia, as did many of the photographs, additional material being kindly provided by Gianandrea Bussi and Giovanni Massimello. Flt Lt Andy Thomas, as ever, kindly raided his private collection to supply certain unique photographs. Many published works were consulted, from which the odd extract is included in this account, and a list of these will be found in the Select Bibliography. Once again Chris Thomas has created an excellent and evocative illustration for the dustjacket, for which he is thanked. The staff of the Public Record Office, Mr Graham Day of AHB5 of the Ministry of Defence, and the staff of Bury St Edmunds Public Library are also to be thanked for their assistance. Last but not least, my special and personal thanks to Mr Jack Lee.

Finally, Don Minterne and I congratulate John Davies of Grub Street for yet another excellent production, the first of this new series.

Brian Cull
Bury St Edmunds 1999

TOBRUK:

A POTTED HISTORY

However seemingly insignificant to the world in 1940, Tobruk Bay was well known to ancient Greek and Roman seafarers as Antipyrgos, which means 'Opposite the Fire' – likely reference to a signal fire maintained by early settlers at a point on the coast to guide mariners on their voyages to distant Carthage. Ruins of Antipyrgos can still be seen near the promontory on which modern Tobruk is built. Before the arrival of the Italian colonists in the early part of this century, Antipyrgos/Tobruk had enjoyed a checkered 2,500 year history. Christianity came to North Africa and there was a Bishop of Antipyrgos. Following the decline of the Roman Empire in Western Europe, this part of North Africa remained within the 'East Roman' or Byzantine Empire until conquered by the Muslim Arabs in the seventh century. Christianity slowly gave way to Islam while Tobruk remained a trading post on both the coastal shipping and land caravan routes. The Muslims also built themselves a fine fortress on the north side of the bay. Later still, in the Middle Ages when the pirates of Barbary roamed the area, Antipyrgos was firstly renamed Tabarka and then Marsa Tobruk, or the Bay of Tobruk. Very rarely did Europeans venture to these parts during the ensuing centuries and, when they did, they did not much like what they found. By the sixteenth century the North African coastline was part of the Ottoman Empire but Marsa Tobruk was of negligible importance as a source of wealth. However, a new fortress was built by the Sultan to ward off any threat from Europe. By the nineteenth century nothing much had changed.

But changes were afoot during the early part of the twentieth century. Italy had long enviously eyed the excellent anchorage at Tobruk Bay, many of her citizens having settled further down the coast at Tripoli. As a means to challenge the Ottoman rulers, in 1911 the Italian government alleged interference by Turkish soldiers with its citizens living in Tripoli and thereby demanded a right to protect its subjects, following which Italian warships appeared off Tripoli and bombarded the town, while large fleets of transports initially carried 40,000 soldiers of occupation across the Mediterranean. Overhead, Italian biplanes dropped bombs on Turkish positions in and around Tripoli, the first-ever operational use of aerial bombing. Six Italian battleships then approached Tobruk Bay, accompanied by destroyers and torpedo-boats. A deputation was sent ashore but the Turkish garrison commander refused to surrender. The flagship opened fire, five shells blasting huge breaches in the walls of the fort, whereby surrender of the garrison quickly followed. With the Italian forces now in occupation, more guns were installed and more fortifications built. After the outbreak of war in 1914, the Senussi Libyans with their Turkish advisors (having sided with Germany) threatened to assault the Italian garrisons at Tobruk, Derna and Benghazi, but these never materialized. During the war years Allied ships used the port at Tobruk on occasion, Italy having joined forces with Britain and France in the world conflict. In 1917, Sayed Idriss, Emir of Cyrenaica and Tripoli and the younger cousin of the Grand Senussi, negotiated successfully at Tobruk with British and Italian representatives to bring an end to the desert fighting. But once peace had returned and Mussolini had become leader of Fascist Italy, with his grandiose schemes for a Second Roman Empire in North Africa, these Italian possessions became a threat to British dominance of the Mediterranean Sea and thereby the seaways to her Middle and Far East empires. Whoever controlled Tobruk (and Benghazi) – with their ports and adjacent airfields – effectively had control the central Mediterranean.

<u>INTRODUCTION and PREAMBLE</u>

THE WAR IN THE DESERT

June – November 1940

"The loss of Egypt will be the *coup de grâce* for Great Britain, while the conquest of that rich country, necessary for our communications with Ethiopia, will be the great reward for which Italy is waiting."

Benito Mussolini, Fascist Dictator of Italy,
to his North African commander, Marshal Rodolfo Graziani

Until Mussolini played his hand and entered the war on the side of Germany on 10 June 1940, British and Commonwealth forces in Egypt and Palestine could only stand by and watch in amazement and with trepidation as German troops steam-rollered their way across Western Europe; with insufficient numbers of men and unsuitable or obsolete equipment they would have been unable to alter the outcome even if they had the means to intervene. As a result of these over-whelming successes, with the Germans having reached the Channel ports and on the verge of invading Britain, Mussolini entered the arena and declared war on both Britain and France. But when the Regia Aeronautica launched its first tentative attacks against targets in Southern France it paid a costly price, as it did in early operations against the tiny British Mediterranean garrison at Malta; and as it did when its Libyan-based colonial air force carried out strikes against Egyptian border targets soon after the declaration of war. Under the command of General Felice Porro, Aeronautica della Libia (renamed 5^Squadra Aerea as from 5 July 1940) possessed a sizeable air force including nine squadrons of CR32 and CR42 biplane fighters, and in excess of 100 SM79 and SM81 tri-motor medium bombers (sixteen squadrons), plus a number of Ba65, Ca309 and Ca310 light bombers (nine squadrons) in addition to four squadrons of Ro37 observation aircraft. A considerable force against which the RAF's 202 Group commanded by Air Commodore R. Collishaw DSO DSC DFC, a Canadian WWI fighter ace, could range three squadrons of Gladiator biplane fighters (33, 80 and 112 Squadrons), five squadrons of Blenheim light bombers, one squadron equipped with Bombay and Valencia transport-cum-bombers, and one squadron (208) of Army Co-operation Lysanders. 80 Squadron also possessed the Middle East's one and only Hurricane (L1669[1] – nicknamed *Collie's Battleship*), which had been undergoing desert trials.

The battle ground over which the bitter contest was to take place comprised the northern coastline of Egypt and Libya, to a depth of some 60 to 100 miles, although most of the ground fighting would take place between Sollum and El Agheila in Cyrenaica, the eastern province of Libya. This area is rocky rather than sandy desert, while along parts of the coast salt marshes were inclined to become very boggy during the rainy season. To the south lies the mighty, impassable salt marsh known as the Qattara Depression and, to the west, the Great Sea Sand, the northern edge of the Sahara Desert. The area of land around the hills of Jebel el-Akhdar was reasonably fertile and had been colonized by Italian settlers, while the coastline was dotted with small towns and villages but within Cyrenaica there were two ports of some considerable importance – Benghazi on the western side of the province, and Tobruk on the eastern coast. Whoever controlled these ports effectively controlled the central Mediterranean.

Tobruk, a small, relatively unimportant town with a population in 1940 numbering about 1,000 Italian civil servants and shopkeepers, and 9,000 Arab civilians, did however possess a good, deep water harbour which housed three destroyers (*Aquilone, Euro, Nembo*) of the Regina Marina's 1^Squadriglia, and two squadrons of submarines (61^Squadriglia with *Sirena, Argonauta, Fisalia, Smeraldo,* and *Naiade*; 62^Squadriglia with *Diamante, Topazio, Nereide, Galatea,* and *Valoroso*, while the old cruiser *San Giorgio* was anchored in the harbour for AA defence duties. The town was dominated by a huge three-storied, concrete building overlooking the harbour which housed the naval headquarters. There was also the small civil aerodrome on the promontory (identified by the Italians as Tobruk 1, T1) and four landing grounds (numbered T2, T3, T4, and T5) within the garrison's perimeter where six squadrons of Fiat biplane fighters were based – 10°Gruppo CT with CR42s under TenCol Armando Piragino, which comprised 84^Squadriglia (Cap Luigi Monti), 90^Squadriglia (Cap Giovanni Guiducci), and 96^Squadriglia (Cap Roberto Fassi); three squadrons of CR32s – 8°Gruppo CT under Magg Vincenzo La Carrubba which comprised 92^Squadriglia (Cap Martino Zannier), 93^Squadriglia (Cap Mario Bacich), and 94^Squadriglia (Cap Franco Lavelli); there were also two squadrons of reconnaissance Ro37s – 73°Gruppo OA under Magg Adolfo Domenici (127^ and 137^ Squadriglie). In addition to the naval and air units there was a sizeable garrison of around 10,000 Italian and native troops stationed within the fortified defences. That, therefore, was Tobruk on the eve of hostilities, 10 June 1940.

Although the first official raid against Italian targets across the border by the RAF occurred at dawn on 11 June, when Blenheims attacked El Adem aerodrome where between 60 and 70 SM79s, SM81s, Ro37s and Ca309s were dispersed, an unofficial 'bombing' sortie was undertaken during the hours of darkness by none other than Air Commodore Collishaw himself, accompanied by a volunteer crew aboard an antiquated Valencia biplane transport nicknamed *Bessie*. With Collishaw at the controls the intrepid aviators took off from 202 Group's HQ at Ma'aten Bagush, a crate of hand-grenades stowed on board:

---

[1] L1669 was written off following a forced-landing at Amiriya on 30 September 1940 while serving with 274 Squadron.

"Drifting casually westwards, *Bessie* rose and fell on each air pocket. Her wing tip lay gently across the sleepy Mediterranean, gleaming in the brilliant moonlight, tumbling playfully against the warm sand of the North African coastline. 'Target ahead ... fingers out.' Collishaw broke the magic spell with unfeeling brusqueness. 'Listen, chaps ... I'm going down to zero feet. There's a couple of searchlights ahead, but they'll be looking for an aircraft, not a bus!' Flg Off Harvey [the co-pilot] swallowed a second time and sank even lower in his harness. For the last minute or so he had been anxiously trying to identify a small red light approaching dead ahead in their path. It was not until *Bessie* had passed about six feet below the red light that he realised it was fixed to the top of [a] transmitting aerial. 'Blimey, sir ...' he ventured, 'if the ack-ack doesn't get us, we'll be skewered on the radio station!' Collishaw grinned across at him 'I told you this would be a low level attack ... stand by, everybody, grenades at the ready ... when I shout, pull the pins and throw like hell ... if you don't get rid of them quick, we'll be about the only aircraft to shoot itself down ... Now!' Scattering grenades left and right, *Bessie* sauntered the length of the camp, her progress marked by pin-pricks of light as miniature explosions, more effective for their nuisance value than for their potence, plotted her erratic course." [2]

Under cover of darkness the Valencia returned safely to Ma'aten Bagush, her crew delighted with their unconventional achievement. With such an adventurous character in charge of 202 Group as Air Commodore Collishaw, it was little wonder that his men were inspired to face up to the challenge posed by such an overwhelmingly superior-in-numbers air force as that of Aeronautica della Libia.

When the Blenheims carried out their raids later in the morning, CR32s and CR42s from Tobruk rose to meet them, two of the bombers being claimed shot down and a further four damaged. Two Blenheims indeed failed to return and a third force-landed with battle damage. The shooting war had started in earnest and Tobruk's fighters had opened their account. The AOC-in-C RAFME[3], Air Chief Marshal Sir Arthur Longmore GCB DSO, wrote:

"By the 14th June reports of the results of this initial offensive had come in to my headquarters. From the Western Desert Collishaw reported successful attacks on El Adem airfield as well as on oil tanks and shipping at Tobruk. On the frontier at Fort Amseat an ammunition dump had been blown up. This was a very promising start, the promptness of our air attacks within a few hours of Mussolini's declaration of war had obviously taken the Italians by surprise."

202 Group's fighters made their first claims on the 14th when a flight of Gladiators from 33 Squadron intercepted a formation of Ca310s and their CR32 escort over Fort Capuzzo. One of each type was shot down by the Gladiator pilots.

---

[2] Keith Hine in *RAF Flying Review*.
[3] Air Chief Marshal Longmore's command covered all RAF units in Egypt, Sudan, Palestine and Transjordan, East Africa, Aden and Somaliland, Iraq and adjacent territories, Cyprus, Mediterranean Sea, Red Sea and the Persian Gulf.

80 Squadron's Hurricane was in action on the 19th, flown by Flg Off P.G. Wykeham-Barnes, temporarily attached to 33 Squadron at Mersa Matruh, who claimed two CR42s shot down in an engagement in the Sollum area. Accompanying Gladiators claimed two more for the loss of one of their own (Italian claims were for three Gladiators shot down). The Fiats were from T2-based 10°Gruppo CT, two of which were totally lost with one pilot killed and the other, the Gruppo commander, TenCol Piragino, taken prisoner. Tobruk's fighters were involved in an unusual action on the 20th when a CR42 and two CR32s engaged and damaged a reconnoitring Sunderland flying boat off Tobruk harbour; the following day Gladiators erroneously attacked HMAS *Sydney*'s Seagull amphibian which was spotted during a bombardment of Bardia by naval forces. The badly damaged FAA aircraft reached Mersa Matruh safely but its undercarriage collapsed on landing.

The Italians suffered a morale-bruising blow on the 28th when the renowned aviator Maresciallo dell'Aria Italo Balbo was killed while flying an SM79 to Tobruk. Approaching the garrison from seaward shortly after a raid by Blenheims on T2 landing ground – which had destroyed a CR42 of 90^Squadriglia, damaged several others in addition to two CR32s and five Ro37s, killed six airmen and wounded three pilots, one of whom died during the night – Balbo's aircraft, one of two SM79s in formation (the other containing General Porro, commander of Aeronautica della Libia) was fired on by the AA cruiser *San Giorgio* anchored in the harbour. All on board were killed – and Italy had lost a champion and a hero. Air Chief Marshal Longmore wrote:

> "At the end of June, Marshal Balbo, the Italian Governor-General of Cyrenaica, was killed in his aircraft by the anti-aircraft guns of one of his own cruisers. This Italian was an international figure in the aviation world, known to many British air-travellers; as a mark of respect I had a suitably worded note dropped over the frontier by an aircraft on reconnaissance. In due course a reply was dropped by an Italian machine from my opposite number expressing, 'Deep thanks for your message of sympathy'. Perhaps it was just as well this colourful personality did not live to see the humiliation of his country in defeat."

Action flared up again on the 29th when Gladiators of 33 Squadron encountered a number of CR32s over the Ridotto-Cappuzo area and claimed two shot down; in addition, an Ro37 and an SM81 were also shot down, the same unit accounting for two more Fiat biplanes the following day. Since the outbreak of hostilities, Tobruk-based fighters had also taken a steady toll of raiding and reconnaissance Blenheims and by the end of the month the Italian pilots reckoned they had raised their tally to 22 RAF aircraft shot down (twelve Blenheims and ten Gladiators), for the loss of three pilots (two killed, one PoW) – an impressive, although exaggerated, record. At the end of the month 8°Gruppo CT changed its CR32s for CR42s, and a few days later reinforcements arrived at Tobruk in the guise of 18 new CR42s of 13°Gruppo CT from Castel Benito, which landed at T2.

80 Squadron at Amiriya also received some welcome reinforcement when three more Hurricanes arrived (on 13 June), these having been flown out from the UK via France and Tunisia, followed by another three on 21 June, and five more by

26 June, the latter having staged through Malta[4]. Other new arrivals included two French Morane MS406 fighters from Syria. When Italy entered the war, RAFME Command had requested assistance from the French in Syria since they were operating the most modern fighters in the area. Accordingly, Général Mittelhauser, the French GOC in the Orient, authorised GCI/7 based at Estabel south of Rayak in the Lebanon to move to Egypt, a vanguard of three MS406s arriving at Ismailia on 23 June. The pilots were Lt Antoine Péronne, who badly damaged his aircraft (No833) on landing, Adjt-Chef Charles Coudray (No826), and Adjt-Chef André Ballatore (No827). Six mechanics to service the aircraft were also sent to Egypt aboard two Fokker VIIIs. Following the armistice between Germany and France, the French contingent at Ismailia was given the choice of returning to Estabel or remaining in Egypt, although it was stressed that the Moranes would not be released. The Frenchmen decided unanimously to remain despite pleas of French officers who were sent from Beirut to persuade them to return. Two days later they were joined by Cne Paul Jacquier of GAO 1/583 based at Koussair in Syria, who landed at Ismailia in a twin-engine Potez Po63-11 reconnaissance aircraft (No699). He was followed on 30 June by a Bloch 81 and two Caudron Simouns. Another Po63-11 (No670) arrived on 3 July in the hands of Sgt-Chef Marcel Lebois of GRII/39 from Damascus, and was joined shortly thereafter by a third Potez (No395) flown by Adjt Albert Lamour-Zevacco. Among the passengers on board these aircraft were Sous-Lts Jean Pompéï and Daniel Clostre, both of whom were destined to retrain on Hurricanes, as were several of the other escapees. Two Martin 167Fs from GBI/30 were soon to join the ad hoc unit, which was then officially named Free French Flight No2[5] (Free French Flight No1 had already been formed in England, see later).

Meanwhile, on the ground the Italians continued to build up their forces in eastern Cyrenaica in preparation for an offensive operation across the border into Egypt. Mussolini – who declared himself to be "the protector of Islam" – was keen to take the initiative but Marshal Graziani hesitated. He complained that his tanks were inferior to those of the British – even British armoured cars could out-gun the Italian light tanks – while the intense summer heat – often reaching 50°C (122°F) – suggested he should wait before launching his offensive. So he delayed, much to Mussolini's annoyance.

Air operations during July followed those already established – raids by Blenheims against airfields and other military targets and border skirmishes by patrolling Gladiators. 33 Squadron claimed a CR32 shot down near Capuzzo on the 1st, two CR42s over Sollum on the 4th, then later the same day caught more CR42s of 8°Gruppo CT taking off from the advanced landing ground at Menastir, shooting down six and damaging four more (although claiming nine shot down) for the loss of one Gladiator whose pilot baled out. Three 2°Stormo pilots were killed including the CO of 94^Squadriglia, three others were taken prisoner and yet three more were

---

[4] The Hurricanes included N2624, N2499, P2544, P2627, P2638, P2639, P2641, P2687, P2695, and P2864.

[5] The two airworthy Moranes were allotted RAF serial numbers AX674 (No826) and AX675 (No827); the Potez Po63-11s were re-serialled AX672 (No670), AX673 (No699) and AX680 (No395).

wounded. The Gladiators of 80 Squadron also achieved some success when they intercepted ten SM79s north of Alexandria, claiming one probably destroyed. There were further engagements on the 15th when 33 Squadron accounted for an SM79 near Mersa Matruh, then on the 23rd the Gladiators encountered 18 CR42s of 10° and 13°Gruppi CT over Sollum and claimed four shot down. More success came the way of 33 Squadron next day when its pilots claimed five CR42s for the loss of one Gladiator, the Italian pilots claiming five. The same unit met more CR42s next day, again claiming five shot down. By the end of the month, Tobruk-based CR42s had increased their tally by 15, having claimed ten Gladiators, four Blenheims and a Sunderland.

There were two major clashes between the Gladiators and Tobruk's CR42s during August, the first occurring on the 4th when 80 Squadron's B Flight, which had replaced 33 Squadron at Sidi Barrani, encountered seven Ba65s escorted by CR42s near Bir Taieb el-Esem. This time the Gladiators came off second best, three being shot down including Flg Off Wykeham-Barnes (who baled out) and another returned badly damaged with a wounded pilot. Although B Flight claimed four victories in the fight none were apparently confirmed; the Fiats claimed four Gladiators and three Blenheims shot down. The second major engagement occurred on the 8th when 80 Squadron claimed nine CR42s (seven actual losses) for two Gladiators; Wykeham-Barnes was again involved, none the worse for his parachute jump four days earlier, and was credited with one of the victories. Patrols over the Fleet, which was returning to Alexandria from a bombardment on Bardia on the 17th, brought further combat for the Gladiators of 80 and 112 Squadrons when the warships came under attack from SM79s, two being claimed shot down. One of 80 Squadron's Hurricanes (P2544) was on detachment at Mersa Matruh, Flg Off J.H. Lapsley also meeting the raiders, three of which he claimed shot down. The two Moranes of Free French Flight No2, temporarily attached to 80 Squadron, also flew operational patrols over the Fleet but failed to encounter any of the Italian raiders. CR42 claims for the month of August totalled 16 including one Sunderland and three Blenheims; the others were for Gladiators. 202 Group was about to be reinforced by the arrival of personnel of 3RAAF Squadron which was to be equipped with a mixture of Lysanders, Gauntlets and Gladiators, although it would be some weeks before the unit was operational. But a new fighter squadron was established on 19 August when ten pilots of A Flight (the Hurricane Flight) of 80 Squadron were detached to form 274 Squadron, which was intended to be the first all-Hurricane unit, while 80 Squadron was to revert to an all-Gladiator unit until sufficient numbers of Hurricanes had arrived for its pilots to convert and retrain. The CO of 80 Squadron, Sqn Ldr P.H. Dunn, took command of the new unit and was joined by experienced Hurricane pilots Wykeham-Barnes and Lapsley, who became his flight commander[6]. The Moranes and Po63-11s of the French Flight, now fitted with desert air filters, were also absorbed into 274 Squadron, becoming its C Flight, while the Martins were sent to Aden – where both were subsequently shot down by Italian fighters – and the light aircraft (the Bloch 81 and two Simouns) joined the Communications Flight as Free French Flight 3 at Heliopolis.

---

[6] The first six operational Hurricanes were P2544, P2638, P2639, P2641, P2643 and P2651, while L1669 was used mainly for conversion and training duties.

The French airmen with the various Flights were offered honorary RAF ranks, Cne Jacquier, the Fighter Flight commander, becoming a Flight Lieutenant, others the rank equivalent to their Armée de l'Air status, but not all accepted the offer and these were allowed to retain their French ranks. Général de Gaulle, leader of the Free French, on learning of the absorption into the RAF of several of his officers, angrily declared his intention to denounce them as deserters and thereby liable to arrest and trial for desertion should they enter French-controlled territory, since Prime Minister Churchill had agreed that de Gaulle's volunteers should be recognised as a French force with its own uniform and discipline! The Prime Minister was forced to intervene and a compromise was reached. However, the French Flight's association with 274 Squadron was soon interrupted when orders were received at the end of the month for it to proceed to Haifa in Palestine[7].

By the beginning of September, Italian troops were massing on the frontier and it was obvious that and attack was imminent, but it was not until the 13th that Marshal Graziani's forces advanced into Egypt. The invasion force comprised four infantry divisions and an armoured group with 200 light and medium tanks. The Commonwealth forces fell back and by 17 September the Italians had advanced 60 miles in just four days, but then they halted and began to construct a line of fortified camps extending from Sidi Barrani on the coast to 50 miles inland. Here Graziani intended to consolidate and improve his supply lines until cooler weather arrived, before continuing his push eastwards. That was the plan. In Cairo, the speed of events fired rumours of imminent British defeat which were tempered by the decision to evacuate to South Africa wives and children of all British military personnel stationed in Egypt, except those women engaged in official war work. The news was not well received in the civilian community and only served to inflame the passions of Egyptian nationalists who wished to see the end of British rule in their country. The Egyptian government had, until now, refused to be drawn into the military conflict by declaring war on Germany and Italy, although under the terms of the Anglo-Egyptian Treaty it was committed to pledge its full co-operation. Indeed, three squadrons of the Royal Egyptian Air Force – two equipped with Gladiators and the other with Lysanders – were attached to the RAF's 202 Group and were based at Helwan, Dekheila and the Baharia Oasis respectively.

There was surprisingly little aerial conflict during the month, despite the Italian offensive. The CR42s were kept busy intercepting mainly Blenheims, of which they claimed two on the 4th, one on the 20th, five on the 18th, one on the 25th, and another on the 27th, and two more on the 30th, also shooting down a Sunderland. Similarly, the Gladiators and Hurricanes reported several engagements with SM79s, Flt Lt Lapsley in Hurricane P2544/YK-T of 274 Squadron shooting down two on the 10th. He got another on the 15th, as did a second Hurricane pilot, Sgt J.H. Clarke (P2641). By the end of September the first five Hurricanes and four Blenheims to operate the air route across Africa from Takoradi on the Gold Coast, via Nigeria, French Equatorial Africa, Sudan, to Egypt, had arrived at Abu Sueir.

---

[7] From Haifa airfield on 6 September 1940, a Po63-11 flown by Flg Off Péronne and a Morane piloted by Wt Off Ballatore were scrambled on the approach of four Italian bombers, but they failed to intercept. The Moranes were scrambled twice more during September on separate occasions (flown by Wt Offs Coudray and Ballatore) but again without success. On the first of these occasions – 21 September – Haifa was heavily bombed with the loss of 32 lives.

More were soon to follow. The Takoradi route was the direct result of the loss of the French African empire to Britain, which generated a masterly piece of improvisation by a small RAF servicing unit which had arrived in August to facilitate and expand the base to be capable of handling up to 120 aircraft a month. Along the route which Imperial Airways had pioneered pre-war, runways had to be built or extended, accommodation improved or constructed, and meteorological and signals facilities installed. The first batch of crated aircraft had arrived in early September.

There was only one major clash between Tobruk's fighters and RAF fighters during October, this occurring on the last day of the month when 33 Squadron with its new Hurricanes[8] encountered SM79s escorted by CR42s over Mersa Matruh. Three of the bombers were claimed shot down – two were seen to be shot down by Flg Off E.K. Leveille who was then shot down by Serg Mario Veronesi and killed, the other by Flg Off P.R. St Quintin, who claimed a second as probably destroyed – but two Hurricanes were lost including P3724 (Leveille), the second (St Quintin) crash-landing after being attacked by Ten Guglielmo Chiarini and Serg Francesco Nanin – the Italian biplanes' first victories against the Hurricane. A CR42 was claimed in return by Flg Off F.S. Holman (P3725), Ten Gianfranco Perversi being killed, while Flg Off H.J. Starrett (P3729) claimed an SM79 as possibly destroyed. Gladiators of 112 Squadron also engaged and claimed three CR42s for the loss of five of their own, two of which collided. The CR42s continued to knock down the occasional Blenheim, claiming three on the 12th and two on the 25th, plus a Wellington and a Lysander. Early November also proved relatively quiet in the air, CR42s shooting down another Lysander on the 13th, but five days later 3RAAF clashed for the first time with CR42s, losing its CO. Three of the Fiats were claimed in return. 112 Squadron also enjoyed some success. Having accounted for an SM79 on the 18th, six Gladiators engaged a large number of CR42s over Sidi Barrani and claimed no fewer than eight shot down (actual losses were three shot down and four damaged) for no loss, while the Italians claimed all six Gladiators. Italian fighter claims were wildly extravagant for November, the CR42 pilots reporting to have destroyed ten Gladiators and two Hurricanes in addition to two Blenheims and the Lysander.

One incident, away from the frontier battle zone, which caused much consternation during the month occurred on the night of 19 October when Italian bombers carried out a raid on Cairo, bombs falling on the suburb of Maadi. However, the city – one of the most sacred to Islam – was not again targeted since the Italians and their German allies were keen not to antagonize the Egyptians into throwing their lot in with the British. And, after all, Egypt was technically neutral. However, as a result of the initial bombing, the priceless treasures represented by the Great Pyramid of Khufu on the Giza Plateau, the smaller Pyramids of Khafre and Menkaure and the attendant Great Sphinx were considered to be endangered by aerial bombing, the Sphinx in particular being afforded a protective anti bomb-blast sand-bag barrier to the vital breast and head areas. In the event, the pharaohs from their lofty thrones high above looked after their legacies and one of the world's seven greatest wonders was spared the ravages of modern war[9].

---

[8] The first ten Hurricanes allocated to 33 Squadron were N2624, N2628, N2640, N2646, P3724, P3725, P3726, P3727, P3728, P3729.

[9] The next intentional bombing attack on Cairo occurred during the first Arab/Israeli war, when, on the evening of 15 July 1948, a lone B-17 bomber flown by an American Jewish

During November 208 Squadron received some Hurricanes for visual reconnaissance duties, and it was joined in these duties by a detachment of Lysanders from 6 Squadron which was based in Palestine. By late November it was becoming increasingly apparent that for the French Fighter Flight at Haifa to remain operational it would need to re-equip with British aircraft, namely Hurricanes, and by the end of the year it was disbanded and the pilots sent to 70 OTU at Ismailia for conversion. By then another escapee had joined their ranks, Cne Jean Tulasne, who had reached Haifa in his Morane (No819) on 5 December[10]. Meanwhile, the Fighter Flight commander, Flt Lt Jacquier, had suffered a broken back as a result of an accident in a Magister which he had force-landed following engine failure. During his period of recovery and convalescence, Jacquier was visited by the AOC-in-Chief RAFME, Air Chief Marshal Longmore, who had been authorised to offer the French pilots a substantial bonus for the aircraft they had contributed to the British cause. Following discussion with his pilots, Jacquier was requested to refuse the offer, at which the Air Ministry cabled the following message:

> "The Air Council are warmly appreciative of the extremely friendly spirit shown by the crews of No2 Free French Flight in offering to turn over their bonus of £767.10s as a contribution to the common defence. We should very much like to give public expression to our appreciation but there are reasons against such publicity which you will appreciate."

By the end of November, with the intensification of activity in the Balkans, 80 Squadron had moved to Greece with its Hurricanes, and was soon followed by Gladiator-equipped 112 Squadron and two Blenheim squadrons, but despite this drastic reduction in his air force, the British GOC, General Sir Archie Wavell decided to make a reconnaissance in force against the Italian defences at Sidi Barrani. With the Italian forces consolidating and apparently content with their successes, Wavell felt it was the right time to strike back (Operation *Compass*). Having received a recent reinforcement of tanks and men, Wavell was able to amass 31,000 troops and 275 tanks, plus 60 armoured cars and 120 guns, all supported by two squadrons of Hurricanes (33 and 274), one of Gladiators (3RAAF), two tactical reconnaissance units with Lysanders and a flight of Hurricanes (208 plus a detachment from 6), three squadrons of Blenheims and three squadrons of Wellingtons, plus one transport-cum-bomber unit with Bombays. A third Hurricane unit, 73 Squadron, was on its way to reinforce 202 Group.

---

crew en route from Czechoslovakia to the new state of Israel, attempted to bomb the Egyptian Army Officers' School and King Farouk's residence, Abdin Palace. The eight 250kg bombs missed their targets, four falling in a crowded area of poor housing near the Palace, killing and wounding a number of civilians – perhaps as many as 85 of whom 30 were fatal: see *Spitfires over Israel* by Brian Cull and Shlomo Aloni with David Nicolle, published by Grub Street.

[10] One further escapee from Syria arrived in Egypt early in 1941 when Sgt-Chef J.M.J. Nevraumont landed at Ismailia in another Po63-11 (No420) from GRII/39, which was renumbered AX691. After retraining and conversion to the Hurricane, Nevraumont joined 73 Squadron.

CHAPTER I

OPERATION *COMPASS*:
THE PUSH TOWARDS TOBRUK

December 1940 – January 1941

"... the Italian Air Force was no longer capable of offering any serious threat
for the time being. It looked as if it would be some time before the enemy
would be able to stage an early counter-offensive in Libya."

Air Chief Marshal Longmore, AOC-in-C RAFME

73 Squadron, under the command of Sqn Ldr A.D. Murray, who had spent a number
of years attached to the FAA, departed the UK on 15 November aboard the aircraft
carrier HMS *Furious*, its air echelon swelled to 34 by the addition of spare pilots
including two temporarily attached from the FAA; they were: Flt Lt M.L.ff.
Beytagh (A Flight commander), Flt Lt J.D. Smith (Canadian, B Flight commander),
Flg Offs D.S. Scott DFC, J.E. Storrar DFC, Plt Offs W.T. Eiby RNZAF, G.E.
Goodman, R.L Goord, C.K. Gray, P. Haldenby, P.C. Humphreys, C.C.O. Joubert
(South African), O.E. Lamb RNZAF, B.P. Legge, J.B. McColl (Canadian),
A. McFadden, K.M. Millist, A.G. Wainwright, and M.P. Wareham; Sgts G.W.
Brimble, H.W. Coussens, R.V. Ellis, G.W. Garton, G.E.C. Genders, J. Griffith, R.I.
Laing RNZAF, A.B. Leng, A.E. Marshall, J. Stenhouse, H.G. Webster, J. White, and
W.C. Wills. The two attached FAA pilots were Sub Lts D.H. Richards and R.W.M.
Walsh. Several of the pilots were combat experienced including both flight
commanders, Flt Lt 'Smudger' Smith with three victories, and Flt Lt Mike Beytagh
(two victories), both Battle of Britain veterans, while Palestinian-born Plt Off
George 'Benny' Goodman (of English father and Russian mother) was one of the
more successful with ten victories of which four were shared, Flg Off Donald Scott
(six and two shared) and Sgts Fred Marshall (one and one shared), Ron 'Monty'
Ellis (four shared), and Geoff Garton (two) had flown in both France and the Battle
of Britain. Flg Off 'Jas' Storrar (eight and three shared), Plt Off Clifford Gray (two)
and Sgt John 'Jack' White (three and two shared) were also veterans of the air
battles over England earlier in the year.

The Hurricanes, their wings removed, were stowed in the carrier's hangars. The
plan (codenamed Operation *Stripe*) was for *Furious* to sail to West Africa from

where the Hurricanes were to be flown via Takoradi to Egypt, a total distance of 3,700 miles. One of 73 Squadron's pilots aboard *Furious*, Sgt Garton, recorded in his diary:

"By 1000 on the 15th *Furious* was out of dock [Gladstone Dock, Birkenhead] and beginning to move under her own steam. There was some excitement at midday when we rammed a small sloop which sank in about ten minutes, although all the occupants escaped without even a wetting in their own boat. We were well clear of land and heading NW around the top of Ireland when CO told us that we were bound for Sierra Leone and the Gold Coast. We would have to fly off the carrier and land at Takoradi, then fly across Africa to Cairo. Brim (Sgt George Brimble) and myself played cards all night with two POs [Petty Officers] and went to bed about 1000, the first time in many weeks that I had gone to bed stone cold sober! The sea was calm and we sergeants were being looked after very well by the POs. On the 16th we met up with the rest of our convoy and escort. Three carriers and five destroyers, plus a Sunderland overhead for most of the morning and three Skuas [of the carrier's resident 801 Squadron] at readiness on deck made for a secure feeling. Again it was cards for most of the evening followed by a stroll around the Flight Deck before turning in. It seemed strange to hear the football results on the [BBC] Home Service hundreds of miles out to sea."

Another of the NCO pilots, Sgt Marshall, also maintained a diary:

"After the first couple of days there was a tremendous sea running, in fact the lower Flight Deck was under water at times. During the night of 15th/16th we missed collision with a large ship by what was stated to be 20 yards. The 17th sticks in my mind as by far the worst day I have ever spent at sea: the wind was gusting to 60 knots and the sea was beyond description, at times reaching the Flight Deck which was 65 feet above the waterline. There was damage to the starboard side and the motor launch was stove in, and in addition there was damage to some of our Hurricane mainplanes. The destroyer escort left us in the morning to seek more sheltered water. There were two lectures on the 18th, the first about the ship by a lieutenant commander, which was just a bind, then one by the CO who gave us maps and all the gen he had about Takoradi. Whether he meant it or not, it all sounded pretty grim. By the 20th the temperature had reached unpleasant levels, and it became very uncomfortable below decks."

Sgt Garton's diary continues:

"By the morning of the 22nd we seemed at last to have shaken off the depression brought on my the yellow fever jabs, and we watched three Skuas take off to search for the two destroyers which we supposed to join us for escort work. We were all somewhat shaken by the way they [the Skuas] staggered off the deck, and the landings appeared even more fearsome. The tannoy came up with the unwelcome news that Jerry submarines were active off Freetown and had already sunk one steamship. Two ships were spotted on the horizon at 1330, and we all assumed that they were French, but our escorting cruiser dashed across to find that they were Spanish trawlers. The temperature in the hangars reached 125 degrees. Then, on the 24th, the evening watch reported that two torpedoes had been fired at us, presumably by an enemy sub. On Monday 25th, *Furious* dropped anchor in Freetown harbour. We were met instantly by dozens of blacks coming out singly in small canoes which were rather primitive and appeared to be made from solid tree trunks. They had all had considerable acquaintance with Englishmen, as their songs were the popular ones current in the UK, and the language would not have been out of place in Billingsgate Fish Market. The were diving over the side for coins, and trying with little success to sell us fruit. The CO told us we could go ashore that afternoon if we wore some decent attire and conducted ourselves in a fit manner as representatives of His Majesty's far-flung Empire. He also warned us of the dangers of eating fruit as the whole town was alive with malaria germs, dysentery etc. We scrounged 'whites' from the friendly POs and spent a lot of effort with coloured chalk to ensure that our tapes [stripes] would satisfy the Duty Officer, but it was to no avail as shore leave – for the sergeants at least – was scrubbed and we weighed anchor at 2230, leaving the harbour under cover of darkness. Next day was to be our last on board and we enjoyed a farewell party given to us by the POs."

Furious arrived off Takoradi on the morning of 27 November, and the Hurricanes began taking-off in sections of four, Sqn Ldr Murray leading the first section. Tasmanian-born Sgt Bob Laing RNZAF was in the first batch:

"I was in the first five or six to take-off. *Furious* had a small but distinct step about half or two-thirds of the way along the Flight Deck which, I understood, was to flip a heavily-laden Stringbag [Swordfish] or whatever into the air. There was a FAA pilot whose job was to stand on the port mainplane to give a few last words of advice, and to make absolutely certain that the man taking off was in fine pitch. I found it all much less trouble than I had anticipated and, aided by the healthy headwind and about +3lb of boost, the Hurricane was off with a light touch on the stick well before reaching the ramp. It was fortunate that it was a short flight to Takoradi – I had, in a moment of forgetfulness, put my helmet in my kitbag, and had to put up with the howl of the Merlin in my unprotected ears for the half hour or so, which just shows how stupid one can be at times."

Sgt Marshall was in the section led by Flt Lt Smith, and recorded:

"We started lining up our machines at about 1330, after the [six] Skuas and [three] Fulmars had flown off, and at about 1630 Smithy, Wainwright, Lamb and myself got all set, then when Wainwright's turn came he went in over the deck – it certainly appeared to me he was trying to get off in coarse pitch. It shook me up a bit, as I was the next to go. We all landed at Takoradi in the dusk: 30 minutes in V7483 for me."

Flg Off Storrar remembered:

"We lost one chap who took off in course pitch, his Hurricane dropping down in front of the *Furious* which then ran over him. Luckily he survived and was picked up by the cruiser HMS *Naiad*. The captain of *Furious* sent a message to the cruiser, saying 'Well fielded, *Naiad*'. Ours were the first Hurricanes to land at Takoradi ..."

Plt Off Alex Wainwright survived his ducking and was plucked from the sea, shaken but uninjured except for a few cuts and bruises. Next day six more Hurricanes flew to Takoradi, followed by the final dozen on the morning of 29 November. Flg Off Scott led the final batch of Hurricanes:

"I led the second batch. *Furious* had some damage to one of her propellers which restricted her speed to 21 knots. It was as well that there was a strong and steady wind blowing that she could steam into – with 15 [*sic*] other Hurricanes on the deck behind me, the available take-off run was far from being the full length of the deck.

I had a talk with Wainwright when he returned, and he said he went so deep that the water was completely black. Like all of us, he was expecting to be hit by the ship's props as it passed over him, but some smart work on the bridge changed course enough to bring him to the side rather than the stern. We all checked each other's cockpit before take-off; I have come to suspect that his prop pitch control might have been connected back to front, so that in selecting 'fully fine', he got maximum coarse pitch."

All aircraft of the second batch landed safely at Takoradi, where the Hurricanes were split into groups of six for the journey across central Africa to Heliopolis in Egypt, each group to be escorted by a Blenheim for navigation purposes. The first group departed Takoradi on the first leg to Lagos on 28 November, Sqn Ldr Murray (V7566) leading Plt Offs Humphreys (V7556), Legge (V7555), McFadden (V7837), and Sgts Laing (V7347) and Brimble (V7563). All went well until the formation reached Fort-Lamy in French Equatorial Africa on 1 December, where McFadden's aircraft developed battery trouble and was left behind; the remainder pressed on to El Geneina in the Sudan but unfortunately, as darkness was descending, the Blenheim lost its bearings owing to W/T failure. Sqn Ldr Murray recalled:

"Our lead Blenheim transmitted increasingly urgent requests for a homing, finally switching to 'Mayday'. I could not hear this, and my first indication that something was wrong was when the Blenheim started a square search. The sun was getting low, and of course in those regions it goes quite suddenly from daylight to dark, so I flew alongside the Blenheim and signalled that we ought to get down while we could still see."

All six aircraft had to carry out emergency landings at a desolate location near Rullu, 60 miles south-east of their original destination. The Blenheim got down safely, followed by the CO whose aircraft tipped up on its nose and one wingtip. Humphreys stalled in from ten feet, his aircraft breaking its back but he was uninjured apart from a cut on his head, while Legge made a creditable landing. Laing's aircraft was slightly damaged but Brimble spun in from 200 feet and was killed. Bob Laing reflected:

> "I hit a soft patch of sand which dragged the wheels and put me over on the
> prop tips despite full back pressure on the stick and using no brakes."

The party had no food other than their emergency rations, and very little water. On the next morning the CO set off in the most promising direction, building cairns of stones every so often as an aid for the return journey. Eventually he came across a native policeman who rounded up some soldiers from the local militia and the party made its way back to the crash site where the soldiers unshipped the shovels they had brought with them and dug down about four feet into a wadi to find water. Meanwhile, the CO, having borrowed a donkey, set off for help and after "an epic ride" got word through to Geneina. A salvage and repair party eventually arrived, took away the wrecks and checked over the damaged machines. The Blenheim and the three airworthy Hurricanes took off from an improvised runway just outside the wadi and reached El Geneina safely, from where they flew to Heliopolis, arriving on Christmas Eve. Plt Off Eiby remembered their return:

> "I picked up old Bob Laing in his shorts – he was as brown as a bloody berry.
> Bob had done a lot for them when they were down there, morale wise. The CO
> sent for me [being a fellow New Zealander and an officer] and said, 'Your
> friend Laing did a magnificent job when we were down and helped a
> tremendous lot ... but he will have to stop calling me 'cock' and treating me
> with great casualness – I just can't have this going on. The reason I am sending
> you to do this for me is that he has done so much good I'd hate to have him in
> the office and tell him that myself and that it was a disciplinary matter.' So I
> went along and saw old Bob in the Sgts Mess and told him to stop calling Sqn
> Ldr Murray 'cock'!"

In the meantime the remaining 27 Hurricanes[1] had all safely reached Heliopolis with the exception of Sgt Marshall's original machine (V7483) which had been left at Maiduguri following fuel pump trouble. At Maiduguri, however, was P3967 which had been left behind by the very first delivery flight, but was now airworthy and, aboard this, Marshall arrived with his group. One or two other pilots experienced delays, while Plt Off Joubert's mount (P3977) was also non-73 Squadron issue but one allocated at Takoradi to replace the one lost on take-off from the carrier. By 9 December all were reunited at Heliopolis except those still at Geneina, and Plt Off Wainwright, who was still at Takoradi following his enforced dip in the sea. The Squadron now learned of the award of the DFC to Plt Off Goodman for his performances earlier in the year, while news of a DFM for Sgt Jack White followed soon after. Both Plt Off Gray and Sgt Genders were posted away to 70 OTU, and the two attached FAA pilots, Sub Lts Richards and Walsh, were sent to the RNAS at Dekheila, to where B Flight with five Hurricanes under the command of Flt Lt Beytagh were despatched to aid the defence of Alexandria; three other pilots travelled by road. About a dozen of the Hurricanes were destined for other units and those earmarked for 73 Squadron were not repainted in desert colours at this stage but retained their dark green/dark earth European-style camouflage, and 73 Squadron's code letters, TP, were applied, together with individual aircraft letters. Thus V7562 became TP-A, V7478 became TP-B, V7371 became TP-C, V7299 became TP-D, and so forth.

* * *

Within three days of the start of Operation *Compass* on 9 December, Sidi Barrani was again in British hands and the Commonwealth forces were poised to move against Bardia. 3RAAF, which had a Gauntlet Flight, carried out dive-bombing attacks while Hurricanes maintained patrols over the battle area, those of 33 Squadron meeting CR42s while ground strafing. Three of the biplanes were claimed shot down (two by Flg Off Woodward), plus one probable, in return for a Hurricane which had to force-land with combat damage. Shortly after midday seven Hurricanes of 274 Squadron led by Sqn Ldr Dunn encountered five SM79s of 229^Squadriglia, claiming one shot down near Bir Zigdin el-Hamra by Plt Off Stan Godden (N2624) and two more near Sofafi; the remaining two were claimed damaged. These were shared by the other members of the Flight – Sqn Ldr Dunn (P3723), Flt Lt Wykeham-Barnes P2638), Flg Off E.M. Mason (P3722), Plt Off P.H. Preston (P3720) and Flt Sgt T.C. Morris (V7300), although Flt Lt Lapsley missed out, as he recalled, ruefully:

> "I was flying a brand new aircraft [V7293] which had just come up from the depot, on its first sortie, and having positioned myself at nice close range behind the leader, pressed the gun firing button to find the guns had not been cocked."

274 Squadron was again in action in the afternoon when 27 CR42s were met over the Sidi Barrani-Sofafi area, the Hurricane pilots reporting five confirmed victories and three probables for one Hurricane damaged, Wykeham-Barnes (plus two probables) and Sqn Ldr Dunn (P3723), who also claimed a probable, again scoring. Flg Off T.L. Patterson (P3720), a Canadian who had joined the Squadron in October, claimed another, while Flt Lt Lapsley (V7293) had his first successful fight with a CR42:

> "The Hurricane was of course vastly superior to the CR42 in speed and armament and also carried armour plating. However, the manoeuvrability of the CR42s in comparison to the Hurricanes made them difficult to shoot down

---

1 2nd Flight: V7546 (Scott), V7483/P3967 (Marshall, see text), V7489 (Wareham), V7561 (Wills), V7562 (Haldenby), V7560 (White); 3rd Flight: V7553 (Smith), V7554 (Lamb), V7478 (Goord), V7492 (Coussens), V7424 (Walsh), V7491 (Richards); 4th Flight: V7544 (Storrar), V7371 (Garton), V7552 (Millist), V7551 (Webster), V7484 (Griffith), V7559 (Ellis); 5th Flight: P3977 (Joubert), V7372 (McColl), V7545 (Gray), V7558 (Genders), V7557 (Stenhouse), V7550 (Leng); 6th Flight: V7299 (Beytagh), V7423 (Eiby), V7353 (Goodman).

once they had seen you unless they were foolish enough to endeavour to disengage by diving, and most of us fought many engagements with CR42s which developed into an unending series of inconclusive, but very frightening, head-on attacks as the Italian fighters turned to meet us each time as we came in."

The fifth CR42 was claimed by Flg Off E.M. Mason (P3722), known as 'Imshi' to his friends, who wrote:

"In the afternoon five of us met 27 CR42s. We had a lovely dog fight and I personally accounted for one (confirmed). He went down with flames coming out but was not properly blazing."

4°Stormo CT reported meeting many Hurricanes and claimed seven shot down and three probables for the loss of one pilot who baled out and was captured (Serg Guglielmo Biffani), while two others were shot down (Serg Nanin and Serg Bogoni, both surviving) and four other CR42s carried out emergency landings, one of which turned over and caught fire; the pilot (Ten Vaccari) was badly burned, and two of the others were wounded. The Gladiator pilots of 3RAAF reported several successes next day (10 December), claiming a Ro37, three CR42s and two probables; two of the fighters fell to Flt Lt G.H. Steege and Flg Off A.A. Gatward. 33 Squadron was again in the thick of the action, shooting down two CR42s and probably a third for the loss of one Hurricane which crash-landed (P3728), losing a second aircraft (P3824) that evening when one of its pilots (Lt J.G. Fischer SAAF) failed to return from a reconnaissance sortie. One pilot (Serg Nanin) of 4°Stormo CT was killed when his aircraft was shot down by a Hurricane and several other Fiats returned suffering battle damage. On the ground the battle was going in favour of the British offensive, Sidi Barrani and Buq-Buq having been retaken with the Italians pushed back to Halfaya Pass. The following morning (11 December), a 274 Squadron patrol intercepted and shot down a SM79 near Qur el-Beid (credited to Plt Off Godden, N2624) although one of the attacking Hurricanes, P3976 flown by Flt Lt R.V. Evers-Swindell, was hit by return fire and force-landed. A further patrol engaged CR42s of 151°Gruppo CT in the afternoon, Flg Off Mason (P3722) claiming one shot down near Qur el-Beid. In a letter to his parents describing the action, he wrote:

" ... late in the afternoon three of us were on patrol when I saw a speck on the horizon going towards Libya. I chased after it, the other two following, and eventually saw it was a lone CR42 making for home (probably after ground strafing our own troops). I chased up behind him without him noticing me and waited until I was right behind him at point blank range and put a burst into him. The other two saw him going down burning."

But the day's honours undoubtedly went to the pilots of 33 Squadron, Flt Lt J.M. Littler and Flt Sgt H.J. Goodchild each claiming a CR42, while Flg Off St Quintin reported shooting down a Ba65, for the loss of one Hurricane (P3726). Six days later the missing pilot, Flg Off C.H. Dyson DFC, returned safely to the Squadron with an amazing story. He told colleagues that on coming out of a cloud bank, he found himself directly behind a formation of CR42s escorting an SM79 over the British lines. He fired two bursts at two sections, each of three fighters, and all six were apparently seen to start smoking and fall away. He was then attacked by others – one of which he claimed as probably destroyed – before being hit by another and forced down near Sollum. Army witnesses allegedly confirmed the action and also reported that one of the stricken fighters had collided with the SM79, bringing this down also. Despite apparent 'confirmation' of this performance by numerous ground witnesses, Italian records do not indicate losses of this magnitude. Only Ten Vittorio Gnudi of 8° Gruppo CT was recorded as having been shot down and killed, although several other CR42s returned with battle damage. Nonetheless, for this performance Dyson was awarded a Bar to the DFC he had won in Palestine in 1938. Two further SM79s were claimed next day (12 December) by Flt Sgt Morris (P3723) of 274 Squadron, while 3RAAF Gladiators reported shooting down three of 17 CR42s met over the frontier, one apiece being credited to Flg Offs Gatward, A.H. Boyd and W.S. Arthur. The Fiats were from 84^ and 96^Squadriglie, the Italian pilots claiming two for the loss of one (Serg Roberto Steppi, who was captured). Friday the 13th was certainly an unlucky day for 202 Group fighters, 3RAAF alone losing five Gladiators (one pilot killed – Flt Lt C.B. Gadon – and one wounded) in combat with CR42s of which two were claimed in return (by Flt Off Boyd, while Flt Lt Steege claimed an SM79), and 274 Squadron lost two Hurricanes including P3976 with one pilot killed (Lt F.J. Joubert SAAF), Flt Lt Lapsley (P2641) claiming a CR42 shot down. The Italian pilots from 73^ and 97^Squadriglie claimed eight Gladiators shot down for three Fiats damaged. Better results were achieved by 33 Squadron later in the day when it claimed three CR42s and two SM79s, on this occasion without loss. Next day (14 December) 274 Squadron claimed no less than six SM79s during morning patrols over Bardia and Sollum, four of these falling to Flg Off A.A.P. Weller (V7300), Flg Off Patterson (P3720), Plt Off Godden (V7293) and Flg Off Mason (P3722); another fell to the combined fire of Flt Lt R.H. Smith (P5175) and 2/Lt R.H. Talbot SAAF (N2627), and the sixth to Flg Off H.C. Down (P2652) and Sgt Clarke (P2627). Three more were claimed probably destroyed, one each by Weller and Patterson, the third jointly by Down and Clarke. Mason, whose victim fell at Bir Chleta, wrote:

> " ... I saw bombs burst. I dived down and finally saw three SM79s. When they saw us they turned and made for home but I dived on the right hand man and taking my time, sat behind him and gave him a burst. Two chaps jumped out and floated down, looking very miserable, and then it burnt up and hit the gound and exploded with a terrific flash and blaze."

The Squadron engaged CR42s of 13°Gruppo CT escorting SM79s over Sidi Aziez in the afternoon, reporting five of the escort shot down, of which two were claimed by Sqn Ldr Dunn (whose aircraft, P5176, was hit and force-landed), and two by Flt Lt Lapsley (V7293) who had now taken his score into double figures to become the top-scoring pilot in 202 Group. The fifth was credited to Flg Off C.F. Greenhill (P2627), while Flg Off Mason (P3722) claimed a probable:

"... two of us met a CR42 which attacked head on but I gave him a long burst and he went down in a spin. We didn't see him smoke or burn or hit the ground so he is unconfirmed. I have also been doing a lot of ground strafing. I fly down a road at nought feet and fire at motors and things. Interesting to fire at the back of a van full of troops. You see your bullets hitting the sand and you just move the cloud of sand up towards and past the lorry. You then see dozens of chaps pile out like nobody's business. Some run away – some can't!"

By 15 December all Italian forces had been driven out of Egypt and some 38,000 prisoners had been taken. The CR42s of 4°Stormo which had been operating from Derna now moved up to Tobruk's T4 airfield. Both 33 and 274 Squadrons carried out offensive patrols during which Flt Lt Wykeham-Barnes (V7300) shot down a CR42 near Bir Galata. On this day also, Flt Lt Smudger Smith together with Plt Off McFadden and Sgts Marshall and Wills of 73 Squadron's A Flight were ordered to Sidi Haneish for attachment to 274 Squadron. Marshall reported that his aircraft TP-A (V7562) suffered bad engine vibration en route, the Hurricanes landing at Amiriya where some effort was made to rectify the problem. On taking off again they ran into a bad sandstorm so landed at Ma'aten Bugush where they stayed the night, flying on to Sidi Haneish in the morning.

At midday on the 16th a patrol from 274 Squadron which included the 73 Squadron quartet met a formation of SM79s of 9°Stormo BT escorted by CR42s near Bardia, and a series of fights ensued. Six of the bombers were claimed shot down, two each by Marshall and Flg Off Patterson (P2544/YK-T), and one apiece by Smith (V7553) and Flt Lt Wykeham-Barnes (V7293), while Flg Off Mason (P3722) claimed a CR42, and Smith probably a second. Three of the bombers failed to return, one flown by the Stormo commander (Col Mario Aramu), one by the commander of 29°Gruppo BT (TenCol Grandjacquet) and the third by the CO of 63^Squadriglia (Cap Girolami); three others were badly damaged. Of the engagement, Sgt Marshall recorded:

"We flew up to Sidi Barrani where we refuelled and took off on an offensive patrol. I flew with Pat [Patterson] and at 17,000 feet west of Sollum we spotted some 79s at about 5,000 feet. We dived and engaged them and I got two in flames. Pat two and Smithy one. There were congratulations from Collishaw [AOC] on our return, but I wished it was all over and I could get back to UK – my cold was still bad, which didn't help, plus the food and conditions were awful with half a gallon of water per day per man."

Plt Off McFadden failed to return from this action, having been chased by CR42s 'up country' where he was forced to land owing to lack of fuel, damaging his aircraft (V6737) in the process. He returned to Sidi Haneish next day, none the worse for the adventure and his aircraft was later recovered and repaired. Another patrol from 274 Squadron sighted an SM79 circling to land at Menistir and this was attacked and "considerably damaged" by Flg Off Down (P2652) and Plt Off T.B. Garland (P3721), the bomber also being strafed after it had landed. Next day (17 December) 33 Squadron reported shooting down a CR42 (Sottoten Natale Cima) in the Tobruk-Bardia area, claiming a second damaged, while the Italians claimed a Hurricane in return credited to Sottoten Magnabosco of 2°Stormo. While flying with a 274 Squadron patrol to the Bardia-Gambut area on 18 December, Flt Lt Smith (V7553) of 73 Squadron claimed another SM79 shot down but on landing reported sick, going down with sandfly fever; both Flg Off Scott and Plt Off Joubert were ill at this time with malaria. Even the Fleet Air Arm joined in the action on this date when Cdr C.L. Keighly-Peach[2], Commander Flying aboard the carrier HMS *Eagle*, paid a flying visit in his Sea Gladiator (N5517) to the Swordfish unit temporarily based at Fuka. Before returning to base he carried out a strafing attack on an Italian-occupied aerodrome, spraying a line of CR42s before making good his escape.

274 Squadron was again involved in a heavy engagement in the Sollum-Gambut area next day (19 December), Flt Lt Lapsley (V7293) and 2/Lt Talbot (P3721) each claiming CR42s shot down, and third being claimed damaged by Flg Off Greenhull (P3822), while Flg Off Weller reported damaging one of seven SM79s he attacked before his aircraft (V7300) was riddled by return fire, although he was able to land safely at Sidi Haneish. 33 Squadron also engaged SM79s and CR42s in the same area, probably part of the same formation, claiming three bombers and four fighters shot down (the latter by Flg Offs Woodward and Dyson, two apiece). The 20th was relatively quiet although a Lysander was lost to ground fire and Sgt White of 73 Squadron was attacked and shot at by a pilot of 274 Squadron who apparently filed a combat report reporting a successful action! Flg Off Patterson (P2544/YK-T) of 274 Squadron bagged another SM79 on 21 December over the Bardia-Sollum area, 33 Squadron claiming two more out of approximately 30 encountered; three members of the crew of one of the downed bombers were seen to bale out but their parachutes failed to open. Next day 33 Squadron reported shooting down a further two SM79s.

There was to be no let up in the intensity of action in the run up to Christmas, two SM79s being claimed by 274 Squadron's Flg Off Mason (P3722) on the morning of 23 December, 2/Lt Talbot (P3721) damaging a second before shooting down an escorting CR42, although Flg Off Greenhill (P5176) was hit by another and obliged to force-land south of Taifa, the victim of a pilot of 10°Gruppo CT. Of his latest victories, Mason wrote this graphic description in a letter to his parents:

> "The first one was well over Italian territory and was all alone making for home and only just off the ground. I got behind him and gave him a short burst. His port engine caught fire and he managed to get his aircraft down with wheels up. I didn't bother to fire again but flew alongside and watched, as I hadn't seen one crash close too, yet. However, he bounced twice, and slid on his belly and tipped on his nose. Out of the crew of five or six, only one got out (one of the two pilots). He stood looking at the wrecked machine so miserably that I hadn't the heart to machine-gun him. After this I climbed up and after a bit I saw a large formation below me of ten SM79s escorted by about 20 fighters (CR42s). I dived past the escort and shot at one of the outside bombers

---

[2] When Cdr Charles Keighly-Peach was appointed Commander Flying aboard *Eagle* in June 1940 the carrier had no fighter defence, so he arranged for four Sea Gladiators to be collected from FAA stocks held at Malta, training two Swordfish pilots to fly these with him. Then aged 38, he led this trio into action against Italian torpedo-bombers and reconnaissance seaplanes during July and August 1940, participating personally in five successful combats.

and dived away. After climbing again I saw that although the chap [at which he had fired] had dropped back at first he had now got back in formation. I hung around above for about ten minutes and then whilst they were dropping their bombs (on our troops) I chose my opportunity and dived very steeply on the same fellow. As the escorting fighters saw me coming in plenty of time I had to continue my dive and away, closely pursued by some extremely angry CR42s. So I did not observe the result of my engagement, although I saw my bullets going into him. I was not going to claim this one. However, another pilot saw an SM79 burning on the ground near this encounter, so I have been told that I can have this as confirmed. Also, a later report from the army states that it was seen going down in flames. So that made it two SM79s for one morning!

I find that I have a bullet in one of the petrol tanks [he wrote later], presumably as a result of this morning's show. Although I did not notice anything, I must have had quite a concentration of crossfire from the bomber formation as well as return fire from the rear gunner of the first lone aircraft. This is the first bullet hole I have had! It was only luck I got the bomber. [And later, he added] The machine I shot down and didn't machine-gun the pilot (as I thought) turned out to be a Caproni 310 [apparently an aircraft of 16°Gruppo Assalto] and not an SM79. The motors I saw rushing towards it turned out to be ours and all were taken prisoner. The two pilots had been both badly wounded and were taken to hospital, but the Radio Op and gunner were OK. I had a most interesting chat with the gunner afterwards at HQ. A very pleasant little chap – a photographer in civil life – just nearly finished his six years in the air force. He said he fired 300 rounds at me! He showed me a bullet hole in and out of his jacket that had not touched him."

3RAAF returned to the fray on 26 December, meeting five SM79s and an estimated 24 CR42s of newly arrived 23°Gruppo CT[3] led by Magg Tito Falconi, claiming two of the escort (credited to Flt Lt Steege and Flg Off Arthur) plus two probables for no loss despite Italian claims for one Gladiator shot down; the CO of 74^Squadriglia, Cap Guido Bobba was killed in this action and Magg Falconi's aircraft damaged. But it was 33 Squadron which took the end of the month's honours when its pilots claimed three SM79s and probably two CR42s on 27 December (Flg Off Woodward claiming a CR42 probable and a second damaged), and one more of each type the next day (Woodward being credited with the CR42 flown by Sottoten Ruggero Coparali of 91^Squadriglia, who was killed, plus two SM79s damaged) to raise it's tally for the month to 37 confirmed, plus 10 probables and 11 damaged, followed closely by 274 Squadron with 36 confirmed, four probables and at least four damaged, while the 73 Squadron detachment had claimed four and one probable, and the Gladiators of 3RAAF had chipped in with

---

[3] 23°Gruppo CT, which had arrived at Tripoli from Sicily on 16 December, was now operating from Z1 landing ground at Ain el-Gazala and comprised 70^, 74^ and 75^Squadriglie commanded by Cap Ottorino Fargnoli, Cap Guido Bobba, and Cap Pietro Calistri, respectively. The Gruppo had seen much action over Malta in the preceding months, Cap Bobba alone having claimed three Hurricanes shot down one of which was credited as a probable but was killed in his first action in Libya.

11 confirmed and three probables[4]. Losses were negligible with just three fighter pilots killed since the start of Operation *Compass* on 9 December. With the arrival of 23°Gruppo CT, 2°Stormo CT ceased operations, handed over its remaining CR42s to 4°Stormo CT and returned to Italy, having claimed 45 British aircraft destroyed and many damaged for the reported loss of 13 aircraft, with ten pilots killed and two captured. Following the departure of 2°Stormo CT, 2°Gruppo CT under the command of TenCol Giuseppe Baylon arrived at Tripoli from Italy, equipped with 13 of the Regia Aeronautica's latest fighters, the Fiat G50bis.

The important part played by the reconnaissance pilots of 208 Squadron, which operated both Hurricanes and Lysanders, was not overlooked, General Richard O'Connor, GOC Western Desert, showing his appreciation of their efforts in a message from his HQ:

> "The GOC wishes to express his appreciation of the work done recently by 208 AC Squadron. In particular he would like to mention the very excellent photographs taken of the Bardia area, and the consistently good reports obtained from visual reconnaissance, all of which are proving of the greatest value to the Army."

Following the recapture of Egyptian frontier territory and its associated depots and airfields, Air Marshal Arthur Tedder, the Deputy AOC, flew to Sollum in his Percival Q6[5]:

> "There were a number of abandoned Italian aircraft on the aerodrome above Sollum, but they had all been pretty well looted by the Australian soldiery, who had rather been like a swarm of locusts. I saw one CR42 in which the looter had been defeated by the metal skin until he had optimistically begun with a tin-opener to cut the rather nice heraldic design on the tail fin! I looked in on a bunch of Australian pilots who were brewing tea in a small mess tent. They were complaining that one of their aircraft force-landed less than a mile away the night before (short of petrol but apart from that quite serviceable) and had been stripped by the soldiery. I remarked that this was what you had to expect from Aborigines – and beat a hasty retreat!"

On the first day of the new year of 1941, 258 Fighter Wing was formed at Aboukir under the command of Grp Capt C.B.S. Spackman, its function to control the front-line fighter squadrons. Spackman's deputy, Wg Cdr D.V. Johnson, a former CO of 3RAAF Squadron, flew to Sollum to select a suitable site for the Advance Wing HQ, and was followed by a road convoy comprising AMES216 (Mobile Radar

---

[4] During the December fighting several RAF pilots had been able to increase their personal scores impressively. For 33 Squadron, Flg Off V.C. Woodward headed the list with at least 9 and two shares; Flg Off C.H. Dyson was credited with a dubious 9, and Flg Off P.R. St Quintin with at least 7; Flg Off F.S. Holman, Flg Off J.F. Mackie, and Flt Sgt L. Cottingham with 6 apiece; for 274 Squadron, Flt Lt J.H. Lapsley had increased his score to 11, while Flg Off P.G. Wykeham-Barnes had 8 and two shares, Flg Off E.M. Mason 6, Sqn Ldr P.H. Dunn 5 and three shares, and Flg Off T.L. Patterson 5.

[5] The Percival Q6 (P5640), a four-seater communication aircraft, was on the strength of 267 Squadron.

Unit) and 17 Wireless Installation Section. 73 Squadron had by now moved up to Sidi Haneish and was ready for action, which was soon to come its way when the Australian 6th Division began an assault against Bardia at dawn on the morning of 3 January, in which it was joined by vessels of the Inshore Squadron carrying out a bombardment from the sea. From Sidi Haneish 73 Squadron was ordered to despatch single Hurricanes at ten minute intervals throughout the day, the pilots tasked with reconnaissance rather than combat. In fact they were instructed to avoid enemy aircraft and to refrain from strafing enemy transport. In all, 27 Hurricane sorties were flown up to 1400, Sgt Garton having sighted a formation of a dozen CR42s escorting three SM79s north of Bardia which he did not attack owing to shortage of fuel. During the course of another sortie Plt Off Goord was attacked by a CR42 of 23°Gruppo CT but was not hit and dived away in accordance with instructions. However, at 1310, Sgt Marshall (V7299/TP-D) went to the aid of the veteran monitor HMS *Terror* of the Inshore Squadron which was under attack by five SM79s near Ras Uenna, part of a larger force put up by 34° and 41°Stormi. He chased them for ten minutes, eventually catching up with them about 20 miles out to sea:

> "At 300 yards I fired my first burst. Within half a minute one of the Savoias had caught fire and was plunging into the sea. I turned to attack another and saw two of the crew bale out as my fire was again successful. The third in my bag got it in the starboard motor, and the aircraft went into a long glide which finished in the Mediterranean. I silenced the return fire from the fourth Savoia, and pieces of metal flew off to starboard. There was little chance of her ever making base. It was a pity my ammunition ran out, as the fifth was a sitter. I felt sorry for two of the Ities who baled out; they were some 20 miles out to sea without a hope of being picked up."

Next day (4 January), 33 and 274 Squadrons were kept busy patrolling the battle area, a pilot from the former unit shooting down a CR42 over Bardia-Tobruk, Plt Off Godden (V7558) of 274 Squadron claiming two more and Flt Sgt Morris a fourth, but the latter's aircraft (V7293) was hit in the radiator and was force-landed. Flg Off Patterson (P2643) was also obliged to force-land. These actions had been fought against SM79-escorting CR42s of 10° and 23°Gruppi, whose pilots claimed two Hurricanes – one by TenCol Carlo Romagnoli, 10°Gruppo commander, and the other by M.llo Leonardo Ferrulli of 91^Squadriglia – for the loss of three of their own, in which Sottoten Ennio Grifoni, also a member of 91^Squadriglia, was shot down in flames, and Sottoten Bruno Devoto force-landed at Tobruk's T5 landing ground, while Ten Gino Battaggion of 70^ Squadriglia was wounded and force-landed at Ain el-Gazala; the latter, who had been escorting SM79s bombing armoured cars in the Bardia area, recalled:

> "At 18,000 feet I saw two Hurricanes in front of me. I began shooting. They shot at me, too. Suddenly, I felt a hit. An explosive bullet broke the windshield into many pieces and I was slightly wounded in the head. The explosion broke my goggles and wounded me in one eye. With blood oozing down my face, I lost consciousness for some seconds, perhaps ten or twenty. I recovered consciousness due to the air rushing into the cockpit and found that the aircraft

was spinning. I managed to recover from the spin and when I was near the ground fired a burst at some trucks. My wingman signalled to me that one wheel of my aircraft was damaged but I managed to land at Ain el-Gazala, near an ambulance. I landed at the slowest speed possible, holding the weight of the aircraft on the one serviceable wheel, and succeeded in stopping without overturning. The personnel near the ambulance recovered me and for about three months I could not fly because the eye gave me a lot of trouble. Some splinters had been extracted from my head – some of them are still there."

Later in the day Flt Sgt J.C. Hulbert of 274 Squadron in N2625 was shot down and killed near Bardia by a CR42 flown by Cap Calistri, CO of 75^Squadriglia. Meanwhile, 73 Squadron put up 24 sorties during the day but only one pilot sighted any enemy aircraft and as these were fighters he avoided combat. On another sortie Flt Lt Beytagh (V7561/TP-X) destroyed a CR42 on the ground at Bardia, as noted by Sgt Garton:

"Webby and I went off with Beytagh to Barrani where we refuelled before going on patrol as section. Saw nothing but shot up Bardia from 0 feet and the flight commander stopped a 42 on the deck."

Although a signal had been received to the effect that the army expected to capture the whole Bardia position by the end of the day, returning pilots reported that the enemy still held on in the south, although that position fell to the Australians late next day. The climax was witnessed by a Lysander pilot of 208 Squadron:

"I was detailed to fly over the Bardia defences. Only one complete Italian battery was firing but other isolated guns were still pumping shells into a wadi to the north where our infantry had established a base. I saw six of our tanks snaking their way towards the battery, pouring out yellow flashes of fire without interruption. Their fire must have been very accurate, because when I was within 200 yards of the enemy the opposing fire ceased and I saw Italian gunners running forward waving their hats and jackets. I was circling round at about 150 feet and got a wonderful view of our infantry, who were following the tanks and mopping up the Italians as they came running from their entrenchments. I dived on a detachment of our troops and dropped a message directing them to some isolated groups of Italians who were obviously anxious to surrender. I saw one column of about 1,000 yards long slowly winding its way from Bardia towards Capuzzo, apparently unescorted."

208 Squadron was again commended by the GOC who sent a personal message to the CO, Sqn Ldr J.R. Wilson:

"I would like to convey to you my appreciation of the work carried out by the Squadron under your command during the operations against Bardia. The reconnaissances carried out, both tactical and artillery, were of a very high order and contributed largely to the ultimate success of the land operation."

Sunday 5 January also saw a resumption of intensive aerial action, the Italians resisting until the end. Flg Off Mason (P3722) and 2/Lt Talbot (P3721) of 274 Squadron were given a free hand to operate further afield and attacked Z1 landing ground at Ain el-Gazala, current home of newly arrived 23°Gruppo CT. Mason reported:

> "In the morning [0840] I ground strafed some 42s and Bob [Talbot] shot down a 79 taking off; in the afternoon [1230] we went there [Gazala] again and circled over the aerodrome. Suddenly I saw two CR42s approaching to land. I dived down and came up behind. I gave the leader a burst and as I shot past him he turned slowly and dived straight in the middle of the aerodrome and exploded. In the meantime the other chap had turned and came for me head on. I gave him a short burst and he did the same thing. This time on the edge of the aerodrome. By then five more, also returning home, had seen me and were diving on me so Bob shot down the leader and they dispersed."

Mason was credited with damaging three CR42s on the ground during the morning strafe. His two victims during the early afternoon were Ten Oscar Abello and Serg Pardino Pardini of 70^Squadriglia, both of whom were reported to have been shot down and killed whilst coming in to land at Gazala. Meanwhile, other pairs of Hurricanes patrolled over the Gambut complex of landing grounds, meeting CR42s and SM79s. During the course of the day's actions, at 1245, eight SM79s of 41°Stormo BT and 17 escorting CR42s from 23°Gruppo CT were engaged five miles south-west of Gambut; Sqn Ldr Dunn (P3723) reported shooting down one of the fighters and Plt Off Wilson (N2646) damaged another, while Flt Lt Wykeham-Barnes (V7558) shot down one of the bombers and damaged a second. Sottoten Sante Schiroli of 74^Squadriglia was shot down and killed, apparently near Bardia, during which combat his newly appointed CO, Cap Mario Pinna, claimed a Hurricane, but it is not known if Schiroli fell victim to 274 or 73 Squadron, since single aircraft of the latter unit were also operating in the Great Gambut area: Sgt Marshall (V7562/TP-A) shot down an SM79 some 30 miles south-east of Gambut – the action witnessed by Plt Off Goord – while Sgt Webster (V7551/TP-K) destroyed one CR42 in flames and damaged another ten miles to the south-east, before Plt Off Goord (TP-M) caught another fighter about 25 miles south-east of Tobruk. All these successes were achieved between 1235 and 1305. During the course of a patrol by the newly arrived G50bis of 2°Gruppo CT, the commander, TenCol Baylon, reported meeting Hurricanes, one of which he claimed damaged, although no record of such an encounter appears in RAF records. Later in the afternoon, at 1420, Flt Lt Beytagh (V7561/TP-X) opened his North African account when he shot down another CR42 near Marsa es Sahal, just west of Tobruk. This latter machine was also an aircraft of 74^Squadriglia, flown by Sottoten Leopoldo Marangoni who was seriously wounded but managed to bale out. He was taken to a British field hospital but died during the night. A wounded British Army officer, Lt Anthony MacDonald, who was in a bed nearby, wrote to Marangoni's mother; the gist of the letter follows herewith[6]:

---

[6] The letter was written originally in English and then translated into Italian before being re-translated into pidgin English, which required much editing. The above is therefore a heavily-revised, concise version and not a copy of the original nor a direct translation of the Italian version.

"I am an English officer who lived with your son on the last day of his life. Your son was shot down by one of our aircraft in the early hours of the afternoon of 5 January. He baled out, landing heavily behind British lines. Before he baled out he had been wounded in the right leg, below the knee. On landing he broke the right leg and lost a quantity of blood before he was picked up. I had been wounded almost at the same time and we were picked up in the same ambulance and sent to a base hospital. We travelled until 10pm and stopped at an infirmary where our wounds were treated. It was evident that your son's leg should be amputated but he was very, very feeble from loss of blood, so much so that the surgeon decided it was not possible to operate until he was stronger. Before he died he told me he was not frightened of death. He related some things about his life and his home. We spoke in French. At 4.30am he awoke and raved for about an hour. During the delirium he appeared to relive the air battle. Ten minutes before he died he regained consciousness and spoke in Italian. I think he prayed because frequently he pronounced the word 'Madonna'. The doctors had tried everything to prevent the loss of blood but he had lost too much before being picked up. He died from weakness brought on by the loss of blood and not directly from the wound. Cheer up, because we know he died in peace with God. He died in perfect peace at 5.30am. An English priest was at his bed."

Italian records note that a Hurricane overflew Derna airfield next day and dropped a message reporting the fate of Sottoten Marangoni, presumably at the same time delivering MacDonald's personal letter addressed to the pilot's mother.

The Deputy AOC, Air Marshal Tedder, made another flying visit to the front-line when he flew to Bardia on 6 January:

"I took off from Bugush [in the Q6] just behind a Bombay loaded up with six Italian generals and a couple of dozen other officers, all exported from Bardia and bound for Heliopolis and prison camps. On the way back we caught up with the Bombay and flew alongside it for a few minutes to give me the opportunity of making a sketch in my little book."

Hurricanes, singly or in pairs, still roamed over the battle area, Flg Off Storrar (V7562/TP-A) and Sgt Laing (V7553/TP-E) meeting CR42s near Ras el-Meheta at 1445, one of which Storrar reported shot down in flames:

"I saw two CR42s which appeared to be playfully dogfighting another – the CR42s observed me just before I opened fire but one 3-second burst in the engine was enough. The e/a fell on the beach. The second CR42 made a head-on attack then dived away fast."

The CR42 engaged by Laing also escaped:

"I was steaming along near Tobruk and found a CR42 doing about the same speed, slightly below me, so I had a few squirts at him as he went down through a cloud layer, and saw some pieces fly off which seemed to put him out of control. I found the biplane quite a tricky thing to attack, as it had a very good evasive flexibility, and this Fiat could easily have turned inside me. I also made the mistake of firing too early, so was very lucky to hit him, and put him down."

CR42s were also encountered by a patrol from 33 Squadron over the Bardia-Tobruk area, one of which was reported shot down by Wt Off Goodchild who also damaged a second. 274 Squadron now begain sending pairs of Hurricanes behind the Italian lines to strafe the airfields and landing ground, Sqn Ldr Dunn (P3723) flying to Gazala on 8 January where he destroyed two SM79s on the ground, while Flg Off Mason (P3722) visited Martuba when he strafed a dozen more SM79s, reporting the destruction of two which were, in fact, SM81s. Next day (9 January) Mason, again accompanied by 2/Lt Talbot (V7484), took off to continue the series of airfield attacks, Mason (P3722) shooting down a CR42 over Derna, while the South African shot down another CR42 over Martuba. As he overflew the airfield, Talbot observed the burnt out wrecks of six SM79s which were assumed to have been the result of the previous day's raid by Mason. About these latest successes, the latter wrote:

"We made a rule never to shoot at people or buildings like messes or tents, only at aircraft. So they got to know us and used to stand watching us set their machines on fire (except those who were using guns and pom-poms at us). In the afternoon we again did this and what I have dreamt of happened. A single CR42 took off and climbed up to engage me. We had a dogfight below the clouds and immediately over the aerodrome. It lasted a long time, about ten minutes. He was very good and much above the average Italian. We believe he is Major Ernesto Botti – a famous Italian ace who has a crack squadron of CR42s [it was not Botti]. I am very glad to say that he managed to bale out successfully when I finally finished him off and I saw him down safely before we went home."

Sgt Garton of 73 Squadron flew an early morning patrol without sighting the enemy:

"Off at 0630. Patrolled over Tobruk and Gulfo di Bomba, again without seeing any Itie aircraft. We are continually flying over their territory without inducing them into the air. Still, air presence keeps them on the ground and leaves our army free from enemy bombing attacks."

While on patrol later that morning Plt Off Goodman (V7546/TP-Q) of 73 Squadron encountered an unusual aircraft, a white-painted, Red Cross-marked SM81S flying eastwards at 1,000 feet just off the coast west of Tobruk, apparently an aircraft of 2°Gruppo APC. Having flown beside and exchanged waves with the pilot, he decided not to attack since it appeared to be unarmed and the obviously relieved Italian crew were allowed to go about their business. On another patrol Sgts Marshall and Wills were fortunate to escape unscathed when caught unawares by a section of G50bis:

"I got bounced by three G50s at 20,000 feet and was lucky to escape. I landed at Bardia after dark. Bill was left behind at Haneish."

73 Squadron now began moving up to Gazala West, as noted by Sgt Garton:

"Left Haneish at 1530 with Monty [Ellis], landing at the new base an hour later. This of course is Italian Libya, and we are on enemy territory for the first time. B Flight was in a cottage, and we partied on some cognac which had been looted from the Wops by two Aussies and handed over to us. Leng, Monty and myself went along and found that Eiby and McColl had already passed out and been put to bed. The Aussies shot a heavy line about how they had mounted a bayonet charge and took Bardia. We were not the most receptive listeners, as all three of us were feeling no pain and had to be carted back to our billet in a lorry."

The run of successes for 274 Squadron's deadly duo, Mason and Talbot, continued next day (10 January) when they again visited Derna; on their first sortie each pilot shot down a SM79 at 1000, while during an afternoon intrusion, at 1600, Mason (P3722) shot down a second SM79 and damaged one of the newly arrived G50bis of 2°Gruppo CT, and Talbot (V7484) claimed a G50bis destroyed with a second damaged. Mason wrote:

"We went there [Derna] again and both shot down SM79s coming to land. I got one in the morning and one in the afternoon. All crashed on the aerodrome. But they set a trap for us. We were purposefully doing these shows at the same time for moral effect. When I saw this SM79 in the afternoon coming to land and went screaming down on it and shot it down as it approached the boundary, a smoke fire was lit. Within five minutes five Fiat G50s (the latest type of Italian monoplane fighter) appeared. We were caught awkwardly because I was below them and we got mixed up. I got a long head-on attack on one and he should have gone, but of course is unconfirmed, and Bob got one who jumped out."

The G50bis had been escorting three Ba65s of 159^Squadriglia, in company with six CR32s of 160^Squadriglia, when they became separated. On returning to Derna, the G50bis leader, Cap Tullio De Prato of 150^Squadriglia, sighted a Hurricane flying in the opposite direction. He signalled by hand gestures and manoeuvres the potential danger to the other two pilots he was leading, then turned to meet the Hurricane – apparently the aircraft flown by Talbot – which was, by then, manoeuvring to attack. The two aircraft exchanged fire and, as De Prato turned again, he realised his machine had been hit in the engine and decided to carry out an emergency wheels up landing near Ain el-Gazala. With the engine of fire, the Italian pilot, despite injuries, managed to get clear before the G50 exploded in flames. Help was soon on hand when a passing Arab and his family provided a donkey, and led him to the nearby airfield where a CR32 could be seen. On reaching the airfield, De Prato introduced himself to the CR32 pilot, Ten Giacomello, who had force-landed after being hit by AA fire. The two pilots decided to await rescue since Giacomello's colleagues had seen him force-land. Shortly after, however, a Hurricane appeared – flown by Flg Off Mason – which strafed and destroyed the CR32. On seeing this, the kindly Arab again came to their aid and led them to the safety of a cave. Just before sunset help finally arrived when a Ca133 appeared, escorted by three CR32s, and soon the two pilots were on their way back to Derna. While the rescue was under way the airfield was strafed by another Hurricane which, however, failed to sight the Caproni and escort. Earlier in the day, presumably during the action with Mason and Talbot, Serg Magg Albino Fabbri of 152^Squadriglia claimed a Hurricane shot down.

Sandstorms during the ensuing four days effectively curtailed offensive operations although, on 14 January, Plt Off Wilson of 274 Squadron successfully strafed five SM79s at Derna although he believed they were already unserviceable. A petrol pump and gun positions were also machine-gunned but on the return flight he was obliged to force-land at Sollum. Sgt Garton of 73 Squadron was also obliged to force-land his aircraft (V7561/TP-X), battle damaged, following a low-level reconnaissance sortie to the Tobruk area ordered by Wing HQ:

> "I took off to patrol Tobruk at 0900. After 45 minutes at 15,000 feet I went down to 2,000 feet or thereabouts, south of Tobruk, to have a recce of the troop positions. I found myself inside the Itie outer defence lines and was about to open fire on some troops when they started waving to me, so I held my fire and had another look – and was fired upon by the defences and hit. Their cannon shell hit the underside of the engine and damaged the cooling system which immediately filled the cockpit with white smoke. Thinking I was on fire, I pulled up to about 500 feet anticipating having to bale out, but finally discovered that the engine was merely shot up and that there was no fire. There was no engine either, as it had seized solid, and I pancaked, wheels up, in the desert without knowing on which side of the lines I was. Fortunately I was greeted by an artillery officer who gave me a whisky and some breakfast, and provided transport to the nearest drome, about 15 miles away. I then scrounged a lift back to base in a Lysander. The artillery wallahs had provided me with an up-to-date map of the Tobruk area showing the Itie defences and our own positions. This is what I had set out to obtain, but a badly damaged Hurricane seemed an inordinate price to pay. I shall keep clear of Tobruk in the future."

Sgt Marshall had also had a narrow escape during a similar low-level sortie over Tobruk and had returned 'very frightened', so much so that he took to his bed with sickness and a bad headache. The Squadron questioned the thinking which put the valuable Hurricanes and their pilots at such risk. Garton added, later:

> "I heard that I am due a rocket from the AOC over yesterday's effort, despite the fact that it resulted from HQ's stupid orders and the total lack of information given to us."

With the situation in Greece deteriorating rapidly, 33 Squadron was ordered to prepare to leave for that destination forthwith. With 80 and 112 Squadrons already operating in Greece, and now 33 Squadron about to follow, 202 Group was left with just the Hurricanes of 73 and 274 Squadrons, supported by the Gladiators of 3RAAF. The fighter pilot shortage was somewhat offset by the return to 274 Squadron of a number of its French pilots who had completed the Hurricane conversion course at 70 OTU.

CHAPTER II

THE CAPTURE OF TOBRUK: ENTER THE LUFTWAFFE

January – February 1941

"I was fairly sure that the Luftwaffe was arriving in Tripoli and would be playing havoc with our recently captured ports and lines of communication ..."
Air Chief Marshal Longmore, AOC-in-C RAFME

It was the fall of Bardia that galvanised Hitler into providing immediate air support for his Italian allies in Libya, with the promise of heavy armoured ground units to follow. Hitler was determined that Tripolitania should not fall to the steam-rolling British advance but first he required an assurance from Mussolini that the Italians would fight for every square foot of Libyan soil. Having readily accepted the conditions, Mussolini promptly authorised the despatch by sea of two of his élite divisions – one armoured, the other motorised – to reinforce Marshal Graziani's disintegrating army. These were to begin arriving at Tripoli from the middle of January. Air protection for the convoys was to be provided by the Luftwaffe's Fliegerkorps X which had arrived in Sicily from Norway at the end of December, ostensibly for operations against Malta and the Royal Navy's Mediterranean Fleet. Fliegerkorps X comprised approximately 200 aircraft, mainly Ju88s, He111s, Ju87s, and Bf110s, and were divided between the airfields at Catania, Comiso, Marsala, Trapani and Palermo, though a small number were stationed at Reggio di Calabria on the toe of the Italian mainland.

During the early morning hours of 16 January 1941 the distinctive drone of Daimler-Benz engines shattered Benghazi's dawn as the first section of a total of 14 He111s of II/KG26 touched down on the dusty runway at Benina at the end of their long flight from Sicily. The crews were greeted by members of 1 Staffel of (F)/121 whose reconnaissance Ju88Ds had arrived shortly before, but the joy was soon cut short when three of the following group of Heinkels crash-landed one after the other on arrival, as did a Ju52/3m of III/Ln.Regt 40, one of several transport machines carrying flak guns and their crews for the defence of Benghazi. Although the crews and occupants of all the machines survived, one of the bombers was badly damaged and subsequently written-off. Events were to go from bad to worse for the small group before the day was out, when a Ju88D in the hands of Obfw Hermann Peters collided with a stationary Italian aircraft on take-off and crashed, killing three members of the crew including the pilot; the remaining badly injured crewman died in hospital next day. However ignominiously, the Luftwaffe had ominously arrived in North Africa. Having surveyed his new surroundings, a newly arrived officer felt compelled to write:

"Cyrenaica is an almost treeless and therefore shadowless lunar landscape. The Jebel el-Akhdar is a wildly fissured mountain range broken only by a few valleys in which sand, usually white or reddish yellow, stunts the growth of any vegetation. Mobility is restricted almost entirely to the desert road, so it is startling in the midst of this barren waste of sand and stone to fly across the tents, flocks of sheep and camels of Arabs of whom no European knows: what caravan trails do they use, what is their living, what laws and customs do they obey? The farther east you go along the desert road, the more inhospitable the landscape becomes: while for about 30 miles east of Benghazi the colonizing work of the Italians is evident, around Derna and Tobruk there are no signs of human habitation. Even the pitiful stunted pines fall off. The thorny shrubs barely struggled up to knee height."

The role of II/KG26's Heinkels at Benina was twofold: one was to provide protection for the convoys from Sicily as they approached the North African coast, but more specifically they were to hamper reinforcements and supplies for Wavell's army then arriving in Egypt via the Suez Canal. Although the Italian island of Rhodes in the Dodecanese was closer for such missions, from where II/KG26 had operated briefly during December and early January, it lacked stocks of fuel, whereas Benina had sufficient quantities for sustained operations. However, to carry out mining and reconnaissance sorties from Benina over the Canal entailed a 1,400-mile round flight, only achievable if flown at the most economical cruising speed.

The Heinkels were soon called into action, for within hours of their arrival German agents in Egypt reported that a British convoy was about to enter the Canal from the south. Under cover of darkness on the night of 17/18 January, eight mine-laden Heinkels set out at half-hourly intervals for their first mission from Libyan soil, the crews briefed to scour the Canal for shipping from both directions. The operation was under the overall command of Maj Martin Harlinghausen, Fliegerkorps X's Chief-of-Staff, who was aboard the aircraft flown by Hptm Robert Kowalewski. After an uneventful but tiring four-hour flight the Canal was reached, but initially no significant shipping was to be seen. Nonetheless, a number of merchant vessels were eventually sighted at anchor in Bitter Lake and mines were laid. With the first part of the mission thus successfully accomplished without undue alarm, the Heinkels commenced the long return flight to Benina but then disaster struck – one by one the bombers ran out of fuel and were obliged to force-land in the desert wastes, until only Lt Kaupisch's aircraft remained to touch down at Benina, its fuel tanks practically dry. Of the seven missing aircraft, Kowalewski belly-landed his machine 175 miles short of Benina without injury to himself or his crew. After setting fire to the Heinkel, the four airmen set out to walk back to the aerodrome believing they were much closer than in fact they were. Four days later a searching Heinkel piloted by Kaupisch eventually located the exhausted men, landed nearby and flew them back to Benina. Of the remaining crews, two men were injured when they baled out of their doomed 6 Staffel machine, and a third was injured when his aircraft came down in Italian-controlled territory. Three aircraft came down in British lines and the crews were taken prisoner including the Gruppenkommandeur, Maj Helmut Bertram, aboard Lt Hans Folter's IH+GM which force-landed west of Tobruk. The crew of IH+JP, which made a creditable wheels-up landing 20 miles east of Fort Maddelena, took five days to walk to Sollum and into captivity. The abandoned Heinkel was located by a pilot of 6 Squadron flying a Magister and was later inspected by a team of engineers before being salvaged and transported to 103 MU at Aboukir. Thus, in just two days, the II/KG26 detachment had lost almost two-thirds of its complement, a situation made worse a few days later when an aircraft of 4 Staffel crashed on landing at Benina. The Gruppe was therefore obliged to await the arrival of 5 Staffel from Sicily before undertaking further operations. The reaction of General Hans Geisler and his staff at Fliegerkorps X's HQ in Sicily to these catastrophic events is not recorded, but can be easily imagined.

Other new arrivals in Libya at this time for FliegerFührer Afrika, as the new command was labelled, included the advance element of 50-60 Ju87s of I/StG1 and II/StG2 commanded by Hptm Paul-Werner Hozzel and Maj Walter Enneccerus respectively, which flew in from Sicily towards the end of the month, while 20 long-range Bf110Es of III/ZG26 accompanied them. The Messerschmitts were dispersed between Castel Benito, Sirte and Arco Philenorum (known as Marble Arch to the British) under Maj Karl Kaschka, the Gruppenkommandeur, the Staffeln commanded by Oblt Wilhelm Matthes (7 Staffel), Oblt Prang (8 Staffel), and Hptm Bord (9 Staffel).

With the arrival of the Heinkels and their subsequent forays over the Suez Canal, the defence of Alexandria and the Canal area became a priority for the British. Among the handful of defenders against the intruders were the pilots of Free French Flight 2, who were joined in the night sky over Alexandria by Gladiators of the Royal Egyptian Air Force's 2 Squadron based at Helwan, one of whose pilots came close to intercepting a marauding Heinkel. However, it was not until May that the first successes were achieved by RAF fighters. By then at least one supply ship and three smaller vessels had fallen victim to mines laid in the Canal by the Heinkels of II/KG26 which had been joined by others from 2/KG4.

* * *

Meanwhile, in the Western Desert, as Sgt Ellis of 73 Squadron was returning from a patrol along the main El Adem to Bardia road at 50 feet on the morning of 16 January, he saw nine CR42s flying in the opposite direction, about 150 feet above. Owing to his obvious disadvantage he increased speed and rapidly outdistanced the Italian fighters. Off duty next day, Ellis was one of several of the Squadron's NCO pilots to visit the Bardia battlefields, where he and Sgt Webster found an almost intact Italian army lorry which was towed back to camp by an Italian tractor driven by Sgts Garton and Marshall. En route several cases of lemons were discovered by the side of the road and these were quickly loaded on board, subsequently providing much appreciated lemon juice for those who wished to partake.

5^Squadra Aerea suffered the loss of an aircraft during the day when a patrolling Hurricane of 274 Squadron flown by Flt Lt Wykeham-Barnes (P2641), encountered another Red Cross-marked SM81S tri-motor of 2°Gruppo APC some ten miles west of Tobruk. This was immediately attacked and the air ambulance promptly crash-landed after which the crew was seen to scramble clear before setting fire to their aircraft. British troops were quickly on the scene and the five Italian airmen were rounded up and taken prisoner. Half an hour later Flt Lt Tulasne (V7423) overflew the wreckage of the downed aircraft, confirming its complete destruction. A Hurricane of 73 Squadron flown by Plt Off Humphreys failed to return from an afternoon patrol, and it was not until the following day that the Squadron learned that he had landed safely at Sidi Barrani, having failed to locate Sidi Haneish in poor visibility caused by one of the frequent sandstorms. He was eventually flown back to Sidi Haneish aboard a Blenheim of 113 Squadron when his Hurricane (TP-L) refused to restart, although the aircraft was later recovered. Further south, at Siwa, British troops were bombed by two Italian aircraft but little damage resulted and there were no casualties.

Hurricanes and RAAF Gladiators continued to put up offensive patrols over the Tobruk area while Blenheims bombed the town's defences on 18 January. The camera-equipped Hurricanes of 208 Squadron meanwhile continued to produce photomosaics of Bardia, Tobruk and El Adem in readiness for the forthcoming assault. Severe sandstorms in the vicinity of Bardia effectively put paid to 274 Squadron's flying programme for the day, although an early patrol was undertaken. Despite orders prohibiting unauthorised ground strafing, gun positions at Sidi Mahmoud were attacked at 0835 by Plt Off McFadden of 73 Squadron. He explained on his return to Sidi Haneish that he had become lost in a sandstorm and had inadvertently found himself at low level over Sidi Mahmoud (Bu Amud). Opening fire on impulse, he believed he had killed several of the gun crew and damaged the position.

Both Hurricanes and Gladiators continued to fly offensive patrols over the Tobruk area during the following two days but met no enemy aircraft, although 274 Squadron's activities were again restricted by local sandstorms on the 19th, but next day the Squadron was able to send up a total of eleven aircraft at half-hour intervals to patrol over the Tobruk area. The fighter squadrons were visited by Grp Capt Spackman, OC 258 Wing HQ, accompanied by an ALO from 202 Group, on the afternoon of 20 January, when they were provided with the latest intelligence information regarding the disposition of British forward troops and the locations of Italian positions in readiness for the ground assault against the Tobruk garrison, which was planned for the morrow.

As British and Australian forces closed in on Tobruk, the town and its defences continued to be the main target for the RAF's nocturnal bombers. Wellingtons and Blenheims carried out nightly attacks commencing 16/17 January, bombing military barracks and shipping in the harbour, even dropping leaflets over the garrison on the 19th calling for its surrender. With the ground assault on Tobruk finally under way early on the morning of 21 January, the advancing troops were ably supported by HMS *Terror* and gunboats *Ladybird*, *Cricket*, *Aphis* and *Gnat* of the Inshore Squadron which bombarded Tobruk harbour and a sandy ravine west of the town known as Wadi es Sehel, where a concentration of Italian reserve troops had been assembled ready to meet and counter attack the first onrush of Imperial forces. With the conclusion of the naval bombardment, Blenheims made the first of a total of 56 sorties against the defences during the day, scoring hits on M/T, gun emplacements, buildings on the wharf and the battered *San Giorgio*. Several fires were started. The Wellingtons had begun their assault at 0300. Aboard one of them was the *Daily Mail*'s war correspondent Alex Clifford:

"The moon, like a luminous slice of melon, was topping the horizon as we screamed down the flarepath and lifted gently into the night. There was nothing to see. I crouched down, trying to keep warm and watching spangles of stars slide past the little glass bubble above me. Vaguely in my earphones I heard the crew chatting about heights, courses, clouds, and navigation signals. I fell asleep.

Somebody awakened me and yelled 'Tobruk!' I fumbled my way forward and peered out of the plane's transparent nose to see earth and sky slashed with flame. Groups of big yellow flashes were bombs landing. Clusters of incendiaries wove crazy patterns of dazzling white flame athwart the landscape. To my unaccustomed eyes the AA barrage seemed terrific. It was our turn to go in. For a second there was an icy panic inside me and I wished I had not come. Then I grew too excited to be afraid. I raced back through the plane's darkened belly, past the bomb-aimer lying flat on his stomach, and over the racks of sleek, yellow bombs waiting to be released. Fumblingly, I eased myself into the rear-gunner's turret.

I swivelled my turret round, manoeuvring to see the bombs land. I had almost given them up when the earth below me erupted in five flaming volcanoes. Stuff was coming up all around us. The sky seemed filled with coloured tracers, and AA guns were going flat out. Back we turned, and plunged again into the fantastic blaze of bursting shells. Another flare was burning, and Tobruk's bay and promontory showed up like a gigantic thumb sticking out into the sea. We made a straight run for the target, but showers of tracers met us and barred the way. The pilot swerved momentarily and tried again from another angle. Again I heard 'Bombs gone!' and this time I saw flames belch up straight across the road junction we were aiming at.

Two blinding flashes to our left made me jump, and I reported to the pilot. For a couple of seconds we swerved and twisted, eluding the gunners. Then we jockeyed into position for a third run. This took us through the thickest barrage. The grounded cruiser *San Giorgio* in the harbour was pumping up stream after stream of tracers. I saw one coming straight for me – a diamond necklace this time. Then it veered off slowly and missed. Right in the middle of the barrage our bombs fell, and flares with them. This time the result was spectacular. A large barnlike building flashed into orange flames, and its roof soared gently upwards, then it fell back in fragments. Swirls of white smoke spiralled up, and as we swung away out to sea I saw two more explosions shatter the flaming walls. Those were our last bombs, and once more we passed Tobruk and watched other people's bombs crash down against the fantastic background of AA fire. The Italian gunners were certainly standing up to their job well.

Dawn was glimmering on the eastern horizon as we raced back to our base. But other slim, black shapes sped past us invisible in the darkness. They would be over Tobruk as dawn broke ..."

Five Hurricanes of A Flt/73 Squadron provided cover for a morning raid by Blenheims. Over Sidi Mgherreb to the west of Tobruk the Hurricanes spotted two G50bis of 2°Gruppo CT which they pursued, as recalled by Sqn Ldr Murray, who was leading:

"I spotted and dived on two G50s below us, and they turned back to the east. As we followed I saw about nine more climbing up from below, then Wainwright's Hurricane went spinning down in flames, shot down by another gaggle from above. He was so close that I was lucky not to be taken down with him. We did well to get out without further losses."

Plt Off Alex Wainwright's Hurricane (P2639/TP-K) was shot down by Serg Magg Antonio Patriarca of 358^Squadriglia, and the British pilot was later reported to have been killed. In the ensuing dogfight one G50 was seen spiralling down and was reported to have been seen by Sgt Griffith burning on the ground. The downed aircraft was credited to Sqn Ldr Murray (V7560/TP-F) since he was the only one able to get a telling shot at one of the Italian fighters although Plt Off Brian Legge reported that he had knocked pieces off the tail unit of the one he attacked before his own aircraft (TP-M) was hit by ground fire. With its engine on fire the Hurricane was successfully force-landed at El Adem where, with the help of a 274 Squadron NCO, Legge was able to douse the flames with sand and water.

There would appear to have been some confusion as to what actually occurred during the whirling series of dogfights. Though no G50bis was lost, Ten Romano Pagliari of 152^Squadriglia was wounded. The burning aircraft seen on the ground was presumably Wainwright's Hurricane. In addition to the Hurricane losses, a Blenheim was shot down and a second damaged. As a result of this unhappy action, Sqn Ldr Murray was later reprimanded by the AOC for attacking fighters when detailed to protect the bombers. Hurricanes from both 73 and 274 Squadrons participated in other escort sorties and, during the course of one, Sgt Garton of the former unit, flying No2 to Flt Lt Beytagh, watched in horror as his leader attacked a Hurricane of 274 Squadron before realising his mistake. When, on returning to base, Beytagh learned that a 274 Squadron aircraft was missing, he feared that he had shot it down. There was relief all round when the missing pilot, slightly wounded Flg Off C.J. Laubscher, a South African, walked into camp and reported that his aircraft (V7213) had been hit by ground fire and, as a result of which, he had been obliged to force-land ten miles south-west of Tobruk. HQ 202 Group now telephoned 73 and 274 Squadrons with instructions that their Hurricanes were not to fly below 12,000 feet while over enemy-occupied territory unless absolutely necessary, orders which contradicted those from 258 Wing HQ to the effect that the Hurricanes could drop down to 6,000 feet to gather information on enemy troop and transport movements. Despite the latest directive Sgt Marshall took a section of four from 73 Squadron to Tobruk and "flew around at ten feet" before returning safely to base.

208 Squadron's Lysanders were also out and about conducting artillery shoots, in addition to tactical reconnaissance sorties, and one of these was damaged by flak over Tobruk, following which it crash-landed. Since the end of December the Squadron had carried out a total of 38 reconnaissance flights over Bardia and Tobruk for the army, of which 26 were considered successful. During this period only two aircraft were damaged by AA fire while two others had successfully evaded attacks by fighters. Following the capture of Bardia the Squadron was advised that General Argentino, commander of the Italian 28^Division, had expressed his admiration for the close co-operation of British air, land and sea forces. He said that he attached little importance to air bombing, whether from material damage or morale point of view, but stressed the great importance of air co-operation with the army, which he admitted did not exist in the Italian forces, adding that during the British advance on Bardia the mechanised units were so well directed by the low-flying Lysanders that they appeared to be "connected to each other by string."

By noon Tobruk's outer and inner defences had been penetrated to a depth of over five miles on a broad front and, as night fell, advancing troops were able to look down on the town which was covered in a great and dense pall of smoke from the blazing oil reservoirs. In the bay lay the smoking hulk of the *San Giorgio* and, in the harbour amidst a dozen wrecked, half-submerged vessels[1], the once proud Italian liner-cum-troopship *San Marco* burned fiercely, as did the smaller freighter *Liguria*, the scene witnessed by a *Reuter's* correspondent:

> "From the top of the final escarpment we saw Tobruk for the first time. Below us lay the white houses of the town, with the large setting sun glinting off the still waters of the harbour. A large liner lay at anchor – ablaze from stem to stern. Smaller craft which were tied up alongside were also in flames. Masts and funnels of sunken vessels showed above the surface. The *San Giorgio* lay in the harbour mouth. A few men wandering through the town were the only signs of life ..."

With daybreak on 22 January the assault continued and the garrison finally surrendered at 1015. Another war correspondent wrote:

> "The streets of the town were almost empty when our troops entered, but there was an impressive little scene when the Brigadier received its surrender. In front of their staffs and guard of carabiniere, the Italian commanders stood at attention in full dress with medals – General Della Mura, commander of the 61st Metropolitan Division, Admiral Vietina, commander of the naval base, and Maj-General Barberis, commander of the garrison troops. The Admiral made a formal speech ..."

On the following morning Australian Broadcasting Corporation war correspondent Chester Wilmot recorded:

---

[1] These included the Italian freighters *Chantala*, *Manzoni*, *Sereno* and *Serenitas*, the destroyers *Zeffiro*, *Ostro* and *Nembo*, plus the minesweeper *Berta*.

"From the top of the naval building I studied the main prize of the battle – the harbour. One pier had been completely demolished by RAF bombs, but the Italian attempt to wreck the other main jetty had resulted in nothing more than a small gap on one side. Lying sunk or beached were a dozen victims of RAF bombing [sic[2]], but fortunately none blocked the channel. Obligingly, the Italians had left undamaged six auxiliary schooners, twenty large pontoons, a couple of dozen lighters and several fast launches. With these available, the demolition of the main jetty and of the two large cranes did not much matter."

Once an inspection of the town and garrison had been carried out Wilmot was able to add:

"Most of the anti-aircraft guns had been destroyed, but there were twenty 105mm and twelve 149mm guns undamaged in an ordnance store – brand new. These were a boon to the Greeks, to whom they were soon shipped together with a mass of other captured war material. The vital Tobruk water supply plant was intact, though, of course, the pipeline by which the Italians had brought water more than a hundred miles from Derna was cut. The two distilleries, however, which delivered 20,000 gallons a day and the sub-artesian wells which could provided a further 20,000 gallons were untouched. The Italians left substantial stores of Chianti, cognac, aniseed brandy and mineral water. The Chianti was good but the brandy was fiery and the aniseed worse. Tobruk was stocked with enough tinned food for a garrison of 25,000 for two months – a windfall for our troops who had been existing on little but bully-beef, biscuits, butter, jam and tea. The tinned fruit and vegetables were as good as Australia's best."

With the fall of Tobruk some 25,000 prisoners were taken including an English-speaking Egyptian officer in the Italian Army, and 3,000 personnel of the Regia Marina. The British and Australian forces had suffered only 500 casualties. Among the 'prisoners' were 14 prostitutes who had been in the employ of the Italian forces. They were promptly despatched to Alexandria, initially aboard a captured Italian schooner, and were eventually incarcerated in a Catholic convent in Cairo for the remainder of the war. The skipper of the schooner later recalled:

"One woman had a pet dog. The dog arrived with the women when they came on board. When we transferred the women to a hospital ship, the dog was abandoned and stayed with us. He was a cute little dog. We named him Dusty because, when he shook, he stirred up enough dust to cause another *khamseen*. He was injured during a bombing raid and had a kink in his middle, which caused him to walk sideways. He was a male, but sat down to piddle, which I attributed to his never seeing a tree in his lifetime."

Of this period of intensive air and ground operations, the *Daily Express* war correspondent (Alan Moorehead) wrote:

---

[2] A number of these had been sunk or damaged by RN bombardment.

"[Air Chief Marshal] Longmore's policy had succeeded brilliantly. From the first he had concentrated on damaging enemy aircraft on the ground by low-level machine-gun attacks. This put the enemy machines out of action long enough to enable our troops to come up and seize the airfields. Around Tobruk I had already seen nearly a hundred aircraft caught in this way. Day after day fewer Fascist airmen came against us. There was still some strafing of the troops, but now Hurricanes flying only 30 or 40 feet above the ground were ranging back and forth over the whole of eastern Cyrenaica, blowing up staff cars and transports, machine-gunning troops and gathering information of the movements of the enemy. By the time Tobruk fell, the Italian Air Force was utterly defeated ..."

Following the capture of Tobruk the mobile radar units AMES216 (then at Acroma) and AMES235 (at Msus) moved to the garrison, followed a few days later by 258 Wing HQ. The Hurricane squadrons were now advised that all ground to the east of Derna was in British hands and that they were not on any account to strafe positions in that area. Other Italian forces meanwhile withdrew to the Mechili area, exposing their 60^Division at Derna and leaving the Mechili-Benghazi track open and unguarded. The barracks at Derna, which had been targeted by seven Blenheims a few days earlier, was again attacked on the night of 21/22 January, this time by eight Wellingtons, when a number of explosions were observed by the crews. Next it was the turn of the Italian barracks at Apollonia near Barce to warrant the attention of the Blenheims. Results of the bombing were unobserved by the crews but the Italians reported that only two of the seven attacking aircraft actually bombed the barracks and these failed to cause any serious damage. Hurricanes from 73 and 274 Squadrons continued to patrol over Acroma and Tobruk and also provided protection for Blenheims and RN vessels operating off the coast, but no enemy aircraft were seen.

Apollonia and Derna landing grounds were bombed by small groups of Blenheims on 23 January, when four explosions and small fires erupted in the barracks area at the former, while bombs were seen to burst among buildings at the latter. Blenheims also attacked Maraua landing ground, where bombs were observed to burst among parked aircraft. Hurricanes meanwhile flew protective patrols between Acroma and Ras el-Meheta and again encountered no aerial opposition. British forward patrols reported eight enemy bombers burning on a landing ground east of Derna, while 50,000 gallons of petrol was discovered abandoned by the retreating Italians between Ain el-Gazala and Bomba seaplane base, where an astonishing total of some 20,000 bombs of varying sizes were found, many of which would soon be put to good use. Although not encountered by the RAF patrols, Italian aircraft were about and further south, near Giarabub, British troops were attacked by six dive-bombers which caused little damage and no casualties. During the evening two Wellingtons and six Hurricanes[3] arrived at Sidi

---

[3] The Hurricanes and pilots had flown to Egypt across central Africa from Takoradi on the West Coast, having arrived there via the carrier *Furious* as had 73 Squadron in November. The nine pilots, all Battle of Britain veterans, were Flg Off C.D. Whittingham, Plt Offs J.F. Pain, P.J. Kearsey, D.J. Thacker, D.J. Hammond, C.E. Langdon, and Sgts A.H. Deacon, C.W. McDougal and C.G. Hodson.

Haneish from Ismailia, all eight aircraft destined for Malta, where they were
urgently needed; three spare Hurricane pilots were passengers aboard the
Wellingtons. 73 Squadron was asked to house the crews although this caused minor
problems, as noted by the Squadron diarist:

> "The officers and NCOs had blankets but we experienced difficulty in having
> them for the night as we had three spare tents but no beds or bed boards to
> spare."

The detachment remained two nights, departing on the morning of 25 January for
Gazala, where the Hurricanes were to refuel and then await the arrival overhead of
the two Wellingtons since it was considered inadvisable for the bombers to land at
Gazala in daylight. In the event, the leading Wellington damaged its tailwheel while
taxying out at Sidi Haneish and the operation was postponed until a replacement
could be flown in from Ismailia. While waiting for this, the second Wellington flew
to Gazala with blankets and kit for the Hurricane pilots – and promptly burst a tyre
when landing. The two replacement Wellingtons arrived early the following
morning but again the flight to Malta had to be delayed because some of the
Hurricanes' guns – some of which had been removed from each aircraft to lighten
the load – were aboard the unserviceable Wellington at Gazala, as was one of the
detachment's spare pilots. A Valencia transport was sent to Gazala to collect pilot
and guns but then intermittent sandstorms prevented the Hurricanes departing for
Malta until the morning of the 29th, accompanied by one of the Wellingtons, the
other having gone unserviceable. Of the débâcle, Hurricane pilot Plt Off John Pain
recalled:

> "We spent an overly long and unexpected four [sic] days as guests of 73
> Squadron. Originally we were to fly to Malta from LG2 at Fort Capuzzo but,
> by moving the rendezvous to Gazala, shortened the water crossing [to Malta]
> by about 60 miles. However, having arrived at Gazala the escorting Wimpey
> went u/s. We returned to [Sidi Haneish] where sandstorms pinned us down for
> two days. This time was spent exploring the battlefields and acquiring
> souvenirs. All told we made three trips to Gazala before we finally got away.
> The mess at Gazala was an old tomb with the mess bar supported at each end
> by a sarcophagus. Outside the drome was still dangerous with S-mines and
> booby traps, and shrapnel was a serious hazard."

Of the long and potentially hazardous flight to Malta, Pain wrote:

> "While our aircraft were equipped with non-jettisonable, unself-sealing long-
> range tanks, our guns were empty. It had been considered in Cairo that the
> weight of the ammo might be decisive in achieving range to Malta with a
> safety margin. A loose vic was formed on the Wimpey and I was on the outer
> starboard. [Flg Off] Whittingham was the appointed leader of the Hurricane
> flight. The first portion of the flight, in beautiful Mediterranean weather, was
> still within fighter range of the Italian Air Force. Consequently, in loose
> formation, we kept up a fairly constant weave which settled down as we got

further out to sea. The majority of the over four-hour flight was uneventful, other than each of us listening to our engine note with considerable concentration. About 100 miles out we saw a destroyer, a small speck with a white wake, some 10,000 feet below us. It lay directly in our path and the Wimpey made no effort to avoid it. The next moment this fly speck erupted and the barrage burst about 2,000 feet below us. The Wimpey made a dignified concession and altered course to starboard by at least five degrees. The next burst was about 500 feet below us and slightly behind. It was quite astonishing how much muck came out of that little ship. We never did find out if it was Royal Navy or Italian."

As the formation approached Malta a number of enemy fighters, probably Italian MC200s, were observed:

"We were almost over Filfla [a rocky outcrop off the southern coast of Malta] when we sighted a formation of ME109s [*sic*]. They sighted us and attacked. There was no alternative but to attack even though we had no ammo. I am not sure of who did what at this stage. We went into them almost head-on and they scattered. Then followed a short dogfight. Two Hurris stayed with the Wimpey which went hell for leather for Luqa and made it safely. The melée was sharp and intense with our continuing pressing the attack, but when they broke we left them to it. It was pointless pursuing them with no ammo, and fuel was getting low. We landed at Hal Far."

Within a month three of the nine reinforcement pilots would be dead and a fourth wounded[4].

Meanwhile, operations to prevent air attack on a special convoy bound for Malta from Alexandria were carried out on 24 January by Blenheims which bombed Sidi el-Magrun landing ground, where two aircraft were claimed damaged, although Italian records reveal damage to one SM79 only and injury to one airman. Other Blenheims bombed dispersed aircraft at Soluch landing ground, where an SM79 was destroyed and a second damaged, plus an airman wounded, while a further group visited Maraua but inflicted little damage. One of the Blenheims was claimed shot down by a G50bis of 151°Gruppo CT, although the targeted aircraft was able to limp back to its base in a damaged condition. Protection for these sorties was provided by Hurricanes from both 73 and 274 Squadrons, which patrolled the Mechili-Martuba line. Despite the Hurricane patrols, G50bis-escorted Ju87s of the newly arrived I/StG1 were able to dive-bomb advanced British forces in the Mechili area, inflicting considerable casualties.

With Tobruk safely secured the next objective was Derna – 40 miles to the west – and, in support of the offensive, Air Commodore Collishaw moved 202 Group HQ to Sidi Mahmoud. In preparation for the assault he ordered 73 and 274 Squadrons to prepare for a move to Gazala, while 3RAAF and 208 Squadrons were to advance to Tmimi, the latter unit flying its remaining seven Lysanders and four

---

4 See *Malta: The Hurricane Years, 1940-41* by Christopher Shores and Brian Cull with Nicola Malizia published by Grub Street.

Hurricanes[5] from Gambut during the morning. 274 Squadron promptly despatched six aircraft to operate from Gazala East, to where an advance party under Plt Off Wilson had been sent by road. However, the vehicle in which they were travelling was blown up by a landmine although all occupants escaped injury, but the incident caused the intended operation to be cancelled. Nonetheless, the Squadron despatched six aircraft to carry out a sweep over the forward area, followed by a second patrol in the afternoon. Apart from minor AA fire over Derna there was nothing to report although Flg Off Patterson failed to return from this sortie. News was soon received, however, advising the Squadron that Patterson had force-landed in the Tobruk area following engine problems. Both pilot and aircraft (P2638) were unharmed and the Canadian returned to Bardia the following morning.

On the morning of 25 January seven Blenheims bombed dispersed aircraft at Maraua, others being despatched to raid Derna and Barce but these were prevented from reaching Barce by the fighter defence. Hurricanes of 73 Squadron and RAAF Gladiators patrolled the Mechili-Martuba line but encountered no enemy aircraft. Nonetheless, off Tobruk the 5,856-ton British tanker *Tynefield* was attacked and damaged by a bomber, probably a Ju88 of LG1 operating from Sicily. Three Blenheims returned to Barce landing ground the next day (26 January) where two Italian aircraft were claimed probably destroyed on the ground; one G50bis was in fact damaged. Nine other Blenheims bombed Maraua and three went to Apollonia. A protective patrol of four RAAF Gladiators over Mechili engaged five G50bis of 2°Gruppo CT, losing one aircraft and its pilot, and two others were damaged. The Italian pilots claimed four Gladiators shot down, while the Australians claimed a G50 damaged in return.

274 Squadron was instructed to send two Hurricanes to operate from Sidi Barrani, Flg Offs Mason and Patterson being selected for the duty. During an afternoon offensive patrol on 26 January, the two Hurricanes encountered three G50bis of 2°Gruppo CT near Derna which Patterson (P3823) immediately chased, claiming two shot down and damage to a third. One of these was flown by M.llo Ottorino Muscinelli of 358^Squadriglia, who was killed. Meanwhile, Mason (P3722) saw seven CR42s of 368^Squadriglia busy strafing Australian troops, the Italian pilots apparently oblivious to the approaching Hurricane; Mason continued relating his experiences in the series of letters to his parents:

> "Chased them and when they turned to attack me I had a quick dogfight with them all round me. The first one I fired at went down and crashed without burning. The second and third each turned slowly over and dived straight in and exploded. All this was over in two or three minutes. By the time the third one was down the others had disappeared which was very fortunate as my motor cut and I had to force-land. All this took place very low over the top of our front-line troops and I landed next to a blazing CR42 amidst crowds of wildly enthusiastic Australians [about 30 miles south-west of Gazala]. Unfortunately the ground was very rough and I burst a tyre and went up on my nose, wrecking the poor old aircraft with which I had got all my victories.

---

[5] V7345 flown by Flg Off L.G. Burnard; V7291, Flg Off L.T. Benson; P3826, Flg Off R.R. Stephenson; N2611, Flg Off R.J. Hardiman.

After I force-landed I learnt that one of the CR42 pilots had tried to bale out but his parachute had not opened. So I had a look at him. He was about 200 yards from his still-blazing machine. I had got him in the right shoulder so he had not been able to open his chute. I went through his pockets and found a lot of interesting snapshots and a lot of letters. Before I left I covered him with his parachute and weighted it down with stones. I hitchhiked by road and air, back to the Squadron. When I arrived there I was accosted by several press representatives who made me pose for photographs."

Mason's aircraft may have been hit in this action since a Hurricane was claimed by Serg Magg Annibale Ricotti, and a probable by Ten Giuseppe Zuffi, both of 368^Squadriglia. Two of Mason's victims were killed, Sottoten Alfonso Nuti and M.llo Guido Papparato from the same unit. These victories raised his total to 13, elevating him to the position of top-scoring pilot in the Middle East and gaining him a DFC. Flg Off Patterson's score was now seven.

From Gazala five Hurricanes of 73 Squadron took off to patrol Mechili and Derna but when they commenced the return flight Flt Lt Beytagh realised one aircraft was missing, at the same time noticing smoke coming from the ground. Dropping down to investigate what turned out to be the smouldering wreck of a crashed CR42 – presumably one of Mason's victims – the Hurricanes were fired on by lorry-mounted machine-guns hidden in a wadi. Sgt Jock Stenhouse's aircraft (V7559) was hit. His companions watched with horror as it dived straight towards the ground but, at the last moment, Stenhouse was able momentarily to regain control, climb to about 1,500 feet and bale out. Sgt Garton, who was leading Green Section, later noted the incident in his diary:

"Took Green Section of Webby, Jock and myself to Gazala, along with Blue Section. Patrolled over Mechili and Martuba from there, with Beytagh leading. Over Mechili we sighted an object burning on the ground. The leader took the formation down but I stayed aloft, out of harm's way Jock Stenhouse was shot up by ground defences and baled out from about 1,500 feet. He was last seen lying face down on the ground with Itie transport converging on him from the west, and our own tanks from the east. Hope he has been found by someone as we believe he was hurt in his fall."

Although he had come down midway between British and Italian troops, Stenhouse was safely rescued and transferred to hospital where he was found to have broken his leg. The 'missing' Hurricane had meanwhile returned to Sidi Haneish, its pilot having merely become separated from the rest of the Flight.

The two Hurricane squadrons were ordered to put up maximum patrols on the morning of 27 January as a major ground battle was developing around Mechili. 73 Squadron was short of aircraft but, even so, A Flight was able to despatch seven aircraft at 0730, followed by four of B Flight an hour later, both patrols refuelling at Gazala. On their return to Sidi Haneish they were refuelled and sent off again, although flown by different pilots. No enemy aircraft were sighted during these patrols but sandstorms in the afternoon compelled three of A Flight and all four of B Flight to overnight at Gazala. By the end of the day Mechili had fallen to the Armoured Division.

Three Hurricane-escorted Blenheims raided Apollonia landing ground during the day, while a patrol from 274 Squadron strafed M/T withdrawing from Mechili, inflicting severe casualties. By the end of the day Mechili had been totally abandoned by the Italians although resistance continued from the forts at Derna where, on the nearby landing ground, 14 unserviceable aircraft were found. Hurricanes from 274 Squadron were also engaged in strafing sorties the following day (28 January), destroying several M/T when a convoy was caught moving towards Barce, Flt Lt Wykeham-Barnes (P2638) leading a further strafe of vehicles seen near Maraua and east of Barce, part of the convoy attacked in the area the previous day. All aircraft returned safely from these sorties.

The remaining days of January were comparatively quiet for the Hurricane squadrons, allowing ground personnel of B Flt/73 Squadron to move forward to Gazala on the 29th, followed by the remainder of the Squadron two days later. 274 Squadron had already moved into Gazala and were saddened to learn that their successful South African pilot, Bob Talbot, had been recalled for service with the SAAF, departing for the Union within days. Of the move to Gazala, one of 73 Squadron's airmen, Ken Rumbold, remembered:

"Our advance party had hung around Gazala for several days but only a few Hurricanes came in to refuel and rearm. One night we could see the Itie aircraft over Tobruk and Plt Off Millist took off without the aid of a flarepath to sort them out. He landed back with the help of truck headlights."

The Hurricanes continued to fly offensive patrols during this period, one from 73 Squadron flying as far west as ten miles from Barce, but without sighting any enemy aircraft. On 30 January, Derna finally fell to the Australians. War correspondent Moorehead wrote:

"The country the men were asked to penetrate after Tobruk was vastly different from the desert. Derna was an oasis of banana plantations and pomegranate groves, of lush vegetable gardens and leafy trees. On Derna aerodrome, a great red plain lying above the thousand-foot seacliffs with the town below, the Italians fought. Wadi Derna, a ragged valley that stuck into the hills, was for few days death to enter. A few companies of Australians charged the aerodrome above with the bayonet and made themselves masters of its storehouses and buildings. The two sides were so mingled at first that the leading Australian platoon lodging in a hangar heard Italian voices through the night.

The aerodrome with its twenty wrecked machines[6] was now ours, but unexpectedly about forty guns firing from the other side of Wadi Derna turned upon it an uninterrupted cannonade of shellfire. This was bad shelling while it

---

[6] Derna was one of the landing grounds which had been attacked by 'commandos' landed by craft of the Inshore Squadron. It was recorded that German-occupied landing grounds were generally assaulted by small groups of mainly British-led German Jews, and Italian-occupied landing grounds by similarly led Senussi Arabs, whose hatred of the Italians was legendary and fanatical; the commandos would place small time-bombs on any aircraft they could reach and swiftly depart into the night.

lasted. And it lasted three or four days. The fall of Derna depended greatly upon the fall of a certain Fort Rudero which the Italians were using as an observation and sniping post. In the first advance one Australian company was all but wiped out, and another company had to be withdrawn. The final attempt came one forenoon, when the red earth was washed and new after a heavy shower at night. The barrage had begun afresh and a staid slow flight of Savoias – the last we were to see – had been bombing until it ran into a lone Hurricane coming back from patrol into Libya. The Australians forgot the shelling, forgot momentarily the wounded nearby and their hunger and raised a cheer as the Hurricane dived straight through the Italian machines and sent one dropping with that breathtaking fateful slowness to the red desert. Its bursting flames rose from behind the wreckage of the other broken aircraft on the field."

The identity of the Hurricane pilot referred to in Moorehead's account is uncertain, but may have been Flg Off Laurence Benson of 208 Squadron who had been briefed to carry out a reconnaissance sortie to Slonte during the morning of 29 January, and had been requested to drop a message container regarding an Italian pilot who had been taken prisoner, undoubtedly Serg Cesare Sironi, a CR42 pilot of 70^Squadriglia shot down on 23 January. Benson may have overflown Derna en route to Slonte and Benghazi and thereby engaged the Savoias, since there is no report of this combat within the records of any of the Hurricane units. Benson failed to return and it was assumed that his Hurricane (N2611) had been shot down by ground fire, although it seems probable that he fell victim to a CR42 flown by Serg Giuseppe Sanguettoli of 74^Squadriglia. The Italians reported that Sanguettoli had intercepted and shot down a Hurricane over K2 landing ground near Benghazi, only realising later that it had dropped the message container. Two days later an Italian aircraft dropped a message over British lines to say that Benson[7] had been buried with full military honours. Sadly, the location of his grave was lost during the course of subsequent battles in the area. Encounters with enemy aircraft were, however, infrequent at this time, although Flg Off Mason (P3722) of 274 Squadron shot down a CR42 near Derna next day (30 January); of his 14th victory, he wrote:

"I decided to have a look at Benina near Benghazi. Actually a hell of a way and much too far for a safe margin. I had Pat [Flg Off Patterson] from Toronto with me. It was teatime. I saw a single CR42 on patrol and went for him. Where we boobed was that instead of taking our time, Pat and myself were each scared the other would get there first. So we were going too fast. I attacked first and overshot him. By the time I had turned, Pat had disappeared. So I started in. But this CR42 was very tough. We kept doing head-on attacks where we rush at each other head-on until point-blank range and then shoot past each other. Usually very successful. But this fellow wouldn't go down. On the fourth attack we were rushing each other, each firing. But this time he didn't pull out but came straight on. I pulled up instinctively and as he passed

---

[7] Flg Off Benson had survived being shot down by a CR42 in November 1940 while flying a Lysander. His gunner, despite a leg wound, managed to shoot down their assailant.

underneath my wing I felt a crash and a bump. I thought we had collided. I had a glimpse of him going straight on and burning. I now realised that I had been hit and not collided. I felt a pain in my right side and saw a great hole in the side of the cockpit where an explosive bullet had come through and burst inside. Also, the wing had had one explode [*sic*] and bits and pieces were flapping about. However, the aircraft seemed OK. I had obviously been caught by an explosive bullet; I felt blood on my side and had hundreds of miles to go. So I pressed my right hand on my side to close the gaping hole and stop my guts falling out, and flew with my left hand as fast as I could go. However, if I flew too fast I would run out of petrol, so I had to use my judgment and compromise. I reached the aerodrome and made an extremely bad landing. I taxied in to be carried, fainting, from my machine. When I got down I expected the movement to cause great agony. However, to my surprise, I walked OK. I went in the mess and looked for blood. Eventually I found a small patch on my shirt. The Doc looked at it and found that the small pieces of shrapnel from the explosive bullet had gone through so much clothing that they had cut my skin and bounced out again!! But the aircraft had been badly shot about."

Mason's gallant opponent in this action was Serg Mario Turchi of 368^Squadriglia, who managed to force-land his damaged fighter on Benina aerodrome. Patterson also returned with his aircraft (P3765) damaged by Turchi, managing to land safely despite a shrapnel wound to his left arm which necessitated a visit to the hospital. A patrol led by Flt Lt Beytagh (V7492/TP-H) of 73 Squadron on the afternoon of the last day of the month (31 January) encountered a large convoy of about 300 M/T and some 5,000 troops on the road from Derna to Barce, while Hurricanes from 274 Squadron escorted Blenheims raiding Barce airfield, where three Ro37 reconnaissance aircraft were damaged and three airmen were killed, with four others wounded. From this sortie Plt Off P.D. Strong (P2651) failed to return but was later found to have force-landed south-west of Gazala due to oil pressure failure. He was returned by the army the following day. Meanwhile, three Hurricanes of 274 Squadron led by Flt Lt Lapsley (V7552) were despatched to attack aircraft and M/T reported at Barce, but very poor visibility was encountered over the target area due to heavy showers, with cloud descending to 200 feet. Nonetheless, a large aircraft seen on the ground was strafed and several lorries proceeding into Barce were similarly attacked.

3RAAF[8] had been advised of its imminent re-equipment with Hurricanes and towards the end of the month pilots of A Flight began to withdraw to Ismailia for conversion. Flg Off John Jackson, a 32-year-old Queenslander, learned that he was to go:

"Hooray! John Saunders and I are to go back to Ismailia to collect two Hurricanes and to join Gordon Steege (Flight Commander) and the rest of our Flight – Perrin, Boyd and Gatward. We went by Lysander, John and I crouching in the back, to Sollum. There we picked up a broken-down Magister

---

[8] 3RAAF had claimed 15 victories while flying Gladiators since its first action on 18 November 1940, Flg Off Boyd having been credited with four, Flt Lt Steege with three, and Flg Offs Gatward and Arthur with two apiece.

in a horrible state and we headed for Amiriya, landing at Sidi Barrani, Mersa Matruh, Fuka. Took about 2½ hours to start the contraption at Fuka and we were terribly anxious to get to Amiriya so that we could go into Alex and spend the night. Flew all day over a long stream of transports heading west. A great sight. Arrived Amiriya just before dark and scrounged a lift on a lorry into Alex – and did we have a time!"

Three days later they were introduced to the Hurricane:

"Yesterday afternoon we were given a bit of a talk on Hurricanes by a pilot – flew them today. They are great. Cruise along at about 200mph and believe, when opened out, will do about 280-300mph. Poor dagoes! But what I like is the increased visibility and I've always liked the low-wing, monoplane-type best. I feel much happier now we have Hurricanes."

At the end of the month six Hurricanes, all second-hand and now sporting the new OS codes of 3RAAF (its Gladiators had been coded NW), set out from Ismailia to join the Squadron which was located at the newly captured Martuba airfield near Derna, a town of considerable size with a peacetime population in the neighbourhood of 10,000. Of his first impressions of Derna, Plt Off Peter Moulding of 6 Squadron wrote:

"The North African seaboard from Tripoli to Alexandria can boast no town more attractive nor yet one with a better natural setting than Derna. The little port rests comfortably on a flat shelf of fertile, sandy soil providing an irregular strip of variegated colour between the deep green thickets on the lower slopes of the escarpment and the clear-cut blues of the lagoon. The southern part of the town is composed mainly of villa-type houses, white or colour-washed, each surrounded by its own vivid display of flowering shrubs. Her aerodrome, high up on the escarpment some three miles outside the town, could be accounted of limited value. The red clay held the moisture and after rain the surface became too soft for safety. On the western perimeter, close to the main road, stood a large, disused hangar with, alongside, several sheds and offices, many of which had suffered damage from British bombs. In such a place as this, the chief problem was to disperse and conceal aircraft to the best advantage. With the precious Hurricanes they took particular care. They cleared tracks along which the machines could be taxied well away from the landing surface."

Derna did not possess a harbour of any value but the little bay on which it stood provided a safe anchorage for small craft. Its most valuable asset to its captors was its good water supply.

During the second half of January submarines of the Royal Navy's 10th Flotilla had commenced operations off the North African coast against the Italian Trapani-Tripoli supply line, HMS *Upholder* sinking a 3,950-ton freighter on the night of 27th/28th, before torpedoing a steamer from the same convoy. Allied vessels in the region did not escape attention, the hospital ship *Dorsetshire*, conveying Italian PoWs from Sollum to Alexandria, being bombed by two Heinkels of 4/KG26 on the last day of the month. The crippled steamer drifted ashore near Sidi Barrani but many of the prisoners panicked and about 50 drowned. The bombers also attacked the minesweeper *Huntley* on her way to Derna. The 700-ton vessel went down off Gatruh although seven officers and 51 men of her crew were saved. One of the Heinkels force-landed at Benina on return due to engine failure. The aircraft was badly damaged and its pilot was injured. The reconnaissance unit, 1(F)/121, also lost one of its Ju88Ds at the end of the month when the crew baled out due to the close proximity of an 'enemy aircraft'. All four survived and returned safely to their unit, but the identity of the cause of their problem remains unclear. Shortly thereafter, a second Heinkel of 4/KG26 force-landed at Benina, burst into flames and was completely destroyed. This crew also survived unhurt.

At the beginning of February more Ju87s arrived at Castel Benito from Sicily, but the five aircraft were the first of the Regia Aeronautica's newly acquired dive-bombers to reach North Africa, although they had been operating from Sicily against Malta for the past five months. Led by Cap Ercolano Ercolani, the 236^Squadriglia Ju87s, nicknamed *Picchiatelli* (literally, crazy dive-bomber) by their crews, flew to Misurata next day where they were joined by five more, these from 237^Squadriglia led by Cap Giovanni Santinoni. The two squadriglie formed 96°Gruppo Aut B.a'T under the command of Cap Ercolani but it would be some considerable time before the mainly untrained crews were ready for operations. With 5^Squadra Aerea reforming and regrouping in Tripolitania under the command of General S.A. Mario Aimone Cat, it could now boast nine squadrons of CR42s and six more equipped with G50bis:

Castel Benito

2°Gruppo CT	G50bis	Magg Giuseppe Baylon
150^Squadriglia		Cap Tullio De Prato
152^Squadriglia		Cap Salvatore Teja
358^Squadriglia		Cap Annibale Sterzi

Misurata

155°Gruppo CT	G50bis	Magg Luigi Bianchi
351^Squadriglia		Cap Aldo Alessandrini
360^Squadriglia		Cap Gino Callieri
378^Squadriglia		Cap Bruno Tattanelli

Tauorga

18°Gruppo CT	CR42	Magg Ferruccio Vosilla
83^Squadriglia		Cap Edoardo Molinari
85^Squadriglia		Cap Giulio Anelli
95^Squadriglia		Cap Gino Lodi

Sorman

23°Gruppo CT	CR42	TenCol Tito Falconi
70^Squadriglia		Cap Claudio Solaro
74^Squadriglia		Cap Mario Pinna
75^Squadriglia		Cap Pietro Calistri
151°Gruppo CT	CR42	TenCol Raffaele Colacicchi
366^Squadriglia		Cap Bernardino Serafini
367^Squadriglia		Cap Simeone Marsan
368^Squadriglia		Cap Enrico Zuffi

Apart from the newly arrived Ju87s at Misurata, based at Tauorga was 53°Gruppo BT with two squadrons of SM79s under the command of Magg Rosario Di Blasi, while Ro37s and Ca311s of 64° and 67°·Gruppi OA (four squadrons) were at Mellaha and Wadi Tamet respectively, and one squadron of SM79 torpedo-bombers (175^Squadriglia RST) was operating from Castel Benito.

For the British defenders of the narrow coastal strip February opened with an early morning raid by an estimated six German aircraft – identified as He111s and Ju87s – against shipping in Sollum harbour, where the Stukas were seen to release their bombs from heights of barely 1,000 feet while the Heinkels dropped at least three parachute mines. The guns put up a fearsome barrage but, although one of the raiders was believed to have crashed into the sea in flames and a second retired emitting volumes of smoke, no German losses were recorded. One of the gunnery officers, Lt Kenneth Rankin of 152 HAA, noted in his journal:

> "Two of our shoots went extremely close ... but these German pilots have the
> most incredible guts ... even the Lewis gunners had opened up and had been
> fairly close with their shooting. We all 'took our hats off' to those brave
> German pilots ..."

The RAF continued its series of raids against various Italian landing grounds west of Derna. Seven Blenheims visited Soluch and dropped bombs among dispersed aircraft, damaging a Ca309 of 23^Squadriglia APC, while a lone aircraft bombed Barce landing ground. 73 Squadron, currently based at Gazala, despatched six aircraft to El Adem from where one section carried out a strafe of Apollonia landing ground. Sqn Ldr Murray (V7560/TP-F) led the attack, claiming a Ghibli twin-engine reconnaissance machine destroyed on the ground, while Flg Off Storrar (V7544/TP-S) and Plt Off Wareham (V7299/TP-D) shared two more in addition to a Ca310. The Italians reported that three Ca310s were damaged as a result of this attack. The other section from B Flight – Plt Offs Millist and Goodman led by Flt Lt Beytagh (V7551/TP-K) – strafed M/T and troops on a road near El Ghebab, destroying many vehicles and inflicting heavy casualties. A further one dozen sorties were flown by the Squadron during the day but only Sgts Marshall and Wills encountered enemy aircraft, being engaged by seven CR42s from 151°Gruppo CT while strafing a convoy near Cyrene at about 1730. Wills (V7544/TP-S) turned the tables on one of his assailants which he claimed shot down south-west of Cyrene. This was possibly Cap Bruno Locatelli of 368^Squadriglia who failed to return from an operational sortie. His colleagues, however, reported that he had shot down by ground fire. A Hurricane was in turn claimed shot down by Cap Bernardino Serafini[9], CO of 366^Squadriglia.

---

[9] On 26 November 1941, Cap Bernardino Serafini, flying a CR42 of 366^Squadriglia, shot down a Hurricane of 33 Squadron flown by Flg Off D.S.F. Winsland DFC, a veteran of the fighting in Greece and the Desert – probably the last Hurricane to fall victim to one of the Italian biplane fighters. Victor and vanquished were reunited in 1984, due to the efforts of Brian Cull and Italian air historian Nicola Malizia, and the two former enemies have remained firm friends ever since.

Blenheims and Hurricanes continued searching out Italian convoys withdrawing from the Derna area, one located west of Faidia on 2 February being bombed by the Blenheims before Hurricanes strafed; some 50 vehicles were claimed destroyed, six of these being credited to 73 Squadron. Another convoy was attacked between El Gubba and Maraua by Blenheims but they were themselves engaged by CR42s of 151°Gruppo CT which shot down two of the bombers. 274 Squadron despatched two aircraft, flown by Flt Lt Tulasne and Flg Off Weller, to attack M/T between Maraua and Slonte, followed by two more two hours later. At least 20 large diesel lorries were strafed.

Next day (3 February), eight Blenheims bombed two ships off the coast near Sirte and also attacked an M/T convoy nearby, while Hurricanes strafed M/T and troops withdrawing to Barce and destroyed an estimated 36 vehicles. 274 Squadron alone flew 14 sorties, sections being led by Sqn Ldr Lapsley (the new CO), Flt Lt Wykeham-Barnes, Flt Lt Tulasne and Flt Lt R.H. Smith, when numerous lorries packed with troops were attacked between Barce and Tocra, causing considerable damage. The Italians also recorded an attack on the landing ground at Berka by five aircraft, presumably Blenheims, which destroyed two unserviceable aircraft. Axis aircraft, although scarce, were out and about, British reports stating that three aircraft bombed Tmimi but caused little damage and no casualties. Ju88Ds of 1(F)/121 were active and, on returning to Tripoli, one of these suffered the indignity of being attacked and seriously damaged by three G50bis over Castel Benito, as a result of which air gunner Gfr Rudolf Nowack was severely wounded, losing a leg.

On the morning of the 3rd, Air Marshal Tedder paid a flying visit in 267 Squadron's Q6 to meet front-line commanders:

"I flew up to Tobruk, and thereon to Bomba where General O'Connor had pitched his headquarters. He and I had arranged that I would come up and be given an insight into his plans and timing, so that I could co-ordinate the operations of the heavy bombers with his own operations. He gave me an outline of the situation regarding supplies, which were inevitably a continual brake on his advance. He told me ... as far as he could see it would be ten days before he could make a definite advance against Benghazi. I said I would adjust our air operations to fit in with his timetable."

During the first few days of February Wellingtons carried out a number of nocturnal sorties against various targets, including attacks against Barce railway station and Berka airfield, both being raided again the following night. Benina was also targeted on this night and two hangars were reported destroyed. Five Wellingtons returned to Benina the following night, Berka and Jedabya airfields also being visited, when one aircraft was claimed destroyed on the ground. In addition to bombs, some 6,000 pamphlets were dropped calling for the surrender of the various garrisons. Submarines of the 10th Flotilla were also active in the Gulf of Sirte, HMS *Truant* sinking one ship of 1,130 tons but missed a convoy approaching Tripoli. Two nights later four torpedo-armed Swordfish of the Fleet Air Arm's 815 Squadron set out from Gazala to hunt down reported shipping leaving Tripoli harbour, but the convoy was not located in the darkness and one Swordfish suffered engine failure during the return flight, force-landing in the desert near Gazala.

With Cirene now in British hands, Blenheims and Hurricanes continued to attack M/T retreating from Barce on the morning of 4 February and claimed ten vehicles destroyed or badly damaged. Six Hurricanes of 274 Squadron led by Flt Lt Tulasne attacked transport and troops west of Bacnis during the morning, inflicting severe damage. Flt Sgt Tom Morris (V7770) was compelled to force-land west of Mechili due to fuel problems but, later, both pilot and aircraft returned safely to Gazala. With the Italians in full retreat, all available Blenheims and Hurricanes were sent into battle – few as they were. Air Chief Marshal Longmore, the AOC-in-C, later wrote:

> "It must be admitted that the scale of our air operations at this stage was somewhat reduced, due partly to unserviceability through many flying hours under desert conditions, and also through our inability to establish airfields sufficiently rapidly to keep pace with the speed of the Armoured Division's advance. The over-ponderous standard squadron formation did not lend itself to such conditions and moreover we had very few transport aircraft left. The need was apparent for some unit, charged with the preparation, construction or repair and subsequently defence of airstrips for fighters, and it should be up with the forward troops in the advance. It was the first time during the war in which we had moved forward at such a pace."

The railway station at Barce was bombed by Blenheims on 4 February, when hits on the track were observed. One of the bombers was shot down by a CR42 of 368^Squadriglia, with the loss of the crew. A second fighter from this unit, flown by Serg Ezio Masenti, suffered engine problems and landed at Barce. British troops were in the area and, as soon as returning pilots reported on Masenti's plight, a Ca133 light transport being used as a hack by 151°Gruppo CT took off from Agedabia in the hands of M.llo Giovanni Accorsi of 366^Squadriglia, who was accompanied by an engineer, 1°Av Mot. Callerani. Three CR42s of 366^Squadriglia led by Cap Chiarini, provided protection but, over Barce, the Ca133 was intercepted at low-level by a section of 73 Squadron Hurricanes and was shot down by Plt Off McColl (V7372/TP-W), both Accorsi and Callerani losing their lives in the subsequent crash. As the CR42s dived down in a vain attempt to assist the doomed transport, the Hurricanes turned to engage, Chiarini being shot down by Flg Off Goodman (V7716/TP-U); Chiarini, one of the Regia Aeronautica's most successful fighter pilots with at least five victories to his credit was also killed[10].

Meanwhile, Plt Off Millist's Hurricane (V7491) was hit in the engine during a head-on attack by Serg Antonio Camerini, necessitating a forced-landing ten miles north-east of Benina. For two days, without food or water, Ken Millist – known as 'Tiny' due to his height, in excess of six feet – walked and hid, being chased on one occasion by an Italian motor-cyclist whom he successfully evaded. On the third day

---

[10] Cap Guglielmo Chiarini had been credited with shooting down a Gladiator on 23 July 1940, followed by two Blenheims and a third shared on 18 September, a shared Hurricane on 31 October, and another Gladiator on 19 November.

he met an Australian army sergeant who gave him food and water before helping him to obtain a lift to Derna, where he met Plt Off Wareham who had taken an advance ground party to the landing ground in readiness for the morrow's operations. Of Millist's plight, his colleague Plt Off Bill Eiby recalled:

> "When he was shot down by the vintage biplane everyone laughed their bloody heads off. He went in head-on. We were told not to tackle them head-on, but Tiny did and got hit in the radiator for his pains."

During the afternoon ground strafing of M/T by the Hurricanes was abandoned due to lack of suitable targets, general offensive patrols being reinstated in the Barce area. With the Australians pushing on towards Benghazi from the north, the Armoured Division made a dash across the desert from Mechili towards the coastal road south of Benghazi. The speed and success of the advance took everyone by surprise, the trapped Italian forces making a belated but unsuccessful attempt to break out at Beda Fomm, where the greater part was captured or destroyed. As the Australians advanced on Benghazi, the RAF continued its assault against Berka and Benina airfields. The Blenheims bombed Benghazi railway station and Jedabya landing ground on 5 February, while three escorting 73 Squadron Hurricanes operating from Derna strafed Benina aerodrome, where eight or nine bombers were claimed damaged on the ground by Sqn Ldr Murray (V7560/TP-F), Flg Off Storrar (V7544/TP-S) and Sgt Marshall (V7553/TP-E). Near Benghazi the crew of a Ju52/3m of KGrzbV.9 reported being attacked by a fighter with the result that the gunner, Uffz Heinz Schneuder, was wounded. This was possibly a combat with a Blenheim or an Italian fighter, since the Hurricane pilots did not record meeting any enemy aircraft in the air on this date.

3RAAF at Martuba, now under the command of newly promoted Sqn Ldr Peter Jeffrey, had been rejoined two days earlier by its Hurricane-equipped A Flight from Ismailia. Within the Australian unit Flt Lt Duncan Campbell had also been promoted to Squadron Leader rank, while Jock Perrin and Alan Rawlinson were made Flight Lieutenants. The Squadron could now boast two Squadron Leaders and five Flight Lieutenants! Five of the Hurricanes were immediately despatched to Mechili landing ground on the morning of the 5th, with the object of refuelling there before undertaking an offensive patrol between Mechili and Benghazi but, on arrival at the designated landing ground, the pilots encountered many problems, as Flg Off Jackson noted in his diary:

> "Three of the Hurricanes would not start again – mine, John Saunders and Boyd. Turned them by hand until exhausted. Nearly upset my back again, will have to be careful. The other two chaps, Gordon Steege and Gaty, took off OK and flew to the correct drome a few miles further south on a huge dried up lake, and they sent back a trolley starter battery. We got off OK and joined the others. The correct ground proved to be an advanced LG for 208 Squadron, but they were out of petrol and the job was called off – bad business."

Benghazi was finally occupied on 6 February, little resistance being experienced in the final stages. When the RAF entered Benina it found some 85 abandoned unserviceable and damaged aircraft, including a Ju88D of 1(F)/121 and a Heinkel of II/KG26. The *Daily Express'* Alan Moorehead reached Benghazi on the tail of the Australian troops:

"Benghazi lay in view. It stood there clearly, a long line of white rooftops by the sea, a cloud of smoke shot with flame rising from the centre of the town. Nearer on the coastal plain were the red and grey roofs of Benina – Benina, through which Mussolini for a year past had provided most of his bombers and fighters with their ammunition for the destruction [*sic*] of Egypt and the Army of the Nile. All of us had been bombed by aircraft from Benina. Now the whole airport was deserted and in ruins. Through glasses I counted 22 wrecked aircraft at one end of the airfield alone. A water-tower had been blown bodily out of the ground by the RAF. Half-a-dozen hangars, each large enough to accommodate a goods train, were shattered and savaged into a state of uselessness. In the airport's living quarters, where we slept for a few hours, Italian pilots had lived well with their private baths and neat dressing-tables equipped with double mirrors and scent sprays. But all was in wild disorder by the time we got in.

Graziani's army of Cyrenaica was destroyed for ever. Of the quarter million Italian troops in Libya something more than one half were either killed or in our hands. At least two-thirds of his equipment in ships, aircraft and land weapons were destroyed or captured. Nineteen Fascist generals were captured including General Annibale Bergonzoli [renowned for his achievements in the Spanish Civil War, and former Commandant of Bardia]. He was ill; I saluted him: 'I suppose you want to know how I kept on eluding you since last December', he said. 'Well, I walked out of Bardia on the third day of the battle. I saw it was hopeless, and with several of my officers we set off, walking by night, hiding in caves by day. It took us five days to reach Tobruk. We passed right through British lines. After Tobruk fell I flew out aboard the last remaining plane to Derna. Derna was in some ways our best stand, but when at last many of our guns were out of action and we had no more ammunition I got my troops away by night and with them drove off down the coastal road to Benghazi. We had no time to prepare defences outside Benghazi. In any case, it was an open town. We had no wish to expose the women and children there to any more misery. We decided to leave with our army for Tripoli. You were here too soon ...'. He wore a plain, undecorated green uniform. Among the Fascist generals he was certainly the bravest of the lot."

Of the successful conclusion to the British advance, Air Chief Marshal Longmore wrote:

"Following the British occupation of Benghazi, the remnants of the enemy forces retreated westward to Tripolitania, while the Italian Air Force was no longer capable of offering any serious threat for the time being. It looked as if it would be some time before the enemy would be able to stage an early counter-offensive in Libya."

Meanwhile, the situation in Greece was causing grave concern and the call was for further reinforcements to be sent. Longmore continued:

> "It was therefore with some relief to me that the decision was made not to continue the advance towards Tripoli. My first move was to withdraw No274 (Hurricane) and No45 (Blenheim) Squadrons to start a reserve. A mere trickle of aircraft was coming across the Takoradi-Sudan reinforcement route and hardly any cased Hurricanes were now arriving by sea. No3 Australian Squadron, now completely rearmed with Hurricanes, was to remain at Benina to provide the air defence of Benghazi; No73 Squadron at Gazala was to move to Bu Amud for the defence of Tobruk, whilst No6 Army Co-operation Squadron with its mixture of Hurricanes and Lysanders was to replace No208 at Barce, keeping one Flight with the forward troops at Agedabia."

In Cairo and elsewhere there was great satisfaction with the successful outcome of the Libyan campaign, and General O'Connor expressed his appreciation of the work of 202 Group in a special Order of the Day addressed to Air Commodore Collishaw:

> "I wish to record my very great appreciation of the wonderful work of the RAF units under your command, whose determination and fighting qualities have made this campaign possible. Since the war began you have consistently attacked without hesitation an enemy air force five and ten times your strength, dealing him blow after blow, until finally he was driven out of the sky, and out of Libya, leaving hundreds of derelict aircraft on his aerodromes. In his recent retreat from Tobruk you gave his ground troops no rest, bombing their concentrations, and carrying out low-flying attacks on their M/T columns. In addition to the above you have co-operated to the full in carrying out our many requests for special bombardments, reconnaissances, and protection against enemy air action, and I would like to say how much all this has contributed to our success."

On this very day, hundreds of miles away in Berlin, a relatively unknown Generalleutnant Erwin Rommel was appointed commander of the German troops now assembling in Tripoli, the advance elements of an army about to be accorded the title Deutsches Afrika Korps. The tide in North Africa was about to turn.

CHAPTER III

IN DEFENCE OF BENGHAZI AND TOBRUK

February – March 1941

"It was about this time that rumours abounded of Messerschmitt 109s having been seen up near Tripoli, and soon after there was confirmation that Jerry was moving in to Africa in some strength. This was serious ..."

Cpl Pete Minterne, 73 Squadron

Flt Lt Beytagh and Flg Off Storrar of 73 Squadron flew an offensive patrol along the Libyan coast on 6 February, overflying the ancient Roman town of Apollonia, as the latter recalled:

"Just for the hell of it we went down to have a look, landing our Hurris in the main street. At first we thought the place was deserted but, after a while, people began to creep out of hiding places and come towards us. They didn't seem hostile, so we just stood there and waited to see what was going to happen – keeping a sharp look-out for anything tricky."

Following the rout of the Italian Army, Apollonia, with its whitewashed villas, had been left completely unprotected and was being preyed upon by marauding bands of Arabs who swarmed down from the hills at night to loot and pillage. The inhabitants, of mainly Italian stock, pleaded with Beytagh and Storrar to remain and protect them. The two pilots agreed to stay the night:

"We parked the Hurris at the end of the street and turned them round so that their guns pointed in the right direction. Then we got into them and waited. As dusk fell we could see dim figures sneaking down from the hills into the village. We held our fire till they seemed to be gathered in a bunch at the far end of the street. Then we let them have it – right on target. Oh, boy!"

At first light next morning they took off from Gazala after radioing for a detachment of the army to take over at Apollonia:

"We got a small rocket (from the CO) but, after all, we'd captured a whole

village practically single-handed. And we had a valid excuse for delay ... it was
hard to start the engines on a winding handle while they were still hot. We
simply had to wait till they cooled down."

While they were away, sandstorms had effectively prevented further flying from
Gazala which allowed Sgts Marshall, Leng and Griffith of 73 Squadron to visit
Tobruk to see what could be scrounged; Marshall noted that it was a waste of time
except for six loaves of bread found on the road, the first bread they had seen since
Christmas.

With the return of 3RAAF to the front-line, 274 Squadron was withdrawn from
operations and advised of an imminent posting to Greece. The Squadron's
Hurricanes were thereby handed over to 3RAAF at Martuba, the remaining
Australian Gladiators being flown to Amiriya by the departing pilots[1]. 3RAAF was
at the same time advised of an immediate move to Benina following its capture, the
advance party leaving at 0800 on 9 February. They were joined by eight Hurricanes,
but the pilots were then ordered to fly to nearby Berka landing ground. That night
German bombers raided Benghazi, as Flg Off Jackson of 3RAAF noted:

"Went to bed early (11pm) and shortly afterwards was woken by bombs being
dropped in the town – scared me stiff to hear the planes diving on the town
with a whistle noise and the explosion and flash of the bombs dropping. I
hurriedly shut the windows and lay on the hard, cold floor – a rotten
experience. It was my first real taste of bombing and I don't like it much. They
had another go just before dawn."

The dawn raid was by a single Ju88 which dropped four bombs on Benina
aerodrome, but caused no damage or casualties since they fell outside the perimeter.
As a result of this attack, the Hurricanes were promptly recalled from Berka. 73
Squadron was ordered to despatch a detachment to El Adem for the protection of
Tobruk, Plt Off Legge leading the four aircraft of A Flight. During this relatively
quiet period, as many pilots as possible were granted long-overdue leave and,
individually, flew to Alexandria, some taking Hurricanes in need of servicing,
others as passengers in Lysanders which were acting as air taxis. With the short
leave period over, pilots invariably returned with replacement Hurricanes. These
returning pilots also brought with them rumours that the Squadron was to be sent to
Greece forthwith. Among those rejoining the Squadron was Flg Off Don Scott, who
had been sick since early December. Almost immediately he was sent to Benina to
assist 3RAAF with its conversion to the Hurricane:

"The two senior pilots were Sqn Ldr Jeffrey, a typical Aussie with a quiet
reserved manner, and the senior flight commander Flt Lt Pete Turnbull, who
was his exact opposite, although both were excellent characters. On my first

---

[1] 274 Squadron was not sent to Greece but remained, albeit temporarily, in Egypt as fighter
defence for Alexandria. One of the Squadron's senior French pilots, Flt Lt Tulasne, was
posted to Haifa in Palestine. On 25 February, with Flt Sgt J.A. Breton as his air gunner in one
of the Potez 63-11s, he made an interception of an Italian reconnaissance aircraft
approaching Haifa although an attack did not materialise.

morning, as I entered the hut which served as the dining hall, I happened to be just in front of Turnbull who greeted me with a resounding thump between the shoulder blades and 'G'morning Pommie bastard'. One learns fast, and I took care to be just behind him the following morning and gave him more than he had given me – the greeting being unprintable!"

The AOC-in-C visited 258 Wing Headquarters on 10 February and inspected the Ops room, when it was announced that the Wing was to provide fighter protection for both Tobruk and Benghazi. The detachment at Benghazi was to be known as Advance 258 Wing. At the same time Grp Capt Spackman was relieved as OC by Wg Cdr Johnson, his second-in-command, and posted to RAFHQ in Cairo. A new command was established at this time, RAF Cyrenaica being formed under Grp Capt L.O. Brown, though Air Commodore Collishaw remained in command of 202 Group.

A new man also arrived in Tripoli at this time, General Rommel flying in from Sicily where his aircraft had landed to refuel. On discussing the situation with General Geisler of Fliegerkorps X he was astounded to learn that Rome had forbidden the bombing of Benghazi because of its Italian population and fine Italian-owned property. He immediately rescinded this order and Luftwaffe bombing raids against this vital port commenced immediately, that very night. Rommel's orders were simple and emphatic – recapture Cyrenaica and thereby keep Italy in the war. He immediately came into conflict with his new commander, General Italo Gariboldi, the new Italian C-in-C in North Africa following Marshal Graziani's removal. The Italians made it clear they intended to consolidate their current positions and defend Tripoli whereas Rommel wished to go on the offensive. The advance element of his ground forces began arriving by sea within a few days, but while awaiting the arrival of the main body of his armoured units, he ordered large numbers of dummy tanks based on Volkswagen cars to be built in an effort to fool British reconnaissance aircraft which kept an eye on the port.[2]

The Luftwaffe's bombing offensive against Benghazi began on the night of 11/12 February, AA gunners shooting down a Ju88 of 6/LG1 which crashed south-west of Soluch. The pilot survived to be taken prisoner but his crew of L1+JP all perished. The following night He111s of II/KG26 laid mines off Benghazi while others bombed Berka aerodrome where four British soldiers were killed. A more serious attack developed against Benina next morning when six Ju88s commenced bombing and strafing at 0520 and continued until 0650, although only one building was seriously damaged and two Australian soldiers injured. Just before the end of the raid Flg Off Gatward of 3RAAF took off in an attempt to overtake the Ju88s as they headed back to base, but was unable to catch them. Following the surprise attack, the Squadron was tasked to provide standing patrols over Benghazi during daylight hours, commencing 0545 next morning, initially by a pair of Hurricanes, then by a single aircraft until dusk, the last sortie to be flown at 1810.

---

[2] Between 1 February and 30 June 1941, some 81,785 Axis troops were landed at Tripoli, plus approximately 450,000 tons of weapons, fuel and ammunition. The first troops to arrive were the Italian *Ariete* and *Trento* Divisions, together with the German 5th Light Division – the first contingent of the Deutsches Afrika Korps.

Sqn Ldr Murray requested permission for a section from 73 Squadron to patrol over Benghazi at dawn on 14 February but, although German bombers continued to intrude the area, no encounters ensued although a single aircraft dive-bombed Terelli barracks at Benghazi where a British soldier and an Italian prisoner both sustained wounds. Further casualties occured when some 20 bombs fell on Maraua, to where 208 Squadron had moved with its six Lysanders and three remaining Hurricanes (P3826, V7345 and V7291). Later in the day three German bombers strafed Jedabya and there were two attacks on British troops at El Agheila although, on this occasion, defensive ground fire brought down two of the raiders; one of those under attack later wrote:

> "Dust was being kicked up by a rough desert wind as, through the haze, unidentified aircraft were suddenly spotted gliding in and then opening up in one of the most ferocious attacks in the 11th Hussars' experience. The Luftwaffe had arrived, its Messerschmitts streaking through to aim deadly cannon fire at dispersed armoured cars and lorries, setting many alight. One of the intruders was shot down by a barrage of anti-aircraft machine-gun fire..."

Both pilot and gunner survived to be taken prisoner when their 7/ZG26 aircraft (3U+FR) force-landed about 15 miles west of El Agheila. Four hours later a formation of Ju87s from I/StG1 dive-bombed the same unit, also losing one of its aircraft, A5+LH of 1 Staffel, in which the pilot was killed although his gunner survived to be taken prisoner. Two days later III/ZG26 lost a second Messerschmitt (3U+FS) to AA fire but on this occasion both crewmen were killed.

With the increase in aerial activity over Benghazi, 73 Squadron was ordered to detach a section from B Flight to El Adem and the other section to Benina, there to assist 3RAAF but the latter instruction was then rescinded, Plt Off Goodman taking his section to El Adem to relieve Plt Off Legge's A Flight detachment. The shortage of Hurricanes at Gazala was further compounded when Flg Off Storrar belly-landed his aircraft (V7544/TP-S) when returning from El Adem:

> "Tale of a lunchtime session. Returning from El Adem in the heat of afternoon. Forgot flaps and wheels. Cost me a small fortune in drinks for everyone for three days. But it must be remembered that we had been flying long hours for some considerable time, and fatigue played its part."

3RAAF was advised that Sqn Ldr Jeffrey was to assume the role of Station Commander at Benina and command of the Squadron was to pass to Sqn Ldr Duncan Campbell. As if to celebrate the changes, the Squadron claimed its first Hurricane victory at 0900 on 15 February, when Flg Off Saunders (P5176), a 21-year-old English-born Australian, chased a Ju88 of 7/LG1 out to sea, as recorded by his close friend John Jackson in his diary:

> "John Saunders had good luck and did a great bit of work this morning. He and Gordon Steege did the dawn patrol. John spotted a raider just making off to sea and followed him up unobserved and poured a volley into him from close range. The raider was a Ju88 and it immediately dived steeply away, and John

lost sight of him. He was not sure whether he got him or not. Later in the day John was on patrol and decided to fly out to sea to about the spot where he fired – about 12 miles west of Benghazi, out to sea – and about six miles out he saw a Very light and spotted a rubber boat with two men in it. He immediately flew back to Benghazi and drew the attention of a trawler by firing off a light and flying to and fro to the raft. The trawler woke up and went out and collected the men – turned out to be four in the raft, two seriously wounded, all Germans."

Lt Wilhelm Grotz and two members of his crew of L1+JR, Fw Erwin Rink and Uffz Walter Tiede – one of whom was severely injured and the other less so – were rescued from their collapsible lifeboat, but the gunner, Uffz Karl Schauer, was dead. A second Ju88 of III/LG1 crash-landed at Tripoli later the same day following flak damage although the 9 Staffel crew survived. Another machine from the same Staffel crash-landed at Tripoli the following day and again the crew survived.

On the morning of 17 February, six RAAF Hurricanes were despatched to Agedabia to patrol the road from there to El Agheila, since Ju87s had been bombing and strafing forward troops in the area, but no enemy aircraft were seen. A further section of three Hurricanes repeated the mission during the mid-morning period next day (18 February), landing at Agedabia to refuel. From there they carried out a second patrol at about 1500 before setting out for Benina, as Flg Off Jackson, who was flying P5176, noted:

"On return run sighted dead below us about 12 Ju87s, though at first only saw three. I warned Gordon Steege and Johnny Saunders who were in front of me – I was acting as swinger or hawk-eye. I turned and dived to attack and, as I turned, I spotted the other nine or ten aircraft following up the first three. We were at about 12,000 feet at about two miles north of Agheila, near a place called Mersa el-Brega. Was very excited as I realised we were unobserved. They were flying at about 1,000 feet and had been dive-bombing. I did a diving attack on a Ju87 and seemed to pepper it well and it eventually sheered away. I attacked another bloke by a shallow quarter attack and peppered him until he also sheered away. Both looked as if they were going to land. Then did a head-on attack on a third bloke and followed and peppered him until he started to break up in front of me and eventually crashed in flames. I had to pull up over him. By this time we were only about 200 feet. I then encountered fairly heavy ack-ack and machine-gun fire from our own troops and climbed like billy-o to get away and lost sight of the other Huns."

Jackson's third victim was apparently the aircraft (WkNr5548) flown by Fw Hans Drolshagen and Uffz Wolfgang Schafer of I/StG1, who were both killed when it crashed near Agedabia. Meanwhile, Flt Lt Steege (V6737) and Flg Off Saunders (V7770) engaged other Stukas:

"Gordon and Johnny chased a couple each, and each thought they had got at least one each though did not actually see them go in. Hope we get them all confirmed. I was a bit ahead of Gordon and John and lost sight of them and

returned to Agedabia, landed and refuelled. The other two returned direct to
Benina."

Although several of the Stukas fled the battle area bearing the scars of combat, all
apart from Drolshagen's machine returned safely to Castel Benito, although one
gunner, Fw Erich Morgenstern, had been severely wounded in the action. Earlier
during the afternoon a small force of Ju88s carried out a raid on Benghazi harbour,
targeting the monitor *Terror* and other ships. Lt Rankin and his gun battery of 152
HAA had just reached Benghazi from Sollum when the raid developed:

> "Had hardly been there 20 minutes when a daylight raid started and I rushed
> over to the spotting telescopes to do my stuff. Managed to spot the first two
> planes and got the section on target. Identified them as Ju88s and watched one
> do a thrilling dive on the jetty. The sky was filled with AA bursts and I watched
> one plane come circling down with white smoke pouring from one wing. Our
> shooting was quite good."

Despite the gunners' claims for two Ju88s destroyed in this action, one of which the
Royal Navy apparently confirmed, none appear to have been lost. There was only
one Hurricane available at Benina that morning and although scrambled it failed to
make an interception. Shortly after the return of Flt Lt Steege's patrol following its
successful encounter, a mixed formation of three Ju87s and two He111s raided the
harbour, dropping mines and bombs. Jackson continued:

> "Had a decent air raid just about dusk – the Huns plastered Benghazi. They
> dropped a hell of a lot of bombs but though they flew over here (Benina) they
> didn't drop any here, though some close by."

While Sqn Ldr Murray was away at RAF Headquarters in Cairo endeavouring to
find out more about the proposed movement of 73 Squadron to Greece, orders were
received at Gazala for the Squadron to provide an experienced pilot to report to El
Adem forthwith, from where he would be flown to an airfield in Crete with a view
to advising on its suitability to operate Hurricanes. Acting CO Flt Lt Beytagh
decided that he would accept the duty and, accompanied by Plt Off Millist,
immediately flew to El Adem. At the same time the Squadron's ground personnel
were ordered to depart for Amiriya in readiness for the posting to Crete, while Flg
Off Storrar was instructed to take Plt Offs Lamb and Goord to Benina where they
were to reinforce 3RAAF. The ground party duly set out for Amiriya, arriving two
days later, only to be told to return with all haste to Gazala since their move to Crete
had been cancelled.

   With dawn on 19 February came two He111s of 6/KG26, intent on bombing
shipping in Benghazi harbour. Several bombs were dropped ineffectively. One of
the raiders was hit by gunfire from HMS *Peony* and crashed into the sea just outside
the harbour. The pilot of IH+MP was recovered, wounded, as was one of his crew,
but the other two crew members perished. Of the raid, Lt Rankin of 152 HAA
recorded:

"Woke up to the sound of the cock crowing, the dawn breaking and inevitably, the sound of the air raid. Planes came over dropping bombs and mines and one was shot down by a little ship in the harbour."

From Benina three 3RAAF Hurricanes again set out for Agedabia, from where they were tasked to carry out an offensive patrol. Three more followed shortly thereafter, one flown by Flg Off Jackson, who wrote in his journal:

"Jeffrey, Saunders and myself went down to Agedabia this morning and refuelled. Jock Perrin, Gaty and Boyd had gone ahead earlier and did an early patrol down to Agheila. We were just waiting for them to return before taking off when we heard bombs being dropped to the south, so we hopped into the air and made south. Passed several villages that had been just bombed and came across Boyd returning on his own so realised something was wrong. He went back to Agedabia and we went on and saw an aircraft in flames. Flew low and found it to be a Hurricane burning furiously, much to our sorrow. However, Jeffrey spotted Jock waving. We finished our patrol and got back to Agedabia and found out from Boyd that they had spotted a number of Ju87s (aircraft of II/StG2) dive-bombing the village just near where we spotted them yesterday. Before attacking, Jock had a good look around but could see no other aircraft. He and Gaty dived to attack – Boyd held back – and Jock got a Ju87. He looked round to see three Messerschmitt fighter-bombers (Bf110s of 8/ZG26) on his tail. One came up from under him and set his gravity tank on fire. Anyway, he turned and engaged to shoot down the Messerschmitt and then had to force-land with his plane on fire. Poor old Gaty was last seen by Boyd in flames and crashing onto the seashore."

23-year-old Flg Off Alan Gatward from Wahroonga, New South Wales, was killed in this action. His aircraft was apparently shot down following a joint attack by two Messerschmitts flown by Lt Alfred Wehmeyer and Uffz Max Hohmann. Wehmeyer then attacked Flg Off Perrin's aircraft (V7557) but was in turn shot down by him. It would seem that Perrin was then shot down jointly by Fw Richard Heller and Oblt Prang, the Staffelkapitän, each of whom claimed a Hurricane destroyed. Wehmeyer meanwhile ditched his crippled Messerschmitt (WkNr3886) in the sea, he and his wounded gunner, Obgfr Wilhelm Wust, getting into their dinghy and being picked up by an Axis rescue craft some 48 hours later. The Stuka (WkNr5455) shot down by Perrin was than flown by Uffz Kurt Steuber and Uffz Walter Nentwig of 5 Staffel, who survived although both suffered wounds in the action.

Perrin, wounded in one eye and severely burned, was picked up by a patrol car and taken to Benina. Here he related to his colleagues that as he staggered from his burning aircraft following the crash-landing he was repeatedly machine-gunned by the Messerschmitts, which dived on him as, half blinded by oil and blood, he made a desperate dash for the shelter of a tree:

"It was the fastest 100 yards I have ever run and, when I barged into that tree in my haste, I saw stars by the thousand."

He was sent to hospital in Tobruk. On the night of his arrival Tobruk was raided and a bomb exploded close to the hospital, with the result that he ended up on the floor with a window frame draped around his neck. His Squadron colleague Jackson noted:

"The CO reckons Jock ought to get the DFC for the show he put up. I reckon he should, too. A great bit of work."

The award of the DFC to Perrin was indeed announced the following month though he was fortunate to receive it. Shortly after the bombing incident at Tobruk hospital the authorities decided to evacuate the patients to Alexandria aboard the hospital ship *Ramb III*, a former Italian vessel. Soon after leaving harbour the ship was dive-bombed and sunk by Ju87s. Perrin was one of the lucky survivors.

While the pilots of 3RAAF were thus engaged with the Bf110s of 8 Staffel near El Agheila, one of 73 Squadron's detached pilots operating from Benina, Flg Off Storrar (V7553/TP-E), encountered six or seven more III/ZG26 Messerschmitts while patrolling about 15 miles out to sea off Benghazi. He attacked and believed he damaged one before making his escape. It was assumed that they were escort for a reconnaissance Ju88 which passed over Benghazi harbour, going eastwards. The intruder was engaged by AA and pursued by a Hurricane on standing patrol but Plt Off Goord (V7562/TP-A) was not able to close the range, as noted by Lt Rankin of 152 HAA:

"A single hostile plane came over and again I was the first to spot it – a reconnaissance plane dropping no bombs – it was out of range by the time we had got our height and we did not open up. It was chased out to sea by a Hurricane and I had both planes in the identification telescope at once. The Junkers seemed to escape, which was very sad."

Apparently the 1(F)/121 crew reported worthwhile targets in the harbour since five Ju88s of Stab III/LG1 arrived from Sicily in the early afternoon and proceeded to dive-bomb the monitor *Terror*. A very heavy AA barrage was fired and four patrolling Hurricanes were called in, while two standby Hurricanes were scrambled, but only Plt Off Lamb (V7371/TP-C) was able to report an engagement. He chased a Ju88 down to sea level, firing all his ammunition, but did not see it go in. In fact the damaged bomber managed to return to Catania with a wounded observer (Obfw Otto Seigner) on board. Lt Rankin wrote:

"Watched a most interesting and exciting raid – the planes corkscrewing their way through terrific AA fire, some of it very close indeed. Each plane carried out a sensational dive, in some cases quite vertical, or so it seemed. No ships were hit but there was damage to the mole. Where were the Hurricanes? Nowhere to be seen, so there is something radically wrong somewhere."

There occurred another raid on Benghazi during the early morning hours of 20 February, the Hurricane patrol again failing to intercept. However, one of the raiders, an Italian bomber, was shot down in flames by AA fire, as recalled by Lt Rankin:

"A sensational start to the day – just at dawn the usual raid started and one plane was caught by the light AA, bursting into flames at the bottom of its dive and crashed near the jetty. The flames lit up the buildings all round us. Clouds of black smoke poured from the flames as the petrol burnt out."

Several bombs were dropped on Benghazi but there were no casualties. One of the raiders was reported to have ground strafed from 700 feet. Another raider was shot down by AA fire the following morning (21 February) during a further raid on Benghazi harbour, this time a Ju88 of II/LG1 falling in flames. There were no survivors from LI+JM. Flg Off Jackson of 3RAAF, who was visiting Benghazi, witnessed the bomber's demise:

"Was watching bombing raid over Benghazi and the fireworks put up by the ack-ack when we saw a plane come down in flames and break up into bits – believe it disintegrated over Ops room in Benghazi, parts falling on the roof and nearby."

Benghazi was raided for the third consecutive morning on 22 February, again by Ju88s of II/LG1 from Sicily. Sqn Ldr Murray (V7551/TP-Z) of 73 Squadron, operating with a section of 3RAAF from Benina, engaged one at about 0730. He was credited with its destrction but, despite severe damage, the 4 Staffel Ju88 was able to reach its base and land safely. Meanwhile, Ju87s of II/StG2 discovered the monitor *Terror* near Derna. Badly damaged, the old vessel attempted to escape but eventually sank the following day, her luck having finally run out.

With the increased activity over Benghazi, three Hurricanes of A Flt/73 Squadron were sent to Benina to again reinforce 3RAAF, Flg Off Storrar leading Flg Off Scott and Plt Off Goord for this duty. The raiders were back with the onset of darkness, AA fire shooting down a He111 of 4/KG26 in which the crew of IH+KN was reported missing. Several bombs fell on and around Benghazi but inflicted little damage and no casualties.

It was the turn of Tobruk harbour to be raided at dawn on 23 February. Two Hurricanes of 73 Squadron led by Sqn Ldr Murray failed to intercept and the raid ended at 0725. At 1115 more unidentified aircraft approached from the sea. The Hurricane patrol, this time led by Sgt Marshall, was ordered to intercept but again without success. At midday Benghazi harbour was visited by a single Ju88, probably a reconnaissance aircraft. Although three Hurricanes of 3RAAF were airborne, no interceptions were made. Of this period, Flg Off Jackson wrote:

"We have a new system now re patrols over Benghazi. Ops have some secret device called *Jumbo* [obviously a reference to the mobile radar unit, AMES235] that can locate and position aircraft within about five miles radius, so we now sit in our aircraft for two hours at a time and as soon as we get a signal we take off pronto and try to intercept the raiders before they drop their bombs. They have dropped a lot of magnetic mines lately and some damage has been done to naval vessels. Did six hours on this standby today, four hours sitting in the aircraft and two hours on patrol. It is very tiring sitting and waiting with all your gear on."

A few days later he added:

> "More standby again today. I think old *Jumbo* gets a bit mixed up sometimes
> and now and again we chase ourselves. At Benina we have two or three
> Hurricanes and their pilots standing by, and on the warning firing of a Very
> light by our own Ops officers we have to be in the air within two minutes of
> receiving the signal. At first we used to sit in our aircraft for the whole standby
> period with all our gear on, but we found we became too cramped, so now we
> are allowed to roam about within a hundred yards or so of our aircraft. As soon
> as two aircraft get the signal to go, two or three more pilots move up to standby
> and so on, so that anything from six to nine aircraft are ready all the time."

Jackson's diary also give an insight into the daily life of the local population, and
how the closeness of the war effected them:

> "Had a long day in Benghazi looking around the markets. Bought a few odds
> and ends to send home, a pair of Arab shoes and two Arab shawls. The poor
> civilians are terror stricken and as soon as the air raid alarm goes they close up
> their shops and won't open again for hours. Most of the bigger and better shops
> are cemented and blocked up and apparently don't intend opening. Most of the
> places open are in the market section and are mostly Arabs."

From 0600 on the morning of 24 February, Hurricanes provided escort for HM
ships approaching Tobruk harbour but could not prevent Ju87s of II/StG2 from
sinking the destroyer *Dainty*. At 1845 the guns reported the presence of an enemy
aircraft over Tobruk harbour but no communication was possible with the Ops
room. Nonetheless, three Hurricanes of 3RAAF were ordered off, as noted by
Jackson:

> "Three of us took off and flew around in the dark. Saw a red flare go off and
> made for it but saw nothing. Boyd saw an aircraft and followed on its tail for
> about 20 or 30 miles. It was a twin-engined aircraft but it was too dark to see
> its markings and he didn't fire as he thought it might be one of our own
> bombers. Anyway, it turned out that it must have been an enemy aircraft. Had
> to land in the dark. My aircraft had no flash plates and exhausts made a
> frightful glare and I couldn't see a damned thing but bumped my way down. I
> was last to land and it was pretty dark."

A Ju88 was spotted by observers over Benghazi harbour the following morning but
eluded three patrolling Hurricanes. Such was its speed that the AA batteries did not
open fire. Tobruk harbour was again targeted at dusk, Sgt Leng (V7716/TP-U) of
73 Squadron being scrambled from El Adem at 1815. Once airborne he entered the
defended area to investigate a probing searchlight but was fired upon by the
defences so promptly returned to base. An attack on the harbour by an unknown
number of unidentified aircraft which started at 1920 finally petered out at 2040.

On the ground Rommel was restless. Although the Axis offensive codenamed
Operation *Sonnenblume* (Sunflower) was not planned to commence until May, by
which time a significant armoured force would have arrived to support the assault,

Rommel was granted permission to send out a reconnaissance unit to test British opposition known to be in the area between El Agheila and Agedabia, as he noted in his journal:

> "On 24 February came the first clash between German and British troops in the African theatre. Without casualties ourselves, we destroyed two enemy scout vehicles, a truck and a car and took three British soldiers, among them an officer, prisoner."

Since it soon became apparent that British forces in the area were weaker than originally estimated, Rommel was impatient to get on with his brief and capture Cyrenaica. He resented being restrained when his experience and intuition suggested the time was right for an offensive, and arranged to fly to Berlin to argue his case, having drawn up plans for the 5th Light Division to make ready to attack the British garrison at El Agheila.

Six unidentified aircraft approached Tobruk during the late afternoon of 27 February, four Hurricanes from El Adem and three from Gazala being scrambled but the raid did not develop. This was followed by an evening raid on Benghazi harbour by the Luftwaffe. AA opened fire and several bombs were dropped, one damaging the telephone link between AMES216 and 3RAAF at Benina which resulted in no communication for 12 hours except by R/T. During the night several mines exploded in the harbour, while bombs were dropped in the vicinity of Berka landing ground, near where a large fire was started.

A few days after arriving in Sicily as reinforcement for III/LG1, Hptm Hajo Herrmann led his 7 Staffel Ju88s out over the Mediterranean, searching for a reported medium-sized British naval formation from Alexandria which was heading westwards in the direction of Benghazi. Taking off during the early morning darkness of 28 February, the crews had been briefed to be off Tobruk at dawn, where it was estimated the British force would be, and to then dive-bomb the ships using the new PC1400 armour-piercing bombs with which they were armed. However, the North African coast was shrouded in cloud or banks of fog as the bombers approached, and the coastline could not be observed. When at last land was sighted, it was realised that the formation had penetrated inland. Accepting the hopelessness of a co-ordinated attack in such conditions even should the ships be sighted, Herrmann ordered his crews to fly at low level over the sand dunes on a north-westerly heading, with the intention of reaching an Axis landing ground before fuel ran out. At this stage a patrol of Hurricanes was spotted about 6,000 feet above the bombers. Of the sortie, Herrmann wrote:

> "I twisted my head round to look until it hurt. Then I saw the section of fighters. They were flying towards us, but not diving down at us yet. They were almost in the sun. Aha! I thought. It's going to be a surprise attack. I looked ahead at the sand dunes I was racing low over, and then back at the Hurricanes. Now was the moment they should be committing themselves to the attack. We hadn't even painted a desert camouflage on our aircraft before we took off. And there was also a bird of doom in the form of black shadows cast by our aircraft on the sand ahead. I crouched down in my seat. We were

sitting ducks. The Hurricanes were exactly above us. Please don't turn. Then they were a short distance ahead and above. They flew off to the left, heading west. They hadn't seen us. Slowly the Hurricanes faded into black dots in the distance. We carried on, right down on the deck. What we had experienced was the victim's mute expectation of the executioner's axe."

Apparently unbeknown to Herrmann, or possibly forgotten by him in the mists of time, the two patrolling Hurricanes – aircraft from 73 Squadron – did sight at least one of the Ju88s at about 0630. Plt Off Wareham (TP-L) reported carrying out a stern attack against a single aircraft but saw no results, while Plt Off Legge (V7551/TP-K) engaged what he thought was a He111 – possibly the same aircraft as that attacked by his colleague – but similarly failed to observe any effect from his attack. Both pilots reported return fire although neither was hit.

As the Ju88s headed for Cyrenaica they were fired on by a small convoy, part mechanised, part camel, Herrmann just having time to gain height and release his bomb in its midst while his gunners strafed. The terrified, heavily-laden camels scattered in all directions as the Junkers sped westwards, eventually making touch down at Sirte, before flying on to Tripoli. There the aircraft were refuelled while the crews rested before embarking on the flight back to Sicily. One failed to reach Sicily, however. Lt Dr Fritz Kratz had been granted permission to carry out a reconnaissance of the Benghazi area before returning to base, as he wished to try out the new bombsight he had helped to develop. Aboard Uffz Peter Müller's 4D+HR, Kratz sighted a large ship moored alongside the docks at Benghazi but low clouds prevented a conventional attack, so Müller flew over and around the harbour for some time awaiting a suitable gap in the clouds. Lt Rankin of 152 HAA was among those watching from below:

"Just after dawn, when our guns had only just come out of action, the most annoying thing happened. A Ju88 shot out of clouds only 2,000 feet high and immediately above us. We could do nothing except look at it and swear like hell. Then another one appeared [in fact the same aircraft] and a Hurricane shot out of the clouds behind and blew it out of the sky – it fell in flames and burnt for over an hour, two of the crew baling out successfully."

The successful pilot was 3RAAF's Sqn Ldr Campbell (P3980) who had been guided on to its track by ground control. The bomber crashed three miles south of Benghazi aerodrome. Kratz and Müller survived and were taken prisoner but Obgfr Hermann Beschorner and Gfr Alfred Grundmann were killed. Of this incident, Flg Off Jackson wrote:

"A German flew over the drome at about 800 feet and did two circuits without our aerodrome defence waking up. Luckily, *Jumbo* [radar] had called our standby team into the air and Duncan Campbell smacked a Ju88 down at about 2,000 feet, his first victory and he's as proud as punch and has gone off in a car to view the wreckage not far from here. One of our other chaps, Lindsay Knowles, chased the bloke who flew over the drome [in fact the same aircraft] but he lost him in the low clouds."

Another witness to the bomber's demise was Australian Medical Officer, Capt John Devine, who later wrote:

"I was stark naked in the middle of a small field, having a sponge bath before breakfast. We had had a number of our own planes over lately, and I heard a large bomber approaching at only about one or two hundred feet. Purely by chance I glanced up, and there was a large, two-engined Junkers bomber with black crosses painted on it. The rear gunner was examining me benevolently. I have never in all my life felt quite so naked. They passed on, and shortly afterwards I saw the plane coming back, and then two [sic] of our Hurricanes dived on it and shot it down. Later we heard from the German pilot that he had been lost and had been coming down to land at the aerodrome near Benghazi, thinking it was the one near Tripoli. This mistake was understandable, for quite a number of Italian Savoia planes were scattered around our aerodrome. When they were almost on the ground, the German pilot told me, they saw a Hurricane and, turning quickly, tried to escape. His first intimation that planes were after him was when bullets commenced to come through his roof and an engine was set on fire. The pilot and one other parachuted, and landed alive. The rest were killed.

To my mind, the interesting part was what happened to the bullets that passed through the Junkers. From all eight guns of the Hurricane, they struck the cookhouse of Berka barracks where there were some ten or fifteen thousand Italian prisoners of war. This so disturbed the Italian prisoners that they made a break and surged away from the cookhouse. It was said that their break to freedom was stopped when one of the Australians guarding them fixed his bayonet."

Severe dust storms during the remainder of the day made further flying impossible in the area until night fell when, at 2045, six aircraft approached Tobruk harbour from the north and the north-west, but a raid did not develop. The Luftwaffe was suspected of laying mines.

The Hurricane-equipped A Flight of 6 Squadron was now attached to 208 Squadron at Agedabia for the pilots to gain operational experience, Flt Lt Saunders commanding the detachment. Their task was to carry out reconnaissances in co-operation with 2nd Armoured Division. B Flight with Lysanders remained at Barce, while C Flight at Heliopolis was being re-equipped with long-range Lysanders. Plt Off Moulding of A Flight wrote later:

"Agedabia had been an enemy maintenance unit and, among the 70 or so skeletons scattered in final dispersal across the sandy waste, almost every type of Italian machine was to be found; bombed, machine-gunned, battered, fired, demolished. A veritable graveyard. The landing surface itself became defined within a perimeter of wrecked aircraft. The aerodrome buildings – square, modern, Italian-built – glaring white and without the boon of shade; many were damaged, more derelict. The big hangar was roofless, burnt out.

The Italians are good engineers, good technicians, good builders. They enjoy digging slit trenches, keeping the sides vertical and angles exact. They like making dug-outs and hide-outs and fox holes. Where the British in the desert tended to improvise in matters of air raid protection, the Italian planned and schemed, allocated and perfected. And when he retreated he left his systems intact. True, he resorted to petty annoyances – he dubbed walls 'Vive Il Duce' and 'British Pigs', put his bilge water into the wells and, at the last moment, deposited his excreta prominently on floors, in doorways and anywhere where the thick stench and the parasite fly swarms would be sure to annoy the incoming troops. Sometimes he left booby traps but they were usually fairly obvious, amateur efforts. Generally speaking, Italian defences and living quarters could be taken over and put in good order in a very short time. Agedabia was no exception.

A Flight soon made themselves snug and comfortable. The buildings in which they were quartered were fitted with wire fly-netting; at each exit there were beautiful, deep slit-trenches. In spite of acute shortage of water, some effort had been made at plumbing. There were wash basins and shower-baths, somewhat primitive in design, but effective. The magnum opus, serving as an Officers' Mess, was something distinctly Italian. It consisted of a subterranean room carved out of the solid rock. Approached by a steep, curving stairway, this extraordinary chamber had been found in good order, properly ventilated and complete with wiring for electric light. So far as A Flight was concerned, the room lent itself admirably to the dual role of Flight Commander's office and air liaison section."

German reconnaissance aircraft continued to visit Tobruk and Benghazi, flying at such a height as to avoid interception. A raid on Tobruk harbour occurred on the evening of 2 March, five Ju88s of 8/LG1 from Sicily arriving from seaward at 1915. One Hurricane from 73 Squadron was scrambled from El Adem but was obliged to return due to faulty equipment, Sgt Leng being despatched at 1930 in V7551/TP-K. Not only was he unable to locate the raiders but his aircraft was fired upon by the guns, sustaining some damage. On returning to El Adem in the dark, he was unable to locate the aerodrome and, with fuel running low, he baled out, his aircraft crashing some 15 miles from Bu Amud.

Sgts Marshall and Webster of 73 Squadron were attached to 3RAAF at Benina on 3 March to provide aerodrome protection while the Australians carried out a mission to the south, as Flg Off Jackson noted:

"Eight of us went south. Flew tight formation with Wilf Arthur acting as tailend Charlie, swinging from side to side behind formation, protecting and watching for surprise attack from rear. If we sighted anything Gordon and I were to form echelon and attack whilst the others stayed up above to watch out for any enemy fighters acting as escort to the dive-bombers. Anyway, flew for about two hours 15 minutes and saw nothing. Heard later, just after we left the area, seven dive-bombers and five ME110s had a crack at Agedabia and cleaned up a few M/T."

At 1215 next day an unidentified aircraft was heard over Gazala at a considerable height, following which it circled the Tobruk area, apparently a Ju88D taking photographs. Plt Offs McFadden and Legge of 73 Squadron took off in the hope of intercepting and climbed to 20,000 feet but were unable to sight the intruder. Another reconnaissance Ju88, which approached Tobruk harbour from seaward on the morning of 5 March, was sighted by a patrolling Hurricane flown by Sgt White of 73 Squadron at 0920, but it escaped in cloud before he could close the range. A second intruder was reported at 1037 but the patrolling Hurricane failed to locate it in the cloudy conditions. Another or the same Ju88 flew low over Benghazi harbour at 1230 and similarly evaded patrolling Hurricanes of 3RAAF. The Australian unit despatched a further patrol to the Agedabia area in search of Ju87s but again nothing was seen. The Squadron also learned that Flt Lt A.C. Rawlinson, who was on loan to 6 Squadron at Agedabia for reconnaissance duties, had been slightly injured near Mersa el-Brega when his Hurricane (V7484) force-landed after engine failure. At 1350 a despatch rider arrived at Gazala West to report that three German bombers had attacked an M/T convoy about 25 miles west of Gazala on the road to Zummar Azen, but 258 Wing would not grant permission for the two pilots at readiness to investigate, much to the disgust of 73 Squadron.

Benghazi was targeted by a lone bomber on the morning of 6 March, its bombs falling harmlessly into the sea. It was reported that this aircraft later crashed into the sea in flames ten miles west of Benghazi although German records do not confirm such a loss. The raider was alleged to have been a Do217 according to Jackson's diary:

> "A Hun was picked up by *Jumbo* [radar] and he eventually flew past Benghazi at 500 feet – we had five Hurricanes after him and one of them flew clean over the top of the Hun without seeing him – the Hun must have seen him though as he went straight off south for the lick of his life. Rather funny – one of our new blokes – [Flg Off] Jewell – came in and reported to have seen a Ju87 near the drome when he was taking off. It turned out that Wilf Arthur had had trouble getting his undercart up and was flying around with flaps and cart down. Jewell mistook him and by the time he got off, Arthur had disappeared – fortunately! The Hun turned out to be a Dornier 217 bomber – very much like a Ju88, only twin fins[3]."

A second attack by a lone raider was carried out during the evening and again no damage or casualties resulted. A Hurricane scrambled to intercept failed to engage. Earlier in the day, five Bf110s of III/ZG26 bombed and strafed a 20th Brigade convoy on the road to Derna, the attackers being identified as He111s. Few vehicles were damaged although two soldiers were killed and a third was wounded. Benghazi was again raided on 7 March, and again next day when Benina also received a visit, but no damage resulted. Jackson of 3RAAF noted:

> "This afternoon an enemy aircraft flew over the drome and dropped a salvo of

---

[3] The aircraft was not a Do217, although it may have been a Do215 strategic reconnaissance bomber from Sicily since these aircraft were known to operate occasionally over the central Mediterranean, but was more likely to have been a reconnaissance Bf110 from newly arrived 2(H)/14.

six bombs right in the middle of the drome – made craters about 10-12 feet
wide, by about four to five feet deep. Two of the bombs didn't go off and just
penetrated the earth. One seemed to break up without exploding and the other
seemed to be intact. Much speculation as to whether they are delayed action –
anyway, most of us went over and had a looksee. Engineers exploded them a
couple of days later."

Due to the increasing tempo of attacks against Tobruk, A Flt/73 Squadron was
ordered to move on 10 March to Bu Amud, 15 miles east of the harbour, from where
it was to provide standing patrols during daylight hours over a hospital ship
departing for Alexandria. Hurricanes were scrambled that evening when an intruder
was reported over Tobruk harbour but this evaded interception and, as it departed,
its gunners machine-gunned a vessel just off the coast. On arrival at Bu Amud
ground personnel were soon put to work checking out their new base, as
remembered by Cpl Pete Minterne:

"Our first task on moving in was to walk in line abreast along the landing strip,
picking up sharpened steel spikes which were sticking out of the sand. They
had caused many punctures and other damage to our Hurricanes and made a
big hole in our supply of spares. The spikes had four legs so that there was
always one more or less upright. We thought the Ities had left them just to
make our lives more difficult, but it turned out that it was a scheme hatched up
by the smart-arses at HQME. A Bombay had flown over enemy territory at
night and tipped them over the landing grounds, scoring an own goal which
caused us a great deal of grief."

El Adem was raided by an estimated 15 Ju87s during the night of 12/13 March,
aircraft remaining over the airfield for two hours. A number of buildings were
damaged but good shelters and thick-walled buildings helped reduce casualties. As
it was, two Italian prisoners and a Palestinian soldier were killed. Sgt Garton of 73
Squadron's B Flight later recalled:

"We were awakened about 0245 by the sound of aircraft; the Officers' Mess
was hit, causing two casualties, then we were machine-gunned from about 500
feet. After that there was more bombing from four or five Jerries which set a
hangar on fire and damaged two or three of our kites."

One bomb exploded only 20 yards from where Sgts Garton and Marshall were
sleeping. Plt Off Millist was among those who made heroic but vain efforts to
reach the three men under the debris, following which, on his own initiative, he
took off in V7716/TP-U during the bombing. Patrolling in the vicinity for an hour,
he encountered one of the dive-bombers which he attacked twice, believing he had
gained some strikes before he lost sight of it in the darkness. Ju88Ds of 1(F)/121
continued to keep both Benghazi and Tobruk under surveillance, but patrolling
Hurricanes managed successfully to provide protection for shipping arriving and
departing the ports. There were no interceptions but all were aware that the lack of
aerial activity could only signify a calm before the storm. While German

reconnaissance aircraft concentrated on coastal regions, RAF reconnaissance was directed to the area west of El Agheila, where troop and M/T movement was noted. A Hurricane of 6 Squadron ventured too low while investigating on 17 March and was shot down by ground fire, Flg Off J.C. Wilson being captured when his camera-equipped aircraft crash-landed. The Luftwaffe lost two of its reconnaissance Bf110s during this period, both aircraft of the newly arrived army air reconnaissance unit 2(H)/14, attached to the Afrika Korps. Both pilot and observer were killed when their aircraft crashed in a sandstorm, while the pilot of the second survived his injuries when his machine crashed near Marada. For the next eight days sandstorms in the Tobruk area effectively curtailed all offensive flying from Bu Amud although there occurred the odd scramble after reconnaissance aircraft, without contact being made. 73 Squadron welcomed the return of its Canadian flight commander, Flt Lt Smudger Smith, now recovered from his severe attack of malaria, and also the arrival of a reinforcement pilot, Sgt John Elsworth, a Rhodesian.

Further efforts were made to strengthen Malta's defences on 17 March by the despatch of one flight of Hurricanes from 274 Squadron. It was possible for RAFME to make available small numbers of Hurricanes from those constantly arriving via the Takoradi route. Since the beginning of the year some 70 Hurricanes, plus 68 Blenheims, a dozen Wellingtons, a similar number of Fleet Air Arm Fulmars and a handful of Marylands and Lodestars, had reached Egypt or Sudan, although these numbers were insufficient to make good losses and requirements. During the months of December, January and February the sand-laden *Harmattan* wind on this route necessitated a complete overhaul of some engines on arrival in Egypt, delaying the issuing of these aircraft to operational units. Nonetheless, seven Hurricanes and eight pilots led by Flg Off Imshi Mason were to be sent to Malta but, on arriving at Benina where refuelling was to take place, one aircraft crashed and its pilot, Flg Off Garland, suffered slight burns. Against advice he continued the journey aboard the Wellington which navigated the aircraft to Malta. One of the pilots was Flg Off Charles Laubscher:

> "My feelings were mixed at this news [of the move to Malta]. On one hand there was at last the opportunity of some concentrated action and, with Imshi leading us, one could feel reasonably confident. On the other there was the undoubted fact that we would be on the receiving end ... the defending fighters had been battered by swarms of ME109s and Macchis. There was one compensating factor, however. We were to fly across, which suited me, as I had a morbid fear of being torpedoed at sea. Long-range tanks were fitted and tested, guns were checked and the Hurricanes generally prepared for flight from Benina to Malta. We set off from Amiriya on 13 March and spent the night with 73 Squadron, as El Adem was unsafe due to the unfriendly attention it was receiving from enemy dive-bombers. Our escorting Wellington was delayed due to phenomenal sandstorms in the Delta area, and it was only on 18 March that it arrived and we set off for Benina to refuel before the sea leg to Malta. 'Micky' Garland crashed on landing, and journeyed to Hal Far as a passenger aboard the Wimpey. It was a pity that he was not left behind with his aircraft, as he was put on standby as soon as we arrived at Takali, and was

killed on his first operation in Malta ..."[4]

While enjoying a few days leave in Heliopolis Flg Off Jackson of 3RAAF arranged to meet one of his convalescing colleagues, Flg Off Lex Winten, who had received a bullet wound in his right hand during one of the December actions:

> "Dressed his hand – it is still draining through a nasty hole in the palm – there must yet be a lot of metal in the hand as it keeps breaking out in different places, fingers have very little use. He's a casual bloke, just puts it under the tap water full of germs. He has a white rat (called 'Sidi Barrani'), which he bought off a gully-gully bloke, and it lives in the sling on his arm. It generally appears suddenly from nowhere on his shoulder or coat lapel. It drinks gin and gets tight, and then has a sleep. It got tight the other night and fell in a glass of gin and lime but is now OK again. Lex used to order two drinks – one for himself and one for his hand, and used to pour the one for his hand down the plaster to kill the odour."

Fliegerführer Afrika lost another Ju88 on 21 March, this from Stab/StG3 on a special reconnaissance flight, which was hit by AA fire near Giarabub. The wounded pilot ordered his crew to bale out while he remained with the aircraft (2F+XA) to carry out a belly-landing, which he survived, only to be taken prisoner. Next day (22 March) 6 Squadron despatched a Hurricane from Agedabia to carry a tactical reconnaissance of Marada, where three or more enemy aircraft had been reported by the army. The pilot was unable to locate the landing ground, ran out of fuel and was obliged to force-land, returning to Agedabia by road. Air HQ was anxious to establish to what extent the enemy was using Marada landing ground and ordered a patrol of 3RAAF to investigate, as noted by Flg Off Jackson:

> "Led a patrol of four down south to Agedabia, where we refuelled, and had to await information re a place called Marada. Boyd dropped out with his aircraft u/s, leaving myself, Edwards and Ellerton. We located Marada and found only one aircraft just off the aerodrome, a u/s SM79, so we had a good look around. We were machine-gunned each time we went down – put a decent couple of holes through one of my mainplanes and got a bullet through my rudder and a bit of shrapnel through my air cleaner. Other blokes didn't get hit but Dave Ellerton got engine radiator trouble and it looked as if he would have to force-land – anyway, he managed to get back to Agedabia. Three ME110s came over very low but went on and machine-gunned the Armoured Division further north. Heard the General's car was machine-gunned the day before and 50 bullets went through it but he managed to hop out and take cover. We arrived back at Benina at 1900."

---

[4] In addition to Mason, Laubscher and Garland, the other pilots were Flg Off J.S. Southwell, Plt Off D.F. Knight, and Sgts T.A. Quinn, M.P. Davies and R.J. Goode. Southwell, Knight and Garland were all killed in the same action five days after their arrival at Malta; Goode and Mason were both wounded within the month (see *Malta: The Hurricane Years 1940-41*). Upon recovery Imshi Mason was given command of 261 Squadron, and later 94 Squadron, with which he was killed leading in action on 15 February 1942.

The Messerschmitts from III/ZG26 remained very active, seven attacking a petrol train at Soluch station during the morning of 23 March. The train caught fire and was badly damaged. On the same day two aircraft from this unit, 3U+NS and 3U+AT were shot down by ground fire, but whether during the attack on the train is not certain; one aircraft came down near el-Magrus, while the other crashed near Mersa el-Brega. Jackson continued:

> "Lex, Duncan Campbell and a few others went off in a car at dawn this morning to examine a ME110 which the army shot down 80 miles south of here. It landed intact and they captured the pilot and observer and brought them up here. The observer wears glasses with lenses as thick as a Tom Collins, so the medical exam can't be too strict."

A single SM79 dropped four small bombs on M/T in the Gialo-Gtafia-Mersa el-Brega area without causing any damage, and next day another SM79 bombed shipping off Mersa el-Brega. Meanwhile, the BR20M-equipped 98°Gruppo BT lost two of its aircraft when they collided while taking-off from Bir Dufan on the night of 22/23 March, all eight crewmen losing their lives.

The first sign that the storm was about to break at last manifested itself on 24 March when a German armoured reconnaissance force overran the British outpost at El Agheila. Rommel and his Afrika Korps were on the move. On his return from Berlin, Rommel wrote in a letter to his wife:

> "... the Führer was extremely pleased with the change that has taken place here since my arrival and the beginning of my activities. He endorsed my measures in every respect. This sort of thing pleases you and gives you energy to go on."

And in his journal he added:

> "On my return to Africa, the 3rd Battalion [of the 5th Light Division] took the fort [at El Agheila], the water stores and the airfield in the early hours of 24th March. The garrison, composed of light forces, had the whole area mined and retreated skilfully on our attack."

Prime Minister Churchill, on learning of the German offensive action, telegraphed General Wavell:

> "We are naturally concerned at rapid German advance to Agheila. It is their habit to push on whenever they are not resisted. I presume you are only waiting for the tortoise to stick his head out far enough before chopping it off. It seems extremely important to give them an early taste of our quality ..."

Wavell brushed aside the threat posed by the Germans:

> "No evidence yet that there are many Germans at Agheila; probably mainly Italian, with small stiffening of Germans ... [adding] I have to admit to having taken considerable risk in Cyrenaica after capture of Benghazi in order to

> provide maximum support for Greece ... Steps to reinforce Cyreniaica are in
> hand ... own chief difficulty is transport."

For the RAF there were also ominous rumours, as remembered by 73 Squadron's
Cpl Pete Minterne:

> "It was about this time that rumours abounded of Messerschmitt 109s having
> been seen up near Tripoli, and soon after there was confirmation that Jerry was
> moving in to Africa in some strength. This was serious ..."

This was indeed serious. The rumours were not unfounded. A Staffel of Bf109Es
had already reached Sicily and had started to take a toll of Malta's fighters, and
these had been joined in early March by the three Staffeln of I/JG27, comprising
30-40 more Messerschmitts under the command of Hptm Eduard Neumann, which
were earmarked for operations over Libya in support of the Afrika Korps.

CHAPTER IV

IN FULL RETREAT:
THE BENGHAZI–TOBRUK HANDICAP

March – April 1941

"There'll be no Dunkirk here. If we have to get out, we shall fight our way out.
There is to be no surrender and no retreat."
Maj General Leslie Morshead, Tobruk Garrison Commander

Although Rommel had been authorised only to make probes in the El Agheila area, and was to await the arrival at the front of the whole of the 15th Panzer Division before undertaking any proper offensive action, he decided in the light of his initial success to keep the British under pressure and, if possible, on the run, thereby denying them the opportunity to organise strong defensive positions. Mussolini was furious; General Gariboldi, to whom Rommel was subordinate, disclaimed all responsibility and was ordered to stop him from advancing any further. Rommel simply signalled Berlin with news of his successes and received the necessary approval to continue his offensive directly from the German High Command.

With the Germans thus making their first move eastwards, causing alarm and panic among the ranks of the British forward forces, Air Marshal Tedder decided the time was right to visit Barce to find out the state of play for himself. Using the Q6 flown by Flg Off M.K. Holland, a 'resting' Blenheim pilot, he set out on the morning of 30 March but 15 miles north-west of Mechili the aircraft suffered oil pressure failure; of the experience Tedder wrote:

"The journey turned out to be an eventful one. We were more than halfway on our journey when a bolt in our port engine gave way and the oil in the sump rapidly drained out. As the aircraft was fairly heavily loaded, we could not maintain height on one engine. The only thing to do was land."

A successful emergency landing was made, as recalled later by the pilot, Maurice Holland, in a letter to his parents:

"I told the passengers to stand by for a forced-landing. We were over some foothills to the south of the mountain range and I could see no place to land the aircraft until, at the last moment, I spotted a rough camel track. I managed to get the plane down undamaged and we found that one cylinder had come loose. At this time we did not know that Barce was being evacuated and that the Germans were pushing us back. I tried to send some SOS signals but the radio was broken. We had a little water and some biscuits and bully [beef] so prepared ourselves for a long wait. We prepared a fire and signals and saw about three aircraft that day, but failed to attract their attention."

The Deputy AOC wrote in his journal:

"Soon after we perched we heard, and saw, a couple of Hurricanes pass some distance away. Apart from that the only signs of life have been one or two pertinacious flies, two butterflies, a couple of ravens which looked a little sinister but, on inspecting us, decided we were not yet ripe..."

Holland continued:

"On the second day we decided there was no one looking for us and that we should do something about making contact with the world. It was arranged that Flt Lt Bray [Tedder's aide] and myself should walk for help and that the Air Marshal and my mechanic [LAC Gratwicke] should remain with the aeroplane. We set off to walk the 35 miles north to the road. We had a bottle of water each and a little food and carried a blanket each as it gets very cold at night. Never again am I going to walk in the desert. The track was rough and the sun sweltering hot and, after four hours, we had apparently got nowhere. We climbed a hill to get our bearings and were shocked to see nothing but sand hills and desert all about us. Our map was as good as useless and we had no compass.

We were on the point of shooting ourselves when we saw a Blenheim. It was circling where we thought the aircraft [the Q6] was and we leapt with joy when we saw it land and send up a cloud of dust. It was some ten to twelve miles away so we turned back as it would probably have been fatal to carry on. When we arrived back we heard that the squadrons were retreating and, by chance, one of the planes had spotted the sun shining on our wing. He [the Blenheim pilot, Sgt Dixon] had landed, left some water and had promised to return that night with a serviceable Blenheim, as that one had been shot up. We just leapt on the water and drank. I never realised before what it was like to be without water.

Towards evening he [Sgt Dixon] came back, left some more supplies and took the Air Marshal and Flt Lt Bray away. I gave the Air Marshal a letter telling my Squadron what we wanted to repair the aircraft and then the mechanic and I set about making camp and some tea. We had a good contented sleep that night."

In the morning a Lysander of 267 Squadron arrived, its pilot explaining that as the Germans had advanced east of their location, he had been instructed to fly them back to Heliopolis and that the Q6 would have to be abandoned. However, HQME, apparently unaware of the full extent of the German advance, ordered 267 Squadron to recover the Q6, whereupon Holland, Gratwicke and three others flew to El Adem in an Anson, from where they re-located the Q6, carried out repairs and flew it back to Heliopolis. By then the Germans were some 120 miles east of the location.

* * *

Rommel's rapid advance revealed the vulnerability of Mersa el-Brega, the gateway into Cyrenaica and, on the morning of 31 March with complete disregard of orders from his Italian superiors, his forces began an assault, as he recorded:

> "A fierce battle broke out in the early hours with British reconnaissance troops at Ma'aten Besker. In the afternoon, troops of the 5th Light Division attacked the Mersa el-Brega position itself, which was solidly defended by the British. Our advance came to a halt. I spent the whole day on the battlefield, trying in the afternoon to find a possible way to attack north of the coastal road. There in the evening the 8th MG Battalion made a fierce attack through the rolling sand dunes, and succeeded in pushing the enemy back to the east, capturing the defile at Mersa el-Brega."

Agedabia, where 208 Squadron and A Flt/6 Squadron were based, was now threatened. The latter unit's Plt Off Moulding observed:

> "There could be no doubt that the enemy had achieved complete surprise. It seemed unbelievable that the broken enemy could have reinforced himself so quickly and to such an extent that he could take the offensive. When tactical air reconnaissance brings the first news of a large-scale offensive, someone on the strategic level has blundered. The size of the blunder was reflected in the implications of the withdrawal. A solid defence position at Agheila was the bastion on which the protection of the whole Cyrenaican bulge depended."

Shortly before midday on 31 March, Agedabia was raided by ten BR20Ms of 98°Gruppo BT from Bir Dufan with an escort provided by Bf110Es of 9/ZG26 led by Hptm Thomas Steinberger, the new Staffelkapitän. On the landing ground a Lysander was damaged and there were five casualties but the raiders did not escape unscathed, a dozen Hurricanes of 3RAAF intercepting, as graphically recorded by Flg Off Jackson in his journal:

> "Acting on secret information received at HQ, 12 Hurricanes went off today to patrol over Agedabia. Had been told to expect ten bombers and five fighters at a certain time, and we went off in three formations of four, lower formation at 3,000 feet, middle at 7,000 feet and top formation at 10,000 feet. I was in the middle formation. We had patrolled area for about one hour when lower formation spotted two ME110s and the four of them pounced on one and brought it down in flames. Duncan Campbell got credit for same though Sqn Ldr Jeffrey and Kloster also got very good bursts into it."

Despite Campbell being given credit for the Messerschmitt's destruction, Sqn Ldr Jeffrey (V7567) had undoubtedly inflicted some damage on it during his initial attack, as his Combat Report would suggest:

"I saw two ME110s circling over Agedabia, apparently about to dive-bomb. I called up on the R/T and led my Flight between the two ME110s. I delivered a front quarter attack on the left-hand e/a, delivering next a beam attack. I saw my fire going into the fuselage. I immediately turned and saw tracers hitting the e/a from someone above and behind me. The e/a turned away and I delivered a quarter attack developing into a beam attack on his underside. I continued to attack and saw the e/a roll over and dive into the ground. The e/a was the same one as attacked by Sqn Ldr Campbell, who had apparently put the aircraft on fire before my last attack."

Campbell (P3980) reported:

"Sqn Ldr Jeffrey attacked a single ME110 which turned away to the left. I anticipated where the ME110 would finish his turn and set out for a head-on attack. I opened fire out of range and throttled back. The burst lasted 10 or 11 seconds during which the ME110 ceased firing and burst into flames between the pilot and the starboard engine. He passed by me and heeled into a vertical dive. He exploded on hitting the ground and burnt. The crew must have been killed before the machine crashed as at one time there was ample opportunity for the crew to jump out while the machine was rolling on its back."

The third member of the section, Flg Off Kloster (V7253) also claimed a share in the Messerschmitt's demise:

" ... when they [Sqn Ldrs Jeffrey and Campbell] dived into attack I was left slightly behind. I saw one enemy circling and turning to the left. He went into a dive and I dived towards him and delivered a quarter attack from above. I held my fire until I was almost on top of him, then climbed away to make a further attack. I then observed the enemy diving towards the ground. He exploded into flames immediately on impact with the ground."

The second Messerschmitt escaped the attention of the other Hurricanes; Jackson, who was flying V7770, wrote:

"Top and middle formations then got mixed up and Hurricanes milled about going hell west and crooked for about ten minutes, and then started to leave the area. Most of us were some miles north of Agedabia and I had just called over the R/T that I was going to go back and land, and refuel, as my aircraft was using a lot of juice, when someone called to look behind. We saw a huge stick of bombs go off over Agedabia drome. I turned and flew upsun but could not see the bombers. I eventually spotted them flying seawards – started to chase them but lost sight of them again and they were too far away when I spotted them again. I then flew west of Agedabia upsun for about ten minutes, looking for enemy aircraft and then landed to refuel. Found drome full of craters, about 25 in all, and a lot of incendiary bombs were still burning. One gunpost had been hit badly. One gunner killed, one officer and three men badly wounded.
    The ME110 brought down by Duncan Campbell [3U+PR flown by Obfw

Josef Bracun and Uffz Werner Kasper] had crashed in flames and nothing was left of same. Found out when I got back to Benina that John Saunders and Lindsey Knowles had got in attacks on the bombers. John had badly damaged one and Knowles probably two. They were the only two to attack the bombers. Good work. Actually we all should have been able to attack the bombers but through breaking the formation and milling about, the Squadron lost its effectiveness and a lot of chaps had gone off home singly or in pairs and didn't even see the bombers. Edwards and Knowles had ME110s on their tails during the mêlée but managed to shake them off. I didn't even see a ME110."

Flg Off Knowles (V7566) reported that although he made eight attacks on the bombers, they remained in perfect formation and did not alter height:

"Saw one formation of four BR20s at about 8,000 feet. I climbed after them and opened fire at about 350 yards from under port quarter. I broke away, deciding to climb higher before attacking again and saw another formation of five BR20s following about one mile behind. I turned and delivered a head-on attack on the starboard aircraft of the formation, breaking off at less than 50 yards range. I then turned and made about seven attacks from about 250 yards on the aircraft on each side of the formation. No results were observed except that the starboard engine of the port aircraft emitted a trail of smoke after I had shot at it. I continued until I ran out of ammunition and then broke away. A few minutes later a ME110 attacked me from above on port quarter. I half-rolled and dived down to 5,000 feet and the ME110 attacked on the starboard quarter. Similar evasive tactics were employed and the ME110 broke away and retired towards the bombers. It is not known what damage was done to the bombers but two of the formation were certainly hit by my fire. During the engagement the bombers kept perfect formation and did not alter course of height."

Knowles' assailant may have been the Messerschmitt leader, Hptm Steinberger, since he claimed a Hurricane shot down north-west of Agedabia in this action. One of the bombers was also claimed damaged by Flg Off Saunders (V6737):

"Enemy aircraft were travelling fast and it took some time to catch them. At 400 yards I started giving bursts at the leader and sweeping fire at the rest. I closed in to 200 yards, firing bursts and broke off due to shortage of petrol. A small fire appeared to have broken out in the rear of the fuselage of the leader, while others were definitely hit. Much machine-gun fire from the rear gunners."

Sqn Ldr Jeffrey was not happy with the outcome of the operation, as noted by Jackson:

"CO gave us a sound talk on our bad airmanship. I think everybody realises what a rotten display we made – should have got those bombers. Our R/T seems very inefficient and practically hopeless – most unreliable and it is continually breaking down in different aircraft – result leads to muddles and misunderstandings in the air and seriously interferes with our efficiency in combats."

The bombing of Agedabia forced the air reconnaissance units based there to beat a hasty retreat. 6 Squadron's C Flight had already withdrawn its Lysanders from Giarabub to Barce, but A Flight continued to carry out reconnaissances, firstly using the landing ground at Antelat before withdrawing to Barce via Msus; of this frantic period, the Squadron's diarist wrote:

"[Flg Off] Fletcher, who is with the advanced Flight at Agedabia, had a spot of excitement with Hurrybus. While on recce he saw a ground party waving to him. How could he ignore such a friendly gesture? Down he went to have a look and they shot a piece out of his prop. Fletcher came home. Jerry got a bit obstreperous today. He started to advance from El Agheila and also bombed hell out of A Flight at Agedabia. The Australians shot up a few, though, to show Jerry that he can't mess about with the forward squadrons. Scotty [Plt Off Scott] got hit with a bit of shrapnel which glanced off his head leaving it rather the worse for wear. A Flight shot back from Agedabia on seeing Jerry tanks come over the horizon. 'Paddy' Weld [the CO] got moving with A Flight ground party, but didn't turn up at Barce."

With the Commonwealth forces now in full retreat – the panic-stricken withdrawal eastwards becoming known, with typical British humour, as the 'Benghazi-Tobruk Handicap' – Rommel pushed forward a two-pronged advance: his Afrika Korps forces and the Italian *Brescia* Division advancing on Benghazi, while the *Ariete* Armoured Division set off through the desert towards Msus. Benghazi was evacuated and a general retreat to Mechili was ordered. Bf110s of III/ZG26 harrassed the retreating forces, one of whom remembered:

"They [the Messerschmitts] moved so fast we could only get off a couple of rounds, but F Section on the shore were more fortunate, and one aircraft was hit. As they approached our hillock a withering fire of all descriptions came up at them, which must have caused some surprise. I quite clearly saw the rear gunner in one aircraft on a level with where I was standing."

Both sides lost reconnaissance aircraft to ground fire during this period, a Blenheim with a naval officer on board being shot down with the loss of the crew, while a Bf110 of 2(H)/14 crashed near El Agheila in which the observer was wounded. The Luftwaffe began concentrating its efforts against shipping at Benghazi but, not wishing to damage the harbour facilities seriously, refrained from intensive bombing. Due to the increased aerial activity, 73 Squadron was instructed to send B Flight to Benina to assist 3RAAF, while A Flight was busily engaged on convoy protection off Tobruk. When Prime Minister Churchill learned of the latest setbacks, he again telegraphed Wavell for reassurance:

"It seems most desirable to chop the German advance against Cyrenaica. Any rebuff to the Germans would have far-reaching prestige effects. It would be all right for you to give up ground for the purpose of manoeuvre, but any serious withdrawal from Benghazi would appear most melancholy. I cannot understand how the enemy can have developed any considerable force at the end of this long, waterless coast road, and I cannot feel that there is at this moment a persistent weight behind his attack in Cyrenaica."

Wavell could only relay the devastating news that he had ordered a withdrawal from Benghazi and that a large part of the armoured brigade had been overrun, resulting in the probability of having to also order the withdrawal of the 9th Australian Division east and north-east of Benghazi. The Prime Minister also cabled Foreign Secretary Anthony Eden, currently in Cairo to assess the seriousness of the situation:

> "Evacuation Benghazi serious, as Germans, once established in aerodromes thereabouts, will probably deny us use of Tobruk. Let me to what point retirement is ordered. Far more important than the loss of ground is the idea that we cannot face the Germans and that their appearance is enough to drive us back many scores of miles."

Eden could not offer a solution or much by way of consolation following his meeting with Wavell and Air Marshal Tedder, although it was believed that the German-Italian offensive in Cyrenaica was nothing more than a major diversion to precede the German attack in the Balkans; he added:

> "This judgment in no way diminishes the seriousness of the indirect threat to Egypt, for quite clearly the enemy must be expected to press any advantage he gains. Unfortunately, his first moves attained a greater measure of success than had been expected, and he is following up his initial success ..."

On the morning of 2 April, two patrolling Hurricanes of 3RAAF flown by Flg Offs Ellerton (V7353) and Edwards (V7566) encountered an Italian reconnaissance aircraft at 20,000 feet west of Benghazi, which they identified as an SM79. Both attacked and pursued the intruder for 30 miles out to sea, where it was last seen at 2,000 feet with smoke pouring from its starboard engine. It was claimed as probably destroyed. Their victim was in fact a Z1007bis of 175^Squadriglia RST from Castel Benito which managed to limp back to its base with a dead crewman on board (Ten Ugo Del Curto, an army observer seconded to the unit). Reconnaissance Ju88s were also evident over both Benghazi and Tobruk, single or pairs of Hurricanes being scrambled on the approach of intruders throughout the day, as noted in Lt Rankin's journal, 152 HAA having now been withdrawn to Tobruk:

> "A Ju88 reconnaissance plane came over at 19,000 feet. We spotted him and fired 13 rounds whereupon he turned away, just as a patrolling Hurricane spotted him. Our shooting was not good, but the plane was taking skilful evasive action – he knew what he was doing. Nevertheless, our bursts gave his position away to the Hurricane and we must hope he gets caught before getting home with his valuable information. Later news was that the Hurricane did a victory roll on landing at El Adem, so perhaps it caught the Jerry."

Later, Lt Rankin added:

> "Went for a bathe after lunch ... another Ju88 was observed right overhead –

there had been no warning and we were evidently taken by surprise ... the few
shots we did fire were no use. A very poor show indeed, and that plane flew
right over us, the harbour, Bill's site, and El Adem aerodrome. I hope to
goodness the Hurricanes get him. Evidently they got one this morning [an
obvious reference to the Z1007bis engaged by 3RAAF]. Another amusing
happening on this eventful day. A Blenheim went over the harbour and one
shot was fired at it. One of the other sites reported it was a Heinkel and the
town siren went off – everyone panicked and then discovered the error. Later
on, no one would admit to having fired that shot ... So ended a day's rotten
shooting, as bad as ever I have seen ..."

Shortly after lunch on 3 April, seven Hurricanes of 3RAAF – now operating from
a landing ground at Got es Sultan about 20 miles north-east of Benina, to where it
had hurriedly withdrawn the previous night – accompanied by B Flt/73 Squadron,
encountered eight Ju87s of II/StG2 about 15 miles south of Sceleidima, escorted by
an equal number of Bf110s of 7/ZG26 led by the newly appointed Staffelkapitän,
Hptm Georg Christl. The Stukas had been attacking British troops near Derna, as
one of those under attacked recalled:

"Two lots of nine [*sic*] planes came over and dive-bombed and machine-
gunned us, but only knocked out one truck. A piece from one bomb blew the
side of the driver away."

One section of RAAF Hurricanes led by Flt Lt Rawlinson waded into the dive-
bombers while Flt Lt Steege's section engaged the escort. B Flt/73 Squadron did not
become involved, as remembered somewhat ruefully by Sgt Garton:

"We were with the Aussies, and they attacked Ju87s and ME110s. Us? We
were led by Tiny Millist who took us off on a long chase after what turned out
to be a Blenheim, and we missed the scrap altogether."

Flg Off Jackson's journal again provides an account of the ensuing series of
engagements:

"Somebody spotted enemy aircraft. We were in three flights, Gordon Steege
[P3967/OS-B] leading bottom flight with myself [V7770], John Saunders
[V6737] and Pete Turnbull [V7492], Alan Rawlinson [V7772] leading middle
flight about 1,000 feet above us, and a flight of 73 Squadron above them. The
top flight did a wild goose chase after one of our Blenheims they spotted out
on our starboard side, which happened to be returning from a reconnaissance,
and they did not see the enemy which turned out to be about ten ME110s
escorting Ju87s who were dive-bombing and ground strafing our ground
forces. I only spotted the ME110s and didn't see any of the other enemy
aircraft. I followed Gordon Steege into attack and got on the tail of a ME110
just after he had fired a few rounds at it. I fired two bursts then my guns
stopped. Rotten luck just as I was getting in close. Pete Turnbull followed me
in on the same ME110 and gave it a burst also. Gordon Steege got the credit
for this kite as he attacked first and probably got in the best attack. I did a steep

spiral to gain speed to get out of the place as it was useless to remain without guns firing, and flew back to Benina.

Pete Turnbull had a go at two more ME110s and blew an engine out of one and bits off another, and fired at a couple of others. Smithy [P3980], one of the three South African pilots[1] attached to us, attacked one of the Ju87s and blew the tail clean off one which crashed in flames. Jimmy Davidson [V7566] also claimed a Ju87. Alan Rawlinson also sent two 87s down in flames [and John Saunders claimed one damaged]. All our chaps returned safely though some had bullet holes – both Pete Turnbull and Jimmy Davidson had holes through their ailerons and both were jamming badly. There were very fortunate to get back."

Despite the claims for three Bf110s probably destroyed, only one (WkNr3885) was shot down in which the pilot, Uffz Georg Stirnweiss, suffered wounds. The Zerstörer crews similarly overestimated their successes, two Hurricanes being claimed shot down by Hptm Christl and a third by Obfw Franz Sander. Two Ju87s failed to return from this operation, a 5 Staffel machine (WkNr5885) crashing about 20 miles south-west of Sollum in which the gunner, Uffz Peter Ott, was killed, although the pilot, Uffz Christian Apmann survived, wounded. The second Stuka (WkNr6034), from 6 Staffel, crash-landed north-east of Agedabia with a wounded gunner, Uffz Erwin Dürr, on board.

For A Flt/73 Squadron at Bu Amud, the day was relatively quiet. During the morning, patrols were flown in protection of an RN minesweeper operating off Tobruk. Then, at midday, Flg Off Scott and Plt Off Joubert were scrambled to investigate two aircraft reported overflying El Adem at 20,000 feet. Soon after take-off Joubert's engine began malfunctioning and he was obliged to return to base, Plt Off Humphreys being ordered off to join Scott in his place. An aircraft was seen high over El Adem but was not engaged. However, Lt Rankin's journal provides an alternative identification of the two aircraft originally reported:

"Had an alarm at midday – various hostiles about but too high for us to pick up in the glare. Suddenly a cry – 'plane' – went up and everyone laid on two great white planes which were tearing in at incredible speed, only to find they were some huge birds, possibly eagles. Everyone was taken in."

Sqn Ldr Murray scrambled at 1805 when another intruder was reported approaching Tobruk. He was ordered to climb to 20,000 feet but failed to locate the aircraft which, in the event, turned out to be a Blenheim going about its duty, as noted by Rankin:

"In the evening we had another alarm, but this time it was on account of a Blenheim which [we] managed successfully to identify, when we were all prepared to open fire – there is so little difference at great heights between Blenheims, Ju88s and Glenn Martins."

---

[1] The three South African pilots attached to 3RAAF towards the end of March were Lt G.K. Smith SAAF, Lt A.A. Tennant SAAF, and Flg Off R.F. Donati, a South African in the RAF.

That night (3/4 April), 6 Squadron was ordered to evacuate Barce immediately and withdraw to Maraua, where ground parties subsequently arrived at all hours during the morning. The Hurricanes of A Flight flew in to join the rest of the Squadron. Plt Off Moulding of A Flight recorded an orderly withdrawal from Agedabia to Maraua:

> "We moved to Maraua more or less according to schedule. Shortly after 0730 on a fine, clear morning, the vehicles of the main road party were straggled out on the flat tarmac road which leads to the base of the escarpment. About the same time the aircraft, five Hurricanes and ten Lysanders took off in flight formation and, with one exception, set course eastwards. The exception was a Hurricane which headed off to the west on its own, keeping low, weaving and turning as it followed the highway to Benina."

The lone Hurricane was searching for A Flight's ground party under the command of the CO, Sqn Ldr Weld, which had failed to arrive at Maraua as scheduled although it did eventually turn up two days later, more or less unscathed. The Squadron diarist wrote:

> "The air party arrived at Maraua after an anxious night. Meanwhile, A Flight have been carrying out almost continuous treks. We have been doing Trojan work with the Lizzies. The CO turned up that night with almost all of A Flight. A very happy reunion."

3RAAF, together with B Flt/73 Squadron, was also ordered to evacuate Got es Sultan landing ground with all haste, as noted by Flg Off Jackson:

> "About 10 [o'clock] that night CO got an emergency signal ordering us to leave Sultan immediately as enemy were expected to arrive any moment – had to go to Maraua. This meant all our Hurricanes would have to be burnt. We [the pilots] all decided that, as we wouldn't be worth a cracker without aircraft, we might as well run the risk of being captured and try to get our aircraft away at dawn. We had to pack up and send off on trailers two or three u/s Hurricanes that couldn't be shifted. There was also a Wimpey bomber which had crash-landed there on its way back from a bombing raid – undercarriage crook and one wing buckled, but CO called for volunteers with Wimpey experience to fly it off. The only bloke who had any experience, very limited, was Donati. He volunteered and called for someone to accompany him. A corporal did so. He got it off OK but then found it wouldn't cruise at much above stalling speed, and wouldn't climb above 1,500 feet. He nearly got to Maraua when it started to get worse and went into two spins. He cut the motors and got it stable again and crash-landed. He took out all the valuable gears, guns and radio, and then burnt it. He found a wee donkey grazing nearby and went riding off up to a nearby hill where he struck some Diggers – they got him back to us. A great piece of work on his part.
>   Anyway, whole Squadron packed up and all our transports were on the move by sunlight. We kept a few blankets each and snatched an hour or so, all wondering if the Huns would walk in during the night. I couldn't for the life of me see how they could possibly arrive so soon as, during our late afternoon

patrol, we did not sight them – but apparently HQ had the wind up and was quite prepared to see us burn our Hurricanes. It would have been impossible to get them off as no night landing facilities could be arranged. All communications seem to be in a mess. We all got into the air at dawn, the CO being the last to leave. Pete Turnbull did a good job – his aircraft had a tyre shot and we had no spares, so he packed the tyre with blankets and flew it to El Adem. We had brought our captured CR42 [upon which the Squadron had bestowed the unofficial RAAF serial number A42-1] with us from Benina. We decided we couldn't bring it with us, so CO strafed it and set it on fire. We arrived at Maraua to find great chaos. Three lorries had tipped over in the dark – one was our mess lorry with £80-worth of beer, an absolute tragedy."

Meanwhile, on the morning of 4 April, Flg Off Storrar and new pilot Sgt Ken Souter of A Flt/73 Squadron were airborne from Bu Amud to fly protection sorties for two ships reportedly approaching Tobruk Harbour, but neither could locate the vessels. Wing HQ telephoned at midday to apologise for the confusion since there had never been a convoy to escort – someone at RNHQ had blundered. Then, at 1440, Sgts Laing, Coussens and Marshall were scrambled to investigate an unidentified aircraft at 20,000 feet west of Tobruk, only to find this was friendly, as were several others encountered by another section of Hurricanes shortly before dusk. The fine weather continued next day (5 April). At Bu Amud, A Flt/73 Squadron had experienced a relatively quiet day. Patrols were maintained throughout the daylight hours, during which a departing RN vessel was escorted beyond Gazala Point in the morning, and two other naval vessels heading eastwards were provided with air cover during the afternoon. There occurred the occasional scramble as unidentified aircraft entered the sector, but there was only one encounter with an enemy aircraft when Flg Off Scott (V7371/TP-C) intercepted a Ju88 near the harbour at 1035. He was however unable to get within 600 yards of the intruder as it fled seawards but nevertheless he fired several bursts which he believed may have hit the target, although no visible result was observed. The Squadron received three reinforcement pilots during the day, Flg Off R.F. Martin DFC (who had served with the Squadron in 1940 in France, where he had gained his DFC), and Plt Offs Roylance Chatfield and Roy McDougall, all three ferrying Hurricanes from Ismailia via Mersa Matruh and El Adem. Leaving the Squadron at this time was Plt Off McColl, the Canadian returning to the UK. Among recent visitors to Bu Amud was Flt Lt J.A.F. Maclachlan DFC who had served with 73 Squadron during the Battle of Britain and had, more recently, flown Hurricanes in the defence of Malta. Although achieving rapid success, he had been shot down (in February 1941) by a Bf109 and seriously wounded, necessitating the amputation of his left forearm. Despite this major disability, Maclachlan[2] persuaded Sqn Ldr Murray that he was capable of flying a Hurricane with just one arm (he had already flown a Magister trainer at Malta within a few weeks of losing his arm), as recalled by airman Ken Rumbold:

---

[2] The gallant Maclachlan returned to England where he was fitted with an artificial arm; he returned to operations and commanded a Hurricane intruder squadron, raising his tally to 16 before being shot down over Northern France. Seriously injured, he died in captivity.

"He might have had trouble convincing the authorities, but none of us had any
doubts after he borrowed one of our kites and put on a memorable display of
aerobatics, beating up the camp at low level."

It may have been quiet in the Tobruk sector, but there was to be plenty of action for
the Hurricanes at Maraua during the day, although not until the afternoon were
enemy aircraft encountered. B Flt/73 Squadron was called upon to provide escort
for a Sunderland flying boat on an ASR mission in the morning, as was a section
from 3RAAF. Four days earlier, a reconnaissance Blenheim had been reported
down in the sea about 25 miles out from Benghazi, its crew having taken to their
dinghy. Conditions had been unsuitable for an earlier attempt to rescue the airmen,
but on this occasion the flying boat was able to complete the operation successfully.
Further patrols were carried out from Maraua before lunchtime without incident, as
noted by Flg Off Jackson:

"First patrol I was on was over retreat of our troops up the Barce Pass where
there was some blockage. They were supposed to be accumulating but were
making an excellent target for dive-bombers; however, we struck no enemy
aircraft. Apparently they were harassing our retreating troops north-east of
Barce and, from Barce, we could see long columns of transport kicking up a
big dust cloud on the desert roads, all heading north-east. It was fairly obvious
that they would be attacked in this sector as the desert was making them very
visible for many miles."

At 1405 however, when Flt Lt Beytagh (V7810/TP-W) and Plt Off Eiby
(V7550/TP-O) set out in company with a section of three from 3RAAF they soon
encountered every fighter pilot's dream target – an unescorted formation of slow,
cumbersome dive-bombers. In the ensuing engagement five Ju87s – aircraft from
6/StG2 – were claimed shot down, one apiece by the 73 Squadron pilots, who also
claimed two others damaged, while Flg Off Ellerton (V7353) claimed two more and
Flg Off Kloster (P5176) one. The fifth Hurricane, V7347 flown by Flg Off
Edwards, was hit by return fire and obliged to force-land without injuring the pilot.
There was a certain amount of over-claiming but the Stuka unit lost its
Staffelkapitän Oblt Peter Riedinger together with his gunner, Gfr Heinz Wilke,
when their aircraft (WkNr6044) crashed about 60 miles east of Benghazi, and two
other dive-bombers were forced down in which both gunners, Gfr Heinz Orlowski
and Obgfr Kurt Loos, were wounded. Of the action, Bill Eiby recalled:

"By now the bloody army was in full flight. They retreated and the Jerries were
knocking hell out of our convoys. We got scrambled and ran into this mob.
I dived at this bastard and hit him and he caught fire. He went straight in. I
should have shot down another one but he eluded me. Soon after that they
withdrew the Stukas as the Hurricanes could shoot them down like flies."

At 1635 another Hurricane patrol took off from Maraua, led by Sqn Ldr Campbell
in V7567, to provide cover for the hard-pressed British forces and, at the same time,
to carry out a search for the missing pilot (Edwards). The seven Hurricanes,
including three from B Flt/73 Squadron, soon sighted a dozen more dive-bombers

– on this occasion 4/StG2 – south of the Barce Pass. Flg Off Jackson participated on this occasion:

> "We decided to do another patrol to search for Mort Edwards and, at the same time, protect our retreating troops from enemy dive-bombers. Had gone no distance before we bumped into a large number of Ju87s, unescorted by fighters. We attacked immediately and I saw Jock Perrin send one down in flames. I then attacked another and gave it a good burst, and reckoned I had damaged it badly when another Hurricane came at it from my starboard and delivered a beam attack, which sent it down in flames. I then attacked two others, damaging them, and had got on the tail of a fourth and given it a couple of bullets, and silenced its gunner, when my guns ceased to fire. I then had the enemy at about 100 feet and felt enraged that he looked like escaping. His rear gunner appeared to be dead so I thought I might dive at him and clip him with my wing. Anyway, decided I was too low to get away with this so made a couple of dummy attacks and much to my delight he crash-landed in a cultivated wadi. His aircraft hit the side of the wadi and spun around in a cloud of dust. I flew around a few times and eventually the pilot got out, looking a bit dazed or stunned. I gave him a wave and returned to Maraua but pinpointed the position in case I ever get back over the area. Jewell saw Duncan Campbell losing height with a stream of white smoke pouring from his aircraft and he has not been seen since. I feel confident that both Mort and Duncan have force-landed safely, although they will be taken prisoners."

Flg Off Edwards was indeed taken prisoner but in rather a bizarre manner. Having been picked up by a British patrol from HQ 2nd Armoured Division, he was, together with his companions, captured by the Germans in a subsequent ground action. Sqn Ldr Campbell, however, was dead, presumably mortally wounded by return fire from the Stuka he engaged. Nine of the dive-bombers were believed to have been shot down in this action, Flt Lt Perrin (P3967/OS-B) and Flg Off Jewell (P3818) each claiming three destroyed, while Jackson (V7772) was awarded one and two probables, Plt Off Millist (V7766/TP-Z) and Sgt Garton (V7716/TP-U) each claiming for B Flt/73 Squadron, Millist reporting damage to a second. Only Sgt Webster (V7546/TP-Q) failed to score, noting ruefully "Engaged Ju87s without effect!!" Sgt Garton summarized the day's events in his diary:

> "Went off on a dawn patrol over Barce, but didn't see anything. Mr Beytagh took a patrol off at midday and they met a Ju87 convoy, shooting down six in all. Mr Beytagh and Eiby got one each. I went off on a later patrol and we met about 12 Ju87s. I got one destroyed, and chased another for miles without being able to take him and knock him out of the air."

As with 6 Staffel earlier in the afternoon, 4 Staffel lost its leader, Oblt Hans Sonntag and his gunner Fw Heinrich Kieselhorst both being killed when their aircraft (WkNr6046) crashed. Uffz Heinrich Ehlers, gunner aboard Obfw Heinz Gragert's aircraft (WkNr5951/T6+GH), was also killed; Gragert was taken prisoner and may have been Jackson's victim. Three other Ju87s were forced down, each with a wounded gunner on board[3]. A few days later, two Australian soldiers trekking eastwards from Benghazi came across a small Arab settlement near Derna where they were given food and water. Once fed and watered, they were shown to a tent which contained a seriously wounded German air gunner whose aircraft, they were told, had been shot down by an RAF fighter; he was almost certainly a survivor from one of the Stukas shot down by the Hurricanes. The two Australians agreed to take the wounded airman with them, intending to hand him over to British troops at Gerdas Abid. With the airman securely strapped to a donkey, the trio reached Gerdas Abid only to find that the troops had departed, local Arabs once again taking charge of the wounded man. The Australians, joined by two more plus five Egyptian civilians, eventually reached the safety of Tobruk. The fate of the German airman is unknown.

Meanwhile, the Hurricanes had returned to Maraua but, on landing, the pilots were told to leave immediately for Derna, since reconnaissance pilots of 6 Squadron, also operating from Maraua, reported enemy ground units outflanking British forces in the area. Sgt Garton continued:

> "Returned to Maraua but left immediately for Derna owing to pressure by the Huns. They were apparently trying to cut us off along the desert road. Arrived at Derna to find considerable panic. Laing and I went into the officers' mess to celebrate, with whisky, my Ju87."

Flg Off Jackson noted:

> "As soon as we landed we were told that we had to clear out for Derna immediately and we pushed straight off without waiting for fuel. We can't understand why our own ground forces don't stop and fight instead of retreating all the time. I felt a bit windy on the way to Derna – short of fuel and my guns had stopped firing during the last patrol, so was hoping I wouldn't strike any enemy aircraft. Passed three fighter Blenheims who gave me a start until I identified them. Landed at Derna and found the place in a great state of turmoil. Eight ME110s had just attacked the aerodrome a few minutes before I landed and destroyed two Blenheims and one Hurricane."

The Messerschmitts, from 7/ZG26, also seriously damaged two Lysanders while bullets and debris caused minor damage to three other Blenheims; one of the attacking aircraft was claimed to have been shot down into the sea by the defences, although none was actually lost[4]. 3RAAF's ground party convoy, which had earlier set out for Derna, was also strafed and two airmen were seriously wounded, one of whom died later, while several of the transports were badly damaged, although all were driveable. On reaching Derna the convoy was ordered to continue on to Martuba, eventually arriving there at 1800 without further interference from the

---

[3] The wounded air gunners of 4/StG2 in this action were Fw Günther Stulken, Ogfr Kurt Heinrich, and Ogfr Walter Rauer.

[4] The Luftwaffe did lose an aircraft to AA fire during the day, a He111 (N6+1A) of Kurierstaffel Afrika force-landing near El Adem (apparently having lost its way) and among those captured was Hptm Baudissin, Rommel's Chief Intelligence Officer.

Luftwaffe. Army HQ had in the meantime decided that the reports of Maraua landing ground about to be overrun were exaggerated and ordered A Flt/6 Squadron to return forthwith, together with a ground party, although the latter was then instructed to proceed to Tmimi. The day's confusing events were noted by the Squadron diarist:

"As Jerry was trying to outflank us, the ground party left for Derna leaving two Lizzies and A Flight at Maraua. When the ground party arrived, Jerry strafed them. [Flg Off] Hillier arrived [in a Lysander] ten minutes after Jerry left, having been frightened while on TacR by seeing seven Ju87s. When he found that the ground party had to leave again immediately for Tmimi and that he had to stay the night, he nearly passed out."

Plt Off Moulding added:

"AHQ sent a message to say proceed to Derna – no sooner had we reached Derna than up comes a ruddy General asking why we were there ... he said the air force must provide a reconnaissance unit at Maraua. He accused us of spreading alarm and despondency and told [the Flight Commander] that if he did not get A Flight back to Maraua by 5pm he would have him court-martialled."

The Squadron diarist continued:

"The army got a bee in its bonnet that the Jerry seen moving along our flank towards Mechili was not Jerry at all. So back we came to Derna and A Flight left Derna for Maraua. A 0740 [next morning, 6 April] Pat Pike saw Jerry entering Derna so he dropped a message to the boys, and aircraft took off in all directions. Further information showed that Gazala was threatened; so off we went again, this time for El Adem, leaving at 1730 just as the new signals officer and six thoroughly browned-off airmen arrived from El Adem in the back of a pick-up to join the Squadron."

3RAAF was also running around in circles. After an overnight stay at Derna the Hurricanes (including four of B Flt/73 Squadron) flew to Gazala East, as recalled by Plt Off Eiby:

"We were under an Aussie at that time. He told us to stay with our machines and we went back to Barce [Maraua]. It was complete confusion there, everybody getting trucks and pushing off to the east – nobody wanted to stay with us. Its amazing when a bloody rout sets in, and we flew back to Derna and were met by fire from Lewis guns and Christ knows what else as we came in to land. They were in the middle of a retreat and they were firing at everything that flew, having been done over a few times. If I remember rightly, we got off again and went back to Gazala."

3RAAF's main ground party, having just arrived at Martuba, was now ordered to Bu Amud. Following an all-night drive through a severe duststorm, Bu Amud was reached, but once there they were ordered to keep moving – this time all the way back to Egypt. Similarly, 6 Squadron's ground party was on the move:

> "After several narrow escapes we arrived at El Adem only to be instructed to move to Menastir near Bardia, at once. The Squadron arrived back at El Adem and found the air party, after having lost them for two days. [Flt Lt] Gordon Saunders, who left Maraua by road, has not turned up and is presumed captured by Jerry [which was, in fact, the case]."

Not only had 6 Squadron lost one of its Flight Commanders in such an unexpected fashion, the army suffered the indignity of having both General Richard O'Connor, Commander of the Western Desert Force, and one of his senior officers, Lt General Philip Neame VC, captured by a German motor-cycle patrol near Derna. By the end of the day Axis forces had reached the coast road at Derna, with Panzer units having penetrated eastwards as far as Msus.

73 Squadron at Bu Amud now found itself caught up in the confusion caused by the general withdrawal. A message was received from the army at about 0715, reporting gunfire at Acroma, just outside the Tobruk perimeter, and Flg Off Storrar was sent to investigate. He returned having seen nothing of any note. Other Hurricanes were ordered to patrol the area, but still nothing untoward was observed. The Squadron was then informed by Ops that parachutists had been dropped in the area – a further report which turned out to be false – and eventually the scare died down. But then, just after midday, came reports that a small outpost near Acroma was surrounded by enemy forces. Plt Off McFadden was sent off to investigate and, on his return, reported having sighted a truck and a Fiat vehicle with an AA gun attached parked near the outpost, the gun opening fire on his aircraft. Steps were immediately taken to despatch a force of troops to the location and, at 1300, a minor engagement took place. The enemy force constituted a small number of escaped Italian prisoners, plus one German, who had penetrated eastwards and had attacked the outpost which they had succeeded in taking. In the subsequent exchange of fire, one Italian was killed and a British soldier wounded before the remainder were recaptured and taken back to Tobruk. With the excitement over, Flg Off Scott and Sgt Wills flew over to Gazala East to reinforce B Flight, while three more pilots – Flg Offs Storrar and Goodman (newly promoted), plus Plt Off Lamb – travelled by road.

In the early morning hours of 7 April, it was the turn of 73 Squadron to receive orders to withdraw from Bu Amud as the retreat eastwards continued. HQ and ground personnel were to move immediately to Menastir, before heading for Buq-Buq. The Hurricanes and servicing crews were to remain, however, with instructions to operate for as long as possible from Bu Amud or until ordered to withdraw, although all unserviceable but flyable aircraft were flown to Buq-Buq. Soon after the road convoy had departed, orders for its withdrawal to Menastir were rescinded and Flg Off Scott was despatched to drop a message to the convoy leader to head for El Gubbi instead. Unable to locate the convoy, he flew firstly to Menastir, then Sollum and finally Buq-Buq, leaving messages to that effect. One of the Squadron's airmen, John Dobson, remembered:

> "A small detachment of armourers and other ground tradesmen were detailed to go to a landing ground near Bardia, to act as an advanced base for Hurricanes and allow them to avoid the return to base between sorties. Some eight or nine of us arrived at the deserted field and started putting up our tents

Top: Flt Lt Peter Wykeham-Barnes (second from right) briefing pilots of 274 Squadron.

Middle left: Sqn Ldr P.H. Dunn's personal aircraft, P2643, when CO of 274 Squadron. *(Andy Thomas)*

Middle right: Sqn Ldr Charles Ryley at the head of B Flight, 33 Squadron (left to right) unidentified, Flg Off C.H. Dyson DFC, Flg Off P.R. St Quintin, Flg Off H.J. Starrett, Flt Lt G.E. Hawkins, Sgt J. Craig, Flg Off J.F. Mackie, Flg Off V.C. Woodward.

Above: Three pilots of 274 Squadron (left to right) Lt Bob Talbot, the SAAF's first ace of the Desert war, killed in action 3 June 1941; Flg Off Charles Greenhill killed in action 30 April 1941; Plt Off John Strange.

Left: Flg Off Imshi Mason DFC of 274 Squadron.

Top left: Cne (later Flt Lt) Paul Jacquier flew a Po63-11 of GAO 1/583 from the Lebanon to Egypt on 25 June 1940 to join the Allied cause.

Top right: Another French escapee was Sgt-Chef Marcel Lebois (centre) pictured here with his mechanics Adjt Djabian and Serg Vergerio, and Po63-11 (No670) in background.

Above: One of the MS406s in RAF markings flown by Sous-Lt Antoine Péronne, also formerly of GCI/7.

Right: Sgt-Chef André Ballatore arrived in Egypt on 23 June 1940 in a Morane MS406 of GCI/7.

Four of the first six 73 Squadron Hurricanes being ferried from Takoradi to Egypt crashed or crash-landed en route while attempting to land at Rullo, 60 miles south-east of El Geneina in the Sudan, on 3 December 1940, resulting in the death of Sgt G.W. Brimble; the other three pilots survived, and their aircraft are herewith depicted:

Top left: Sgt Laing's V7347 was repairable...

Top right: So was Sqn Ldr Murray's V7566, which remained incredibly balanced on its nose and port wingtip until lowered for repair...

Middle left: But Plt Off Humphrey's V7556 was a write-off, the pilot receiving a superficial cut to his head in the process.

Above left: Sgt Fred Marshall DFM of 73 Squadron (later Flt Lt DFC DFM, killed in a flying accident in 1944).

Above centre: Sgt Bob Laing of 73 Squadron (later commissioned and awarded a DFC).

Above right: Sgt Geoff Garton of 73 Squadron (later Wg Cdr DSO DFC).

Some of the leading personalities of 3RAAF Squadron...

Top left: Sqn Ldr Peter Jeffrey DFC, the CO (later Grp Capt DSO DFC).

Top centre: Flt Lt Peter Turnbull DFC (later Sqn Ldr, killed in action).

Top right: Flg Off John Jackson DFC (later Sqn Ldr, killed in action) whose diary is extensively quoted.   *(David Wilson via Dennis Newton)*

Middle left: Flt Lt Jock Perrin DFC (later Wg Cdr).

Centre: Flg Off Wilf Arthur DFC (later Grp Capt DSO DFC).

Bottom: Majority of 73 Squadron's officers photographed at Gazala circa March 1941: (standing, from left to right) Flg Off Lewis (Cyphers Officer), unknown, Plt Off K.M. Millist, Plt Off J.B. McColl, Flg Off Hoole (IO); (sitting, left to right) Plt Off P. Haldenby, Plt Off W.T. Eiby, Flg Off G. E. Goodman DFC, Plt Off C.C.O Joubert, Plt Off O.E. Lamb, Sqn Ldr A.D.Murray, Flt Lt M.L.ff. Beytagh, Plt Off M.P. Wareham, Plt Off P.C. Humphreys.

Top left: CR42 of 96^Squadriglia force-landed near the Bardia road following dogfight with RAF fighters. *(Nico Malizia)*

Top right: G50bis of 150^Squadriglia force-landed in the desert . *(Nico Malizia)*

Middle: Ju87s of 239^Squadriglia en route to Tobruk escorted by G50bis of 150^Squadriglia. *(Nico Malizia).*

Bottom left: Hurricane P3822 of 3RAAF Squadron. *(Dennis Newton)*

Bottom right: Rare picture of 3RAAF Squadron Hurricane wearing OS code - P3967 OS-B. *(Andy Thomas)*

Top left: P2646 TP-K of 73 Squadron.

Top right: V7544 TP-S of 73 Squadron following force-landing at Gazala by Flg Off Jas Storrar DFC on 2 February 1941.

Middle: Hurricane E of 208 Squadron wrecked at El Adem – possibly P3826, abandoned at El Adem on 22 April 1941 during the retreat.

(Andy Thomas)

Bottom: A group of pilots from 73 Squadron pose with a Hurricane at Gazala, probably in March 1941; (from left to right) Plt Off P. Haldenby (killed in action, Tobruk), Plt Off C.C.O. Joubert, Plt Off W.T. Eiby, Plt Off K.M. Millist DFC (killed in action, Tobruk), Sqn Ldr A.D. Murray DFC, Plt Off P.C. Humphreys, Plt Off M.P. Wareham (DFC later), Plt Off O.E. Lamb (killed in action, Tobruk).

Top left: Flg Off Donald Scott DFC, 73 Squadron.

Top centre: Flg Off Jas Storrar DFC, 73 Squadron.

Top right: Cpl Pete Minterne, 73 Squadron airman.

Above: Four of the French pilots at Tobruk (left to right) Sous-Lt Albert Littolf, Wt Off André Ballatore, Sous-Lt James Denis, and Sous-Lt Louis Ferrant.

Left: Plt Off Jean Pompéï seen at the moment of his rescue by men of the Long Range Desert Unit.

T0BRUK UNDER ATTACK

Top: Tobruk harbour photographed from attacking German aircraft.

Above: Bombs falling on Tobruk waterfront.

Right: The hospital ship *Vita* on fire after being bombed on 14 April 1941; the vessel was later beached and became a total wreck after 490 patients and staff had been evacuated.

Top: A view from air gunner's position as a Ju87 of 239^Squadriglia Aut B.a'T completes ts attack on installations at Tobruk.

(Nico Malizia)

Centre: A view from the ground as a Ju87 attacks positions within the Tobruk garrison perimeter.

Bottom: Army transport HMT *Chalka* under attack by Ju87s in Tobruk harbour 29 April 1941.

Top left: Sous-Lt Albert Littolf, attached to 73 Squadron.

Top centre: Sous-Lt James Denis DFC, leader of the French detachment.

Top right: Sous-Lt Noël Castelain, attached to 73 Squadron.

Middle left: Cne (later Flt Lt) Jean Tuslane, attached to 274 Squadron, flanked by Sous-Lts Albert Littolf (left) and James Denis.

Bottom left: Hurricane V7716 TP-U of 73 Squadron which Flt Lt G.E. Ball DFC force-landed outside the Tobruk perimeter on 12 April 1941 to become a prisoner of war.

(Cesare Gori via Gianandrea Bussi)

Bottom right: Flt Lt George Ball DFC of 73 Squadron, taken prisoner of war on 12 April 1941; during the Battle of Britain he had flown with Sqn Ldr Douglas Bader's 242 Squadron.

Top left: Sqn Ldr Peter Wykeham-Barnes DFC took command of 73 Squadron on 20 April 1941; two days later he was shot down in combat with Bf109s of I/JG27 having claimed two victories first.

Top right: Flt Lt Smudger Smith of 73 Squadron. On 14 April 1941 he shot down two G-50bis of 351^Squadriglia including that flown by Ten Carlo Cugnasca, who was killed. The Canadian flight commander was then shot down and killed by another G-50bis.

Above: The remains of Flt Lt Smith's Hurricane (P2652) and his temporary grave.

Left: Ten Carlo Cugnasca of 351^Squadriglia, killed in action over Tobruk on 14 April 1941. *(Lino Pellegrini via Gianandrea Bussi).*

Hurricane V7811, 73 Squadron. Tobruk, April 1941. Forced down by two E.A just behind front line. Pilot wounded and machine gunned on ground by Germans after crash landing.

Top left: Wreck of an unidentified Hurricane which crashed inverted into a building at Tobruk.

Top right: The remains of Sgt H.G. Webster's 73 Squadron Hurricane (V7553) and his temporary grave.

Middle left: 274 Squadron Hurricane after enemy action; rare view of NH codes which soon gave way to code letters being substituted by a painted lightning flash bisecting the fuselage roundel.　　　　　　(*Andy Thomas*)

Middle right: Painting on "the flash" on 274 Squadron's V7830.　　　(*Andy Thomas*)

Bottom left: Sqn Ldr John Lapsley DFC, CO of 274 Squadron, shot down and wounded by Bf109Es of 1/JG27 on 19 April 1941.

Bottom right: Drawing of Sqn Ldr Lapsley's crash-landed Hurricane V7811, erroneously recorded as a 73 Squadron aircraft by the artist, 73 Squadron airman LAC Ralph Grace, who was one of those selected to guard the damaged machine.

Top left and right: Ju88 2F+XA of St.St/StG3 shot down near Giarabub on 21 March 1941; Lt Hermann Schiesel, the pilot, broke his thigh in the crash and is pictured being tended by his captors, who used a pillow and pieces of camp-bed to set his broken limb before transporting him to hospital.

Middle left and right: Bf109E Black 8 of 1/JG27 flown by Lt Werner Schroer (pictured right)

who survived being shot down twice in three days by Tobruk's Hurricanes in April 1941, before going on to become the second-highest Luftwaffe scorer in the Western Desert (61 out of a total for the war of 114).

Bottom: Ju87 of III/StG1 which crash-landed on the beach near Tobruk, probably J9+BH of 7 Staffel brought down on 12 April 1941.

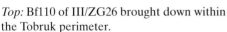

Top: Bf110 of III/ZG26 brought down within the Tobruk perimeter.

Middle left: Hs126 of 2(H)/14 shot down by Lt Adriaan Botha of 1SAAF Squadron near the Derna Road on 1 June 1941.

Middle right: Deputy AOC RAFME Air Marshal Tedder enjoys a joke with Sgt Fred Marshall, 73 Squadron's most successful pilot, following the withdrawal of the Squadron survivors from Tobruk. On the left is Sous-Lt

James Denis, centre position is occupied by Plt Off Bill Eiby.

Bottom left: One that did not get away! Captured Hurricane being inspected by Italian pilots and groundcrew, possibly at Martuba.

(Nico Malizia

Bottom right: Rare photograph showing Hurricane OL-H of the Royal Navy's ad hoc Fighter Flight at Sidi Haneish.

Top left: Flg Off A.A.P. Weller DFC, 274 Squadron.

Top centre: Flt Lt J.E. McFall DFC, 6 Squadron.

Top right: Flt Lt D.G.S. Honor DFC, 274 Squadron.

Middle left: Flg Off O.V. Tracey DFC, 274 Squadron.

Bottom left: Flg Off D.J. Spence, 274 Squadron.

Bottom right: Plt Off Peter Moulding, 6 Squadron.

Top: Obfhr Hans-Joachim Marseille of 3/JG27 with one of his early victims, a Hurricane of 274 Squadron (part of the letter N of the NH code can just be discerned).

Above: Three of the senior pilots of I/JG27 (from left to right) Oblt Ludwig Franzisket, Hptm Karl-Wolfgang Redlich, and Hptm Gerhard Homuth.

Right: Oblt Ludwig Franzisket (right) with Capt Ken Driver DFC of 1SAAF, whom he had just shot down (on 14 June 1941).

in the early afternoon, but this was disrupted by a sandstorm. We heard an aircraft circling overhead and thought we could recognise a Merlin; it went out to sea and then came in on an approach to land a short distance in from the beach. A tricky manoeuvre, even for a pilot who knew the area. The problem was then to find each other. When we finally met up he gave us a message to get out of there fast as Jerry had captured Gazala and was even then swinging south and east around Tobruk to aim for Bardia and Sollum. He took off again, and we loaded our three lorries and ran hard west for Tobruk, and learned later that the Germans were in Bardia the following morning."

Whether the Hurricane pilot was Flg Off Scott, or an unidentified member of 6 Squadron, is not clear but, either way, he probably helped save the small group of airmen from being taken prisoner. Of the move from Bu Amud, one of the Squadron's airmen, Colin Pring, recalled:

"I travelled in a captured Italian gun-tractor towing a large trailer, but the clutch gave up the ghost and we had to abandon the tractor and pile onto the trailer which was then towed by another vehicle. Somewhere between Bardia and Tobruk a tyre blew on the trailer and two men were left to guard it, while the rest of us went on to Tobruk. I went back to retrieve them with no trouble. It was only afterwards that we realised that nearly all the Allied forces were, by that time, inside the Tobruk perimeter."

Meanwhile, from Bu Amud 73 Squadron continued to carry out routine patrols over Tobruk harbour during the morning. Sqn Ldr Murray and Flt Lt Beytagh had just landed when a plot appeared on the radar, Sgt Ken Souter (V7553/TP-E) being scrambled at 0740 to support two other Hurricanes still on patrol. However, it was Souter who sighted the intruder, a Ju88D of 2(F)/123 from Sicily, as it passed over the harbour at 0800. He engaged the reconnaissance aircraft and fired all his ammunition, but was only able to report on his return that whilst all his ammunition had found its mark, it had little visible effect.

Although Souter – who had only recently joined the Squadron – had to be content with an apparent lack of tangible success, Obfw Werner Reinicke's 4U+FK was mortally wounded and, unobserved by assailant or radar plotters, eventually crashed into the sea off Bardia with the loss of the crew. During the afternoon the Squadron flew a total of 14 sorties strafing M/T on the Gazala to Tobruk road, during which at least 26 vehicles were claimed destroyed and several more damaged. A Blenheim fighter also joined in, strafing a column advancing on Mechili. The Hurricanes operated in pairs, and from a sortie which departed Bu Amud at 1400, only Plt Off Lamb returned, his leader, Plt Off Millist[5] having been shot down by ground fire just outside the Tobruk perimeter; on this occasion he did not return on foot as before, having been killed when his aircraft (V7550/TP-O) crashed. Taking off five minutes later (at 1405), Flg Off Scott (V7299/TP-D) and Sgt Marshall (V7560/TP-F) joined forces with a pair of Hurricanes from 3RAAF flown by Flt Lt Rawlinson and Flg Off Knowles (P3980) to carry out a further offensive patrol. About ten miles south of Mechili, two Ju52s of III/KGzbV.1 were

---

[5] On 14 November 1941 news of the award of the DFC to Flg Off Kenneth Millist was announced, with effect from 15 March 1941.

sighted on a landing ground, both being claimed destroyed by Marshall although the two Australians also attacked, each claiming one destroyed. Despite being hit by ground fire, Marshall's aircraft was able to return safely to Bu Amud, but Knowles was obliged to force-land at Gazala due to fuel shortage, as related by Flg Off Jackson in his diary:

> "Lindsey Knowles couldn't make it for [lack of] fuel and landed back at Gazala to find everybody had left. He struck some army chaps who said the Huns were hot on their tracks and he had better burn his Hurricane and go with them, which he did. Meanwhile, our blokes had sent a truck back with a volunteer crew to refuel Lindsey at Gazala, but before they got to Gazala they struck some army chaps who tried to stop them going any further. Anyway, they refused to be stopped and pushed on, only to find a burnt-out Hurricane and that Knowles had gone."

Among the aircraft milling around in the battle area was Rommel's personal Fi156 Storch, which was fired upon by British troops west of Fort Mechili. The General was lucky, for only one bullet hit the aircraft, this drilling a hole through its tailplane. Rommel considered the capture of Mechili vital to his plans, and against which he intended to concentrate his forces:

> "... it was becoming clear that the enemy was greatly overestimating our strength. At all costs it would be necessary to keep up this illusion by generating the appearance of a major offensive. Naturally, I was not in a position to push the enemy hard with my main force, but we were probably able to maintain enough pressure with our advance elements to keep him on the run. The Italian Commander-in-Chief, General Gariboldi, berated me severely, mainly because our actions were in contravention of instructions from Rome. He said that supplies to the Italo-German troops were so limited that no one could assume responsibility for such an undertaking. He demanded that I discontinue all such authority. I couldn't stand for that so I explained that I would continue to react to each situation as it arose as appropriately as I thought at the time. This brought the argument to a head when, like an avenging angel, a message arrived from the German High Command giving me the complete free hand I demanded."

With German troops rapidly approaching the Tobruk perimeter, the garrison was strengthened by the timely arrival by sea of the 7th Australian Division, hastily diverted from its original destination, Greece. Tobruk was becoming the centre of attraction. In his journal, Lt Rankin of 152 HAA wrote:

> "Planes – Hurricanes, Blenheims and Bombays – started pouring back from forward positions. This gave colour to the suggestion that an evacuation was in progress."

His perception was as accurate as his observation, except that there was to be no evacuation of the Tobruk garrison, as harshly emphasised by the Garrison Commander, Maj General Morshead:

> "There'll be no Dunkirk here. If we have to get out, we shall fight our way out. There is to be no surrender and no retreat."

CHAPTER V

INTO THE LIONS' DEN

8 – 18 April 1941

"We must operate Hurricanes from Tobruk as long as it is humanly possible..."
HQ RAFME to 204 Group[1]

Despite severe demands on men and supplies, the Germans were driven on by a commander who knew an opportunity when he saw one. With the capture of Derna successfully completed, Rommel was confident that the garrison at Tobruk could be contained, if not immediately taken, his eyes set firmly on driving the British all the way back into Egypt, even contemplating the capture of the Suez Canal in the foreseeable future. It seemed that only the lack of petrol and supplies could prevent him from fulfilling his ambitious aims, but there was to be another factor which was to thwart his progress – the determination of the three British commanders – General Wavell, Admiral Cunningham and Air Chief Marshal Longmore – to hold Tobruk; Cunningham believed his ships could keep the garrison supplied by sea, while Longmore promised to operate every available front-line aircraft in Egypt from the multitude of landing grounds east of Mersa Matruh, although the Hurricanes of 73 Squadron were to operate from within the Tobruk perimeter, together with those and the Lysanders of 6 Squadron.

Within hours of the fall of Derna a formation of Ju52/3ms began landing there, their arrival preceded by five G50bis which were to cover the landings. Four of the G50bis were from 378^Squadriglia led by Cap Bruno Tattanelli, the other flown by Ten Carlo Cugnasca of 351^Squadriglia. Shortly thereafter, a Ca133 arrived with mechanics and two more pilots on board, this being followed next day by two further G50bis one of which was flown by TenCol Luigi Bianchi, 155°Gruppo CT commander. That evening Cap Gino Callieri's 360^Squadriglia flew in with its G50bis before the third squadron of the Gruppo – 351^Squadriglia under the new command of Cap Angelo Fanello – landed two days later. The G50bis were immediately called upon to escort formations of Ju87s.

Meanwhile General Wavell, accompanied by General Lavarack, who was to take temporary command of the Western Desert Force following the capture of General

---

[1] RAF Cyrenaica became 204 Group on 12 April 1941.

O'Connor, flew to Tobruk on the morning of 8 April aboard Lodestar AX682 of 267 Squadron, arriving in a raging sandstorm and armed with the Prime Minister's latest cable, which read:

> "You should surely be able to hold Tobruk, with its permanent Italian defences, at least until or unless the enemy brings up strong artillery forces. It seems difficult to believe that he can do this for some weeks. He would run a great risk in masking Tobruk and advancing upon Egypt, observing that we can reinforce from the sea and would menace his communications. Tobruk therefore seems to be the place to be held to the death without a thought of retirement. I should be glad to hear of your intentions."

Having consequently advised the Garrison Commander and his senior officers of the decision to defend Tobruk, Wavell then visited 6 Squadron and personally thanked Sqn Ldr Weld for the way in which his Squadron had behaved during the withdrawal. It was late in the afternoon by the time Wavell and his party were ready to depart for Cairo, the sandstorm still blowing fiercely. Despite this, 73 Squadron continued to maintain a standing patrol over El Gubbi, which it had done since Wavell's arrival in the morning. As the Lodestar taxied to the runway one of its wheel-brakes seized, necessitating an on-the-spot repair before take-off could commence. Barely 15 minutes into the flight, the oil-pressure gauge on one engine dropped rapidly and the pilot was forced to turn back to a landing strip near Tobruk.

The grounded aircraft was sighted by Flg Off Storrar of 73 Squadron, who was returning to Bu Amud from a sortie to the Bomba area where he had been instructed to drop a message bag to troops located there. Having completed the mission he encountered a lone Ju87 of II/StG2 near Derna, which he engaged and forced down, the crew surviving unhurt. As he approached the Lodestar a member of its crew fired a Very light into the air, so he landed nearby and was obviously surprised to discover such distinguished personages on board. Assisting the crew in clearing sand from the filter, he then drained some oil from the Hurricane (P3818), enabling the Lodestar to take off again, just as the sun was setting. Twenty minutes later, however, the suspect engine again lost oil pressure and the pilot informed his passengers that he would endeavour to keep the aircraft flying on the one good engine but, before long, that too began overheating, necessitating a force-landing. Although the pilot carried out a skilful landing aided only by moonlight, one of the brakes seized, causing the aircraft to swing wildly before it tipped over, tearing off its port wing and part of the tail. None of those on board was hurt and, in quick time, as was the custom of the services, tea was brewed and rescue awaited. Within a very short time it came, in the guise of an armoured car of a Sudanese desert patrol. General Wavell and his party, plus the aircrew, were duly driven to Sollum, arriving just after 0100. From Sollum the same morning, the General was flown back to Cairo where, in the meantime, GHQ had been thrown into a near state of panic over his disappearance.

Meanwhile, 73 Squadron at Bu Amud was beginning to worry about the non-return of Flg Off Storrar from his afternoon sortie to Bomba. It transpired that following the departure of the Lodestar, he had been unable to restart his own engine:

"I knew that I was just about due south of Tobruk, and was faced with a 30 mile walk back to the Squadron. I walked at night, hiding in the shade during the day. I had get past a German Panzer encampment until I reached the road near Tobruk and I had to use the stars to get direction. It took me two nights, and I was grateful for my Boy Scout training as I headed directly at the Pole Star. The worst part of the trip was that I was wearing flying boots which kept filling with sand and did my feet no good at all. Just before dawn on the second night I heard voices – Aussie voices, from troops guarding the Tobruk perimeter. I had walked into a minefield being laid to close the perimeter. The Australians led me safely through and took me back by truck to the Squadron."

Following his return to Cairo, General Wavell cabled the Prime Minister and, after giving a detailed statement of troop positions, added:

"Although first enemy effort seems to have exhausted itself, I do not feel we shall have long respite and am still very anxious. Tobruk is not good defensive position; long line of communication behind is hardly protected at all and is unorganised."

Churchill was not impressed with Wavell's response and, having consulted the Chiefs-of-Staff, drafted a response:

"We await your full appreciation. Meanwhile you should know how the problem looks to us. From here it seems unthinkable that the fortress of Tobruk should be abandoned without offering the most prolonged resistance. We have a secure sea-line of communication. The enemy's line is long and should be vulnerable provided he is not given time to organise at leisure. So long at Tobruk is held and its garrison includes even a few armoured vehicles which can lick out at his communications, nothing but a raid dare go past Tobruk. If you leave Tobruk and go 260 miles back to Mersa Matruh may not you find yourself faced with something like the same problem? We are convinced you should fight it out at Tobruk."

However, before the message could be sent, Wavell's latest cable arrived, advising of his decision to make a stand at Tobruk, the PM immediately acknowledging same:

"We will cordially endorse your decision to hold Tobruk, and will do all in our power to bring you aid."

By a strange quirk of coincidence, Wavell's counterpart, Rommel, also experienced problems in the air during the day, his Storch coming to grief as it landed near Mechili, having only just avoided being shot down by Italian troops[2]:

---

[2] With the aircraft of both Generals Wavell and Rommel having suffered force-landings, four of the prominent leaders in the desert campaign had now experienced similar mishaps, following Général de Gaulle's forced-landing in French Equatorial Africa (see Appendix I) and that of Air Marshal Tedder the previous month.

"At about 0600 I flew off in a Storch to the front east of Mechili, to follow the course of the battle. Flying at about 300 feet, we approached a *Bersaglieri* battalion which had been brought up the day before. Apparently the Italians hadn't seen a Storch before, and were so taken aback by our sudden approach over their heads that they began firing at us from all directions. It was truly a miracle that from a range of 150-300 feet we were not shot down, and it didn't say much for Italian marksmanship. We immediately turned round and put a hill between ourselves and our allies. Not wishing to be shot down by our own troops, I straightaway ordered the pilot to climb to 3,000 feet, where we could safely observe the situation without being shot down. Clearly the attack on Mechili was gaining headway. A large column of enemy vehicles was rolling eastwards from Mechili, and we flew on expecting to find Olbrich's force [Oberst Olbrich, OC 5th Panzer Regiment] which was surely due. Still no sign of them. We did see an 88mm gun positioned about a mile from the British vehicles. I expected to find more German troops there, and as we came in to land, the Storch struck a sand dune and nosed in. By chance the gunners had a truck left and we made off in it to the south-east, where we soon found a salt marsh that I recognised from my flight the day before. From there we finally found our way back to Korps HQ."

With the Germans tightening the noose around Tobruk, an all-out effort to strengthen the garrison's original Italian-constructed perimeter was made. The first line of defence was a series of concrete posts and barbed wire, an anti-tank ditch and what remained of the minefields. For two days while the sandstorm was at its peak, soldiers laboured round the clock preparing and repairing the defences; new minefields were laid, signalling posts established and 25-pounder guns dug in. The perimeter was manned by seven of the garrison's 13 infantry battalions, while its armoured units comprised a regiment of armoured cars and 45 tanks, of which one third were lightly armoured and armed; there were three regiments of field artillery, plus a few captured 75mm and 105mm medium-range guns, and two anti-tank regiments. The harbour was protected by 75 anti-aircraft guns of which only 16 were heavy calibre.

Dawn on 9 April arrived like thunder for the defenders of Tobruk, the early morning raid being greeted by an intense barrage of gunfire, while a section of Hurricanes was scrambled from Bu Amud, but neither Flt Lt Smith nor Sgt Marshall was able to intercept. Lt Rankin noted:

"Then a reconnaissance plane came over at 14,000 feet and the HAA loosed off furiously. We fired 77 rounds at it, and other sites must have done the same, and yet it got away, chased out by Hurricanes who did not look like catching it. The plane was reported to be a Breda 88 [*sic*], and it dropped some bombs in the harbour without damage to shipping as far as could be seen."

73 Squadron was now ordered to move to El Gubbi landing ground, one of four within the Tobruk perimeter. The RAF contingent at Tobruk was commanded by Wg Cdr E.R.F. Black RAAF, a former CO of 3RAAF, who also acted as Air Liaison Officer attached to Army HQ. By midday, 73 Squadron's ground party from Bu

Amud had safely arrived although there was no news from the convoy which had set out for Buq-Buq, to where all flyable but unserviceable Hurricanes were flown, some of the pilots continuing eastwards to the Delta for a well-deserved break from operations, including Plt Offs Joubert, Legge, Humphreys and Haldenby, plus Sgts Coussens and Leng, one or two of whom were apparently showing signs of fatigue. Sgt Bob Laing was one of those earmarked for El Gubbi:

"Early in April we moved into Tobruk. The airfield was about 100-200 feet above the harbour, and I think really just a bit too central. There was another big drawback in that good routine maintenance and repairs to airframes, undercarriages etc was very difficult with all the bombing and strafing – and really the place was too vulnerable."

One of the Squadron's airmen, Ron Waite, added:

"El Gubbi was a small plateau with just sufficient level surface to give the Hurricanes room to take off and land. After some frantic digging in between the air raids of trenches around the landing ground, we were given some time to sort out our own accommodation."

By the time the ground party arrived, the Hurricanes had already been in action. At 0730, A Flight's Sgts Marshall (V7562/TP-A) and Souter (V7552/TP-J) were scrambled on the approach of an enemy aircraft, meeting not only a lone G50bis flown by Ten Cugnasca of 351^Squadriglia, but also Plt Off Eiby (V7810/TP-W) of B Flight who was just arriving from Bu Amud. Following a brief skirmish, during which he believed he had shot down one of the Hurricanes before his guns jammed, Cugnasca was pursued towards Derna where, upon landing, his aircraft swerved off the runway and was damaged. Meanwhile, Marshall and Eiby returned to El Gubbi believing they had probably shot down his aircraft, presumably having witnessed the landing accident. At 1030, three Hurricanes were scrambled to intercept a further raid on Tobruk harbour, on this occasion invloving He111s of II/KG26 escorted by Bf110s of 7/ZG26; Sgt Garton noted:

"Harbour bombed almost as soon as we landed [from Bu Amud] and I scrambled but was unable to catch up with them."

Flg Off Goodman (V7546/TP-Q) was more successful, however, shooting down Fw Helmut Jaculi's Messerschmitt near the Derna road. The pilot was killed and his gunner, Uffz Johann Wala, seriously wounded. Goodman's aircraft was then engaged and damaged by Hptm Christl, the Staffelkapitän, necessitating a force-landing within the outer defences. He was unhurt and was promptly driven back to El Gubbi. A second of the escort failed to return, apparently falling victim to the AA defences, as did one of the bombers, as noted by *British United Press* correspondent Jan Yindrich:

"Seven big black German planes with swastika markings bombed Tobruk harbour at 1020 this morning while I was banging out on my typewriter the stories I had collected the previous day. The planes missed all the ships in the harbour, although they dived down to within a few hundred feet of the surface of the water. The anti-aircraft batteries shot down three [*sic*] of the bombers, and a Hurricane brought down one Messerschmitt 110. The ack-ack batteries are hot stuff. The racket they make with their barrage is terrific. It is more frightening than the raid."

Ground strafing was carried out by 73 Squadron during the afternoon, two aircraft from each Flight being ordered to attack vehicles near Mechili at 1240, Flg Off Martin (V7553/TP-E) leading Plt Off McDougall (V7562/TP-A) plus Sgts Garton (V7766/TP-Z) and Webster (V7716/TP-U) of A Flight to the area but, en route, a Hs126 of 2(H)/14 was encountered about one mile south of Gadd el-Ahmar, as reported by the leader:

"Intended strafe of roads around el-Mechili – used all our ammunition on Hs126 which was shot down."

The Henschel (WkNr4372) was reported to have force-landed rather than crashed although it was totally destroyed. The pilot, Uffz Heinz Straeten, was nevertheless killed and his observer, Oblt Kurt Weith, wounded. Presumably both had been hit during the attacks by Martin, Garton and Webster. Apparently McDougall did not participate in the action and it would seem that he had become separated from the others, returning to El Gubbi some 30 minutes later.

Flg Off Goodman was obviously none the worse for his emergency landing during the morning, joining Flt Lt Beytagh and Plt Off Lamb for a patrol over the harbour at 1450, the trio landing just as seven Hurricanes of A Flight were preparing to take-off for an attack on the landing ground at Derna where a number of Bf110s had been sighted by reconnaissance Blenheims. The plan was for Flt Lt Smith (V7371/TP-C) to lead five aircraft (the others being flown by Plt Off McDougall, plus Sgts Laing, Elsworth and Wills) in an initial strafe while Flg Off Martin (V7553/TP-E) and Sgt Marshall (V7562/TP-A) were to provide cover. Sgt Bob Laing (P2646/TP-K) remembered:

"So off we went. As we drew near the Derna field we saw a Ju52 just taking off to the west, so two men looked after it [Martin and Marshall], and a little later came back to join our party. I don't really remember how many we fired at and, of course, one couldn't tell if they were really badly damaged as very few caught fire, but I would say about 20 to 30 could well have been shot up. There was not much ground fire, so we had it all our own way and returned to Tobruk well pleased with ourselves."

On returning to El Gubbi, Plt Off McDougall (V7560/TP-F) told *BUP*'s Jan Yindrich:

"We saw about 21 Messerschmitt 110s neatly laid out in rows. We roared down to about 20 feet, with our machine-guns blazing. One pilot flew down each line of eight machines, firing a burst at each. At each burst there was a 'pop' and the machine burst into flames. He alone definitely destroyed eight machines and the remainder were rendered unserviceable. It was all over in ten minutes.

There was little ack-ack fire. I think the German pilots were eating and had no
time to get a plane in the air. After a few runs up and down the aerodrome, we
returned at full speed."

McDougall was obviously slightly carried away with the excitement of the
occasion. The Squadron was officially credited with the destruction of six Bf110s,
one SM79 (in fact an SM81 used by 96°Gruppo Aut B.a'T which was only
damaged, as was a G50bis of 378^Squadriglia) and one unidentified aircraft on the
ground, plus the Ju52 – an aircraft of III/KGzbV.1 flown by Fw Schneider – which
crashed in flames on the beach at Derna having been shot down by Sgt Marshall.
Surprisingly, neither account mentions the sad fact that Sgt John Elsworth failed to
return from the sortie, his aircraft (V7552/TP-J) crashing into a small hill at Marsa
Jahal. The Rhodesian was killed in the crash, probably the victim of ground fire.
Within minutes of the Hurricanes landing there occurred a further raid on the
harbour, as noted by Yindrich:

"Ten German planes bombed Tobruk at 6pm. I watched them follow one another
down in a dizzy dive at an angle of 75 degrees, pulling out after they had dropped
their bombs and when they seemed certain to crash into the sea. They flew off at
low altitude, to dodge the ack-ack fire. One plane zoomed away to avoid
bursting anti-aircraft shells which exploded close to his tail, and dropped a bunch
of four bombs to lighten his load and speed his getaway. They fell with an
unpleasant whistle near where I was standing to watch the spectacle."

For 73 Squadron the day ended when Flt Lt Smith and Flg Off Martin carried out a
dusk attack on enemy vehicles and troop concentrations on the Derna road near
Gazala. Both returned safely. In addition to recording the day's events, as seen from
Lt Rankin's vantage point, his journal providing an insight into the morale-boosting
appearance of the Hurricanes in the skies above Tobruk:

"Six [sic] Hurricanes, which we had seen go out, had gone to strafe some
Messerschmitt 110s at Derna. We went out to count them in, rather anxiously,
and saw one do a victory roll. Counted in only five. More Hurricanes came
back and one did a perfectly superb dive, climb and two victory rolls. They
must be doing wonderful work."

At Crum el-Chel landing ground (Tobruk West) where 6 Squadron was residing, the
diarist had time for reflection:

"After all our excitements of the past few days, we are settling in at an
aerodrome three miles west of Tobruk. All things considered, the Squadron has
done well to lose so little equipment. One or two lorries and trailers were
abandoned. Two Lizzies and a Hurricane had to be burned as they could not be
flown off from the forward aerodrome. Practically no personnel lost. The
aircraft have suffered heavily owing to lack of spares but not once during the
withdrawal has a recce been turned down."

Plt Off Moulding's graphic description of Tobruk West is worth recording:

"... a reasonably flat piece of desert running from the foot of the stony slopes
some 450 yards towards the sea. In width it is about 300 yards. It is doubtless
a salt flat, for many years covered by a thick blanket of sand and stones. This
little, blank space on the earth's surface, probably for the first time in its
history, achieved a name, got itself marked on maps and blossomed forth into
a fully operational aerodrome – rotten little dangerous swine of a scratch
landing ground though it was. Landing diagonally you had a maximum of 450
yards in which to pull up. Easy enough in a Lysander, which you could
pancake without a wing dropping; but in a Hurricane, even with full flap, it
was dicey, particularly with added hazards such as down draughts from the
escarpment, pitfalls and patches of soft sand."

During the day one of the Squadron's Lysanders flown by Flg Off J.E. McFall
returned having achieved an unusual victory. While flying low on reconnaissance
near Mechili a grounded tri-motor transport aircraft was observed, tentatively
identified as an SM82, into which McFall's gunner, Cpl D.G. Copley, emptied his
Vickers gun, the machine bursting into flames.

   Help arrived for 73 Squadron shortly after dawn on the morning of 10 April,
when seven Hurricanes[3] landed at El Gubbi having been despatched from Ismailia
via Sollum, where the pilots had stayed overnight. With the exception of Flt Lt G.E.
Ball DFC, a Battle of Britain veteran who was to take over B Flight from Flt Lt
Beytagh, all the pilots were Free French volunteers and were under the command
of 35-year-old Sous-Lt James Denis. The unit – officially titled Free French Flight
1 but known locally as *Escadrille Denis* – was a welcome reinforcement and, apart
from Denis, comprised Sous-Lts Albert Littolf, Louis Ferrant and Noël Castelain,
plus Sgt-Chefs René Guédon and Xavier de Scitivaux. Both Littolf and Guédon had
seen action in defence of their country in 1940 (see Appendix I). All six had
completed a Hurricane conversion course at 70 OTU and they had only just
returned from a brief detachment to Greece where they had flown in defence of
Athens. Of the arrival at El Gubbi, Denis later wrote:

"Sqn Ldr Murray, the CO, welcomed us and told us we would form C Flight
of 73 Squadron. We were placed immediately on standby at the dispersal. The
surrounding of Tobruk was in progress."

Flt Lt Beytagh took the first patrol of the morning, leading Plt Off Lamb and Sgt
Ellis over Tobruk harbour but without encountering any enemy aircraft, landing
back at El Gubbi at 0750. Before the patrol returned, Sqn Ldr Murray departed at
the head of six A Flight Hurricanes to strafe troop transports in the Derna-Gazala
area, and within minutes of these returning to El Gubbi, two more Hurricanes were
sent off to attack a concentration of vehicles reported south of Gadd el-Ahmar.
These were located and strafed with some success but, at 0905, Sgt-Chef de
Scitivaux's aircraft was hit by ground fire and crash-landed on the beach at Umm
Ghene Gniah, about 25 miles from Tobruk. The French pilot suffered slight facial
injuries but was able to walk back to Tobruk. Meanwhile, the standby section at El

---

[3] The new Hurricanes probably included V7816, V7853, V7856, V7859, W9195, W9198 –
and possibly P2652.

Gubbi – Sous-Lts Denis (V7716/TP-U) and Ferrant (W9195) – was scrambled when a formation of Ju87s escorted by CR42s was reported approaching Tobruk at 0840, as Denis recalled:

"At 8am [*sic*] we took off to intercept Stukas escorted by fighters. I was lucky to shoot down a CR42, for it was our first sortie, and the first victory for Free French Fighter Flight 1"

At 1025 Flg Off Martin led a section of three to carry out further attacks on troop transports, and shortly thereafter Flt Lt Ball took a patrol of four, including Ferrant and Sgt-Chef Guédon, to the Acroma area. The fourth member of the patrol, Sgt White, was unable to find El Gubbi in the swirling dust on returning to Tobruk and carried out an emergency landing on the beach, V7766/TP-Z breaking its tailwheel in the process. The incident was one of several noted in Lt Rankin's journal:

"Took over as GPO [Gun Position Officer] at lunchtime, when the sandstorm became intense again. We had two quick alarms and our little position was enveloped in sand. We were warned of a Henschel 126 flying low, and spotted him for a few seconds as he slipped through the sand clouds. Then the local aerodrome was bombed – could hear the bombs without being able to see anything. After that El Adem was bombed, but it was very difficult for us or the RAF to do anything about it. Conditions were very bad. One Hurricane made a forced landing quite near us."

Among the Axis aircraft involved in attacking retreating British transport columns south-east of Tobruk were six Ju87s of 96°Gruppo Aut B.a'T (three from each squadron) led by newly promoted Magg Ercolani, escorted by nine G50bis of 155°Gruppo CT and three Bf110s of III/ZG26. It was the operational début for the Italian Stukas in North Africa, the crews claiming much success in attacking M/T. The afternoon saw no let up in activity although there occurred only one further aerial engagement, which cost 73 Squadron a Hurricane. First off after lunch was Plt Off Chatfield at 1330, followed five minutes later by Sgt Ellis, with Sgts Garton and Webster being sent off at 1410. Due to the intensity of the sandstorm, Webster landed at Bu Amud, where he awaited an improvement in visibility before attempting to return to El Gubbi. In the meantime Flg Off Goodman scrambled at 1715 when Ju87s were reported attacking gun positions within the perimeter, and was followed ten minutes later by Flt Lt Ball and Sgt Wills. Lt Rankin continued:

"Late in the afternoon we were attacked by 12 Ju87s, all at the same time. It was most confusing, and unfortunately very few of us kept our heads. As a result, our shooting was rather wild and we were only credited with one possible and two damaged. We ought to have shot down at least two – they came terribly close to us. Bombs were dropped close to us, and in the town they hit the hospital, with 24 casualties. Hurricanes were in the sky at the same time to add to the confusion, and I believe some of our bursts were uncomfortably close to one of them."

At 1750, six Bf110s of 8/ZG26, apparently part of the escort, sighted a lone

Hurricane near Bardia, W9195 flown by Sgt Webster who had just taken off for the return flight to El Gubbi. Before he could take evasive action, Webster's aircraft was engaged by Lt Wehmeyer, causing him to carry out an emergency crash-landing at Bu Amud, which was achieved without injury. His friend, Sgt Garton, commented: "Luckiest man alive. He returned by road late that night." An hour later, A Flight scrambled four Hurricanes to patrol the harbour with Flg Off Goodman leading, B Flight sending two more to join them, but no enemy aircraft were encountered. With the onset of dusk, both Flights maintained dusk patrols over the harbour without event. A total of 36 sorties had been flown by the Squadron during the day, and despite the successes achieved in attacking troop transports – during the course of one strafe by Hurricanes, GenMaj Heinrich Kirchheim of the 5th Light Division was wounded – the Squadron diarist concluded his report with a hint of discontent within:

> "All the pilots seemed browned off with this ground strafing – we are losing too many machines which we can ill afford to do and the ultimate result puts us very much on the debit side."

Good Friday (11 April) brought no respite for 73 Squadron, a total of 23 ground strafing sorties being flown throughout the day, during which eleven M/T were claimed destroyed and others damaged. Sgt Laing recalled this intensive period:

> "... strafing the columns of Jerries advancing from the west, most of them on the one good road with all their machine-guns giving you a good solid hail of lead, while your own eight guns were doing their thing as long as you could keep the nose pointing down the road. This was the reason I found myself more than once flying through the telephone lines at the side of the road, and getting back to unwind 20 or 25 yards of copper wire from just behind the spinner. Not for the first time I had reason to be grateful to Rolls-Royce and their mighty Merlin."

Both A and B Flights sent out offensive patrols during the morning, most pilots using their ammunition in ground attacks without sighting any enemy aircraft, although one section reported an engagement, as Sgt Garton later admitted:

> "Took Monty [Ellis] and Webby on strafing patrol in Mechili area, and on the way back chased two aircraft presumed to be enemy aircraft. Opened fire and discovered they were our own!"

At 0945, Sous-Lt Denis set off with four aircraft of C Flight to the Gazala area where a number of Bf110s were sighted, one of these apparently being claimed shot down jointly by Sous-Lt Castelain (V7853) and Sgt-Chef Guédon (V7859). One of the Messerschmitt pilots reported possibly shooting down a Hurricane in return, but it would appear that neither side lost an aircraft in this engagement. While C Flight was thus engaged, A Flight scrambled four more Hurricanes led by Flt Lt Smith when enemy aircraft were reported approaching Tobruk although none were sighted. The next offensive patrol departed at 1135, Flt Lt Ball leading three aircraft to strafe M/T. On their return, two more Hurricanes flown by Sgts Laing and Wills were scrambled to cover them as enemy aircraft were reported. Ten minutes later Sgts Marshall and Garton were scrambled to join them as a formation of German and Italian Ju87s including six from 236^Squadriglia led by Ten Ettore Marcozzi, accompanied by nine G50bis of 155°Gruppo CT led by TenCol Bianchi, arrived, covered by the usual umbrella of Bf110s from III/ZG26; reported Lt Rankin in his journal:

> "At lunch time we were in the thick of it again and Junkers dive-bombers appeared all over the sky. We engaged one by shrapnel control, but our fuse was too short. Then one came, sensationally, straight at us, dived to a few feet of the ground and went clean through our position with machine-guns firing. We filled him up with machine-gun bullets, and smoke came pouring from him as he staggered and side-slipped, regained control and disappeared over the brow of a hill. This we claimed as ours without dispute. A Hurricane came in, shot one down, banked steeply and pounced on another which he shot down in flames – we cheered madly. Then four Messerschmitt 109s [*sic*] appeared from nowhere and all went for our lone Hurricane, which put up a terrific dogfight but turned tail and rushed for the aerodrome with smoke coming out, but still under control. We engaged the Messerschmitt which had been chasing the Hurricane and put in some effective bursts, the result of which could not be properly observed owing to clouds of dust."

Lt Rankin's report is graphically interesting but not entirely accurate. The Hurricane observed being chased by four 'Messerschmitts' was undoubtedly that (V7560/TP-F) flown by Sgt Marshall, who noted:

> "Scramble for dive-bombers. Destroyed one G50 which crashed on beach west of Tobruk. This enemy aircraft was one of four which had attacked me. Confirmed by gun battery in vicinity."

His companion, Sgt Garton (V7295/TP-T) added:

> "Met 15 ME110s and three G50s, who jumped me from a great height. Tried to do a bit of dog fighting but superior numbers forced me to evacuate that part of the sky mighty quickly – pretty rough."

Of the other two pilots airborne during the raid, Sgt Wills (P2646/TP-K) had landed within 15 minutes of taking off, following on the tail of Flt Lt Ball's section returning from its sortie. Sgt Laing (V7371/TP-C), the other pilot involved in the action, recalled:

> "I got in a burst or two at a Stuka over the harbour, but there were [fighters] about and I didn't hang around to see what happened."

One Ju87 of 236^Squadriglia failed to return, M.llo Enrico Bassi and his gunner 1°Av Mot. Giacomo Colombo seen by their colleagues falling to the guns of a Hurricane. Only the pilot was able to bale out, being captured. Other dive-bomber crews claimed damage to the British freighter *Draco* in the harbour, while escorting G50bis pilots claimed one Hurricane shot down and one probable, as noted in 378^Squadriglia's diary, in which recorded details of the action differ somewhat to those reported by their opponents:

"After the end of the Stukas' dive, a Hurricane attacked one and shot it down. Cap [Bruno] Tattanelli shot at the Hurricane, and also Ten [Manlio] Biccolini managed a burst. In the meantime, the aircraft of M.llo [Lorenzo] Serafino had been hit with one shot in the left wing from a Hurricane coming from the rear. While manoeuvring in order to disengage, Serafino saw a third Hurricane and shot at him: the English fighter went down trailing black smoke and went out of sight of the Italian pilot. Then, during the manoeuvre in order to get his place in the formation, he saw another enemy fighter and gave him a burst. In the meantime, Cap Tattanelli got nearer to the first fighter and gave him many bursts, making him dive until he crashed."

Apart from the minor damage to Serafino's aircraft, a second G50bis, from 360^Squadriglia, returned severely damaged and was written off although the pilot was not injured. It would seem that Sgt Marshall had in fact fired initially at a G50 (Serafino's aircraft) but then in fact shot down Bassi's Ju87, the aircraft which crashed on the beach near Tobruk town[4]. Despite the claims and reports of a Hurricane being shot down and others damaged, none of the four aircraft involved suffered any serious damage, if any damage at all, since all were operational during the afternoon. The Hurricane believed to have crashed may have been that of Sgt Wills carrying out a hurried landing.

Sqn Ldr Murray and Flt Lt Smith each led sections engaged in ground strafing during the afternoon. These sorties were directed against an Axis motorized infantry force escorted by two tanks which had cut the Tobruk to El Adem road, as *BUP* correspondent Yindrich reported:

"The Germans and Italians cutting the road were not left in peace. RAF fighter planes roared down over the truckloads of infantry, machine-gunning them from 50 feet and scattering the entire convoy."

Elsewhere, the Germans attempted to penetrate the perimeter defences under cover of a dust storm but when this subsided at about 1700, about 60 tanks of the 5th Panzer Regiment supported by a number of Italian light tanks were sighted five miles south of the perimeter by Blenheims overflying the area, which then bombed and strafed these and concentrations of troops and trucks. These attacks did not prevent an attack being launched, in the first instance by infantry, before the tanks lumbered forward to be met by artillery fire. Before darkness ended the skirmishing, battle had been joined by 11 British cruiser tanks which accounted for one of the German heavies for the loss of two of their own. Altogether, the attackers lost seven tanks in this first probing action.

During the afternoon, C Flight put up two separate patrols over the harbour without meeting any enemy aircraft, although a further dive-bombing raid on shipping and gun positions came in shortly after the second patrol had landed. Sgts Garton, Webster and White were scrambled but failed to engage the raiders. Lt Rankin noted in his journal:

---

[4] See Appendix IV for reproduction of Sgt Marshall's relevant logbook entry.

"Spent the afternoon digging a new hole in the ground ... just as well we did ... for those dive-bombers came over again, and this time they attacked us direct. Two came for us and terrific explosions seemed to be right on top of us. I dived into a hole. The planes machine-gunned us and one lad got a flesh wound in the leg."

By the light of the silvery moon German tanks continued to probe the defences, searching for a way through while pioneers attempted to bridge the ditch and destroy the barbed-wire barrier. They were unsuccessful. As soon as it was light on the morning of 12 April, four Hurricanes were prepared to undertake reconnaissance flights to establish the closeness of enemy ground units. Plt Off Chatfield and Sgt Wills departed El Gubbi at 0730 to fly along the road to El Adem, Flt Lt Smith and Plt Off McDougall setting out 15 minutes later on a similar mission to Gazala and Mechili. At 0815 Chatfield returned alone to report that Sgt Bill Wills had been shot down by ground fire while strafing, his Hurricane (V7560/TP-F) crashing near El Adem; although he was recovered from the wreck by German soldiers, he had been seriously injured and soon succumbed to his wounds. Flg Off Goodman and Plt Off Eiby were the next pair to be sent off on local reconnaissance flights, both returning safely. They were followed by Sgts Garton and Webster who carried out a 30-minute patrol over El Gubbi as cover for three aircraft of C Flight led by Sous-Lt Littolf which took off at 0915 to carry out a strafing attack on a convoy near Gadd el-Ahmar. During the attack they became separated, Sous-Lt Castelain landing at 0950, followed by Littolf 25 minutes later, but Sgt-Chef Guédon (V7853) failed to return, his aircraft having been hit by ground fire and consequently crash-landed; he was taken prisoner.

By mid-morning the sandstorms returned and visibility over the garrison deteriorated rapidly, catching out Flt Lt Ball and Sgt Ellis both of whom had taken off at 1040. Sometime later the two Hurricanes could be heard circling overhead but could not be seen from the ground, nor could the pilots see the ground. Some two hours after take-off, with fuel dangerously low, Ellis force-landed V7372/TP-W at Tobruk West; but Ball simply disappeared. It was later learned that, having run out of fuel, he had force-landed V7716/TP-U outside the perimeter and was taken prisoner. Lt Rankin noted:

"A sandstorm descended and it was sad to hear the poor Hurricanes circling round and round trying to find their base ... I was glad when the wind changed and it cleared up. Then we had a raid – dive-bombers escorted by fighters; only six bombers this time. We fired at the fighters without effect."

The Ju87s were from 7 and 8 Staffeln of III/StG1 – which had just arrived at Derna as replacements for I/StG1 which was being withdrawn for operations over Greece – and were after shipping which had just arrived in harbour, strongly protected by destroyers and other small naval craft. AA fire was intense, both from shore batteries and from the naval vessels, and one aircraft (J9+JH of 7 Staffel) was shot down into the sea, the victim of ships' gunfire. Two more Stukas were shot down – J9+BH of 7 Staffel and 6G+HS of 8 Staffel, one force-landing on the beach west of Tobruk town. Both crews were captured. A Henschel of 2(H)/14 was also hit by ground fire while spotting near the perimeter, the observer being wounded. Although two Hurricanes had been scrambled to intercept the raiders, neither Sgts Marshall nor Griffith was able to engage. With poor visibility hampering their return, Marshall decided to fly eastwards and landed safely at Qasaba near Mersa Matruh. On his return to El Gubbi next morning, he was personally congratulated by Grp Capt Brown for saving his aircraft.

When carrying out the emergency landing at Tobruk West, Sgt Ellis' Hurricane had suffered punctures to all three tyres, two of TP-W's groundcrew, Bill Musson and Ron Luff, being detailed to travel to the location to carry out repairs and await the arrival of a pilot to fly it back to El Gubbi; Bill Musson recalled:

> "We took a tailwheel with us and managed to change it for the damaged one before dark, then spent the night on guard. There were Australian troops in the area and they looked after us and fed us well. Next morning a lorry load of erks turned up and we were able to change one wheel at a time. We spent the afternoon clearing a makeshift runway, moving large rocks and levelling the clumps of camel thorn, while all the time Jerry shells were falling just to the west of us. One of those on target would have spoiled our day. Monty Ellis came to collect the kite, and ran up hard against the brakes before making a short take off."

With the loss of three Hurricanes and their pilots during the day's abortive operations, 73 Squadron signalled HQ for urgent replacements. Six Hurricanes and pilots were promised for the morrow. Not only had bombs been dropped by the raiders, but also bundles of leaflets which showered over the garrison; they read:

> The General Officer Commanding the German forces in Libya requests
> that the British troops occupying Tobruk surrender their arms. Single soldiers
> waving white handkerchiefs are not fired on. Strong German forces have
> already surrounded Tobruk and it is useless to try to escape. Remember
> Mechili. Our dive-bombers and Stukas are waiting for your ships which are
> lying in harbour.

Rommel had clearly underestimated the determination and morale of the defenders, and expected the garrison to be evacuated by sea. He had been surprised, annoyed and then obviously angered by the punishment his troops had already taken, and by their apparent lack of strong leadership, as revealed in his diary:

> "On 12 April reinforcements arrived, and it was decided to mount the first main assault that afternoon. The *Brescia* [Division], which had meanwhile taken over the western front of Tobruk, began the afternoon attack. The 5th Light Division was unhappy with its orders for the attack, and I had to overrule a number of objections its staff raised. The Division's attack was finally launched about 1630. The enemy fired shells all over the area, causing few casualties. The tanks came under fierce fire when they slowed at the point of attack, and halted in front of the anti-tank ditches which we were not yet able to breach. After we left off the attack I decided to try again in a few days.
> I ordered a reconnaissance battalion from the 5th Light Division to advance

on the crossroads inside the Tobruk defences, and if possible blow the anti-tank ditches. Because of their earlier failure, the 5th Light Division was lacking in confidence and was unrealistically critical of my plan to get the main attack under way. The leadership of the Division did not understand the tactic of making a breakthrough, securing the flanks and then pushing deep into the enemy rear before he has a chance to retaliate. It was unfortunate I had not the opportunity to train my divisions personally before raiding into Cyrenaica, otherwise we should have been much more successful at Tobruk."

A few days later, in response to the German leaflets, the British tried their own form of psychological warfare when Blenheims showered leaflets over enemy lines:

Soldiers of Italy!

For you and your companions the day of peace and happiness
is close at hand. In all Africa your comrades have given up the battle.
In Abyssinia the war is over. The Ambassador from the Duke D'Aosta[5]
has already made preliminary peace terms with British GHQ.

Yesterday, thousands of your countrymen were taken prisoner at Tobruk.
It is quite useless to make any further sacrifices of this kind. All Italian
soldiers who have been captured by the British have been treated in the
finest manner. So make an end of this before your losses become
considerably larger.

The sandstorms continued causing havoc with flying operations on the morning of 13 April, though this lack of activity provided some respite for pilots and troops alike. The six promised Hurricane replacements duly arrived in the morning, two flown by new pilots posted to the Squadron – Flt Lt H.A. Olivier who was to take command of B Flight despite his lack of operational experience, and Wt Off André Ballatore, another of the Free French airmen – the others by returning pilots including Plt Offs Humphreys, Wareham and Haldenby. A further batch of unserviceable aircraft were then despatched in the opposite direction, including V7562/TP-A flown by Sgt Marshall, which required an engine change, and another piloted by Sgt Souter who was posted sick following a severe attack of tonsilitis. It seems as though two of the u/s aircraft were flown out of El Gubbi by two of the pilots who had just arrived, Haldenby and Wareham. Of his posting to 73 Squadron, Ballatore recalled:

"My training finished, I was posted to the Free French Fighter Flight – C Flight of 73 Squadron – based at Tobruk. I came as reinforcement. Our missions were varied, to prevent, as much as possible – since we were outnumbered twenty-to-one – enemy planes from flying over Tobruk, and to fire at anything outside Tobruk's perimeter."

There was some action after lunch, Ballatore flying two operational sorties; recorded Lt Rankin:

---

5 Viceroy and Military Governor of Italian East Africa, he died in captivity in Kenya in 1942.

"I took over as GPO after lunch and soon went into action against two
Messerschmitt 110s, one of which we shot down by direct hit, as reported by
the RAF. Later we had an alarm with planes reported all round us. Hurricanes
buzzed into action, but we saw nothing else."

Nor did the Hurricanes sight the enemy. Sgt Garton was scrambled at 1420, followed
30 minutes later by three more from C Flight led by Sous-Lt Denis but no contact
was made with the raiders which comprised three Ju87s from 236^Squadriglia,
escorted by nine G50bis and two Bf110s. The target for the Stukas was the freighter
Bankura which was about five miles from the harbour. Two direct hits were claimed
by the Stuka crews, the explosions inflicting a number of casualties among the troops
on board the vessel. The Squadron continued to send up pairs of aircraft throughout
the afternoon, one pair as cover for four returning A Flight Hurricanes which Flt Lt
Smith had led on a strafing mission to Gambut, where large concentrations of enemy
forces had assembled. All returned safely. In the evening there was an alarm when
two Blenheims arrived unexpectedly, Plt Offs Eiby and Lamb being scrambled on
their approach, while harbour guns opened fire. It was feared that one of the
Blenheims might have suffered damage but apparently both landed safely.

Easter Monday, 14 April, was heralded by a determined attack on Tobruk just after
0730, when an estimated 70 aircraft – Ju87s of III/StG1 and II/StG2 plus seven from
96°Gruppo Aut B.a'T, escorted by eight G50bis of 155°Gruppo CT, four CR42s of
18°Gruppo CT and five Bf110s of III/ZG26 – began bombing the harbour. *BUP*
correspondent Yindrich witnessed their arrival and the subsequent action:

"... 30 big black German dive-bombers, escorted by Messerschmitts, staged
the biggest raid on the perimeter defences as well as the town itself. For over
an hour they were flying over the semi-circle of Tobruk and its defences. I saw
eight in line dive-bomb the harbour and then swoop over the outer line of
defences with their machine-guns blazing. The infantrymen manning the
machine-guns and Bren guns stood up to the attack wonderfully and brought
down three of them. Hurricanes brought down two others in a series of
whirling dogfights. I saw two wounded German pilots with bandages on their
heads being taken to hospital in a lorry."

73 Squadron had only eight serviceable Hurricanes, and two of these flown by Flg
Off Goodman (V7673/TP-P) and Sgt Webster (V7553/TP-E) were just returning
from a successful early morning patrol during which they reported shooting down
a Henschel over the perimeter. No sooner had they landed when Webster was
ordered to join Sgt Ellis (V7299/TP-D) and two pilots of C Flight to assist Flt Lt
Smith who had taken off alone some five minutes earlier to investigate the harbour
bombing. A number of Ju87s were encountered over the harbour, Ellis promptly
shooting down two but Webster, who had just latched onto the tail of another Stuka,
was attacked by two G50bis flown by Ten Cugnasca and M.llo Angelo Marinelli of
351^Squadriglia, the blazing Hurricane crashing at 0743 within the perimeter and
taking Webster to his death. This was probably the combat witnessed by Captain
Devine, or at least part of it:

"I saw my first real dogfight. Way up in the sky little specks were twisting and turning, and faint zooming noises as engines were tortured by each dive, came to us alternately with deep purring roars as planes climbed steeply. A noise like tearing of calico told us when Hurricanes were firing off all their machine-guns at once. Gradually the fight came lower, and close within view came one plane twisting, turning and diving steeply as it was pursued by two others. All the troops cheered and threw their hats in the air, and urged the two planes to catch that '....... Jerry'. The planes passed into the distance, with the pursued one still twisting and turning violently. We heard later it was a Hurricane that was being pursued, and that it had been shot down. The irony of all things warlike!"

It seems probable that CR42s also engaged the Hurricanes at this stage, Sottoten Franco Bordoni Bisleri and M.llo Guido Fibbia of 95^Squadriglia each claiming one destroyed, but Webster's aircraft was the only one lost in this action. Meanwhile, watchers on the ground saw a single Hurricane engage in a series of dogfights with the G50bis. This was Flt Lt Smith (P2652[6]). They cheered as he first shot down one of the Italian fighters, then a second, and was seen to damage a third before he himself fell victim to another flown by the 351^Squadriglia commander, Cap Angelo Fanello, who had lost sight of his two colleagues, Cugnasca[7] and Marinelli after they had shot down Webster's Hurricane; both were killed. 351^Squadriglia's diarist noted:

"Cap Fanello came back over the place of the combat and he saw, near the Hurricane in flames, two G50s: one had flames near the engine and the other one, which perhaps had tried to land without undercarriage, was hidden by a cloud of sand. These were the aircraft of Ten Cugnasca and M.llo Marinelli, who were posted missing."

Another eyewitness to the one-sided action was Lt Joachim Schorm of the 5th Panzer Regiment, who entered in his diary:

"Storming of Tobruk. Above us Italian fighter planes come up into the fray. Two of them crash in our midst."

27-year-old Flt Lt James Duncan Smith from Winnipeg was a very popular member of the Squadron, about whom the Squadron diarist wrote:

---

[6] There remains some confusion as to the serial number of the aircraft Flt Lt Smith was flying on this occasion. The Squadron ORB records it as P2643, an aircraft which may have arrived as a replacement on the morning on 10 April, and which is shown as having been flown operationally twice on the 12th and again on the 13th, but information provided by AHB5 records Smith's aircraft as having been P2652, of which there is no mention in 73 Squadron's ORB. Both P2643 and P2652 were at one time on the strength of 274 Squadron; the former was originally the CO's aircraft and was apparently written off while serving with 274 Squadron on 19 April 1941.

[7] Ten Carlo Cugnasca, born in Switzerland, was well-known in Italian aviation circles having been a pre-war aerobatic pilot of some note. He had fought in the Spanish Civil War, and had flown operations against England in 1940 when 351^Squadriglia was based briefly in Belgium as part of 20°Gruppo CT. He was a close friend of Italian film actress Alida Valli who was deeply shocked by his death.

"Flt Lt Smith, probably the most popular officer in the Squadron and one who lived up to being always an officer and a gentleman. Smudger will be sadly missed by officers and men alike, for his cheerfulness and courage were an inspiration to us all."

It was widely felt that Smith should have been a candidate for the Victoria Cross, albeit posthumously. Flg Off Storrar noted in his logbook:

"Smudger – Flt Lt Smith – fought all through France and the Battle of Britain. Took off alone in Tobruk to attack 110-plus fighters [*sic*]. Shot down two before being shot down himself. Reward – six feet of sand 5,000 miles from home, and a wooden cross. Decorations – nil. Except Canada flash on shoulder."

His death had unfortunate repercussions for certain members of the Squadron, as Sqn Ldr Murray remembered:

"Smudger was a quiet, thoughtful Canadian. His popularity with some of the Squadron personnel was close to hero-worship, with none more so than young McFadden. He [McFadden] was a highly-strung character, seeming to live most of the time on the ragged ends of his nerves. The Equipment Officer displayed a singular lack of common sense in taking Mac along with him to visit the scene of the crash. The sight of the incinerated body still in what was left of the cockpit cracked Mac up completely."

The two French pilots also engaged the dive-bombers, Sous-Lt Littolf (V7856) claiming one shot down and two others probably so, while Sous-Lt Denis (W9198) reported shooting down another. Meanwhile, out of ammunition, Sgt Ellis landed back at El Gubbi, jumped into a fully armed Hurricane (V7810/TP-W) and took off again to rejoin battle, claiming another Stuka shot down. By now Flg Off Martin was airborne in the Hurricane (V7299/TP-D) Ellis had abandoned, meeting a Bf110 which he claimed damaged. Four Ju87s were shot down, including J9+CH of StabIII/StG1 from which Lt Hans Martinez and his gunner Uffz Helmet Pohl were taken prisoner. But it was 4/StG2 which took the brunt of the Hurricane attacks, losing three aircraft. Fw Heinrich Rass and Uffz Fritz Weber were both captured when their aircraft T6+JM was shot down, Weber having been wounded; Lt Erich Hummel, the gunner aboard another 4 Staffel machine was also captured when he baled out, the aircraft force-landing outside the perimeter, while the crew of the third machine escaped capture when their aircraft crash-landed in German lines although the gunner, Uffz Heinrich Kroll, had been wounded in the action. Of the raging air battle, Lt Rankin noted:

"Three Hurricanes went up and then we saw two Macchi 200s [*sic*] and four CR42s moving in. Our guns opened up on them, and soon the air was filled with Ju87 dive-bombers – 30 at least – slipping in and out of the low clouds, bombs dropping, hundreds of guns and rifles firing and a terrific noise. Messerschmitt 110s appeared. Saw four planes come down, one pilot getting out by parachute."

Eyewitness Jan Yindrich, the *BUP* correspondent, added:

"I saw one Junker fleeing out towards the sea and home, with a Hurricane on his tail, his guns rattling away. The Junker fell out of the sky and hit the desert.

A thick cloud of dense black smoke rose 100 feet into the air. Almost the entire garrison downed tools to watch the dogfights. Men stripped to the waist, digging weapon pits, slit trenches and shallow pits for trucks, whipped off their tin hats in spite of falling bullets and shrapnel from the ack-ack guns, and waved them excitedly in the air, cheering the Hurricane pilots as they whirled round in the sky."

When 3RAAF at Sidi Haneish learned of the latest attack on Tobruk, Sqn Ldr Jeffrey, who had resumed command following the death of Sqn Ldr Campbell, despatched two Hurricanes flown by Flg Off Arthur (V7728) and Lt Tennant SAAF (P3725) to investigate. At 1045, when about ten miles east of the garrison while flying at 1,000 feet, they encountered three Bf110s of III/ZG26 which they engaged. Arthur attacked one which was last seen diving steeply towards the sea with blue smoke issuing from its fuselage but, owing to low cloud, he did not see it crash. The Messerschmitt attacked by Tennant – in all probability the same aircraft as that engaged by Arthur – was similarly last seen in a steep dive, upside down, with smoke also issuing from its fuselage. While both pilots claimed only probables, both claims were apparently upgraded later and are shown as such in 204 Group records; however, III/ZG26 reported only one loss (WkNr3418) on this date, the crew of which survived. The two Australians meanwhile continued their patrol and sighted a Ju52/3m on the landing ground at Menastir. Each carried out two strafing runs when bullets were seen to strike the transport aircraft although it did not burn.

73 Squadron also put up four Hurricanes led by Flg Off Goodman to investigate the activity to the east but failed to sight the enemy. Flg Off Martin and Plt Off McDougall were scrambled at 1240 but were recalled within 15 minutes. Plt Off Eiby led another scramble at 1325 when enemy aircraft were reported south-west of Tobruk but no engagements resulted then, nor at 1500 when Flt Lt Olivier and Eiby were sent up, but at 1715, when four Hurricanes were scrambled on the approach of another raid, a small force of Ju87s accompanied by G50bis and Bf110s was sighted. The French pair of Sous-Lts Littolf and Castelain formed one section, Plt Off Lamb and Sgt White the other. The dive-bombers were intercepted, Littolf (W9198) claiming one shot down but the escort then intervened and Owen Lamb's aircraft (V7766/TP-Z) was seen to dive straight into the ground from about 3,000 feet. Lt Rankin witnessed the demise of the New Zealander:

"An air raid in the evening by about 15 enemy planes – those blasted dive-bombers went for a lone hospital ship [the SS *Vita*[8]] which had set out unescorted, and with no protection. She must have been hit for she raced back to shore and all destroyers went out to meet her. Then Hurricanes arrived. During the action we saw a fighter plane drop vertically out of the clouds – it dropped faster and faster and hit the ground with a terrific flash and explosion. We could not say whether it was a Hurricane or a Fiat G50. It was an awe-inspiring sight, such as one had only previously seen on the films."

---

[8] The Australian destroyer HMAS *Waterhen* gamely attempted to tow the crippled *Vita* into harbour but, when this proved impossible, took on board a total of 437 patients, six doctors, six nurses and 41 sick berth attendents and ferried them to Alexandria. The hospital ship was beached and eventually became a total wreck. The Australian destroyer was itself lost at the end of June 1941, sunk by Italian Ju87s.

Two Messerschmitt pilots of 7/ZG26 – Lt Karl-Heinz Bittner and Fw Werner Reiner – each claimed a Hurricane shot down but since only Lamb was lost they probably both attacked the same aircraft. Five G50bis – two from 378^Squadriglia led by Cap Tattanelli and three from 360^Squadriglia led by Ten Vittorio Galfetti – were also involved in this action, as close escort to a dozen Stukas. Tattanelli reported engaging a Hurricane which was attacking a Stuka. The Hurricane broke away and was last seen diving towards the ground. This was probably Castelain's aircraft (V7856) which may have been damaged since he returned to base within ten minutes of taking off, at about the same time Lamb was shot down. The Squadron diarist recorded his loss:

> "Plt Off Lamb – 'Kiwi' – the joker and one the grandest fellows ever, also failed to return from patrol."

While Sgt Garton summarised the day's grievous losses in his diary:

> "Flt Lt Smith bravely tackled five G50s single-handed and succeeded in destroying two before being shot down himself. He and his victims all crashed within a few hundred yards of each other, all burnt out. Another tragedy was Webby, who was shot down in flames while attempting to force-land. Thus, in one engagement, two of the very best types were lost. B Flight, in Webby, lost one of its oldest members and an amazing personality who will be greatly missed. Later on today, Lamb was shot down and killed. Thus ended a very black day for the Squadron, with a firm resolve that new tactics must be evolved, as to carry on any longer operating singly is approaching suicide."

The intense aerial activity directed against Tobruk during the day was in support of a major Axis assault on part of the southern perimeter. Despite initial successes when the leading panzer battalion penetrated the defences, the attack turned into a defeat with the defenders destroying 16 out of a force of 38 German tanks employed. A delighted Wavell cabled the Prime Minister:

> "Between 200 and 300 German pow [sic] captured at Tobruk morning 14 April stated they were badly shaken by our artillery fire and were very short of food and water. These troops wept when their attack was driven off, and their morale is definitely low."

To which the PM responded:

> "Convey heartiest congratulations from War Cabinet to all engaged in most successful fight. Bravo, Tobruk! We feel it vital that Tobruk should be regarded as sally-port and not, please, as an 'excrescence'. Can you not find good troops who are without transport to help hold perimeter, thus freeing at least one, if not two, Australian brigade groups to act as General Fortress Reserve and potential striking force?"

With some good news at last over which he could enjoy a cigar and brandy, the Prime Minister compiled an assessment of the situation in the Mediterranean and

Middle East, as he perceived it, and issued a Directive to the Chiefs-of-Staff (see Appendix III). He also cabled the US President with news of the success, emphasising the importance of the repulse of the German attacks on Tobruk as "the first time they have tasted defeat" in the land war.

The ensuing four days were remarkably quiet for the airmen within the garrison, if not necessarily for the defending troops, due partly to sandstorms which sprang up again, curtailing much flying, and partly to a lack of aggression from the Axis air forces. Nonetheless, the pilots of 73 Squadron, no longer operating as separate Flights owing to lack of available aircraft, carried out three patrols during the daylight hours of 15 April with their seven serviceable Hurricanes but failed to meet any enemy aircraft. Next day there was no flying at all thanks to severe sandstorms while, on the evening of 17 April, with an improvement in visibility locally, two sections were scrambled when Ju87s from III/StG1 carried out an attack on part of the garrison's inner defences, although no contact was made with the raiders. Sgt Laing remembered:

> "Throughout April the harbour area, as well as the gun positions everywhere around the perimeter, were pretty well bombed by the Jerries, but not every day I guess, and we could relax at times. At night, of course, they gave the whole harbour area a real pasting, and got a very hot reception from the ground gunners, so it all made a really magnificent sight."

And Sgt Garton wrote in his diary:

> "Monty [Ellis] and I had the complete day off today so this afternoon we went along to the spot where Webby crashed and took one or two photos of his grave. On returning we called in at the Aussie canteen and were invited to join them in a jug of ale and also to return later for dinner and a few beers. This, of course, we did and enjoyed a goodly beer which went down extremely well."

Meanwhile, there continued to be some aerial activity outside the confines of the Tobruk perimeter, Blenheims operating from just across the border flying not only armed reconnaissances but also supply missions, as recalled by Sous-Lt Denis:

> "We were supplied by Blenheims which landed by night, and also a few ships which, with much courage, got through the blockade. We never lacked for petrol or ammunition. But we lost many aircraft, destroyed mainly by German artillery. They approached very close to our lines with their guns, fired for three or four minutes and left, attacked by Australian infantry which fought with ferocious courage. If we never lacked for petrol or ammunition, on the contrary we suffered from lack of food and water. For the duration of the siege I survived on pickles and tea. Tea was made with briny water, with a lot of sugar to make it drinkable."

At Sidi Haneish 3RAAF was advised of its imminent re-equipment with the American P-40 Tomahawk fighter, numbers of which were now arriving in Egypt. The Squadron's Hurricanes were to be handed over to 73 and 274 Squadrons. With

3RAAF about to be withdrawn to Aboukir for re-equipment, 274 Squadron had moved up to Sidi Haneish to replace it. The Squadron's ground party was despatched to Gerawla to organise a new camp and landing ground, from where the Hurricanes were to operate once arrangements had been made. In the meantime, Flt Lt Turnbull led a patrol of 3RAAF to the Tobruk area, as noted by Flg Off Jackson:

"While on patrol Pete Turnbull spotted what he thought were enemy aircraft and went over on his own to investigate. They turned out to be fighter Blenheims ground strafing. Believe they got a hell of a fright when Pete approached them and they wobbled their wings violently to indicate they were friendly. Anyway, Pete joined them and did a bit of ground strafing with them, much to their amusement. He sent a chap spinning off a motor-bike and cleaned up a few trucks."

Jackson's journal also provides an account of a solo operation flown by Sqn Ldr Jeffrey (V7770):

"The CO did a great job today. A TacR report stated there were two enemy aircraft [SM81s] on Menastir aerodrome near Fort Capuzzo, and they had to be ground strafed – not a nice job as it was probable the Huns had some ack-ack guns covering same, so CO decided to do the job himself and went off alone. He found the aircraft had gone but on another drome near Fort Capuzzo spotted four Ju52s [aircraft of 1/KGzbV.9] just about to land, evidently loaded with supplies for Fort Capuzzo and Bardia garrisons. It seemed most unlikely that there was no fighter escort with them but the CO couldn't see any, so waded into them and shot down one whilst the other three were landing. One of them evidently saw him and crash-landed. The CO then ground strafed them, setting two on fire and burning them up completely. He ran out of ammunition on the other one and had to leave it just riddled with bullets, but not on fire – a magnificent piece of work. All the time one of our photographic-reconnaissance Hurricanes was watching from about 15,000 feet and saw the whole thing.

Six of us went back in the afternoon. Lindsey Knowles and Donati dived down and strafed the fourth Ju52 and it went up in a heck of a blaze – must have been loaded with petrol. I spotted an aircraft on the ground a few miles away and identified it as a Lockheed Hudson [sic], one of our own which had force-landed a few days previously with the AOC [sic] and had to be abandoned as it was in enemy territory. I decided it would be best to burn it so I dived down and strafed it and set it on fire – 30,000 quids worth."

On 16 April the Navy carried out a bombardment of Bardia and Fort Capuzzo, a section of Hurricanes from 3RAAF flown by Flt Lt Turnbull, Flg Off Arthur and Sgt J.T. Berridge (a new pilot) providing cover. Three Bf110s were seen approaching and these dived on the Hurricanes but neither side was able to engage and the Messerschmitts dived away towards Tobruk, the Hurricanes following. After about 15 minutes Turnbull suspected they were being decoyed and ordered his section to return to the ships until it was time to head back to Sidi Haneish. Next day, Flg Off Jackson was briefed to lead another 3RAAF patrol over the Tobruk area but poor visibility prevented the Hurricanes reaching the garrison so they patrolled over Fort Capuzzo and Bardia instead, without sighting any enemy aircraft. The operation was repeated on 18 April, Jackson leading Flg Offs Kloster and Bracegirdle plus Lt Tennant SAAF to El Gubbi, while three 274 Squadron Hurricanes flown by Sqn Ldr Lapsley, Flg Off O.V. Tracey, a New Zealander, and Plt Off Jean Pompéï, another of the Free French contingent, also arrived on detachment. The welcomed reinforcements were placed on standby by Sqn Ldr Murray but were not called to action, as noted by Jackson[9]:

"We had to be very careful getting into Tobruk as our forces there are a bit on edge as they have had so many air attacks. We flew in from the sea along a specified corridor and pooped off plenty of identification colours, and prayed that our own ack-ack would recognise us and wouldn't fire.

73 Squadron are very down in the dumps. They had lost eight pilots during previous few days and only had five aircraft left. It seems incredible that their aircraft numbers and pilots had not been reinforced immediately, but strange are the ways of HQME.

We four chaps took over standby duty for the 73 Squadron chaps whilst they had a bit of a spell. In the afternoon another sandstorm worked up when we were given warning of the approach of a large number of enemy aircraft, picked up by *Jumbo* [radar]. I offered to take off though visibility was foul and landing after a scrap might have been dangerous. Group HQ decided that it was not worth the risk. Anyway, 21 dive-bombers arrived and gave Tobruk harbour a pasting – it was pretty to watch, to see dive-bombers taking advantage of two big cumulus clouds, diving out of one to attack in vertical dives and then climbing up to take cover in the other cloud after releasing their bombs. They certainly seem to work with great system. The bombs were no distance away but nobody took cover, all stood and sat out in the open, watching. The RAF groundcrew didn't seem a bit perturbed – personally I felt like getting down a deep, deep dugout. The bombing did not do much harm, no shipping suffered.

We left Tobruk about an hour before dusk and got to Sidi Haneish just at dark."

The 274 Squadron detachment stayed the night. Shortly after the departure of the 3RAAF detachment, four Lysanders of 6 Squadron, each fitted with long-range fuel tanks, took off from Tobruk West accompanied by the Squadron's Magister, bound for Ma'aten Bagush to where they had been ordered. Three 73 Squadron Hurricanes provided escort for part of the way, and all reached their destination safely. However, 6 Squadron's A Flight was to remain at Tobruk West with its five Hurricanes and two Lysanders under the command of Sqn Ldr Weld. Several of the

---

[9] After participating in the Syrian campaign with 3RAAF during which he claimed further victories, John Jackson – whose diary is extensively quoted in preceding chapters – returned to Australia where he was promoted to command 75RAAF Squadron, which was sent to defend the Port Moresby area of New Guinea in early 1942. Having been awarded the DFC and, after shooting down one Japanese aircraft, he was shot down and killed by another. Subsequently, Jackson's Strip at Port Moresby was so named in his honour.

Lysander pilots had undergone a rapid conversion course on 73 Squadron's Hurricanes over the past few days. Once familiarised with the controls, pilots carried out circuits and bumps under the noses of the enemy, as recalled by Plt Off Moulding:

> "We didn't have much to do with 73 Squadron at all – trying not to be noticed – since every day the bombers came over and we didn't want them knocking us to bits. We used to fire at them with rifles. Then one day I was told to go over to El Gubbi, was shown what to do, got into the Hurricane and flew it. It was quite fast after the Lysander."

Of this period he added:

> "Most of the pilots had by now grown beards but we were ordered to shave by General Morshead who said that pilots with such growth would give the wrong impression if taken prisoner."

Following two such flights totalling some 50 minutes, Moulding was sent out on a reconnaissance and on 18 April, during his second operational flight in a Hurricane, his aircraft (V7814) was hit in three places by AA fire from El Adem although he was able to get back to Tobruk and land safely.

For the Axis forces mustered around the perimeter it was a time of great frustration following their earlier sweeping victories, although the German press endeavoured to reassure an anxious public:

> "Tobruk is surrounded by hills which had already been made practically impregnable by the Italians. Tobruk's lines are similar to the Siegfried Line, if not better. Behind these lines the British troops fight with extreme tenacity, protected by excellent shelters which are not only strong but well camouflaged. General Rommel has therefore surrounded Tobruk by an iron ring which is now unbreakable. The near future will bring an enormous concentration of the German air force to crash in [sic] each fortress by bombing, making Tobruk a hell."

Frequent raids by Blenheims were beginning to take their toll on the besiegers while German fighters were conspicuous by their absence. Panzer Lt Schorm, entrenched outside the perimeter with his colleagues, entered in his diary:

> "The rumour is going around that Obstlt Galland is coming with his squadron. It would be splendid if it were true."

The rumour had some substance. The renowned Luftwaffe fighter leader Adolf Galland, one of Germany's leading aces, was not about to take part in the offensive against Tobruk, but the advance element of the Bf109-equipped I/JG27 – 1 Staffel commanded by Oblt Karl-Wolfgang Redlich, a ten-victory ace – had just arrived at Gazala, a mere 30 miles to the west of Tobruk. The Gruppe's other two Staffeln were soon to follow.

CHAPTER VI

ODDS OF SEVEN OR EIGHT TO ONE

19 April – 8 May 1941

"I met the men of 73 Squadron, or rather, I met those who were left. They had just flown out of Tobruk, and I do not think I have ever seen a tougher looking gang, bearded, with tousled hair and wild eyes."

Air Marshal Tedder, Deputy AOC-in-C RAFME

With the arrival of dawn on the morning of 19 April, Flg Off Weller (P3977) of 274 Squadron set off from Sidi Haneish to carry out a lone strafing attack on Gazala aerodrome in the hope of catching the defences unaware, which he succeeded in achieving. Making one pass over a line of CR42s and SM79s, he reported on his return, some three hours later, probable damage to six of the biplanes and the destruction of at least one tri-motor, which was left in flames. Shortly after midday Sqn Ldr Lapsley, having returned from El Gubbi early in the morning, took off to patrol to the west of Tobruk with Plt Off H.J. Baker and Sgt George Kerr, followed half an hour later by another section led by Flt Lt Down with Flg Off Patterson and newly arrived Flg Off D.J. Spence, another New Zealander. They were to refuel at Sidi Barrani to enable extended patrols to be maintained.

Their arrival in the Tobruk area coincided with a raid on the harbour by 20 Ju88s of III/KG30 escorted by Bf109s of 1/JG27 from Gazala, making their first operational appearance in North African skies. The Messerschmitts soon proved their superiority over the Hurricanes, Plt Off Baker's aircraft (W9296) falling in flames near the El Adem road after the pilot had baled out, probably the victim of Oblt Redlich, the Staffelkapitän; Baker survived but was taken prisoner. Shortly thereafter, Sqn Ldr Lapsley (V7811), hotly pursuing one of the bombers, came under attack from two of the German fighters, one of which was flown by Redlich and the other by Lt Werner Schroer; the damaged Hurricane crash-landed near El Gubbi and was then strafed on the ground, Lapsley being wounded in the leg and shoulder. Only Sgt Kerr managed to escape the onslaught and returned safely to Sidi Haneish. By now the second section had arrived but only Spence reported meeting the Ju88s, one of which had fallen to AA fire over the harbour, as they raced for their base, shooting down one over Ras-el-Meheta and damaging a second. He then sighted a Messerschmitt below, which he also claimed shot down.

The German pilot, Lt Schroer, recalled later:

> "I was attacked by a Hurricane from out of the sun and had 48 bullet holes in my
> aircraft [WkNr3790], but was able to force-land close to our airfield at Gazala."

Two Ju88s failed to return, both 8 Staffel machines. None of the crews
survived[1].The crew of a third bomber flown by Lt Hecking of 9 Staffel reported
being attacked by a Hurricane during which their gunner, Uffz Alfred Klinkhardt,
suffered wounds. Meanwhile, the wounded Sqn Ldr Lapsley was taken away for
treatment as noted by Capt Devine:

> "The Squadron Leader was brought in with a broken leg. He was on the tail of
> a Ju87 [sic] when a Messerschmitt 109 shot away his ailerons. He tried to
> escape, but the Messerschmitt was too fast for him in his damaged condition
> and shot away all his instrument panel. He himself was not hit, but did a
> pancake landing and got out of his plane. Then, while walking away from it,
> he was machine-gunned by the same Messerschmitt and hit in the leg."

Sqn Ldr Lapsley therefore had good reason to comment later on the merits of his
first, and last, encounter with Bf109s:

> "The impact of the Messerschmitts was very great. These aircraft had a very
> significantly better performance than the Hurricane in climbing, diving and
> level speed. The manoeuvrability of the two aircraft was comparable. Our
> results against the Italians had been so good that perhaps we were a little over-
> confident and had not sufficiently absorbed the tactical lessons of the war in
> Europe. This all combined to give us a very rough time for the first few weeks
> after the Messerschmitts arrived."

A guard was placed on Lapsley's damaged Hurricane, as was recalled by 73
Squadron airman Ralph Grace:

> "V7811 had crash-landed not very far away from the front-line perimeter, and
> I was sent out to guard it, not so much to protect from the Afrika Korps as to
> prevent the Australian troops from looting it for instruments etc. I had to spend
> the night there, and slept in a grimy, sandy dugout with a view of the machine."

73 Squadron put up four patrols from El Gubbi during the day, Sqn Ldr Murray
leading two personally, but no enemy aircraft were encountered. Flg Off Goodman
led the section which scrambled when the Ju88s of III/KG30 attacked the harbour
but, as Sgt Garton noted, no contact was made:

> "Raided by about 20 Ju88s and had the pleasure of seeing one spin off into the
> harbour, shot down by AA. Took off but failed to do any good."

---

[1] 4D+KS crewed by Hptm Alfred Neumann (Staffelkapitän), Uffz Paul Gildenberg, Uffz
Wenzel Wanek and Fw Rudolf Pech; and 4D+GS crewed by Obfw Kurt Distel, Uffz
Wolfgang Sterzel, Uffz Kurt Kraft and Uffz Eugen Popp.

The pilots of A Flt/6 Squadron meanwhile continued to carry out tactical reconnaissance, and the occasional photographic sortie, using both Lysanders and Hurricanes, the former evoking a diary entry from Panzer Lt Schorm:

"The Lion has wings; we have one above us. These hateful birds immediately direct arty fire over our post. Likewise smoke bombs, which sail down on parachutes, producing a screaming wail."

The Lysanders were carrying out similar duties to those of the Henschels of 2(H)/14, about which Capt Devine wrote:

"Daily along our front wire, at a height of not more than a few hundred feet, would fly 'Schmidt the Spy' or 'Betty Henschel'. This Henschel reconnaissance plane was apparently heavily armoured underneath, and though our chaps fired everything possible at it, it took no more notice than that occasionally the pilot dipped into a bag and dropped a few hand grenades over the side. Since 'Schmidt the Spy' directed German artillery fire, and because of their inability to bring him down, the troops had taken a hearty dislike to him."

Surprisingly few of these slow-flying spotter aircraft from either side were shot down during the siege; in fact, 6 Squadron suffered no Lysander losses in the air over Tobruk but, as Flg Off Pat Pike later admitted:

"It wasn't much fun roaming round in Lysanders in those days, they were like sitting ducks. Most of us got very jumpy after a time. As soon as you took off you were over the enemy lines. Our job in Tobruk was to keep a constant recce round the perimeter defences and beyond."

Though A Flight's Hurricanes were camera-equipped, these were seldom used at this stage of the fighting. Plt Off Moulding recalled:

"We didn't use the cameras very much because it was better not to waste film since the army couldn't wait to analyse it. However, I do remember taking line overlaps over Bardia. I'd never done it before and somebody told me what to do and how to switch the camera on and all that sort of thing. I went off. Ack-ack was about 6,000-7,000 feet so you had to take the photographs just above that height. It took quite a lot of skilful flying. At the end of the run you had to turn round and do the return – all straight and level. When I got to the end I found I'd forgotten to turn the camera on."

The Messerschmitts scored a further success when, at 1530, Uffz Hans Sippel intercepted a Hurricane flown by 6 Squadron's Irish CO, Sqn Ldr Rowland Weld, who was engaged on a reconnaissance over Gazala. The Hurricane crashed in the desert, taking Weld to his death. Plt Off Moulding commented:

"We didn't know what had happened to Paddy, he just didn't return from a

sortie. We hoped that he had come down safely somewhere, and perhaps was
a prisoner, but we didn't hear any more."

So ended a highly successful début for I/JG27's Messerschmitts in North Africa.
For the loss of one of their own aircraft badly damaged, the German pilots had
claimed four Hurricanes shot down – the first of many successful actions due to
come their way in the ensuing weeks and months. The Gruppe's Kommodore, Hptm
Neumann, later reflected:

"The Gruppe was equipped with the Bf109E-type; the *Emil* was superior to all
enemy fighter aircraft then operating in North Africa and the initial successes
gave the pilots the feeling of safety and superiority although we always felt
ourselves to be inferior in numbers. The main strength of the Bf109E lay in its
excellent performance, high diving speed and good armament. This aircraft
was allowed to fly in the smallest formations and through this offered ideal
chances for gifted and aggressive pilots to show their qualities. Some pilots
took advantage of this to a high degree – apart from the leading pilots it was
very hard for newcomers and less-gifted pilots to achieve similar success."

The arrival of the Bf109s allowed 155°Gruppo CT at Derna to return to Benghazi,
since its G50bis were plagued by sand getting into their engines and all three
squadrons were ordered to prepare to depart forthwith to have filters fitted,
360^Squadriglia leaving on 19 April when 150^Squadriglia (Cap De Prato) from
similarly equipped 2°Gruppo CT arrived to take its place; next day 152^Squadriglia
(Cap Teja) arrived to replace 378^Squadriglia and, finally, 358^Squadriglia under
the command of Cap Sterzi arrived two days later to replace 351^Squadriglia.

For the defenders of Tobruk, 20 April turned out to be relatively quiet. Two
Hurricanes of 274 Squadron flown by Flg Off A.M. Ross and Lt A.J.B. Bester
SAAF arrived at El Gubbi just after dawn, returning to Sidi Haneish two hours later,
their services not required under the circumstances. Later in the morning 73
Squadron carried out two patrols over the harbour area but no enemy aircraft were
sighted. Just after 1115, three Hurricanes flown by Flg Off Goodman, Sous-Lt
Denis and Sgt Garton patrolled over the forward positions to protect them from
dive-bombers during a mopping up operation near the perimeter of the defences,
indulging in some ground strafing at the same time. It was possibly during this
operation that Rommel had a further lucky escape when his armoured control
vehicle was strafed by Hurricanes flying at ground level. His driver was seriously
wounded, a truck driver and a despatch rider killed, and the radio truck destroyed.

As the situation worsened for the defenders, 73 Squadron was issued with orders
covering action to be taken should Axis forces succeed penetration in depth of the
defences:

Resistance: Since the ground resistance which could be put up by this
squadron would be futile against a large body of enemy troops or
mechanised vehicles, in order to save needless loss of life, personnel will not
resist attack by overwhelming forces. All personnel must realise that defence
action will be initiated by officers and that any rash move might result in the
mowing down of all personnel.

Secret Documents: Holders of secret documents to destroy by fire.

Destruction of Equipment: W/T and M/T personnel will proceed to their vehicles if (a) ordered to do so (b) it is obvious that enemy forces are about to overrun the camp.

On Capture of Aerodrome: All personnel to proceed quietly to collect small kit, bedding, personal belongings and rations, and report outside the orderly room.

Destruction of Aircraft: On approach of enemy troops, flights acting under flight commanders will set fire to all aircraft which are unable to fly off.

Flying Off of Aircraft: Serviceable aircraft will, as far as possible, be flown away to rear on approach of enemy troops. Aircraft flying away must be prepared to combat enemy aircraft en route but must NOT carry out ground strafing.

Note: The following vehicles will NOT be destroyed:-Ambulance, water wagon.

Sqn Ldr Murray, recent recipient of the DFC, who was sick and exhausted, now relinquished command of 73 Squadron, being flown to the Delta area via Sidi Haneish aboard a Blenheim; Sgt Garton recorded:

> "At midday the CO, Griff, Monty [Ellis], Goodman and myself left El Gubbi per Blenheim for Sidi Haneish to bring back replacement kites. Landed at Ma'aten Bagush where the AOC had a quiet chat with us and gave us all the gen. Things don't appear to be too good. Stayed the night at Haneish where our advance party is stationed."

At 0915 on the morning of 21 April, five replacement Hurricanes landed at El Gubbi, one of which was flown by the new CO, Sqn Ldr Wykeham-Barnes DFC, former flight commander of 274 Squadron and veteran of the desert war. Prior to the Hurricanes' departure from Sidi Haneish, Flg Off Storrar, who had just arrived in an unserviceable aircraft from El Gubbi, was confronted by the new CO:

> "I flew a Hurricane that had an internal oil leak out of Tobruk rather than having it destroyed on the ground. I landed at the first available airfield [Sidi Haneish]. Wykeham-Barnes was just leaving for Tobruk. He was as keen as mustard and inspired me so much that I nearly went back with him."

The new CO made a fine impression on the Tobruk veterans. Sgt Laing commented:

> "Sqn Ldr Wykeham-Barnes was a very tough lad and was a hell of a fine bloke, cool and efficient – just the job."

Three more Hurricanes arrived during the day, Plt Offs Haldenby and Wareham (who had been hospitalised following illness) plus Sgt Marshall ferrying in replacement aircraft, while Sgt White flew an operationally unserviceable aircraft to Sidi Haneish. One of the French pilots, Sous-Lt Ferrant, also departed eastwards for the Delta, having contracted an eye condition due to the sand and intense brightness of the sun. The morning was again relatively quiet for 73 Squadron, one section flying a protective patrol over RN warships active off Bardia where Royal Marine Commandos were preparing to carry out a night raid[2]. Hurricanes from 274 Squadron also provided patrols during the period of the operation, and over the forward area. During one of these at 0800, six Hurricanes led by Flt Lt Down encountered a patrol of Bf109s from I/JG27. Flg Off Spence (V7354) engaged one from such close range that he collided with it, but nevertheless was able to glide back to British lines and carry out an emergency landing. The Messerschmitt pilot, believed to have been Lt Schroer, also force-landed with a badly damaged aircraft (WkNr4170), having been slightly wounded. It seems that this was the second time in three days that Spence had shot down Schroer. Flt Lt Dudley Honor, who had taken over temporary command of 274 Squadron following Sqn Ldr Lapsley's injury, led a further patrol of six Hurricanes over the front-line at 1000, but failed to meet any enemy aircraft.

73 Squadron continued to send up patrols to meet approaching aircraft, one section being engaged by five Bf109s during which Sous-Lt Castelain's aircraft was attacked and badly damaged by Obfw Albert Espenlaub. While attempting to carry out an emergency landing at El Gubbi, the French pilot suffered a broken arm when the Hurricane flipped over onto its back. The Ju87s returned in force at 1900, carrying out an attack on the harbour, as noted by Sgt Garton (V7673/TP-P), who scrambled with Flg Off Goodman (AS990/TP-V), Sous-Lt Denis (V7834) and Sgt Ellis (V7716/TP-U); however, the latter's engine cut on take-off and he was unable to join the others:

> "This evening we scrambled after 60 Ju87s and 20 ME110s did a fierce attack
> on the harbour. We three immediately got split up and I engaged and managed
> to shoot down one Ju87, whilst Benny [Goodman] and the Frenchman [Denis]
> got one each. I was then tackled by an overwhelming number of 110s and had
> to retire gracefully into the AA barrage for safety."

Bf109s were also present, Denis shooting down one in addition to his claim for a Stuka. His victim was undoubtedly Uffz Sippel (WkNr3777) who failed to return from this sortie. Of the day's action, Capt Devine wrote:

> "... there was a small raid in which we shot down four German planes but lost
> two Hurricanes. What supreme courage these fighter pilots have! Four or five
> of them go up again and again against hundreds. Even though shot down once

---

[2] The Commandos landed near Bardia where they were tasked to destroy a bridge, a dump of stores and to do the maximum amount of damage possible to the coastal defence guns; the bridge was blown, the dump set on fire and four coastal guns put out of action, but about 70 of the Marines were captured.

or twice, they go up again until they are killed. No knights of old ever reached their peak of courage. Today I saw one Jerry diving into the sea closely followed by a Hurricane sitting on his tail."

It had been a day of mixed fortunes for I/JG27. In addition to the loss of 1 Staffel's Sippel and the temporary incapacity of the wounded Schroer, 2 Staffel had experienced another of those not infrequent, but always tragic, incidents of misidentification in the air, when one of its pilots, believed to have been Obfhr Heinrich Pompsch, accidentally shot down an Italian bomber, as recalled by Lt Schroer:

> "An Italian bomber was shot down by one of my friends in error. My friend died mentally from this mistake, and said to me: 'It is of no use living any more.' Next day he did not come back from a mission."

Despite a highly successful attack (on the night of 14/15 April) by RN destroyers from Malta on an Axis convoy making for Tripoli, which sank all five freighters and two of the three escorting Italian destroyers within a few minutes of commencing action, thereby denying the Afrika Korps some 350 men, 300 vehicles and 3,500 tons of equipment in one fell swoop, troops, equipment and supplies nevertheless continued pouring into Tripoli. In desperation, the Admiralty hatched a plan by which this vital port could effectively be put out of use; the plan required Admiral Cunningham to agree to sacrifice the battleship *Barham* and the AA cruiser *Calcutta* by deliberately scuttling them in the entrance to the harbour. Cunningham would not comply with such a drastic solution to the problem but offered to carry out an equally potentially hazardous dawn bombardment of Tripoli, using three battleships and three cruisers, while Swordfish from the carrier *Formidable* and aircraft from Malta would assist the Naval force by bombing and illuminating the port. The attack took place on the morning of 21 April – with surprisingly little reaction from the Axis – but the actual damage inflicted was not severe even though 530 tons of 6-inch and 15-inch shells were lobbed into the harbour area. The town and port were severely battered but the facilities were not put out of action and only one freighter, loaded with fuel and bombs, was sunk, though several others were damaged. During the operation, FAA Fulmars from *Formidable* had provided cover for the task force, the Navy pilots claiming three Italian tri-motors, a Do24 flying boat, and four Ju52/3m shot down for one loss. The transports, from I/KGzbV.9, were on their way to Cyrenaica and were apparently laden with fuel. One only of the five encountered was seen to escape.[3]

Dawn on 22 April arrived with a raid on Tobruk by an estimated 30 Ju87s, including five from 236^Squadriglia[4], and six Bf110s escorted by a dozen Bf109s and a similar number of G50bis, as witnessed by Panzer Lt Schorm:

---

[3] For further details of this operation see *Air War for Yugoslavia, Greece and Crete, 1940-41* by Christopher Shores and Brian Cull with Nicola Malizia, published by Grub Street.

[4] 96°Gruppo Aut B.a'T disbanded on 19 April, 237^Squadriglia handing over its remaining aircraft to 236^Squadriglia which continued to operate under Cap Santinoni, awaiting the arrival of more Ju87s from Sicily.

"0650, alert and ready for action. Then there is a humming in the sky. Hurrah! Six ME110s protected by four ME109s bomb and harrass the enemy's defences. Then a long row of dive-bombers follow. They form into formations of three. Their objective is the harbour. The dull thuds of heavy bombs detonating roll over us. 'Give it to them', my men shout. They will do that all right without our pious wishes, and despite the strong defence."

Four Hurricanes led by Flg Off Scott were airborne from El Gubbi and engaged the raiders, one Ju87 being claimed shot down by Plt Off Wareham (V7837) who also damaged a second, while Plt Off Chatfield (V7492/TP-H) claimed the probable destruction of a third. One of the German air gunners reported shooting down a Hurricane but none was lost nor, apparently, even damaged since, at 1050, Flg Off Martin led the same four Hurricanes into the air when Ju87s and Bf109s were reported approaching the harbour. The Hurricanes were engaged by the escort, one of which Martin (V7810/TP-W) claimed shot down; he noted:

"Attacked by ME109s while attacking Ju87s. One ME109. Chased back to harbour minus elevator controls. Force-landed on aerodrome."

Half an hour later, five more Hurricanes were scrambled to provide support, Sous-Lt Littolf (V7353/TP-A) also reporting the destruction of a Bf109. However, since only one of the Messerschmitts (WkNr4112) was lost, that flown by Obfhr Pompsch of 2 Staffel, who was believed to have baled out but succumbed to his wounds next day, it seems probable that both Martin and Littolf had engaged the same aircraft. Sgt Marshall (W9299/M) meanwhile encountered the Italian fighters and shot down Serg Enzo Falcinelli of 358^Squadriglia, who was also killed. In return Cap Teja, CO of 152^Squadriglia, claimed a Hurricane shot down. Of his 13th victory, Marshall noted:

"Enemy aircraft was at 200 feet escorting Ju87s with ME109s – crashed outside Tobruk defences, confirmed by Lt Littolf. Heavy machine-gun fire from German troops."

German records suggest that a Ju88 of 8/LG1 was lost to fighters over Tobruk during the day, in which Uffz Gerhart Pfeil and his crew perished, but this probably fell to the AA defences.

Despite the desperate plight of 73 Squadron in its life or death struggle, the RAF adminstrators continued to operate by the rule book, as indicated by an entry in Sgt Garton's diary:

"On returning [from the morning action against the Ju87s and Bf109s] I was told to make ready for a trip down to the Delta for interview with AOC re [my] commission. Set off with shot up kite [V7856] and eventually reached Sidi Haneish after going about 20 miles out to sea. Refuelled and reached Heliopolis about 7pm. Stayed there the night. Grand to have a good meal and bath again in decent surroundings, and one has the feeling of relief to be out of Tobruk although it was tough leaving all our boys there."

During a lull between the raids, two Hurricanes from 274 Squadron arrived at El Gubbi, having escorted a 6 Squadron Lysander returning from a flight to Ma'aten Bagush, but Plt Off P.L.V. Hutt and Sgt C.K. Glover did not remain and returned forthwith to Sidi Haneish. Late in the afternoon, two more Hurricanes from 274 Squadron were ordered to strafe a suspicious aircraft reported on the ground at Gambut, which turned out to be a force-landed Wellington. Rather than return with their ammunition, Flg Offs Ross and Noel Agazarian (a former Battle of Britain pilot with several victories to his credit) strafed a convoy of 30 M/T on the Bardia to Tobruk road.

The first scramble for 73 Squadron on the morning of 23 April came at 0705 when an intruder was reported approaching, but no enemy aircraft was sighted. This was apparently a reconnaissance Ju88, its crew undoubtedly observing a number of freighters in the harbour. Flg Off Scott clearly remembered this particular morning:

> "After lengthy discussions we got agreement from Group that unless we could put up a minimum of three machines – leader, wingman and weaver – we would stay on the ground. This was the right arrangement, some days too late. The new CO, Wykeham-Barnes, was not impressed with what he regarded as a somewhat timid approach. After his calling for a volunteer from a group of us standing outside the mess, he and Pete Haldenby took off as a section of two ..."

At about 1000, four Hurricanes – two sections of two led by the CO and Flg Off Martin respectively – took off on another scramble. Shortly afterwards another three were scrambled when an estimated 20 Ju87s including five from 236^Squadriglia led by Cap Santinoni, 30 Bf109s and ten Bf110s approached the harbour. Lt Rankin wrote:

> "Streams of hostile planes came in – 15 dive-bombers rolled up followed by numerous ME109s at a great height. We fired our new harbour barrage. Then came a whole series of dogfights over the aerodrome and we saw two Hurricanes crash – one pilot baling out all right; tremendous crashes, both of them!"

The pilot seen to bale out was Sqn Ldr Wykeham-Barnes (V7837) who came down in full view of the aerodrome, having been attacked by three Bf109s although he claimed a Messerschmitt and a Ju87 before his own aircraft was shot down. He landed on the edge of the harbour wall. His only injury was a strained leg. Capt Devine was another witness to the brief air battle:

> "I saw one Messerschmitt on the tail of a Hurricane which dived straight down to the ground and burst in flames and smoke; but above, we could see its pilot floating down to safety on a parachute. Another Hurricane, which was just about to land on the aerodrome across the harbour and had put down its landing flaps, was swooped upon from a cloud above by an almost vertically diving Messerschmitt. Going at only about 100 miles per hour, the Hurricane was helpless. We could see the flash of the Messerschmitt's cannon as he fired.

> The Hurricane landed hurriedly in flames, and the Messerschmitt zoomed
> straight up in a terrific climb, with ack-ack bursting all round it."

So died Plt Off Peter Haldenby. His body was recovered from the wreck of V7834
and buried in the nearby cemetery. A third Hurricane failed to return, V7810/TP-W
flown by Flg Off Martin, who had also been forced to bale out when attacked by a
Bf109. He returned later, wounded in one arm, as recalled by Ron Waite:

> "Later in the day Dickie Martin, missing from a morning engagement, turned
> up on the running board of an army truck with his parachute loosely bundled
> under his arm. This got the cheers ringing out again."

Three more Ju87s were claimed by the remaining pilots, one apiece by Sgt Marshall
(V7353/TP-A), who reported his victim crashed 15 miles west of Tobruk, and Plt
Off Chatfield (W9299/TP-M), the latter returning with battle damage to its rudder;
the third Stuka was claimed by Sous-Lt Littolf (V7728), the French pilot also
claiming a Bf109 shot down; he was fortunate to escape a similar fate to that which
befell Haldenby; Capt Devine witnessed his return to El Gubbi:

> "Two Messerschmitts were hard on the tail of a fleeing Hurricane at a height
> of only a few hundred feet. The Hurricane was swerving wildly, and leading
> his pursuer around and around the Tobruk ack-ack gun positions. The gunners
> had to aim at the Hurricane in front to hit the Messerschmitt behind, and after
> many shots a red Bofors shell burst fair in the centre of the Messerschmitt's
> fuselage, and it crashed in flames. The Hurricane went off to land, and its pilot
> came back and collected the anti-aircraft gunner who had saved him, thanked
> him, and took him over to his mess for celebrations."

73 Squadron's Bill Davies added:

> "We heard the scream of approaching engines and looked up to see one of our
> Frenchmen coming back over the field with a 109 right on his tail. As they
> banked into a tight turn we all feared the worse, but then one of our Bofors
> guns put a shell right through the Jerry cockpit almost at ground level. The 109
> went hard into the ground and rolled up into a ball, while we stood and cheered
> like idiots as the French pilot landed."

It seems that Littolf's Hurricane had been badly damaged in this engagement and
was belly-landed on the aerodrome; Ron Waite continued:

> "I had stood within earshot of our CO as he tried to explain to two of our
> French pilots what our combat tactics were. He was down on his haunches
> drawing aeroplanes and clouds in the sand, and tried to make them understand
> that they should make full use of any cloud cover. Before the day was out one
> of them force-landed wheels up on the drome, undid his straps and stood up in
> the cockpit firing his handgun at the strafing 109s."

Sgt Laing also witnessed the demise of the Messerschmitt (WkNr4163), in which

Fw Werner Lange of 1/JG27 perished:

> "We watched a ME109 roar past at about 150 feet and the Bofors gunner got his deflection right with the fifth or sixth shot and blew the plane to pieces. In what wreckage we saw close by the field, all we found was a boot."

Shortly afterwards, Sgt Marshall's Hurricane was attacked on the ground by Lt Eugen von Moller, who had also claimed a Hurricane shot down in the air; Marshall recalled:

> "I was strafed in the cockpit by a ME109, wounded in head and shoulder. LAC Webster and another [LAC Jock Boyd] seriously injured at wing tips."

Sgt Laing was standing nearby and also witnessed the incident:

> "Sgt Marshall was wounded as well as two of the fitters. I was only about a dozen yards away, and it was quite a shock to see it happen so fast."

One who narrowly escaped injury was Ron Waite:

> "I was driving the armoury lorry when the strafing began, and dived out and under as quickly as I could. I could see dust kicked up by bullets marching across the sand towards me, but they missed the lorry and finished up at Sgt Marshall's kite, where he was just climbing out of the cockpit. He got a nicked ear but Willie Webster who was just clambering on to the port wing was hit (eight times, we learned later). Even so I saw him slide off the wing and run 20-30 yards towards the Flight Tent before collapsing."

Another was armourer Bill Davies:

> "Willie [Webster] and I walked out to service Marshall's kite, with me laden with belts of ammo, when I looked up and saw 109s coming towards us. I had dropped the ammo and was running for shelter when I realised Willie had been hit. I went back, picked him up and carried him to the Flight Tent. They wouldn't send an ambulance because of the risk, and Willie died that afternoon."

The other wounded armourer, LAC Boyd, despite having been hit nine times, amazingly survived. The Stuka attack on the harbour had inflicted much damage, the freighters *Urania* and *Draco* both taking hits while bomb splinters and debris damaged the corvette *Gloxinia*, the mine-dredger *Fareham*, and the former South African whaler turned anti-submarine vessel, *Southern Sea*. The pilots of I/JG27, which now comprised all three Staffeln, submitted claims for the destruction of four Hurricanes in the air – two by Oblt Ludwig Franzisket (his 15th and 16th victories) and one apiece by Lt von Moller and Obfhr Hans-Joachim Marseille (his eighth victory); the latter, a member of 3 Staffel, was to become one of the Luftwaffe's top fighter aces[5]. At 1500, a further raid by Ju87s escorted by an estimated 20 Bf109s was met by four Hurricanes, one section led by Flg Off Goodman with Plt Off Wareham, the other comprising Sous-Lt Denis and Wt Off Ballatore. The gunnery officer, Lt Rankin, saw the Stukas approaching:

> "Before the Hurricanes had time to recover, the alarm went again and I counted a long line of 15 Ju87s pouring in near C site who were firing furiously. This time they attacked a different part of the harbour and really did not seem to do much damage. Every now and again immense columns of water would shoot up from the old harbour as bombs fell harmlessly in the middle of it. The planes this time drew away to the south instead of our way. A tragedy – the NAAFI ship was bombed and large stocks of beer just unloaded went for six!"

Wt Off Ballatore recalled:

> "Stukas regularly attacked the supply ships in the port. If not able to prevent the bombing, our job was to at least disturb the pilots so they would miss the target. We didn't shoot down many of them but, personally, I never saw a ship receive a direct hit. When attacked by ME109s our planes were more manoeuvrable. We could avoid them with tight turns."

On this occasion the Messerschmitts managed to keep the Hurricanes away from the dive-bombers, only Denis (AS990/TP-V) achieving any success:

> "I was lucky to shoot, in one combat, a section of two German fighters. I fired at them from three-quarters astern at 30-40 yards. One fell on the airfield, almost on the landing lights. I landed immediately afterwards as I wished to have a souvenir, but when I arrived at the spot the Australians had already taken parts, and I had to content myself with a parachute cord."

It would seem that Denis confused this action with that of the earlier crash of Fw Lange's Messerschmitt. However, the second aircraft he claimed was that flown by Obfhr Marseille of 3 Staffel who had attacked him from astern; Denis later reflected:

> "I was well-trained and a confirmed fighter[6]. What's more, I was considered an élite shooter. I knew my job well, and it explains why during my fight with this pilot, presumably Marseille, I was patient enough to act as if I hadn't seen him, wait until the last second and skid, avoiding his bullets which passed very close to my right. I saw them well."

---

[5] Before his death in a flying accident on 30 September 1942, Marseille – a flamboyant character who achieved great success and became known as the 'Star of Africa' – had increased his tally to an incredible 158 including an amazing 17 (eight Hurricanes, eight P-40s and one Spitfire) in one day (1 September 1942), the majority of which can be verified in British records.

[6] Denis had joined the Armée de l'Air in 1925 as a 19-year-old and initially served as a gunner before undergoing pilot training, gaining his wings as a fighter pilot in 1929. He was posted to the fighter group of the 33^Aviation Regt, which became III/GC3 in 1930, later joining II/GC3, but following high blood pressure problems in 1938 was posted to the Wireless Operators School at St Jean-d'Angély (flying Potez 540s) from where he escaped to England in June 1940 (see Appendix I).

As the Messerschmitt flashed past, Denis opened fire. Hit in the engine, it crash-landed in no-man's land from where Marseille was able to make his way back to German lines. His aircraft (WkNr5160) had received some 30 strikes and Marseille apparently related to his colleagues how two bullets had passed behind his head when he had leaned forward for a split second, while two more passed within a few inches of his face. This was effectively the swan-song for the Hurricane defenders of Tobruk. That evening Air Commodore Collishaw wrote to Air Marshal Tedder, Deputy AOC:

> "I am of the opinion that the air situation at Tobruk is critical for the following reasons. The enemy has concentrated two new fighter wings at Derna and Gazala which permits him to escort his bombers over Tobruk with ME110s at approximately 15,000 feet with ME109s flying a good deal higher. The striking forces arrive in overwhelming numbers over Tobruk within ten minutes of the warning being received so that our comparatively few fighters at Tobruk are still well beneath the escorting enemy fighters when the bombing commences. In these circumstances the enemy fighters will always have a great advantage over our fighters as they retain the initiative. During recent days the enemy has acted aggressively in the Tobruk area, both against our fighters and against our ground forces in the Tobruk defended area. Enemy fighters have ground strafed our troops some two or three miles inside the Tobruk defences and have taken the initiative in every way possible and a serious reduction has occurred in our fighter force.
>
> I sent all available Hurricanes to Tobruk so that on 21.4.41 they had 15 serviceable aircraft. On 23.4.41 the enemy made a succession of attacks on Tobruk which caused our pilots to be continuously on the alert and engaged in combat from daybreak until noon. Group Captain Spackman decided that the pilots must be given a rest and they were instructed to stand off for the afternoon. A succession of enemy raids developed during the afternoon without fighter protection and the enemy bombed and ground strafed El Gubbi aerodrome. Several of the 73 Squadron pilots took off during the enemy attacks but the ME109s assaulted them as they were taking off and landing with the result that Sqn Ldr Wykeham-Barnes was wounded and several other pilots killed and wounded. The result was that out of 15 serviceable Hurricanes which were available at 21.4.41 only five remained serviceable on 23.4.41. Group Captain Spackman considers that we ought to produce a minimum of nine aircraft on patrol at a time which means that we must have at least 18 serviceable Hurricanes at El Gubbi continuously.
>
> No. 274 Squadron have approximately 13 aircraft available but, I understand, that these represent a major part of the Hurricanes available in Egypt at the present time and I am loathed to send them to Tobruk as the enemy fighters have taken the initiative, so that we may expect further Hurricane casualties in fights and ground strafing at Tobruk which would obviously reduce our available Hurricane fighter force in Egypt to a more dangerous level. It is for consideration, therefore, whether we ought to continue to send large numbers of Hurricanes to El Gubbi where we shall obviously lose some, or whether some alternative plan must be adopted. This

is, of course, a matter for the AOC-in-C's decision. On the one hand it is vital that we must maintain our air protection of Tobruk, while on the other hand we must not lose what available Hurricanes we have for the defence of Egypt in readiness should the enemy continue his advance in the Western Desert.

I am sending this letter by an officer early on 24.4.41 and request that I may be informed early as to what decision is taken in this matter."

Next day (24 April), at 0710, the Squadron put up one patrol of five Hurricanes led by Flt Lt Olivier but these encountered no enemy aircraft. The afternoon was relatively void of aerial activity and it was not until teatime that a formation of 18 Ju87s escorted by Bf109s appeared, the Stukas carrying out a dive-bombing attack against previously damaged shipping in the harbour. AA guns claimed one shot down but the Hurricanes were not scrambled on this occasion. Shortly after dawn on 25 April, HQ 258 Wing asked 73 Squadron for a nominal roll of available aircraft and pilots remaining at El Gubbi. On being advised that the Squadron possessed just five serviceable Hurricanes, orders were received to prepare to withdraw to Sidi Haneish, but first four of the five remaining Hurricanes were scrambled to meet an early morning raid by about 20 Bf109s escorting Italian Ju87s. On observing the odds, Olivier wisely decided that discretion was required and brought his charges safely back to base. By evening there were eight Hurricanes[7] capable of being flown, of which only four were operational, and these left at 1800 for Sidi Haneish, to where the CO, Flg Off Goodman, Plt Off Humphreys and the Intelligence Officer had earlier departed aboard a Blenheim. The Hurricanes however, landed at Gerawla, where 274 Squadron was based, with the exception of Flg Off Scott:

"V7673 [TP-P] was in the 'flyable' category with a coolant leak. I did not climb after take-off but headed out to sea and kept it low and slow to Sidi Haneish, just about making it with the temperature gauge off the clock."

Sous-Lt Denis commented:

"We landed at Gerawla after some confusion. There Littolf, Ballatore and I were very happy because this mistake enabled us to meet Jacquier and Pompéï, both with 274 Squadron. It had been a trying time, 24 [sic] days in those conditions – it was like a whole war! We took off and fired on anything moving outside Tobruk's perimeter. It soon became obvious we could not keep going any longer. German artillery was firing endlessly, destroying our planes, making supplying hard and sleeping difficult for the aircrews and groundcrews. My ambition was only to live until dusk. Nothing more. During the days we [the French Flight] spent in Tobruk, we carried out 167 ops and gained ten confirmed and two probables, plus many vehicles on the ground."

---

[7] The eight Hurricanes flown to Gerawla were P3725 (Olivier), V7673 (Scott), V7858 (Chatfield), AS990 (Eiby), V7566 (Laing), W9198 (Denis), V7295 (Littolf), V7492 (Ballatore).

Of his brief period in command of 73 Squadron at Tobruk, Sqn Ldr Wykeham-Barnes later reflected:

> "It was a very bad time, as we were outclassed by the 109s, heavily outnumbered, and hopelessly placed tactically. We shot down a fair number of Stukas and 109s. Our rôle was to keep up some appearance of participation, so that the Army should not feel deserted by the Air Force, but the heavy cost of this was known and we were urged to hold out."

Since moving into El Gubbi on 9 April, 73 Squadron had claimed 31 enemy aircraft shot down plus five probables, together with eight aircraft and many dozens of M/T destroyed on the ground, for the loss of about 25 Hurricanes of which 15 had been shot down, with six pilots killed, two taken prisoner and a further four wounded. Although the Hurricanes had been withdrawn, there remained at El Gubbi 73 Squadron's servicing crews and other ground personnel. Some were told to pack up and make for the docks from where they were to be evacuated by sea, while a small party was to stay behind to salvage what they could from the various wrecked Hurricanes, as Ken Rumbold recalled:

> "We had the job of getting all the pranged Hurricanes down to the port and loaded on the A lighters. This was no easy task, as they had to be lifted to get the wheels down and locked, then the outer wing panels removed. I remember the Aussie infantry men were keen on keeping the Brownings, which they set up for firing around the perimeter. At eight per aircraft, we were happy to supply them, and we even rigged up a couple of pairs ourselves. When all the kites that were retrievable had been moved, we expected to be returning to Egypt, but there was no such luck."

Also still in Tobruk was Flt Lt Beytagh, former 73 Squadron flight commander. His continued presence is somewhat of a mystery since he apparently attached himself to the 6 Squadron detachment, where he had a number of friends and acquaintances. Since local air reconnaissance was vital, A Flt/6 Squadron was to remain at Tobruk with its two surviving Hurricanes (V7814 and P5173, named 'Alma Baker' and 'Alma Baker II' by the pilots) and four Lysanders under the command of Flg Off Fletcher. The third Hurricane (V7759) had apparently been damaged on the ground by a strafing Bf109, probably the incident recorded by Plt Off Moulding:

> "The little burst of fire which the Messerschmitt pilot put into 6 Squadron's camp didn't hurt anyone. In order to be sure his machine didn't hit the escarpment, most of the bullets were fired as the pilot began to pull the stick back and were, therefore, wasted on the rocky face, well above the heads of the sheltering troops ... [but] two of its straying bullets caught the end of the camouflage net and went straight through the wing fabric of one of the Hurricanes, missing the spar by inches."

A system of red and green Very lights was devised in conjunction with the RDF unit and this gave the Hurricanes a certain amount of immunity from the marauding

Messerschmitts which attempted to catch them when landing. Moulding recalled one such flight:

> "I was given a recce to go outside the area and told to look at a Bedouin encampment because the army was quite certain it was full of Germans. I went off and found the camp and let them have all eight guns in one go – if there were Germans inside, well jolly good – but if there were women and children and dogs, it leaves a nasty feeling. That's what happened to me. I didn't like that very much but the army was adamant we had to find out."

Air Chief Marshal Longmore sent a cable to the Air Ministry in London, explaining the precarious position in which his force now found itself:

> "We have to maintain periodic offensive patrols over Tobruk by refuelling at Sidi Barrani. Fully realise that this will give enemy, which you must remember are both German and Italian, far too free a hand over Tobruk but am convinced that at the moment there is no alternative. 73 Squadron losses in personnel and aircraft when operating from Tobruk were prohibitive. Under those conditions they were being outnumbered in their encounters with large formations to the tune of seven or eight to one. They have had three squadron commanders in two weeks. Tedder has seen the remnants of them in the desert today and reports that the majority of the pilots will have to be replaced at once. Including four operational/serviceable aircraft left in 73, total immediately available Hurricanes in the Western Desert today was 14. We are taking every possible step to re-establish the position but I am sure you will agree that when our fighters do engage the enemy they must do it with reasonable strength – i.e. we must employ occasional strong patrols instead of trying to cover long periods with penny packets. When we have sufficient Hurricanes to maintain air cover of refuelling at Tobruk, we shall resume refuelling and rearming there. Without such cover, aircraft on the ground at Tobruk are a hostage to fortune we cannot afford."

On learning of the news of the withdrawal of 73 Squadron, the Prime Minister recalled:

> "General Wavell reported that the air fighter situation was serious. All Hurricanes in Greece had been lost, and as a result of recent enemy air attacks on Tobruk a large proportion of Hurricanes there had been destroyed or damaged. Air Marshal [sic] Longmore considered that any further attempt to maintain a fighter squadron inside Tobruk would only result in heavy loss to no purpose. Thus the enemy would have complete air superiority over Tobruk until a fresh fighter force could be built up. However, the garrison had beaten off an attack that morning, causing the enemy heavy casualties and taking 150 prisoners."

To the Chiefs of the Imperial General Staff he wrote:

> "We must not forget that the besieged are four or five times as strong as the

besiegers. There is no objection to their making themselves comfortable, but they must be very careful not to let themselves be ringed in by a smaller force, and consequently lose their offensive power upon the enemy's communications ... We must not put our standards too low in relation to the enemy."

The Hurricanes of 274 Squadron at Gerawla meanwhile continued to take the fight to the enemy, pilots being ordered to fly special missions in attempts to destroy transport aircraft and other ground targets in addition to carrying out TacR sorties. From one of the latter, on the afternoon of 26 April, Flg Off Tom Patterson (V7763) failed to return and it was learned later that he had encountered three Bf110s of 8/ZG26 at about 1630 west of Bardia. The Canadian promptly shot down the aircraft (WkNr3870) crewed by Lt Oskar Lemcke and Uffz Rudi Petters (his eighth victory), but then collided with that (WkNr3404/3U+JS) flown by Uffz Max Hohmann, which crash-landed near Sollum. Both Hohmann and his gunner Uffz Wünsche survived and were able to walk back to their base, but Patterson was killed, as were Lemcke and Petters. Later that afternoon, at 1840, loud explosions were heard by personnel at Gerawla from the direction of Mersa Matruh and all available Hurricanes were scrambled. Once airborne, the pilots were instructed to fly to Amseat, where it was believed that the three Bf110s which had carried out the raid had landed, but on arrival over the landing ground no enemy aircraft were observed. Next day (26 April), Sgt F.H. Dean (P3977) was sent on a special mission to destroy petrol lorries reported to be operating from Benina to the forward area. He returned safely to report the destruction of one bowser which went up in flames and four others thoroughly strafed.

A pilot from 6 Squadron at Qasaba, Plt Off R.A. Griffiths, was now attached to 274 Squadron to help with TacR sorties, but it was Plt Off Godden (V7780), flying such a sortie at dawn on 27 April, who encountered a Bf110 strafing troops at Buq-Buq. He engaged the Messerschmitt and it was seen to force-land near the escarpment south of Sollum, his sixth victory. A further successful sortie was flown by Flg Off Weller in a long-range Hurricane (P3977) when he strafed ten Ju52/3m at Benina. One of the transports was seen to burst into flames following his attack, and he claimed a further seven damaged. Weller, who had carried out a similar lone attack against Gazala a few days earlier, was awarded an immediate DFC. The Ju52s at Benina had earlier been sighted by a reconnaissance Maryland crew from 39 Squadron, whose Canadian pilot Flt Lt 'Butch' Lewis[8] related a graphic description of his subsequent attack:

"We had completed our recce and were coming back over Benina, when we were confronted by a sight of what looked like a hundred Ju52s lined up wingtip to wingtip. It was too good to miss, but it was not our job to attack, so I called up the crew and asked them what they thought about it. 'Let's wreck them, sir', they said. So from about two and a half miles up in the air I pointed the nose down into a steep dive. It looked as if the Junkers had just landed, for

---

[8] Flt Lt W.M. Lewis had flown Blenheims during the Battle of France, had been shot down, evaded capture and reached England aboard a stolen French aircraft.

there were groups of soldiers gathered about the landing ground. We dived right down to about 50 feet, and flashed along the line of German aircraft giving them all we had. One of the aircraft burst into flames immediately, and smoke poured from others. The soldiers were too startled to raise their rifles. They just closed up like penknives and toppled to the ground. As we mowed through them at the bottom of our dive, the belly of our aircraft must have almost been skimming the ground. My observer told me afterwards that we had done a good job. My other gunner fired a burst into a CR42 which was standing away from the line of German aircraft."

Four of the transports, aircraft of KGrzbV.104, were totally destroyed in these attacks and others were damaged. Lewis was also decorated for this feat but other Maryland crews were not so fortunate to escape the attention of I/JG27's Messerschmitts, Oblt Gerhard Homuth, Staffelkapitän of 3 Staffel, shooting down two during this period (one of which he claimed as a Blenheim). Homuth's protégé, Obfhr Marseille, also added to his score on 28 April when he shot down a Blenheim of 45 Squadron over Tobruk. This aircraft had been sent specially to evacuate staff officers of 258 Wing HQ, including Wg Cdr Johnson, the commanding officer. Also on board was Sqn Ldr the Rev J.E. Cox, Chaplain to the RAF in the Western Desert. The Blenheim's demise was witnessed by *BUP* correspondent Yindrich:

" ... a Blenheim came roaring down over our heads at about 50 feet. There was a terrific rattle of machine-gun fire and at first I thought the Blenheim had made a mistake and was firing at us, or choosing an awkward spot to clear her guns. Bullets whistled around, so we dived into a slit trench. A Messerschmitt, hot on the tail of the Blenheim, was responsible for the bullets. The Blenheim roared down the wadi, out to sea, trying to escape, but the Messerschmitt was too close. The Blenheim fell out of the sky and crashed into the sea. The plane disappeared completely, not leaving a trace. The Messerschmitt banked and flew inland again."

Although all seven[9] on board lost their lives, it was a lucky let off for Bob Low of *Liberty Magazine* who had been due to depart aboard the ill-fated Blenheim, as he later related:

"My kit was put on board and I was to go. There were seven people on board and the pilot said that if it was urgent for me to go, he would take me, although that would make eight and a bit too much of a load. I said that I would wait until there was another plane. So I took my kit off and I did not go."

Ju87s and Bf110s continued to attack Tobruk and on 29 April HMT *Chalka*, an army transport vessel was sunk in harbour. One aircraft of 236^Squadriglia was badly damaged by AA fire and crash-landed in the desert. Next day the guns gained further revenge when a Stuka of StabII/StG2 was shot down, both pilot and gunner being killed. A German war correspondent, R.W. Billhardt, writing for the Berlin

---

[9] Lost on board the heavily-overcrowded Blenheim, in addition to Wg Cdr Johnson and Sqn Ldr the Rev Cox, were the pilot Plt Off B.C.deG. Allan and his air gunner Sgt L.W. Morling, plus Sqn Ldr D.P. Barclay, Plt Off S.E. Bellow, and Capt R.S. Oughwright, an army officer.

Nationblatt gave a glowing account of these attacks:

"Over Tobruk the sky is seldom silent. The sound of our motors continually terrifies the Tommies, chases them to their guns and forces them to hang the sky with steel curtains and black anti-aircraft clouds, until dive attacks by our Stukas with bombs and machine-gun fire destroy them or force them to take cover. The anti-aircraft artillery of Tobruk enjoyed our highest respect – once. Then the Stukas dropped their bombs, and since then the anti-aircraft shelling from Tobruk has become very much weaker. After each attack the younger pilots are twice as eager next day to fly still more madly into the middle of the anti-aircraft barrage – to get on to their objectives still more exactly. To batter Tobruk till it is ready for storming will be a nice piece of work."

73 Squadron returned to the fray on the last day of the month, albeit in a limited role owing to lack of aircraft and pilots, many of whom had been posted to the Delta for a rest, while Flg Off Goodman and Plt Offs Chatfield and McDougall were recalled to duty. Another French pilot, Plt Off Jean Pompéï of 274 Squadron, was now attached to 73 Squadron where he joined his fellow countrymen Denis, Littolf and Ballatore, while other new arrivals included Plt Offs R.H. Likeman, J.S. Logan, F.M. Moss, J. Irwin and J.H. Ward, all inexperienced pilots from the Middle East Pool. Sgt John Berridge, also an inexperienced pilot, transferred from 3RAAF Squadron about this time but was killed two or three weeks later in a flying accident. Starting at dawn, four Hurricanes were sent off singly at hourly intervals to strafe M/T travelling between Gazala East, Gambut and Sollum, but Littolf was the only one to find a large convoy – which comprised an estimated 80 vehicles – destroying at least six of these. The others found small isolated convoys and destroyed at least four vehicles, while Pompéï encountered a Hs126 of 2(H)/14 near Gambut which he shot down. He reported that it crashed and turned over on landing. 274 Squadron also despatched aircraft at similar intervals on ground strafing sorties, Flg Off Charles Greenhill's aircraft (V7734) being seen to spin in while attempting to destroy an abandoned fuel dump near Buq-Buq; he was killed in the crash. While out searching for a convoy between Sidi Omar and Sofafi, Plt Off Godden (V7825) encountered four Bf110s strafing British troops, shooting down one and damaging a second, but Flg Off Doug Spence (V7555) was shot down and killed. From the location of his gun site Lt Rankin witnessed the action:

"... saw a dogfight between a Hurricane and two ME109s. The Hurricane put up a marvellous show and must have been a most experienced pilot. Then the most awful thing happened – he finished his fight and came away, ammunition expended, to land at the emergency landing ground. Some mad LAA gunners started shooting at him, and to my horror, shot him down in a great burst of black smoke from only about 300 feet. This was one of the worst things I had yet seen in the war and oh how I cursed and swore at those complete idiots!"

It seems probable that Spence's aircraft had been damaged in the fight with the Messerschmitts, since Oblt Redlich of 1/JG27 reported shooting down a Hurricane which had been strafing M/T between Gazala and Sollum. Presumably Spence, pursued by the Messerschmitts, had made for the comparative safety of Tobruk's defences, only to be shot down by them.

That evening, four hours before midnight, Axis forces attempted to penetrate the perimeter defences again, this time in the south-west at Ras el-Medauar. Rommel's plan was for the 5th Light Division to attack from the right of Ras el-Medauar, a small hill, and the 15th Panzer Division from the left, while assault groups from the Italian *Ariete* and *Brescia* Divisions would hold the flanks, and German troops would push eastwards to Fort Pilastrino and the harbour – but the Australian defenders were resolute. General Morshead sent 20 tanks to challenge the German armour and, although five were lost, the enemy gave up its attempt to advance along the perimeter. Although sporadic fighting continued for a further two days, the assault fizzled out, the Germans having made only minor gains.

May opened with yet another heavy air attack on Tobruk, unopposed by the RAF, as noted by Lt Rankin:

> "There was a terrific air raid – all kinds of German planes all over the sky, and some very rude things were said about the RAF. The battle continued all morning. Then some ships came into the harbour and we feared the worst on their behalf. Everyone feeling too depressed for words. Too much work, too few men, the great heat, cases of nerves, enemy tanks, all contributing to the depression. But the complete lack of RAF support was what upset most people."

73 and 274 Squadrons had endeavoured to help the beleaguered garrison, the latter unit despatching six Hurricanes when news of the latest attack reached them at Gerawla. On arrival over the Tobruk area Bf110s were sighted but, before they could be engaged, eight escorting Bf109s of 3/JG27 intercepted. In a series of whirling dogfights both Flt Lt Honor (W9269) and Flg Off Agazarian (V7829) claimed Messerschmitts destroyed, and Plt Off Hutt (V7755) claimed a probable but was then hit by another and carried out an emergency landing at El Gubbi. A second badly damaged Hurricane, V7482 flown by Sgt Milburn, also crash-landed at El Gubbi, but 7-victory ace Plt Off Stan Godden (V7825) was shot down in flames and killed. Flt Lt Honor later related a rather distorted picture of the action:

> "We were patrolling the area when we saw four ME110s engaged in bombing. We dived down and as we did so we became involved with the escort of ME109s. There was a hectic dogfight. The combat was, however, of short duration and three ME109s, one of them in flames, were seen crashing away to the ground a few minutes later. The other German aircraft scattered."

The 'Messerschmitt' seen falling in flames was undoubtedly Godden's Hurricane, since only one Bf109 (WkNr3805) was damaged in this action in which Gfr Hermann Köhne was wounded, and he managed to reach Derna safely. Oblt Homuth and Obfhr Marseille each claimed two Hurricanes shot down, the Staffelkapitän reporting that one of his victims baled out. It would seem the fourth Hurricane claimed by the Messerschmitts was V7814 of 6 Squadron, as noted by Plt Off Moulding:

> "The Messerschmitts seemed to take-off when we took-off – they were only

20 miles outside the perimeter. You could see them take-off and you could only fly round for about 20 minutes, otherwise they'd get you. That's what happened to Pat Pike – he didn't get down quick enough. I saw him coming into land and was hoping he wouldn't because I could see what was going to happen – a Messerschmitt was following him on his approach. A two-seconds burst, and that was that. He managed to pull up but got a couple of bullets in his backside. Everybody including the padre went out to help in case the Hurricane caught fire, and got him out."

Flg Off Pike was taken to the hospital where Capt Devine treated his wounds; the Australian MO recorded the gist of the conversation in his diary:

"[He] told me how four Messerschmitts had waited until his landing flaps were down and his wheels had touched the ground before shooting him up. His was one of the last remaining Hurricanes here, and he had been told to stay out to sea until twelve Messerschmitts circling over the drome area had gone away. When the wireless people gave him the all-clear, he came in to land. Then the wireless suddenly warned him there were four Messerschmitts a few hundred yards behind, on his tail. His plane was shot to pieces. He was furious that they had bothered to warn him when it was too late to be of use, for he said the few seconds of suspense before the cannons opened fire on him were the worst. In fact he seemed angrier with the wireless people than with the enemy."

73 Squadron had also despatched six Hurricanes but two of these went unserviceable at Sidi Barrani where they landed to top up their tanks. The remaining four flew to the Tobruk area but by then the raiders had departed. It was left to the guns to defend Tobruk the following day (2 May) when Bf110s of III/ZG26 carried out fighter-bomber attacks, these meeting fierce resistance resulting in four of the Messerschmitts being shot down, one of which crashed within the perimeter with the capture of the crew; the other three force-landed, one reaching Gazala with a wounded pilot on board.

From Gerawla four Hurricanes of 274 Squadron, now under the command of Sqn Kdr G.E. Hawkins, a former flight commander of 33 Squadron, were despatched to carry out ground strafing of M/T between Tobruk and Sollum, the operation being flown in conjunction with a single fighter Blenheim IVF which carried a gun-pack in the bomb bay with four forward-firing .303 Brownings. Approximately 20 M/T and two staff cars were thoroughly strafed on the El Adem-Sidi Aziez road. On their return to Gerawla, one of the Hurricane pilots told an enquiring *Egyptian Mail* war correspondent:

"We definitely fixed up some of the trucks and we shot down a good number of enemy troops as they piled out of the vehicles and ran for cover. We saw them tumbling down under our fire."

It was a relatively quiet day for 73 Squadron at Sidi Haneish, Hurricanes being scrambled on one occasion to investigate aircraft over Mersa Matruh but these turned out to be RAF machines which had either not identified themselves or had wandered out of the specified air corridors. Next day (3 May), the Squadron carried out a number of ground strafing sorties during which several M/T were claimed destroyed. On one of these sorties Sous-Lt Denis engaged three Bf110s near Bardia but the fight was inconclusive.

A Flt/6 Squadron was finally ordered to withdraw from Tobruk on 8 May since it was impossible to continue operating owing to the repeated shelling and dive-bombing. There remained just one flyable Hurricane (P5173) and three pilots cut cards to see who would fly it back to Egypt. The successful pilot was Plt Off Moulding:

"The prop wouldn't go into pitch so the Flight Sergeant hammered it into half fine, half coarse. Took off into darkness. Blinded by sand I almost crashed into Tobruk harbour. I thought I was flying eastwards and it wasn't until half an hour before sunrise that I realised I was flying northwards, out over the sea. I set course for Qasaba to refuel, where I ground-looped but didn't do any damage. I then flew to Dekheila."

The four Lysanders departed at the same time, the wounded Flg Off Pike being evacuated in one, as he later recalled:

"From Tobruk hospital I was moved to the top aerodrome for evacuation by air and was looked after by Mike Beytagh, the MO and the IO. I believe they were all that was left of 73 Squadron. We were all pretty bomb happy and I believe we lived in a cave in a wadi near the landing ground. Eventually I was evacuated by air to Heliopolis."

Tobruk no longer possessed its own air force. That the Hurricanes and Lysanders had performed heroically was not denied by German war correspondent Billhardt's report:

"Tobruk is not only a town to be defended but a huge defensive system, well built-up and cleverly suited to the ground. In this defensive system ships have played a great part; we have sunk or seriously damaged them. The harbour was important – it was, because our Stukas have smashed up the quays. English fighters played a decisive part. They have had to give up the role which our Messerschmitts and Italian fighters have now taken over . . ."

With the departure of the last operational Hurricane and the remaining two Lysanders, Tobruk no longer possessed its own air force. And, following the withdrawal of A Flt/6 Squadron, official RAF war correspondent Sqn Kdr George Houghton lamented:

"Somewhere in Cyrenaica, probably in Tobruk, there is an old board which has *West Ham* lettered on it in fading white. When the last war broke out, 6 Squadron was already eight months old. At the end of August 1914 news came that the squadron would go immediately to France. During embarkation leave one or two of the gayer spirits were feasting with friends in London. An adventurous pilot climbed on to the top of a London horse bus and commandeered the destination board. Since that day in 1914, the *West Ham* board has been part and parcel of the Squadron. Pilots came and went, but always the board took its place on the lading vehicle when the Squadron was on the move. All over France it went in the last war; then, during peace, out it came to the Middle East, Sudan, Somaliland, Eritrea, Palestine, Iraw, Syria,

Western Desert, Libya. When time came to withdraw the squadron from Tobruk, the pilots flew out and the groundcrews came out by destroyer. For the first time in 27 years the Squadron moved without their lucky talisman. The board was lost."

Tobruk remained under siege and now its air defence relied on 73 and 274 Squadrons providing patrols from Sidi Haneish and Gerawla, using Sidi Barrani as an advanced landing ground, with 6 Squadron flying TacR sorties from Qasaba. The harbour and garrison were left to the mercy of the dive-bombers, its immediate defence in the hands of the gunners. It was time for consolidation for the Axis troops surrounding the garrison, impatiently awaiting the Stukas to pound the defences into submission, as Panzer Lt Schorm confided to his diary with some scepticism:

"Dive-bombers begin their work again. Let us hope they will accomplish something this time. Up to present they have done nothing to speak of. It is only over the harbour of the town that there are strong defences. In the fortified area they could circle around quietly and make out quite a lot, and then pop in – so what! The commander dives, chucks his eggs haphazardly, and of course the thirty follow his example. Blockheads!"

War correspondent Yindrich, still eagerly recording events as they happened, wrote of this period:

"I met OC Ack-Ack in the tunnel. He had just completed a report of the aerial activity over Tobruk during the period 9 April to 30 April and the part played by the anti-aircraft batteries. In that period, Tobruk area received 677 [sic] visits from German planes, of which 386 were from JU87s, 120 from JU88s, 83 from ME109s, 37 from ME110s, 11 from Dorniers [sic], 4 [sic] from Henschels and 32 from unidentified planes. The ack-ack batteries had shot down 31 planes, or over one a day, and the RAF had brought down approximately 60 [sic], or over two a day, so that in three weeks the Germans have lost 91 planes, or thirty a week [sic]. But the RAF no longer operate from the Tobruk area. The German pilots have roused the gruding admiration of the troops for the daring way in which they dive through a hail of exploding anti-aircraft shells when they bomb the harbour. They still dive almost vertically at their target, but generally at an angle of 75 degrees, until only a few hundred feet from the surface of the water and then release their bombs. They peel off and follow each other down, then back up and down again, in an endless chain. Occasionally, if the ack-ack bursts get near, one pilot will pull out of his dive sooner than the others . . . [adding] 'Digger' Black [Wg Cdr Black] told us an interesting thing about the German pilots raiding Tobruk. He said that one shot down had a diary which showed that 36 hours before he was shot down over Tobruk, he was bombing London. Looks as though the Germans are getting short of planes or pilots, or both."

Despite the lack of its own air defence the garrison was undoubtedly determined to hold on, enouraged by a message received from Prime Minister Churchill:

"The whole Empire is watching your steadfast and spirited defence of this important outpost of Egypt with gratitude and admiration."

CHAPTER VII

TOBRUK STALEMATE:
OPERATIONS *BREVITY* & *MERCURY*

May 1941

"You saw little of the RAF and may have thought yourselves deserted by them;
I can assure you that, in circumstances of extreme difficulty, they did all they
could to come to your assistance, and suffered heavy casualties in doing so."

General Wavell to survivors of the evacuation of Crete

Severe sandstorms with very hot winds persisted throughout the daylight hours of
9 May and all flying was cancelled over the battle front. With an improvement in
the weather next day, 274 Squadron despatched two long-range Hurricanes to carry
out reconnaissance of the forward areas. Sgt Glover (P3469) sighted a Bf109 taking
off from Gazala South landing ground as he approached, reporting that after a brief
engagement he shot it down. He then returned to the landing ground on which
approximately 50 aircraft could be seen and strafed four or five Messerschmitts
before escaping unscathed and returning safely to Sidi Haneish. Another Bf109 was
claimed shot down the following day (11 May) by Plt Off Griffiths of 6 Squadron
(V7753) on a photo-reconnaissance sortie covering M/T concentrations outside
Tobruk. He was engaged by three Messerschmitts but managed to get in a telling
burst at one, which was apparently seen to crash by the army unit over which the
action took place.

During this period of relative inactivity, a number of dummy Hurricanes were
constructed at El Gubbi in an attempt to bluff the Germans, as Pat Marsh of 73
Squadron recalled:

"... the Royal Engineers built five or six dummy Hurricanes from wood, which
we helped assemble and mounted on 50-gallon oil drums. It was our job to
move them now and again and to drive a lorry round and round at the back to
stir up clouds of dust, with a bit of luck foxing Jerry into thinking we were
running up engines ready for take off."

Over the preceding few days Hurricanes of 1SAAF Squadron had begun arriving at
Sidi Haneish from Alexandria where they had been operating in defence of the great

port. Under the command of Maj T. Ross-Theron, the Squadron had seen much action in East Africa and had gained an impressive number of victories against the Italians but facing the Messerschmitts of I/JG27 would present severe problems for the young pilots. The senior flight commander and most successful pilot was Capt Ken Driver, who had recently been awarded the DFC for nine victories, although Lt Bob Talbot had rejoined the unit following his service with 274 Squadron, a unit with which he had gained some seven victories, and Lts Smith and Tennant[1] from 3RAAF. While 204 Group struggled to find sufficient Hurricanes to meet its needs, both German and Italian air forces were increasing in strength, new units and replacement aircraft flying in from Sicily. For the continuing assault on Tobruk's defences and the British forward ground units, these were dispersed mainly in the Derna area:

Luftwaffe – FliegerFührer Afrika (GenMaj Stefan Fröhlich)

Ain el	I/JG27	Bf109E	Hptm Eduard Neumann
Gazala	1/JG27		Oblt Karl-Heinz Redlich
	2/JG27		Hptm Erich Gerlitz
	3/JG27		Oblt Gerhard Homuth
Derna	StabIII/ZG26	Bf110E	Maj Karl Kaschka
	8/ZG26	Bf110E	Oblt Fritz Schulze-Dickow
	8/LG1	Ju88A	
	2(H)/14	Bf110E, Hs126, Fi156	
	II/StG1	Ju87R	Hptm Anton Keil
	II/StG2	Ju87R	Maj Walter Enneccerus

7 and 8 Staffeln of III/StG1 had returned to Sicily in early May in preparation for operations over Crete, their place taken temporarily by II/StG1 from Sicily until the return of I/StG1, from which 3 Staffel arrived on 19 May, the other two Staffeln following a month later. At Benina was based the Ju88Ds of 1(F)/121 and He111Hs of II/KG26. The total number of aircraft available to FliegerFührer Afrika seldom exceeded 150 at this time, comprising approximately 40 Ju87s, 30 Ju88s and He111s, 40 Bf109s, 10 Bf110s and 30 reconnaissance Ju88s, Bf110s, Hs126s and Fi156s.

Regia Aeronautica – 5^Squadra Aerea

Derna	2°Gruppo CT	G50bis	TenCol Giuseppe Baylon
	150^Squadriglia		Cap Tullio De Prato
	152^Squadriglia		Cap Salvatore Teja
	358^Squadriglia		Cap Annibale Sterzi
	85^Squadriglia	CR42	Cap Cesare Giuntella
	95^Squadriglia		Cap Gino Lodi

---

[1] Both Lts Smith and Tennant were soon lost on operations with 1SAAF, the former on 17 June 1941 and the latter on 2 August 1941, both victims of the Messerschmitts.

236^Squadriglia Aut B.a'T	Ju87R	Cap Giovanni Santinoni
239^Squadriglia Aut B.a'T	Ju87R	Cap Giuseppe Cenni

With the arrival of 239^Squadriglia, 236^Squadriglia withdrew its battle-scarred Ju87s to Castel Benito, where it re-equipped with the CR42.

Martuba	20°Gruppo Aut CT	G50bis	Magg Mario Bonzano
	151^Squadriglia		Cap Mario Montefusco
	352^Squadriglia		Cap Luigi Borgogno
	353^Squadriglia		Cap Roccardo Roveda
Berka	98°Gruppo BT	BR20M	TenCol Vito De Vittembecchi
	240^Squadriglia		Cap Ugo Machieraldo
	241^Squadriglia		Cap Alfredo Sordini
Benghazi K2	18°Gruppo CT	CR42	TenCol Ferruccio Vosilla
	83^Squadriglia		Cap Edoardo Molinari
	279^Squadriglia AS	SM79sil	Cap Orazio Bernardini
	175^Squadriglia RST (detach)	SM79	
Ain el Gazala	115^Squadriglia OA	Ca310	

In support of the front-line units, 5^Squadra Aerea could speedily call up reserves based in Tripolitania. One of the units about to move forward was MC200-equipped 374^Squadriglia of 153°Gruppo Aut CT (Cap Andrea Favini) at Castel Benito, which would soon introduce this useful fighter to the North African campaign. Also arriving were fighter-bomber versions of the versatile CR42. Fitted with underwing bomb racks, supplementary fuel tanks and an armoured seat for the pilot, the aircraft had been specially adapted for operations over Tobruk. A number of these were about to be issued to 18°Gruppo CT at Benghazi K2. 151°Gruppo CT was currently based at Mellaha with CR42s under the command of Magg Antonio Giachino, and comprised 366^Squadriglia (Cap Bernardino Serafini), 367^Squadriglia (Cap Giuseppe Costantini), and 368^Squadriglia (Cap Giuseppe Zuffi). Another unit being held in reserve, at Sorman, was CR42-equipped 276^Squadriglia CT under Cap Ippolito Lalatta.

Bomber support was provided by 53°Gruppo BT at Misurata (Magg Rosario Di Blasi) with SM79-equipped 216^ and 217^Squadriglie; 28°Gruppo BT, similarly equipped and also at Misurata with 10^ and 19^Squadriglie (Magg Michel Bianchino), from where 174^ and 175^Squadriglie RST also operated SM79s and 129^Squadriglia Ca311s.

* * *

On the morning of 12 May, Maj Ross-Theron and Capt K.A. Quirk of 1 SAAF patrolled over the front-line, meeting three Italian twin-engined aircraft, possibly a flight of Ca310s of 115^Squadriglia OA from Gazala on a reconnaissance patrol. As the Hurricanes manoeuvred for an attack, two of the aircraft dived away to the south but the third turned westwards and dived to sea level. Two attacks were carried out on this aircraft as it crossed the coast between Sidi Barrani and Sollum but it made good its escape, possibly with some damage inflicted. In the afternoon, SAAF Hurricanes were despatched in pairs at ten-minute intervals to carry out patrols between Buq-Buq and Sofafi in an effort to hamper the German advance. One Hurricane was damaged when Lt M.S. Uys force-landed due to lack of fuel following a strafing attack. They were joined in these activities by Hurricanes from 73 and 274 Squadrons, the latter unit losing Flg Off K.P. English (V7820) who was shot down by ground fire. By the evening the German columns had turned back, leaving a number of burning vehicles in their wake. Still operating from Qasaba, 6 Squadron was well into its stride flying mainly tactical reconnaissances with the occasional photographic sortie, usually managing to avoid the marauding Messerschmitts from Gazala although on this date Flg Off Scott (P3967) was intercepted by three Bf110s when approaching the Sidi Suleiman area. He fired one burst in defence before his guns jammed and was able to escape without damage to his aircraft. As with many of the landing grounds, Qasaba was a fairly barren place as noted by Plt Off Moulding:

"Qasaba landing ground was no more than a bit of level desert which had been cleared of stones and camel thorn. It was about 40 miles east of Mersa Matruh and 90 or so from the Sollum escarpment which, at this time, marked, roughly, the front-line between the opposing armies. It was a well laid-out camp. The so-called 'sea party' had been there before and to them it was like coming home again. They pitched their tents in the same old spots and trod again the paths to the best bathing beaches. Within a week [of evacuating Tobruk] four more Hurricanes had been delivered. All four Lysander pilots had done circuits and bumps, familiarisation flights and gunnery practice in the Hurricanes and at least one short operation each. Reconnaissance activity was kept to a minimum; never more than three sorties a day. The army requirements, relayed to them at Ma'aten Bagush, were modest. A quick look here, a quick look there, but nothing detailed; no photographs, no definite identifications required. Just a general picture."

Operation *Brevity*

With the Germans having occupied Sollum and Capuzzo, Wavell mounted a hastily-conceived offensive operation (codenamed Operation *Brevity*) designed to drive them out before Rommel could use his armoured force to strike into Egypt. Wavell, secure in the knowledge that a convoy had just reached Alexandria with 238 tanks and 43 crated Hurricanes on board, now had back-up forces should the latest offensive fail. He was aware that Axis troop convoys were experiencing severe problems with vehicles and troops worn out and weary following the long haul from Tripoli, and he wanted to strike whilst the iron was hot. The destruction and disruption of supplies of fuel and ammunition carried aboard these convoys would prove vital to the forthcoming battle and Air Commodore Collishaw ordered his squadrons to concentrate on these targets, but severe duststorms prevented any telling attacks for several days before the commencement of the British offensive, set for 15 May. The three squadrons of Hurricanes were tasked to provide standing patrols over the advancing troops and to avoid combat unless enemy aircraft attacked the armoured vehicles and M/T. Collishaw sent a signal to his squadron commanders:

> "We are on the eve of a major effort by our army to defeat the enemy and to advance to the relief of our besieged garrison at Tobruk. The RAF will contribute to the success of our arms. Commanding Officers are to acquaint all ranks with the necessity to defeat the enemy wherever he is found."

With the approach of the British force, the Germans began withdrawing along the Capuzzo-Bardia-Tobruk road, sections of Hurricanes departing Sidi Barrani at ten minute-intervals. Flying out to sea, they recrossed the coast at Tobruk and then attacked the retreating vehicles. A section from 274 Squadron encountered Bf109s of 3/JG27 escorting Ju87s in the Sofafi-Halfaya-Sidi Aziez area, Flt Lt Honor (W9269) claiming one Messerschmitt shot down with a second probably so, while Plt Off Hutt (V7831) also claimed a probable, but Sgt Frank Dean (V7829) was shot down and killed by Oblt Homuth, the Staffelkapitän. A Bf109 (WkNr3213) force-landed at Derna with engine damage, presumably as a result of Honor's attack. 6 Squadron was called upon to fly as many sorties are required, Flg Off Hardiman (V7710), who had recently been posted in from 208 Squadron, flying one such sortie to the Sollum-Gambut area shortly after midday, located 34 enemy tanks moving towards Capuzzo from Bardia. A further 20 were sighted three miles west of Bardia. During this sortie nine Bf109s passed by without noticing the low-flying Hurricane. Having safely avoided detection, Hardiman encountered a Hs126 which took evasive action and escaped after being damaged by his first burst. Several other reconnaissances were carried out during the day, the final sortie being flown between 1700-1930 by Plt Off Moulding (V7777), who sighted a number of Messerschmitt patrols before returning safely to Qasaba.

By nightfall Halfaya Pass had been recaptured and Fort Capuzzo occupied but the British had suffered heavy losses in tanks and many units were exposed to air attack. Fearing the worse, the British commander, Brigadier William Gott, ordered a withdrawal which allowed Rommel to push forward with his armour. The Hurricanes were ordered to attack landing grounds and M/T on the morning of 16 May, Lts Talbot and Uys of 1SAAF meeting a Ju87 head-on at 400 feet near Gazala. Talbot opened fire, setting it on fire, and then swung round onto its tail and shot it down. A wounded crewman was seen to emerge from the wreck. Other SAAF pilots were out and about, Capt Quirk and Lt H.J.P. Burger strafing M/T and light tanks near Acroma. AA fire hit Burger's aircraft and he belly-landed a mile west of the town. Quirk circled overhead and saw his colleague set fire to the Hurricane. He also saw German troops approaching and decided to land nearby in an attempt to rescue Burger. Both men squeezed into the cockpit with Burger sitting on Quirk's lap, the latter having discarded his parachute pack. The heavily-laden Hurricane shedded its tailwheel as it became airborne but Quirk made a creditable landing at

Sidi Haneish, and was awarded an immediate DSO for this action. 73 Squadron similarly despatched pairs of Hurricanes throughout the day, Plt Off John Irwin (V7424) returning slightly wounded by shrapnel. For the second day running 274 Squadron met Bf109s of I/JG27, Sgt Glover (P3469) claiming one shot down near Gambut but the Squadron lost Flg Off Noel Agazarian (V6633), victim of Fw Franz Elles of 2 Staffel. One of the unit's French pilots, 35-year-old Flg Off Daniel Clostre (W9302), a native of Pornic, was also shot down and killed, the victim of ground fire. During a later sortie Hurricanes were tasked to accompany five Blenheim IVFs of 45 Squadron on a ground strafing operation, one of the latter also falling to the Messerschmitts. The British intention to re-establish superiority east of the Egyptian/Libyan border had failed completely; indeed, Operation *Brevity* had proved to be just that – brief.

While these ground and air actions were being fought over the border area, the Tobruk garrison also came under further pressure from Rommel's forces resulting in fighting and skirmishing on the northern flank of the salient, lasting three days. But the defences held and the latest assault repulsed. The German press, with surprising frankness, explained to a disappointed public, unaccustomed to military reversals, the problem facing Rommel:

> "The British garrison is offering considerably more resistance than was expected, and at the same time is harassing our forces by constant patrol actions. The defence lines around Tobruk, which were erected by the Italians, are quite good, but the artillery fire of the British garrison has an intensity comparable with that of the Battle of the Somme in the last war. Our troops suffer from a lack of water and enormous heat, but it can be safely assumed that the British garrison suffer even more, as all water pipes and reservoirs at Tobruk have been destroyed by Stuka dive-bomber action. Lack of heavy artillery is a setback to our operations, as the Stuka is insufficient to replace heavy guns."

During one raid bombs blew up one of Tobruk's largest ammunition dumps and for some weeks the guns were limited to ten rounds per gun per day. Fortunately, there was almost unlimited ammunition for the captured Italian medium-range guns. The garrison continued to rely on destroyers to bring in supplies and reinforcements, unload and get away under cover of darkness.

Meanwhile, 274 Squadron continued to send out sections of Hurricanes on ground strafing duties, Flg Off Ross (W9268) and Wt Off Coudray (V7821) shooting up 16 M/T on the Trigh Capuzzo road on 17 May, leaving one on fire and the others damaged, Plt Off A.J.C. Hamilton (P3469) strafing a Bf109 sighted on the El Adem landing ground the following day. 6 Squadron's Flg Off Scott narrowly avoided becoming a victim of the Messerschmitts on 19 May when his Hurricane (V7721) was intercepted by five of the deadly fighters near Capuzzo during the early afternoon. He evaded and raced for home. Six lorries were attacked by 274 Squadron's Sgt Glover (P3469) on this date, one of which was left in flames, while next day Flt Lt Honor (P3977) reported shooting down a Bf110 which attempted to take off from Mechili landing ground, before setting fire to a Ju52 on the ground. He also strafed a number of lorries, two of which were left ablaze.

21 May proved to be a disastrous day for the Blenheims of 14 Squadron, seven of which were tasked to bomb transport on the Capuzzo-Tobruk road early in the morning. They were intercepted by Bf109s of I/JG27, five of the bombers falling to the Messerschmitts with the loss of all 15 crew members. Shortly thereafter, at 0930, three Hurricanes of 73 Squadron flew to Sidi Barrani from where they were to carry out a similar attack, as noted by Sous-Lt Denis:

"With Pompéï and Ballatore I went to Sidi Barrani for a supply-line attack. During take-off, Ballatore [V7429] touched a water tank and damaged his propeller, so I went with Pompéï only. Instead of flying very low, as we usually did, I decided to take some altitude. When we arrived near the target, I dived quite steeply and realised my wingman was following shyly. Pompéï was a very good pilot but had never trained as a fighter pilot[2]. Worried to see he was following so far behind, I kept looking back and noticed a ME109 attacking him. Having no radio, I could not warn him. He was hit and then the ME109 flew in my direction. I acted as if I hadn't seen him, but never stopped watching, and when he was within range I throttled back violently and skidded to the left. Since I was going very fast, my Hurricane [V7859] reacted violently. I saw the hail [of bullets] pass on my right, and the ME109 could not slow down and flew in front of me. We then started a dogfight, for which the Hurricane was quite good due to its manoeuvrability. At that moment my plane was flying nose up, hooked to its propeller, when I saw the ME109 in the sun. I fired a burst so close that we almost collided. I noticed my bullets enter its fuselage.

After that I had to return to base. I was 180 miles inside enemy lines and I had the rest of the German unit behind me. They wanted to avenge their friend. I headed for Sidi Barrani, flying very low, a mere ten feet high. I must say that they were not very skilful, otherwise they would have had me. I could see their bullets hit the sand, exploding just in front of me. I was flying at full power. I landed without any bullets in my plane. But everybody had shot at me, first the German fighters and then the allied infantry when I flew above the lines. I was furious after landing. I asked a mechanic to refuel and rearm the plane. During this time I sat in the sand and, after a moment, started to shake to a point that I couldn't stand up. I didn't feel afraid but I realised that if I didn't go back immediately I would never fly again on ops. As soon as the plane was ready, I took off and flew around in search of a target. I found only a truck and a cyclist. They paid for the fear I had felt."

Unbeknown to Denis, his main pursuer had apparently broken away on sighting two approaching Hurricanes, Capt Driver and Lt Jarvis of 1SAAF arriving on the scene just in time. They reported seeing a Messerschmitt on the tail of a Hurricane which appeared to have been hit since it made no attempt to manoeuvre, and that the German fighter veered away as the two SAAF Hurricanes closed in. On his return to Sidi Haneish, Denis submitted a claim for a Messerschmitt shot down and

---

[2] Plt Off Pompéï was another escapee from Syria and had commanded Free French Flt 3 (the Communications Flight) at Heliopolis before taking the Hurricane conversion course at 70 OTU, on completion of which he was posted initially to 274 Squadron and then 73 Squadron.

reported that he feared Pompéï was dead since he had not seen him bale out. Nonetheless, the popular, rotound and jovial Pompéï had survived his encounter with the Messerschmitts, although his version of events differs to that of Denis:

"I was flying with Lt Denis over enemy positions. The sun was shining, the air was cool, everything was quiet. Suddenly, I noticed a group of seven Messerschmitts flying an easterly course. Denis saw them at the same time and made the attack sign. I dived and turned. But there was another enemy plane over us and I saw a Messerschmitt dive vertically on Denis' tail. To warn him and try to frighten the German, I fired two or three bursts with deflection to be sure he'd see the tracers in front of him and stop his attack. In fact, he was so fast that my deflection shot was very precise: he received the bullets, flew over onto his back and crashed before he could shoot.

At about the same time I felt a violent shake and a pain in my right thigh. I saw a big hole in my right wing. Hot oil and glycol poured into my face from severed connections. I pulled off my goggles and protected my eyes with my hand. The engine temperature was 120 degrees, with no oil pressure. It was clear I wouldn't go any further. I decided to land near the coast. Three Messerschmitts were following me but, as they attacked one after the other, I only had one enemy at a time. When I saw a German arrive in the mirror, I started a turn, once to the left, once to the right. Then, to avoid losing space, I made only flat turns, just with the rudder. The enemy, seeing me flying flat, fired with no correction but, as I was skidding, it passed on my right or my left. I arrived over the coast, flying at 3,000 feet. Then, what was left of my glycol and oil started to vaporise into white smoke. The Germans thought I was in flames and stopped the fight. The engine seized and I glided down towards the coast. Close to the ground I found a place between rocks and decided to land, wheels-up. After a skid to the right, another to the left, the plane suddenly stopped against a rock. I undid my harness and jumped out. The Hurricane [V7813] had broken in three parts but did not burn. I returned to it, took the water bottle, the watch and the flare gun. I looked at my leg. My battle dress was torn and I was bleeding, but I could walk. I proceeded eastwards."[3]

Since only one badly-damaged Bf109 (WkNr1567) of I/JG27 crash-landed, near Tobruk, in which Obfhr Marseille of 3 Staffel survived unscathed, it would seem that both Denis and Pompéï had fired at the same aircraft. If, indeed, Denis was the victor, it would then be the second occasion on which he had forced Marseille to crash-land his Messerschmitt. Meanwhile, another section from 73 Squadron comprising Sous-Lt Littolf and Sgt Guillou strafed a motor convoy, one ammunition-carrying vehicle exploding following their attack. Both returned safely, but 274 Squadron lost two pilots during the day when the Magister they were flying from Sidi Haneish to Sidi Barrani disappeared. On learning of its non-arrival at its intended destination, two Hurricanes were despatched to search the route but no sign of the aircraft or the pilots, Flg Off Bert Ross and Plt Off Phil Hutt, was found. Next morning three Lysanders joined the search, sweeping from 25 miles

---

[3] See Appendix II for further details of Plt Off Pompéï's adventures and eventual rescue.

inland to the coast, but to no avail. 6 Squadron also lost a Hurricane (V7753) and the services of one of its experienced pilots when Plt Off Griffiths was seriously injured as a result of a crash-landing at Berg el-Arab during the day.

Next day (22 May) 1SAAF was instructed to despatch all available Hurricanes to Sidi Barrani but only three aircraft were ready, these being flown by Lts A.J. Botha, D.L. Taylor and Uys, who were ordered to carry out a standing patrol over the gunboat *Aphis* operating just offshore. As the section flew out to rendezvous with the gunboat, six or seven Ju87s were seen flying in a westerly direction. As soon as they spotted the Hurricanes, the Ju87s dived towards the sea with Botha following. He reported that he shot down one into the sea and, as he pulled up following the attack, found himself below another on which he delivered a belly attack. The dive-bomber apparently burst into flames and followed its companion into the sea.

Tobruk was about to take a side seat as the fighting in the Balkans reached a crescendo following the fall of Greece. There now remained one British outpost, the island of Crete.

Operation *Mercury*

At 0805 on the morning of 20 May, the first of almost 500 heavily-laden Ju52/3m troop-carrying transports and glider-tugs began disgorging paratroopers over the Maleme area. The invasion of Crete had begun, given the codename *Merkur* (*Mercury*) by the Germans. By 23 May the situation had reached crisis point and, with the island's sole Hurricane unit, 33 Squadron, having been decimated, RAF Egypt was ordered to become more involved in the fighting, with Air Commodore Collishaw's 204 Group being given responsibility for air operations over the island. Collishaw had little enough available to supplement the replacement Hurricanes already being despatched piecemeal to Crete. However, in the knowledge that two dozen Hurricanes (213 and 229 Squadrons) had just arrived in Egypt from the carrier *Furious*, via Malta, and would soon be available for operations, he ordered a strike by five Blenheims on the morning of 23 May against Maleme airfield which had been overrun by the German paratroops and was being used as a landing ground for Ju52s ferrying in more troops and supplies. An escort for the Blenheims was provided by three Hurricanes of 274 Squadron, each aircraft fitted with long-range, non-jettisonable fuel tanks normally used for ferrying duties. The Hurricane pilots were not happy for not only did the auxiliary fuel tanks slow the Hurricanes down and make them less manoeuvrable, but also the armour plating behind the seats had to be removed and ammunition reduced to compensate for the weight of the extra fuel. Stated one:

> "The additional tanks gave the Hurricane a range of 900 miles compared with
> the normal range of 600 miles. There were two additional tanks – one port, one
> starboard. The port tank emptied first, then the starboard tank. Air locks were
> liable to develop owing to bad refuelling or severe bumps in the air and throw
> the system out of commission. You never knew, when the port tank emptied, if
> the starboard tank was going to feed through. If your starboard tank refused to
> work over the sea, that was the end."

In the event, the leading Blenheim developed a fault just after take-off, all turned back and the raid was aborted. Later in the day seven SAAF Marylands were despatched to attack Maleme but only five completed the operation which was thought to have caused considerable damage. The next raid, by four unescorted Blenheims, encountered Bf109s and one bomber was shot down. 73 Squadron was also involved in the day's operation, six Hurricanes being despatched to operate from Crete's Heraklion aerodrome, their task to intercept the unescorted Ju52s flying in to Maleme, and to strafe enemy troops there and those around Heraklion. At departure time a Blenheim arrived to undertake the navigation, the formation setting out over the sea at 1135 with Flg Off Goodman leading the Hurricanes. Two hours later five Hurricanes returned to Sidi Haneish, Goodman reporting that they had flown over a number of RN vessels which had put up such a tremendous barrage that the formation had been scattered. He feared that the Blenheim and one of the Hurricanes – V7424 flown by Sgt Laing – might have been shot down into the sea. In the circumstances, Goodman had decided to return with the remaining aircraft of his flight.

73 Squadron was ordered to try again and, at 1520, the same five pilots plus one replacement set off again, this time led by a SAAF Maryland. Just about dusk in the midst of a raid by about a dozen Ju88s, the Hurricanes arrived over Heraklion. Despite being low on fuel they attempted to intercept, both Flg Off Goodman (W9198) and Plt Off Ward (V7816) claiming bombers damaged during a brief skirmish as they pursued them over Canea and out to sea. The aerodrome was heavily pitted with bomb craters and two of the Hurricanes broke their tailwheels on landing as a result. Here they were delighted to find their missing companion, Sgt Laing, who later related:

"Having passed over the bleak-looking slopes of the mountain range I soon sighted the crossed runways of Heraklion, close by the township of Canea. Having circled the landing strip I noticed some good-sized bomb craters in the runway but as the place seemed deserted I decided to land. I made a good landing, running down to the south-east towards the beach. The propeller clanked to a standstill and there was not a sound, which to say the least was most eerie. I stepped out of the aircraft and decided to walk to the nearest building, a stone hut some 300 yards away. Having gone a few yards, a machine-gun opened up on the aircraft and myself, with some degree of accuracy, and I realised I was not alone. Bullets began to whistle round and I dived for a small depression in the ground, which gave me a little cover. I remained there, with my head towards the direction of the machine-gun fire to make a smaller target; also my dark blue tunic against the runway was quite fair camouflage. They gave the Hurricane and myself the works for quite a time and I tried to pluck up courage to make a bolt for it – luckily my mind was made up for me by the approach of a British tank, which rumbled up and shielded me from the fire of the machine-gun. The tank commander, a major, lifted up the trap door of the tank, greeted me with a smile and apologised for the reception I got. Having exchanged views on the situation and the Bosch in particular, he suggested I taxi the aircraft down to the revetment area, about half a mile down the runway, where I would find some shelter. Apparently he wanted to save the Hurricane as pilots were more easily replaced than aircraft!

> Fortunately the engine was not damaged and I was able to taxi down at high
> speed, helped along with bursts from the Bosch machine-gunners, who were
> very active at this time."

His efforts were to no avail however, for within half an hour of his arrival at
Heraklion six Bf110s appeared and commenced strafing British gun positions. The
Hurricane was soon sighted and was quickly reduced to a blazing wreck. Further
raids followed. Laing continued:

> "We could do nothing about it, except the Aussie-manned guns accounted for
> several aircraft but at a very high cost to themselves. Without my plane I was
> a mere spectator of the operation in progress, and one experienced a terrible
> feeling of frustration to witness Heraklion being reduced to a shambles."

The airfield was still under small-arms fire from paratroopers positioned on the
ridge and behind rocks on the perimeter when the remainder of the Hurricanes
arrived, and as the pilots headed for shelter they had constantly to throw themselves
flat for cover. Nonetheless, two Hurricanes were rapidly refuelled and were sent up
to patrol until dusk, but no enemy aircraft were sighted. After a hurried consultation
with the local army commander, Flg Off Goodman learned that there was no stock
of .303 ammunition for the Hurricanes and only limited fuel available. It was
decided that as the Hurricanes could offer little assistance they should return to
Egypt in the morning. Following a night's desultory sleep, the six Hurricanes
prepared to depart at dawn, Laing and Goodman squeezing into the cockpit of the
latter's aircraft, Goodman using his companion's lap as a seat, the parachute pack
having been discarded and stowed into the fuselage. Before heading for Egypt all
pilots were to use up their remaining ammunition by strafing enemy positions
around the airfield, which they did. Of the long and uncomfortable flight, Laing
recalled:

> "Our journey back across the Mediterranean was uneventful from the enemy
> point of view, but we struck a head wind during the last hundred miles and,
> with petrol low, we were feeling anything but comfortable. We finally landed
> at Sidi Haneish in a sandstorm with our petrol gauge registering zero. Surely
> Allah had been with us and my only complaint was that I was so stiff and
> numbed after sitting for three hours in a cramped cockpit and used as a cushion
> for the pilot. However, I gave the flight commander a big hand."

They were the first to arrive, landing at 0830, and were followed shortly thereafter
by Plt Off Ward, but no others returned to base. It was later learned that Flg Off
Donati had run out of fuel and force-landed V7802 at Fuka, Plt Off Frank Moss
coming down just inside Ras el-Kanazis with V7879 also out of fuel. Of the other
two – Plt Offs Bob Goord (V7736) and Bob Likeman (V7764) – nothing was ever
heard. It was assumed that both had come down in the sea, the severe sandstorm
over the coast and out to sea probably contributing to their loss.

Although the aerial assault on British and Commonwealth forces on Crete was
relentless, 204 Group did not commit its aircraft to the fray the following day, but

re-entered the battle area with increased vigour on 25 May. Four unescorted SAAF Marylands and six Blenheims carried out raids in the morning, while four long-range Hurricanes of 274 Squadron led by Flt Lt Honor were tasked to accompany two Blenheims to attack Maleme. As the Hurricanes prepared to leave for Maleme at 0530 one burst its tailwheel on take-off and aborted, but the other three rendezvoused with one of the Blenheims, the other having crashed on take-off from Sidi Barrani. Near Crete the formation entered dense, low-lying cloud and became separated, all but one returning separately to Egypt. Only Plt Off Hamilton (V7562) continued alone towards Maleme, meeting a Ju88 over Suda Bay, claiming this shot down into the sea. Hamilton's Hurricane then developed the feared fuel problem and he decided to land at Heraklion, damaging the aircraft's undercarriage severely on the cratered runway. Unable to take-off again, Hamilton was eventually taken prisoner with the fall of the island. There were further Blenheim raids during the afternoon, three being shot down by Bf109s. The final strike of the day was to be made by three SAAF Marylands and two Hurricanes from 274 Squadron. Off at 1530, one Maryland soon developed a fault, turned back, and force-landed at Sidi Barrani. On arrival over the Maleme area the two remaining bombers went in first, bombing and strafing, but one was hit by ground fire and then pursued by Bf109s until it eventually crash-landed on the coast near Tymbaki. Meanwhile, the two Hurricanes – W9266 flown by Flt Lt Honor, and P3469 piloted by Flt Lt Down – had followed the Marylands in, as Dudley Honor later recalled:

"As we crossed over the mountains there were so many enemy aircraft in the sky that I was undecided whether to have a crack at the ones in the air or carry out my original orders and attack the aerodrome. I decided that I had better carry out my original orders. Down and I dived along the river valley. As we approached we saw two transport aircraft circling to land. There were so many aircraft on Maleme that it was just a congested mess. Some were on their noses, some obviously burnt out. It was difficult to decide in that mass which of the aircraft on the ground to attack. I decided to have a crack at the two which were landing. I thought they were probably full of troops and equipment. They came in too fast for us. We were still about 2,000 yards away as the second one started to touch down. I opened fire at this range and continued firing as I approached the aerodrome. I passed over at about 50 feet, spraying everything I could see. Down's aircraft was about 300 yards astern of me.

I saw three 109Fs [sic] taking off from the aerodrome, going in an easterly direction. I thought they were going after the Marylands. I got to the north boundary, still at 50 feet, and noticed some troop-carriers, German and Italian, coming into the aerodrome along the line of the Cape Spada peninsula; they were about 1,000 feet. As I passed over the northern boundary the AA guns opened up; the sky was black around me with ack-ack bursts. I pulled up to the line of troop-carriers, head on. They stretched right along the peninsula, with about half a mile between each. There was an endless line of them, away to sea. I managed to get up to the same height as the leading aircraft – it was an Italian S79 [sic] – and gave it a very short burst at dead range. It made no attempt at evasion and burst into flames and went straight down into the sea. I carried straight on and had a crack at a second, a Ju52 loaded with troops. He half turned away from me and went down. I saw him as he turned over on his back and hit the water."

Meantime, Flt Lt Hugh Down was being pursued out to sea by Bf109s of II/JG77 – possibly those seen taking off by Honor; he did not return. The other German pilots then gave chase to Honor, apparently joined by at least one Bf110, as he recalled:

"Suddenly there was a series of explosions and my control was gone. A 110 had attacked me from underneath and behind. I did not observe it before the attack. I started to take what evasive action I could. My controls were very badly damaged. I could only try to dodge him. The chase lasted about 15 minutes and I got closer and closer to the sea. I worked in as close to the cliffs as possible, watching him in the mirror. Each time I saw a white puff coming from the front of him I did a skidding turn. I saw the cannon shells bursting in the sea alongside. He must have used up all his ammunition without hitting me again because he sheered off. A 109F [sic] then took up the fight. He employed the usual tactics on me, diving and then climbing. I was unable to turn with him but managed to get him round the north of the peninsula, out of sight of the aerodrome. There was cloud at 2,500 feet but I could not climb to get up there. After about five minutes a burst of fire hit my engine; there was a horrible bang and an awful smell of cordite in the cockpit. I was about 20 feet from the sea when I was hit. I could not pull out so I steered straight ahead to make a landing on the water at high speed, at about 220 mph. I reduced speed in order not to hit the water too hard and touched down at about 120 mph. After about 15 seconds the aircraft began to sink. I still had the cockpit hood closed and my safety harness was still fastened. I went down 40 feet before I realised what was happening. I noticed the sea turning from blue to dark green. I opened the hood, which luckily had not jammed and turned the knob of my Mae West. I was wearing a German Mae West [retrieved from a Ju87 gunner shot down in the Battle of Britain] which inflates automatically, whereas the RAF type had to be blown up by mouth. I drifted to the surface slowly, noticing the water grow lighter and lighter. It seemed a long time. I broke surface to find the 109 still circling overhead at about 50 feet. Fortunately the pilot did not appear to see me and, after a couple of circuits, made off round the peninsula towards Maleme.
   The sea was very rough. I was about half a mile from the cliff and after swimming for about a couple of minutes, I realised I was floating stern upwards. I still had my parachute on. I jettisoned it and my trousers, which were hampering me. I carried on swimming for about three hours until I was just about 20 yards from the cliffs, which were about 100 feet high, not only sheer but overhanging. Each time I tried to get a handhold I was dragged away again by the suction of a retreating wave. My nails and flesh were torn by the rocks. I found it impossible to get to the shore so I relaxed and allowed myself to drift round into a small cave. By this time it was nearly nightfall. I saw a German seaplane fly along the cliffs very near me. I thought he might be searching for me. Eventually I was washed into another cave and although

smashed up against the end of the drive of the sea, managed to hang on by grabbing a rock stalagmite and crawled up onto a little ledge ..."

In the engagement with the 274 Squadron pair, the II/JG77 pilots actually claimed three Hurricanes shot down, one by Fw Otto Köhler of 4 Staffel, one by Uffz Rudolf Schmidt of 5 Staffel, and the third by FjGfr Günther Marschhausen, also of 5 Staffel. The identity of the Bf110 pilot who engaged Honor's Hurricane has not been established. Back at Gerawla, where 274 Squadron anxiously awaited news of its missing pilots, six more long-range Hurricanes arrived in readiness for a continuation of operations over Crete; they were manned by reinforcement pilots from 229 Squadron who had flown from the deck of the aircraft carrier *Furious* to Malta, and from there to Egypt, a few days earlier. At Sidi Haneish 73 Squadron also received six reinforcement pilots, these from 213 Squadron, who had similarly arrived in Egypt via *Furious*. During the day Hurricanes from 1SAAF, 73 and 274 Squadrons provided air cover for the carrier *Formidable* and the destroyer *Nubian*, both of which had been damaged by air attack during operations off the south coast of Crete. Three Hurricanes from the South African unit provided initial cover but were treated as hostile and were greeted by a barrage of AA fire. They were relieved by three more from 274 Squadron, and then by a further three from 73 Squadron. Another section from the same unit arrived an hour later, these engaging a Ju88 which Sqn Ldr Wykeham-Barnes (V7012) managed to hit before his reflector sight failed at the crucial moment, allowing the reconnaissance aircraft to escape.

While the Hurricanes were thus involved in sorties over Crete, German and Italian Ju87s made the best of the opportunity by carrying out sorties against shipping off Tobruk. Seven dive-bombers of the newly arrived 239^Squadriglia led by Cap Giuseppe Cenni, escorted by eight CR42s of 83^Squadriglia, attacked and sank the 3,741-ton merchant vessel *Helka* at 1720, also damaging the sloop *Grimsby*. The latter was later attacked and sunk by Ju87s of I/StG1, this unit losing one of its aircraft in the process. A day earlier the requisitioned trawler *Aurora II* had similarly fallen victim to air attack off Tobruk, while I/JG27 lost a pilot on the 26th during an attack on shipping off Bardia, Lt Erich Schröder becoming a prisoner after ditching in the sea. Serg Magg Ennio Tarantola participated in the attack on the *Helka*, together with his gunner AvSc Giuseppe Tempo:

"I was fortunate that my commander was one of the best in this field, Giuseppe Cenni. The actual methods employed were quite diverse, and depended really on targets allocated to us. Against shipping there was initially the classic dive-bomber approach of diving at 90 degrees vertically in groups of two or three aircraft at a time. This was the system the Germans used so effectively and it was the way that they taught us when we trained with them. Their method was to thus attack the ships from ahead and therefore, no matter which way the target vessel put her helm over to avoid the leading Stuka, numbers two and three following could adjust their attacks and ensure that they scored hits. The German pilots extended their dive brakes and commenced their dives from 12,000 feet, pushing on down vertically to around 2,000-2,500 feet before bomb release and letting their sirens scream on the way down to increase effect. We too adopted this method most successfully."

Throughout 26 May aircraft of 204 Group were again very active over Crete, four SAAF Marylands bombing and strafing Maleme while two others dropped supplies; one of the latter, with an all-Free French volunteer crew, was shot down by Bf109s and flak. From Gerawla, 274 Squadron despatched its six long-range Hurricanes to seek and destroy the transports which were ferrying men and supplies to the island, three setting out at 15-minute intervals commencing 1310, followed by the other three at 1415. Flg Off Tracey (Z4511) was first to arrive over Maleme, where he encountered and shot down a Ju52 before being engaged by a Bf109. He dived towards the steep cliffs, his Hurricane taking several hits in the fuselage, fuel tanks and propeller. Reaching sea level, Tracey pulled clear at the last moment, believing that the pursuing Messerschmitt had plunged straight into the sea behind him. Having nursed his damaged aircraft back across the sea to Sidi Barrani, he was able to carry out an emergency landing. While Tracey was fighting for his life, a second Hurricane (Z4312) flown by Sgt Kerr had arrived off Maleme, and he too claimed a Ju52 shot down in flames to the sea. Like Tracey, he was also pounced upon by a Messerschmitt and soon followed his victim into the sea. Kerr survived the crash, managed to get ashore and next day, by chance, met his flight commander, Flt Lt Honor. In fact, Honor had witnessed the fight in which Kerr had sent the transport aircraft into the sea. It seems probable that Tracey and Kerr were victims of Hptm Herbert Ihlefeld and his wingman Lt Fritz Geisshardt of Stab I(J)/LG2, each of whom claimed Hurricanes shot down over Crete on this date.

The next lone Hurricane, Z4250 flown by Frenchman Flt Sgt Marcel Lebois, evaded the now-alerted Messerschmitts and encountered the Junkers transports, one of which he claimed shot down. He arrived safely back at Gerawla at 1800, where he anxiously awaited news of two of his fellow countrymen flying in the final section to Maleme, but only Flg Off Péronne was to return, landing Z4538 back at Gerawla at 1915. During his five-hour sortie Péronne had also shot down a Ju52 but his leader, Flt Lt Paul Jacquier (Z4632), was missing, as was Sgt Colin Glover (Z4606), the latter having been shot down into the sea by Oblt Walter Höckner of 6/JG77; whether he had encountered any transports before his demise in not known. Jacquier however, had survived and was taken prisoner; he later recalled:

> "I was flying at approximately 10,000 feet about 12 miles north of Maleme when I noticed a single Ju52 flying very low, heading for Crete. I attacked from the rear, made a single pass, disengaged above and banked upwards to the right. I saw it disappear into the sea. Some minutes later I saw a second lone Ju52 at the same altitude. Again I attacked from the rear and broke away upwards, and this also went into the sea. In both attacks the Ju52s only returned fire at the last moment. I regained altitude and continued to Maleme to strafe. While I was attacking, five ME109s and two ME110s on aerial defence were circling at about 300-600 feet, at slow speeds – with undercarriages down – no doubt for identification by German airfield defences. I dived at great speed from 9,000 feet, going west to east (sun behind me). I shot a Ju52 which blew up, and levelled out some feet above the ground. On the eastern edge of the airfield I received a shock – the engine was hit. It cut and petrol flooded into the cockpit. Using my speed, I glided along the beach between Maleme and Canea and landed wheels-up amongst the German

forward positions. I was captured immediately. Apart from rough handling by Austrian mountain troops on capture, I was treated well in accordance with the Geneva Convention. I was wearing the badges of my rank in the RAF and at my first interrogation by the Germans at Maleme I indicated that I was French-Canadian. Some time later I met in the POW camp Lt Courcot and two others in French uniform, surviving crew of the Maryland, and I decided that I would share the same fate as my compatriots. Thus, at my second interrogation, in Athens, I stated I was French."

For the loss of three Hurricanes and their pilots, six transports had been claimed shot down – an extremely poor rate of exchange. German records suggest at least seven losses to fighter attack, three of which managed to crash-land at Maleme, therefore the missing Sgt Glover may have scored before his own demise. 274 Squadron despatched two more Hurricanes at 1700 which were to carry out a dusk attack on Maleme in conjuction with six Blenheims. Both Sgt P.B. Nicolson and Wt Off Coudray, another of the French contingent, returned safely but two of the Blenheims were shot down by Bf109s while a third crashed in the desert on return.

By 27 May there were almost 27,000 German and Italian troops in Crete. The Germans had even managed to land two tanks, towed across from the mainland in an open barge. The German High Command was now as convinced of victory as was General Wavell of defeat. Early on this day Wavell signalled Prime Minister Churchill that Crete was no longer tenable and that troops must be withdrawn. He acknowledged the enemy's overwhelming air superiority, which made reinforcement impossible. The Chiefs-of-Staff reluctantly signalled their agreement. Despite the approaching evacuation, Air Commodore Collishaw considered 204 Group should continue to frustrate the German advance – but the next 24 hours were to prove more costly than effective. During the night Wellingtons from Egypt raided Maleme, while three Blenheims were tasked to make a dawn attack on the same target but one crashed on take-off and the raid was aborted. Further Blenheims were readied for an afternoon attack, but two of the nine aircraft involved collided on take-off, one returned early with engine trouble and four became lost in darkness on returning to Egypt and crashed in the desert. The Blenheim strike had achieved little success and six of the nine bombers had been totally lost – none due to enemy action – with the loss of nine crewmen. The final operation of the day was launched at 1530 when two Hurricanes of 274 Squadron rendezvoused with a Blenheim IVF, the trio directed to attempt further interception of the Ju52 air convoy still streaming into Maleme. As they headed towards the south coast of Crete however, six Ju88s of II/LG1 were encountered and engaged. The Blenheim pilot made a port beam attack on one low-flying bomber, the crew claiming that considerable damage had been inflicted and that the Junkers had probably been destroyed although they did not see it crash. Both Hurricane pilots, Flg Off Weller (Z4250) and Sgt Nicolson (Z4536) also engaged, each believing they had shot one down and, indeed, the Blenheim crew reported seeing one Ju88 falling in flames and two others hit the sea; possibly the latter were bombs being jettisoned as, in fact, only one bomber was lost, Lt Georg Freysoldt and his crew perishing when L1+EW crashed into the sea. Presumably all three fighters had attacked the same aircraft, each unaware of the others' involvement. Following the fight the Hurricanes became separated from the Blenheim and, after an uneventful patrol hunting for transport aircraft, both landed at Heraklion, from where they returned to Gerawla next day.

As a consequence of the losses on 27 May, few sorties were made by 204 Group aircraft next day, only two Blenheims making a strike on Maleme, returning without incident. With the onset of evening two SAAF Marylands were scrambled from Fuka to cover returning warships, while patrols were carried out by two Blenheims each escorted by a 274 Squadron Hurricane. At Gerawla, 274 Squadron was further reinforced by five pilots on attachment from 73 Squadron. A Royal Navy task force had arrived off Heraklion to commence the evacuation during the night, the ships coming under constant aerial attack, the task force commander calling on 204 Group for air cover as the ships entered the Kaso Strait. Although five Hurricanes of 274 Squadron were despatched at the appointed time, these were unable to locate the ships. In consequence, the attacks on the departing vessels continued without respite and two cruisers crowded with soldiers were seriously damaged by Ju87s, many casualties being inflicted to both naval and army personnel. Despite the failure to protect the cruisers, a total of 21 protective sorties were undertaken over various returning warships by 274 Squadron during the morning and early afternoon of 29 May. These patrols consisted of two or three Hurricanes at a time, usually accompanied by a single Blenheim or SAAF Maryland. At midday, the crew of one of the latter spotted a lone aircraft at 13,000 feet which turned out to be a reconnaissance Ju88 of 2(F)/123. The Maryland followed as it dived away, the pilot opening fire and inflicting damage to its starboard engine, but was forced to break away when hit by return fire. By this time Flg Off Tracey (V7830) had arrived on the scene and promptly despatched the Junkers into the sea, Fw Ernst Chlebowitz and his crew of 4U+EK perishing. Meanwhile, the other Hurricane, V7855 flown by Plt Off Sumner, engaged an aircraft identified as a Do17, claiming to have damaged it before it evaded his attack and disappeared. During one of the earlier escort sorties, Sgt Peter Nicolson (Z4634) was detailed to break away and make a dash over central Crete to the Retimo area, where he was to drop a message bag to the besieged garrison. This contained orders for a withdrawal to Plaka for evacuation, but as Nicolson attempted to carry out this duty his Hurricane was intercepted at about 0900 by a Bf109 of Stab/JG77 flown by Oblt Erich Freidrich and was shot down into the sea. He did not survive.

Ju87s returned in force over Tobruk during the day, an estimated 60 aircraft attacking the harbour, shipping and gun positions. With no fighter opposition they were free to select targets at random. Lt Rankin noted:

"Started going to sleep in the afternoon when about 60 dive-bombers came in to bomb shipping in the harbour. They swarmed all over the place and we fired for all we were worth, damaging two for certain. One came for us but, as he dived we got a burst almost straight at him and he immediately swerved off and disappeared. A piece of shrapnel or something went past my head at incredible speed. Something was hit in the harbour and an enormous column of black smoke went up. It was not nice to see these infernal Stukas again."

During lulls between air raids impromptu cricket and football matches were often played by and between British and Australian troops – all quite natural – but a rather bizarre 'sporting' incident occurred about this time, according to an Australian soldier who witnessed the event whose account was recorded by Lt Anthony Heckstall-Smith RN of the Inshore Squadron:

"A Stuka, hit by the Bofors of an ack-ack battery, came skimming over the escarpment from the direction of the harbour, its engine spluttering, to crash-land near the gun site. Out of the wreck scrambled the pilot, shaken but unhurt, to be confronted by a long-legged Australian armed with a rifle. Pulling off his goggles and flying helmet, the German threw his revolver on the ground, and stared at his captor. Then he laughed. 'You're quite a hero when you have a rifle in your hand!' he taunted. 'I wonder how you'd get on without it?' For a full minute the two men stood glaring at each other. Then, slowly, the Australian laid his rifle on the ground and threw his slouch hat down beside it. 'Okay, if that's the way you want it,' he drawled. As the German stripped off his flying kit, tunic and shirt, the rest of the gun crew clambered out of their pit and came running across the sand. Soon, they were joined by others from the nearby slit-trenches and dug-outs, to form a circle round the two men, now both naked to their waists. They were about the same weight and height; both broad-shouldered, lean and darkly tanned by the African sun. Then, surrounded by a ring of cheering Australians, the blond young Luftwaffe pilot and the lanky Digger went for each other with their bare fists. Both knew something about boxing and both were game fighters, and the soldiers yelled themselves hoarse as they fought it out in a whirling cloud of dust. For twenty minutes without a break, the two men pounded each other until the sand was splattered with their blood. Then, the German's knees sagged and his arms fell limply to his sides. 'All right. You didn't need that rifle!' he grinned, wiping the blood from his mouth. 'I'm certain that if the Hun had won, the boys would have let him return to his own lines,' a young gunner wrote home to his mother, describing this strange interlude in the desert war."

On 30 May, 274 Squadron flew 30 sorties over the returning naval forces, sometimes accompanied by a single Blenheim or Beaufighter, and shared in the destruction of three German aircraft. The first contact with the opposition was made just after 0800 when Sqn Ldr Hawkins' section of three Hurricanes encountered three bombers which were identified as He111s. Flg Off Péronne (Z4536) and Wt Off Ballatore (W9303) engaged the nearest bomber and reported that it crashed into the sea. It would seem that the bombers were Do17s of I/KG2 rather than Heinkels; Uffz Heinz Hövel and his crew aboard U5+GL were lost. Of the action Ballatore recalled:

"We shot down a He111 [*sic*] which was attacking a boat. Victory was confirmed. Péronne had been hit by return fire from the rear gunner. With a damaged aileron he managed to land back at Sidi Barrani."

Late in the afternoon Plt Off G.A. Tovey (W9329), another new arrival for 73

Squadron, was accompanying a Beaufighter when they came across Lt Walter Fischer's He111 (IH+KN) of II/KG26, which was on a ferry flight to Cyrenaica. The Beaufighter attacked first but closed so rapidly that it collided with the Heinkel, although both aircraft seemed to escape serious damage. This did however allow Tovey the opportunity to nip in and shoot the bomber down into the sea. As dusk approached, the final sorties were flown by three Hurricanes and a Beaufighter. In the fading light a reconnaissance Ju88 (7A+HM) of 4(F)/121 was seen, and was apparently attacked by both the Beaufighter and a 274 Squadron Hurricane (V7855) flown by Plt Off Sumner, although each was ignorant of the other's presence. The Beaufighter pilot claimed a probable, Sumner a definite victory; whoever fired the telling burst, the Junkers crashed into the sea with the loss of Oblt Franz Schwarz-Tramper and his crew. At Gerawla 274 Squadron received a further influx of pilots to aid in the long patrols, three South Africans from 1SAAF – Capt Driver and Lts Talbot and Bester – and three more from 73 Squadron, the two Frenchmen Sous-Lts Denis and Littolf, plus Sgt Laing.

At 0850 on the morning of 31 May, a dozen Ju88s from II/LG1 attacked RN destroyers *Napier* and *Nizam* as they withdrew from the Cretan coast loaded with evacuees, the action continuing for some 25 minutes during which *Napier* was near-missed. Although suffering damage to both engine and boiler rooms, she managed to continue at reduced speed. One of the bombers was believed to have been shot down by ships' guns, and a second damaged. Overhead a SAAF Maryland and three Hurricanes of 274 Squadron, flown by the attached South African pilots, arrived on the scene and promptly gave chase to two Ju88s. Lt Talbot (Z4510) fired two bursts at one bomber but it evaded him, then Capt Driver (Z4614) and Lt Bester (P2646) made beam and stern attacks on the other, which dived towards the sea. Talbot and the Maryland pilot gave chase for some 70 miles before Talbot succeeded in getting in a burst which hit an engine. The Maryland, with its engines at full boost, overhauled the Hurricane, closed in on the damaged bomber and inflicted further damage. The Junkers was last seen flying just ten feet above the sea. It was assumed to have crashed but in fact the German pilot managed to nurse his aircraft back to Heraklion where he carried out a crash-landing. Meanwhile, Capt Driver reported meeting three or four more Ju88s and claimed to have shot down one of these into the sea.

It would seem that the relieving section of Hurricanes also met the Ju88s reported by Driver, Sous Lt Littolf (W9329) claiming one shot down. He then reported meeting a lone Z1007bis, apparently a reconnaissance machine out from Libya, claiming this damaged before it escaped. One of the Hurricanes, W9273 flown by Sgt Auguste Guillou, failed to return; it may either have been hit by return fire from the Ju88s, or shot down by an escorting Messerschmitt. Bf109s of II/JG77 were certainly in the area, a second patrol flown by Flg Off J.B. Hobbs (W9303) and Plt Off G.B. Johns (Z4322), led by Wt Off Ballatore (W9270), being pursued by two or three as they returned from a sortie, as the French pilot later recalled:

"Returning from a mission over Crete with two British wingmen, we were attacked by a section of ME109s. We were in close formation for security because we had already flown about 100 miles. As they were faster than us, and it was not possible to fly away, I flew with my wingmen very close to the sea, so close that I could see the foam of the waves blown away by the propeller's wind. A ME109 anyway succeeded in making a pass [at one of the other Hurricanes] and a burst of fire damaged an aileron; another shell, after having destroyed the radio set, hit the armour plate behind his head."

Despite the damage to his aircraft, Flg Off Hobbs was able to land safely at Sidi Barrani where the damage was temporarily repaired to enable him to return to Sidi Haneish. Early in the afternoon the three SAAF pilots (Capt Driver, Lts Talbot and Bester) were up again on patrol when an intruder was seen. While Driver and Bester stayed with the ships, Talbot (W9322) set off in pursuit, identifying another Z1007bis. After chasing his quarry for 100 miles westward he finally got in a position to attack, reporting that he shot it down into the sea 50 miles off Tobruk. During the day Hurricanes of 73, 274 and 1SAAF Squadrons had flown 44 sorties, mainly in protection of shipping returning from Crete. The three South African pilots attached to 274 Squadron now returned to their unit, Sqn Ldr Hawkins praising their efforts in a note to Maj Ross-Theron:

"I would like to express appreciation of the work your pilots did – Capt Driver, Lts Talbot and Bester – during their short stay with us. They came to us when we were a bit short, helping us considerably, and were most successful in the patrols. I trust you will acquaint them with the Squadron's appreciation of their efforts."

That night two Sunderlands flew to Sphakia on the Cretan south coast to pick up key personnel, flying low and slowly along the coastline, flashing pre-arranged signals at places likely to conceal parties of evacuees. No response was observed, so after ten minutes one flying boat alighted. An SOS was then seen flashing from the shore. This signal came from Flt Lt Honor, the 274 Squadron flight commander shot down six days previously. He and fellow pilot Sgt Kerr had made their way south, aided by Cretans and Greeks, but so lacerated were Kerr's feet that he had temporarily been left behind as Honor scrambled over the rocks to the shoreline. Using his flashlight, Honor signalled a Morse message and eventually a one-man rubber dinghy arrived, paddled by the Sunderland's second pilot. Just managing to squeeze in, Honor was rowed out to the flying boat, but while six Greeks were also taken on board, it was decided with regret that there was no time to go back for Kerr, who as a result subsequently became a prisoner.

While the German Army and Luftwaffe were winning sweeping victories in Greece and Crete, those stationed in Cyrenaica with Fliegerführer Afrika were not rejoicing, feeling that their war was being overshadowed by that in the Balkans. They pleaded, to no avail, for extra fighter squadrons, believing that the three Staffeln of I/JG27, aided by just one Staffel from III/ZG26, were too stretched to provide proper cover for the supply lines of the Afrika Korps. One senior officer later commented:

"I remember Feldmarschall Milch of the Luftwaffe [Inspector-General] coming over to inspect in May 1941. We all prayed that the RAF would favour us with a good heavy raid while he was there. Fortunately the RAF obliged.

Milch was wearing a beautiful white uniform. I could not have been more delighted than when I saw him dive into a slit trench. When he came out, I was even more pleased to see that it was the trench into which the servants had thrown the refuse from the kitchen."

While undoubtedly the Luftwaffe detachment in Cyrenaica could not fulfil all its tasks in the desert, the Messerschmitt pilots of I/JG27 performed magnificently under the conditions imposed upon them. With fewer than 30 aircraft available at any one time, the German fighter pilots dominated whenever they came into contact with opposing fighters and bombers. It was Air Commodore Collishaw's 204 Group which was at a constant disadvantage, for whenever reinforcement Hurricanes arrived, invariably the pilots were vastly inexperienced, often straight from fighter OTUs, while Hurricanes were no match for Bf109s, particularly when the latter were flown by combat-hardened pilots.

With RAFME still licking its wounds from the disastrous but mercifully brief operation in support of the the evacuation of Crete, hostilities broke out in Vichy-controlled Syria, where the Luftwaffe had been using French bases en route to Iraq during the fighting there the previous month. Since mid-May the RAF had been mounting infrequent small-scale bombing raids against Syrian bases, but now a full-scale invasion was about to be launched to deny these important bases to German forces which it was believed were about to take over from the French in Syria. Mustering a small contingent of Hurricanes, American-supplied P-40 Tomahawks (3RAAF), Gladiators and FAA Fulmars operating from bases in Iraq, Palestine, Transjordan, Cyprus and Egypt, sorties were to be flown to protect the token Blenheim bomber force. Just how the Vichy-French forces would react was an unknown factor, particularly as amongst the invasion force was a weak Free French contingent. Sous-Lt Denis, the senior Free French fighter pilot was among those consulted:

"I was summoned by Général Catroux, French commander in Egypt, who asked two things: first to make a radio broadcast, which I did; and second, to take part in the combats in Syria, which I refused. I explained to him that I knew every pilot there, that they were friends. I asked him to let me keep fighting the Germans and not send me to fight against other Frenchmen. The Général was marvellous. He told me, 'You're right, Denis. Let's not talk about this telegram from London. Général de Gaulle wanted the unit [the Free French Flight] to take part in the war in Syria, but stay here and keep on doing a good job.'"

In the event, none of the Free French pilots fought against their countrymen.

CHAPTER VIII

OPERATION *BATTLEAXE*:
THE ATTEMPTED RELIEF OF TOBRUK

June 1941

"... the whole thing is a complete flop. The only bright spot is that our chaps
have been simply grand and have done more than even the army could have
called for. There'll certainly be a hunt for scapegoats after this ..."
> Air Marshal Tedder, AOC-in-C RAFME,
> to his journal following the failure of Operation *Battleaxe*

With the arrival of the latest convoy with its consignment of tanks and Hurricanes,
General Wavell felt confident despite the disappointment of Operation *Brevity*, and
the subsequent loss of Halfaya Pass at the end of May, that he was now in a position
to strike a blow against Rommel's armoured force poised on the frontier. His hand
was also being forced by Prime Minister Churchill, to whom he cabled certain
misgivings as to the extent of success which he felt could be achieved. The
ambitious plan called for the recapture of the Bardia-Sollum-Capuzzo-Sidi Aziez
area before engaging the enemy forces holding the Tobruk-El Adem area in an
attempt to relieve the besieged garrison, after which the advance was to continue
towards Derna and Mechili; he advised the PM:

"I think it right to inform you that the measure of success which will attend
this operation is in my opinion doubtful. I hope that it will succeed in driving
enemy west of Tobruk and re-establishing land communications with Tobruk.
If possible we will exploit success further. But recent operations have
disclosed some disquieting features. Our armoured cars are too lightly
armoured to resist the fire of enemy fighter aircraft, and, having no gun, are
powerless against the German eight-wheeled armoured cars, which have guns
and are faster. This makes reconnaissance difficult. Our Infantry tanks are
really too slow for a battle in the desert, and have been suffering considerable
casualties from the fire of the powerful enemy anti-tank guns ... We shall not
be able to accept battle with perfect confidence in spite of numerical
superiority, as we could against Italians ..."

The operation was codenamed *Battleaxe* and its commencement depended largely on the readiness of the 7th Armoured Division currently re-equipping with the newly arrived tanks. The RAF's task was to carry out an offensive against the Axis landing grounds and to prevent supplies and reinforcements coming from the rear prior to the British advance, and then to provide close support once the ground battle had commenced.

At this crucial stage of the war in the Middle East, Air Chief Marshal Longmore was relieved of his command by the disgruntled Prime Minister who was unhappy with his performance over the preceding months, Longmore's deputy, Air Marshal Tedder, being appointed AOC-in-C Middle East in his place. General Wavell was also unpopular in London for his failure to mount an offensive earlier. Longmore, who had been called to London for discussions on the situation in the Middle East, was naturally disappointed, and wrote:

> "The results of conferences and discussions had given promise of a good supply of aircraft and equipment to Middle East. My passage by air to Cairo via Takoradi had been arranged, but the Fates decreed that I was not to return to my command. I was informed of the decision by Sir Archibald Sinclair, Secretary for Air. He told me that Air Marshal Tedder's appointment in my place would now be confirmed. My personal feelings are better left to the imagination. It seemed that the change had already been planned when the signal recalling me to England for consultations had been sent."

He added, in his memoirs:

> "I am confident that the historian will not fail to do justice to the successful achievements of that period. I suggest they might be summarized on the following lines:
>
> **A.** Malta still held firmly. It was even in use for offensive operations by naval and air forces. The morale of the islanders had been built up and was at a high level.
>
> **B.** The Navy had complete ascendancy over that of the Italians. The Fleet base at Alexandria had not yet been threatened by land or much inconvenienced from the air. The Suez Canal was in use.
>
> **C.** In Libya the Italian Army and Air Force had been completely defeated. 180,000 of them had been taken prisoner and 20,000 killed. It was the Army's first victory of the war and had obviously acted as a welcome stimulant to all the British Empire.
>
> **D.** Italian East Africa was in our hands and in consequence the Red Sea was entirely safe for shipping. American ships were authorized to use it.
>
> **E.** In Greece we had implemented our promise of assistance to that brave little country to the best of our ability. The RAF had given valuable support to the

Greek Army from the very start of the Italian invasion.

All these achievements were the result of grand teamwork at all levels between the three services in which, I am happy to think, the RAF played a very full part. Some measure of its contribution may be judged from the figure of 1,359 German and Italian aircraft destroyed on all fronts by our aircrews for a total loss from all causes, crashes included, of 584 of our own. We had achieved much with very little, and it was quality in personnel which had made it possible."

Tedder was equally surprised by his appointment:

"I sympathised with Longmore. Nor did I admire the fashion in which he was told to join the ranks of those unfortunate British commanders who are called upon in the early months of the war to face the situation foisted upon them by the neglect and fecklessness of others. I doubted whether I should last long as AOC-in-C. Churchill, for his part, showed much impatience with our slow progress on land. He signalled to Wavell that he had 530,000 soldiers on his ration strength, together with 500 field guns, 350 anti-aircraft guns, 450 heavy tanks, and 350 anti-tank guns. In the five months since the beginning of the year, more than 7,000 mechanical vehicles had reached the Middle East."

Operation *Battleaxe* was designed to make use of these men and the wealth of assembled matériel, and to clear Cyrenaica of the German threat once and for all. 15 June was finally earmarked as D-Day but for 204 Group losses had to be made good before any offensive could be mounted. In the recent fighting over Crete and while protecting naval forces 11 Hurricanes and nine pilots had been lost, consequently both 73 and 274 Squadron were severely affected by a shortage of experienced pilots. At the beginning of the month 73 Squadron received six newly trained pilots from 70 OTU; a few days later six pilots of 213 Squadron under Flg Off C.B. Temlett DFC arrived at Mersa Matruh and were subsequently attached to the Squadron as C Flight, while ten pilots of 229 Squadron under Flt Lt W.A. Smith were attached to 274 Squadron at Gerawla. Another French pilot joined 73 Squadron a few days later, Sgt Marcel Milan having completed his training on Hurricanes at 70 OTU following his escape from Senegal via Gambia earlier in the year. A detachment of ten Hurricanes from 2SAAF Squadron arrived at Sidi Haneish under the command of Capt D.H. Loftus to lend support to 1SAAF. Some of the reinforcing South African pilots had also seen action in East Africa.

* * *

Meanwhile, on the first day of the month, 73 Squadron at Sidi Haneish found itself responsible for carrying out shipping protection patrols, Sous-Lt Denis and Sgt Ellis being despatched in response to an urgent signal from the AA cruiser *Calcutta* that she was under attack. On arrival in the area no enemy aircraft were sighted but the cruiser had sunk following an attack by two Ju88s, with the loss of 117 lives; 255 survivors were plucked from the sea. Later, Sqn Ldr Wykeham-Barnes carried out a similar patrol over the Australian destroyer *Vendetta* but only after a long search to locate her, approximately 40 miles from the given position. Flt Lt P.O.V. Green, a newly arrived flight commander formerly with 112 Squadron, relieved the CO, and he was followed by a section flown by two more new pilots, Plt Off R.W.K. White RNZAF and Sgt J.R.D. Henderson RAAF, who landed back at Sidi Haneish at dusk. No enemy aircraft were sighted during the course of these patrols. 274 Squadron also provided patrols over the naval vessels, using its long-range Hurricanes. The third Hurricane unit, 1SAAF, despatched patrols inland and shortly after 1500 Lt Botha intercepted a Hs126 of 2(H)/14 flying at about 700 feet, some 15 miles east of Sidi Rezegh. The two aircraft approached each other head-on, the Henschel taking evasive action by diving even lower but Botha was able to carry out a beam attack. The spotter aircraft caught fire and crashed with the loss of its crew, Fw Josef Haase and Uffz Georg Scholten.

The South African unit lost one its finest pilots next day (2 June) during an operation to ground strafe Great Gambut landing ground, where a reconnaissance aircraft had reported sighting 13 Bf109s and four Bf110s. In the event, only two Bf110s, six Ju87s and several unidentified aircraft were observed as the Hurricanes swept down to carry out a thorough strafe, three of the Stukas and one unidentified aircraft being claimed destroyed, of which three went up in flames while ten others were believed to have been severely damaged by the combined fire from the six Hurricanes flown by Capts Quirk, G.J. Le Mesurier, Lts Talbot, Uys, Durose and A.A.L. Tatham, but Talbot's aircraft was hit by medium AA fire and was seen to trail black smoke. One of his colleagues wrote:

> "About half a mile from the aerodrome the nose of his aircraft suddenly dipped. The Hurricane struck the ground almost vertically and burst into flames immediately."

Lt Bob Talbot, victor of ten combats and the SAAF's first fighter ace in the Desert war was killed. As a result of this raid 8/ZG26 reported the destruction of one of its Bf110s while II/StG2 lost two Ju87s. Meanwhile, 73 Squadron's two senior French pilots, Sous-Lts Denis and Littolf accompanied by Flg Off Temlett (213 Squadron detachment) escorted a photo-reconnaissance Hurricane (V7774) flown by Flg Off Hardiman of 6 Squadron over the Capuzzo area. Sporadic AA fire was experienced but no enemy aircraft were encountered and all returned safely. Plt Off Logan and Sgt Ellis flew a further patrol over RN vessels off the coast, as did three Hurricanes from 274 Squadron. With the Hurricanes thus engaged and unable to provide any defence for Tobruk, the harbour and its shipping was again at the mercy of the Stukas, an estimated 60 German and Italian dive-bombers carrying out a series of raids. One Ju87R of 239^Squadriglia was shot down by AA fire. This unit lost a second aircraft in similar circumstances a few days later. The Tobruk gunners had not lost their sting. Of this period *ABC* war correspondent Chester Wilmot[1] wrote:

> "Rommel made an all-out attempt to silence the ack-ack guns in the week

---

[1] Chester Wilmot was one of 34 victims of a Comet jet airliner crash in 1954.

ending 2 June, but they found that the Tobruk defences were stronger than ever. There were now 28 heavy guns in action compared with 16 in April and the harbour was ringed with 12 Bofors guns instead of six. The gunners even manned the 3-inch dual-purpose gun on the deck of the gunboat *Ladybird* which lay half-sunken in the harbour. The enemy's most serious losses had been in dive-bombers and their crews, since 80 per cent of the planes shot down were Ju87s. Unfortunately for Rommel, his most courageous pilots – those who dived lowest – were the ones generally brought down, and almost invariably they crashed to death. For all these losses [Tobruk's AA Command estimated it had shot down 57 aircraft by this date, with 44 more probably destroyed and 96 damaged; actual losses were far fewer] Rommel had little to show. His aircraft had sunk in Tobruk harbour only two small naval vessels, two troop transports and one small cargo ship. In addition, a larger number of vessels was sunk outside the harbour approaching or leaving Tobruk. In defying the dive-bombers, the Tobruk anti-aircraft gunners did more than keep the harbour open and destroy enemy aircraft. They gained a moral triumph. For the first time in this war, ack-ack gunners showed that Stukas could be beaten by men who stood to their guns."

Lt Rankin's journal gives some idea of the frequency and intensity of these attacks during the first week of June:

"**1 June** -Up until ten o'clock we were in and out all the time for one alarm or another. Much activity by aircraft all round us, but only one dropped bombs on us. Had various raids during the day and engaged a Henschel in the evening. We turned him back at once, as we evidently shot down the one operating last night ... about fifty dive-bombers appeared and went for the distillery and harbour. We put up a terrific barrage and I myself saw three planes in difficulties. Several were reported down ... four ME110s dropped bombs on our perimeter.

2 June – Up at dawn ... first alarm for a whole fleet of fighters and bombers – three ME110s and then eight Italian bombers, accompanied by eighteen fighters. They flew all round and back again, looking like some air display, while AA blazed away at them. After a quiet evening, just at seven-thirty, same time as yesterday, in they came again. A long stream of Ju88s passed right along the coast – I noticed a Ju88 coming our way. Between us we got him down and he crashed in the sea. Len Downing had a machine-gun bullet clean through his tin hat, which saved his life undoubtedly.

3 June – had a series of alarms and raids by single planes, and patrols by ME109s. A Hurricane was reported once, and we thought we heard it. Sandstorm gathered pace at lunchtime.

4 June – A bit of a sandstorm came up in the afternoon. One or two raids and fighter patrols.

5 June – A biggish raid at dawn ... watched bombs fall out of a Ju88 from a great height, and they took an astonishingly long time to reach the ground ... we had a series of moonlight raids, probably by Italian planes, which dropped incendiary bombs ... they hit one dump of Italian oil which blazed furiously.

6 June – we had both guns in action by three o'clock by which time we had three Ju88s flying in high and dropping bombs on the town. One was knocked about by AA and twisted and turned in making good his escape.
7 June – a fair raid again at and around dawn, mostly dropping incendiary bombs."

Meanwhile, continuous patrols over the naval ships proceeding to Tobruk from Mersa Matruh were maintained throughout the daylight hours of 3 June by 73 Squadron, including a section led by Sgt Ellis. To his amazement, on looking down at the ships below, he saw a stick of bombs drop near them. The Hurricanes immediately climbed for altitude but were unable to locate the aircraft responsible for the attack, but three long-range Hurricanes of 274 Squadron's C Flight (the 229 Squadron detachment), despatched on a shipping protection patrol at 1500, encountered Ju87s of II/StG2 attacking two ships near Gambut, the Stukas protected by six Bf109s of 2/JG27. During a brief skirmish with the Messerschmitts, Flg Off Ron Bary (Z4510) succeeded in shooting down Uffz Reichstein whose aircraft (WkNr4127) crash-landed between Gambut and Gazala and was totally destroyed, but the Hurricane flown by Sgt Peter Crump (Z4369) was shot down into the sea by Fw Elles. The downed German pilot survived the action but the British one did not. Two of the Stukas fell to the guns of the ships they were attacking.

   Much to the annoyance and discomfort of the Hurricane pilots, shipping patrols continued for the next four days, 73 Squadron's diarist noting: "... almost any operational orders would be preferable to the monotony of the hours spent staring and watching for the Hun who rarely turns up." The monotony was somewhat relieved on 6 June when 73 Squadron was ordered to supply escort to two Marylands tasked to carry out photo-reconnaissances of the Tobruk area. Flt Lt Green led the first section of three and the Maryland successfully carried out its mission, but the section led by Flg Off Goodman saw six Bf109s taking off from Great Gambut landing ground as they approached, followed by a dozen more. Goodman signalled the Maryland to abort the recce and to follow the Hurricanes southwards into the desert. The Messerschmitts were evaded and all aircraft returned safely. Two days later, on the eve of 9 June, instructions were received for a dawn attack by two Marylands and eight Hurricanes against the Gazala landing grounds. One section of Hurricanes was to be led to Gazala North by Sous-Lt Denis, the other to Gazala South by Flt Lt Green, but the operation was hastily planned and poorly executed. The Marylands failed to rendezvous with the Hurricanes in the dark skies above Sidi Haneish and Denis, having orbited Sidi Barrani with his section for a considerable time, returned to base. Green, however, decided to press on to Gazala South with his section, navigating the 200 miles in darkness with accuracy although one Hurricane had to return early. Arriving over the landing ground just as dawn was breaking, the three Hurricanes swept down for a strafing attack, machine-gunning a number of Bf109s and G50bis. Before a section of Bf109s appeared, six fires were observed on the ground by Green. He also spotted a Messerschmitt closing on the tail of Sgt Laing's Hurricane, at which he fired a burst and saw it dive away towards the sea. He then set course for Sidi Barrani, where he was the only one of the three to return. Both Laing and Plt Off

Greville Tovey were shot down by the Bf109s of 1/JG27 flown by Oblt Redlich and Uffz Günther Steinhausen, Tovey being killed when his aircraft (Z4118) crashed into the sea, although Laing survived:

> "We were ordered off early in the morning to fly the 30 or 40 miles west to Gazala, to try to knock out any 109s we could find on the ground. It was not a good idea because it was just before dawn and you could not see enough to get yourself into position for a decent burst. I found two 109s but good not get a decent squirt at them although a Storch lit up quite nicely – not that it would bring the end of the war much closer! One of the Jerry ground gunners managed to hit my radiator: I felt a solid bang underneath which gave rise to a steady leak of steam and glycol, leaving a distinctive trail as I set off east. I was quite happy that I could at least reach Tobruk, but rather stupidly forgot that I made an excellent target against the dawn sky to which I was heading. I began to relax a little when I got a solid burst from a 109 up the tail, and I found it quite startling to hear the banging on the armour plate behind my seat, while the instruments on the top and sides of the panel disintegrated. I found myself thinking thank God that armour plating really worked. Perhaps they were not using armour-piecing ammo. Some of the firing must have hit the control surfaces as the Hurricane [Z4429] grew steadily more nose-heavy. Just to add to my predicament the ether in the glycol was rising up from the floor and causing me to become anaesthetised. Anyway she hit the ground more or less level, with a bounce or two. My straps were none too tight and I banged my face on the gunsight, doing wonders to my natural beauty. She began to burn so I jumped out and started to walk a few miles towards Tobruk, feeling none too chipper. A small cave came into view and I laid down in it to recover a bit. I realised later that I had been concussed in the crash, and that I was not in any condition to do any steady thinking or walking. After an hour or two I was found by an Indian patrol and taken into Tobruk, and to hospital."[2]

274 Squadron also particpated in the strafing operation, five Hurricanes (newly arrived Flt Lt D.L. Gould and Sgt Marsh, together with the veteran French pilots Flg Off Péronne and Wt Off Coudray led by Flg Off Weller) being despatched to attack aircraft on the ground at Derna. In the dawn light the pilots were only able to identify four Ju87s among the aircraft assembled there, an accompanying Wellington crew reporting that eight fires were seen on the ground following the Hurricane attack. All aircraft returned safely. Next day (10 June) Blenheim IVFs strafed M/T including tankers along the Barce-Derna road which were believed to be conveying diesel disembarked at Benghazi, while others attacked M/T including tankers on the Maraua-Bir el-Gandula road, one of which burst into flames. 274 Squadron joined the action the following afternoon, Flt Lt Gould's section strafing M/T along the Tobruk-Bardia road while Flg Off Hobbs' section attacked along the Trigh Capuzzo road, resulting in claims for the probable destruction of at least 15 vehicles. A tented encampment at Sidi Aziez was also machine-gunned.

---

[2] A day or two later Sgt Laing was conveyed by the destroyer HMAS *Waterhen* to Alexandria. After a short spell in hospital he returned to the Squadron, later being commissioned and awarded the DFC.

In preparation for the commencement of Operation *Battleaxe*, 274 Squadron received a flight of seven experienced pilots from 33 Squadron, mainly evacuees from Crete under the command of Flt Lt Vernon Woodward DFC, now one of RAFME's top-scoring pilots with at least 17 victories to his credit. A newly-formed fighter unit, 250 Squadron equipped with P-40 Tomahawks, arrived at Sidi Haneish from Egypt, its ranks bolstered by one of 73 Squadron's former senior pilots, newly promoted Flt Lt Dickie Martin DFC. By the eve of *Battleaxe*, 204 Group had assembled a total of 98 Hurricanes and Tomahawks, and could call upon the services of 105 Blenheims, Wellingtons and Marylands for bombing operations:

204 Group:

73 Squadron	Hurricanes	Sqn Ldr P.G. Wykeham-Barnes DFC
plus 213 Squadron detachment	Hurricanes	Flg Off C.B. Temlett DFC
274 Squadron	Hurricanes	Sqn Ldr G.E. Hawkins
plus 229 Squadron detachment	Hurricanes	Flg Lt W.A. Smith
plus 33 Squadron detachment	Hurricanes	Flt Lt V.C. Woodward DFC
1SAAF Squadron	Hurricanes	Maj T. Ross-Theron
plus 2SAAF Squadron detachment	Hurricanes	Capt D.H. Loftus
250 Squadron	Tomahawks	Sqn Ldr J.E. Scoular DFC

6 Squadron with its mixture of Hurricanes and Lysanders was at Qasaba under Sqn Ldr P. Legge.

FliegerFührer Afrika:

At Gazala I/JG27 had been reinforced by the arrival of six Bf109s of 7/JG26 from Sicily led by Oblt Joachim Müncheberg, one of the Luftwaffe's foremost fighter pilots with 43 victories to his credit; he and his small band had ravaged Malta's Hurricanes since their arrival in February, Müncheberg having personally accounted for 20 of the 42 victories achieved by his Staffel in that period:

I/JG27	Bf109E	Hptm Eduard Neumann
1/JG27	Bf109E	Oblt Karl-Heinz Redlich
2/JG27	Bf109E	Hptm Erich Gerlitz
3/JG27	Bf109E	Oblt Gerhard Homuth
7/JG26	Bf109E	Oblt Joachim Müncheberg
StabIII/ZG26	Bf110E	Maj Karl Kaschka
8/ZG26	Bf110E	Oblt Fritz Schulze-Dickow

The bomber force comprised two Gruppen of Ju87s (I/StG1 and II/StG2) and one Staffel of Ju88s from III/LG1, while tactical and photographic reconnaissance remained in the capable hands of crews from 2(H)/14 and 1(F)/121.

In support of their ally the Italians could offer about 70 fighters – G50bis of

2°Gruppo CT and CR42s of 18°Gruppo CT – and 25 bombers although, in the event, only occasional flights of G50bis and CR42s would be encountered over the battle front by RAF patrols. The single Italian Ju87 squadron (239^Squadriglia) was mainly involved in operations against shipping and gun positions at Tobruk, safely out of reach of RAF fighters although the guns steadily took their toll, the unit losing its third crew for the month on 12 June. Bomb-carrying CR42s of 18°Gruppo CT also took part in these latest attacks on Tobruk. Among the pilots serving with the Gruppo's 95^Squadriglia was newly promoted Tenente Franco Bordoni Bisleri, later to become the Regia Aeronautica's top-scoring pilot of the war, and who had claimed a Hurricane over the Tobruk garrison during the April fighting, in addition to four Blenheims; of this period he wrote:

"The CR42 was a good aircraft, easy to fly, strong and manoeuvrable, but it lacked sufficient speed and armament. It was possible to fight Gladiators, Blenheims and Wellingtons in this aircraft, but against other aircraft it was outclassed. The fighter pilots I flew against were generally very skilful, and the bomber crews were also good. Our allies, the German fighter pilots, were very brave and had a wonderful aircraft which they knew how to employ the right way, particularly making the best use of its good armament."

Again Lt Rankin's journal provides an account of the continuing daily raids on Tobruk harbour and garrison:

"**8 June** – A most disturbed night when we were bombed by Italian (probably) planes from a great height. Once again about half the bombs did not go off. One dropped quite near and it was an eerie thing listening to it screaming and tearing down and then only a dead silence. Had nine Italian fighter planes, G50s, parading overhead at breakfast time for nearly an hour. They look good, fast little planes. A Ju88 dropped what looked like an anti-personnel bomb – it burst 2,000 feet off the ground and was followed by explosions on the ground behind a hill nearby ... the alarm went and there were those blasted Stukas again. This time they bombed our forward artillery positions but many of them would not go into their dives properly. I only saw three out of thirteen do a proper steep dive. It really looks as though the Germans have lost many of their best pilots now.
9 June – After a night of continuous raids by single planes we were called out at dawn for a Ju88 and were delighted soon to hear the familiar roar of a Hurricane and several bursts of its multiple machine-guns split the air. Exit one Ju88, as far as we could tell! Another Ju88 came high over us after breakfast but we could not pick it up. 'Harry the Henschel' made his usual teatime appearance. Two saucy ME109s came and did stunts high up over the harbour.
10 June – Had very little sleep what with fleas and air raids, gunfire and bombs. Whilst firing at one raider a stick of bombs fell quite close to us – between us and our dummy bomb site. An ME110 went over dropping bombs and was heavily engaged by AA, going away in difficulties. Saw a lot of thermos bombs which had been dropped; evidently 157 of them were dropped in the ration dump enclosure alone. Saw two which no one else had found yet

and reported them – lethal looking objects.

11 June – A quiet dawn after a good many raids last night. Alarm went and we told of twenty planes coming in. Anticipated a spot of bother and then three CR42s did a power dive, obviously trying to draw our fire to the north. Not to be caught out this time I looked to the south, and there they were – the duty Stukas following up behind. And we were the objective. Got both guns on to them and when the first one came over us we blazed away. But he was determined and came on straight at poor little us. The guns went on firing and the bombs went just over our heads, landing with a terrific crash amongst our dug-outs. More planes followed up – six bombs fell among us.

12 June – After another very disturbed night I woke up around dawn expecting the usual Stuka raid. Sure enough at about 0745 I heard the roar of the CR42s trying the same game as yesterday and knew the Stukas would be following up. Soon the bombs started whistling and crashing. There seemed to be a lot of AA burst around us and I realised we were being protected by the other sites firing from inside the danger zone. One plane was shot down, the crew baling out, and two others were probably shot down. We counted fifteen Stukas and five CR42s.

13 June – An appalling night troubled more than ever with these blasted fleas. Also a number of raids and some activity round the perimeter.

14 June – The raids started and went on non-stop all night. We fired one barrage after another, occasionally getting back to bed and the fleas, only to be called out again a few minutes later. They were trying to prevent our use of the docks by continuous bombing, and we with our AA fire were trying to put them off their aim. Finally it began to get light and we were told of large numbers of planes coming from the east, suspected as friendly. We were too tired even to get excited about it, and no one even raised as much as a cheer when some Glenn Martins, Tomahawks and Hurricanes put on a show for us – what we have been waiting for for months!"

Capt Devine, the Tobruk-based Medical Officer, recorded the increase in air activity with a touch of light-hearted sarcasm:

"The anti-aircraft [command] was warned from Egypt that Hurricanes would fly over the town at a certain time. It is said that the brigadier in charge of the ack-ack returned a message, 'Please send us silhouette of a Hurricane. It is so long since we have seen any friendly planes that the gunners would not be able to remember what a Hurricane looks like.'"

With the offensive's imminent commencement, SAAF Marylands were called upon to make further strikes against the landing grounds at Gazala and Derna at dawn on 14 June, three aircraft each to lead six Hurricanes drawn from 73, 274 and 1SAAF, the latter to attack Gazala South while the first two groups were to strike at Gazala North and Derna respectively. Take-off time at Sidi Barrani coincided with a heavy ground mist and 274 Squadron's designated Maryland crashed on take-off, leaving the Hurricanes to find the Derna landing grounds in darkness and mist, which they failed to do. The sortie was aborted and the Hurricanes returned to base.

Meanwhile, the six Hurricanes of 73 Squadron led by Flg Off Goodman were airborne at 0430 to strafe Gazala North where, on arrival, the Maryland crew claimed an enemy aircraft destroyed on the ground by bombing and reported that the Hurricanes destroyed seven more, but two Hurricanes failed to return. A third (V7383) crashed on returning to Sidi Barrani, in which Flt Sgt John (Jack) White DFM was fatally injured. That evening one of the missing pilots, Plt Off Roy Chatfield, arrived back at Sidi Barrani aboard an army vehicle, having walked 25 miles before being picked after his flak-damaged Hurricane (Z4384) had crash-landed near Capuzzo, but the other missing pilot, Flg Off George (Benny) Goodman DFC, victor of 14 combats, was killed when his aircraft (Z4507) was shot down by flak. His body was later recovered and buried in the temporary cemetery at Zi el-Mrassas.

The third Maryland took-off at 0515 together with the six Hurricanes of 1SAAF, but Lt Durose was soon forced to return. In the darkness and mist the others became separated until only Capt Driver remained to escort the Maryland to Gazala South. When the target area was finally reached, the Maryland bombed from 3,000 feet while Driver (V7818) flew cover at 6,000 feet. A Bf109 suddenly appeared, climbing hard from Gazala South and flown by Oblt Franzisket of 3/JG27, who recalled:

> "While still climbing at 3,000 feet a single Hurricane closed on me from in front, and somewhat higher. As my aircraft was climbing very slowly I had no other choice than to point my 109 at the Hurricane and to fire. The Hurricane fired likewise but his burst was too high, as I could see very clearly by the tracer. We both fired until the last second, and the aircraft touched each other. Just before this I had seen hits on the engine of the Hurricane. When both aircraft collided, my airscrew touched the right wingtip of the Hurricane and his airscrew smashed the right wingtip of my 109. I saw the Hurricane going down in a steep dive and watched the pilot bale out. I turned and flew back to the airfield when suddenly I observed a Maryland north-east of the airfield at 4,000 feet. Although my aircraft was flying with one wing slightly low because of the damaged wingtip, I closed in and fired. The Maryland made a slight right-hand turn. I fired again, my burst going from the right engine along the whole of the fuselage to the tail. The engine caught fire and the Maryland went into a flat spin and one man baled out."

Only the pilot of the Maryland survived to be taken prisoner, as was Capt Ken Driver DFC, the third decorated Allied fighter ace to be lost on the morning's operation. The latter, slightly injured, was taken to meet his victor. Oblt Franzisket continued:

> "Driver was very quiet and reserved, and we chatted for about two hours in my tent. He showed me a photo of his wife and a blonde curl he carried. I promised to drop a message container over Sidi Barrani with a message for her, as she was in Cairo at the time, having come to visit him. He was very glad about this."

While A Flt/73 Squadron was engaged in the dawn attack on Gazala, the Squadron was required to despatch sections of three aircraft at 40-minute intervals to patrol over the Capuzzo battle area and to also provided a shipping patrol, at one stage having all 21 Hurricanes including those of the 229 Squadron detachment in the air at the same time. A busy morning for the pilots and groundcrews alike, a total of 63 sorties being flown during the day. 274 Squadron meanwhile despatched six long-range Hurricanes on a ground strafing mission, three aircraft designated to search and destroy along the Bardia-Tobruk road where five M/T were located and attacked, the other three locating a tented encampment four miles south-west of Sidi Bu Amud where some 40-50 widely dispersed vehicles were sighted. Following a strafing run, a result of which was probable damaged to at least eight vehicles, several small fires were observed which suggested to the pilots that fuel dumps had been hit. Later in the morning a single cannon-armed Hurricane II (V7348, an aircraft delivered by the 213 Squadron detachment) was employed to assist army units in the forward area, the pilot strafing three tanks and a convoy of 20 M/T encountered along the Gazala-Capuzzo road, claiming 18 of the latter destroyed or damaged.

Three Hurricanes of 1SAAF departed at 1910 as escort to another Maryland but the formation was intercepted near Rabia by Bf109s of 1/JG27, which were themselves escorting Ju87s. Apparently Lt Adriaan Botha was seen by army witnesses to shoot down two aircraft (subsequently credited as his 4th and 5th victories) before being shot down and killed by a Messerschmitt, his aircraft crashing some 35 miles south of Bir Hacheim. Lt Ralph Christie was also shot down, in flames, and killed south-east of Halfaya Pass, their victors being Oblt Redlich and Oblt Hugo Schneider. Only Lt A.A. Webb, the third member of the patrol, survived to report on the disastrous action. While army witnesses apparently reported Botha's victims as Stukas, it would seem that one was a Hs126 of 2(H)/14 from which the crew survived the action. SAAF pilots also accounted for a second aircraft from this unit when Capt Loftus with Lts J.R.R. Wells and L.A. Stone of 2SAAF intercepted Fw Otto Unger's Bf110 about three miles east of Halfaya Pass and shot it down. Unger and his observer Lt Friedrich Giesselmann survived the crash and were taken prisoner.

On the eve of Operation *Battleaxe* the squadrons were briefed including 6 Squadron at Qasaba, as recalled by Plt Off Moulding:

> "At about three-thirty that afternoon the pilots were given a general briefing. In the Mess hut, behind closed doors, Captain M produced a large-scale map pinned onto a big drawing board covered with talc. On it, in red chinagraph, were marked the positions of the Allied forces and, in black, those of the Axis troops. Slowly distinctly, as if he were addressing a class at Staff College, he described the situation, illustrating it on the map with a swagger cane. He came out glibly with figures indicating the strength and armament of divisions, battalions and even quite small special purpose units. He discussed in detail the importance of certain topographical features and gave a clear resume of the thinking behind the overall plan. It all looked very easy. 6 Squadron, on the following day and throughout the operation, would be asked to do continual reconnaissance, dawn to dusk, Tobruk to Bardia, down the wire to Capuzzo

and thence as far south as Giarabub. With only eight aircraft it was a big assignment.

Then came the really interesting part, the assumptions on which the plan had been made, the probable reaction of the enemy in general and in detail. The most important of these concerned the Panzer divisions known to be sitting, widely dispersed, astride the coast road between Bardia and Tobruk. The assumption here was firstly that, while the Germans were expecting the Allies to move, they had been given every reason to believe this would not happen until early July, and they would not therefore be able to react quickly. Certainly, reconnaissance over the past few days had shown no signs of activity among the Panzers. It would, the army believed, take them several hours to get mobile. It was a very polished piece of briefing and it left everyone with a feeling that every eventuality had been accounted for and that the operation must be a success."

As British heavy tanks and Indian infantry opened their attack on the defences at Halfaya Pass simultaneous with an assault on Hafid Ridge and Fort Capuzzo, eight Hurricanes of 274 Squadron took off to ground strafe M/T along the Gazala-Tobruk road to Sidi Aziez. Some 15 miles east of Gazala a large concentration of vehicles was located and thoroughly strafed. On the return flight a single CR42 was sighted near Sidi Aziez, engaged and shot down by Plt Off Jim Briggs (Z4612); the Italian pilot survived. At 0600, Plt Off Sumner in the cannon-armed Hurricane (V7348) took off with the task of neutralizing a field gun position between Fort Capuzzo and Halfaya Pass, being led to the area by Plt Off A.W.J. McBarnet (V7710) of 6 Squadron. On approaching the target they were attacked by three Bf109s from 2/JG27 and both shot down, falling victim to Fw Elles and Uffz Rudolf Stöckler, the latter's first victory. McBarnet crash-landed, slightly wounded, and was able to make his way back to his unit, but Sumner was killed. Six of the seven 33 Squadron detachment Hurricanes were led off by Flt Lt Woodward when news was received at Sidi Haneish of enemy bombers attacking forward troops but, by the time they arrived over the battle front, no hostile aircraft were seen. Hurricanes from the detachment also provided protection for another 6 Squadron aircraft carrying out a photo-reconnaissance sortie from which all returned safely on this occasion.

A patrol from 73 Squadron's C Flight took off after breakfast, the three Hurricanes returning at 1000 to report an action with two Bf109s, one of which was claimed shot down by Flg Off J.A. Sowrey[3] (Z4471). Shortly thereafter, Flg Off Temlett led another patrol from C Flight to the Sollum area. Nearing the target the section was initially attacked from astern by four Bf109s, followed by a further eight. In the ensuing combat Temlett (Z4323) and Sgt P.P. Wilson (V7673) each claimed Messerschmitts, although both Hurricanes were badly shot about in return, while Plt Off P.J. Pound (V7710) was shot down; the latter baled out with shrapnel wounds to one knee, and was picked up by an army unit and taken to a casualty

---

[3] Flg Off John Sowrey, from a distinguished Air Force family, had been attached to 73 Squadron at about the same time his younger brother James had joined 6 Squadron. Six days after the end of Operation *Battleaxe*, on 24 June, James was shot down and killed by Oblt Müncheberg of 7/JG26.

clearing station for treatment. For I/JG27, Oblt Redlich of 1 Staffel claimed one Hurricane as did Obfhr Hans-Arnold Stahlschmidt of 2 Staffel, but the Gruppe lost two pilots killed during the morning's combats – Uffz Stöckler (WkNr4123) and Uffz Heinz Greuel (WkNr2943) both of 2 Staffel – while 1 Staffel's Oblt Hugo Schneider was obliged to bale out of his aircraft (WkNr6428).

At 1140, 274 Squadron despatched six Hurricanes to ground strafe along the Trigh Capuzzo road, where a concentration of M/T was located and thoroughly machine-gunned. All returned safely from this operation but the next carried out by 274 Squadron was intercepted by a swarm of Bf109s from all three Staffeln of I/JG27 – with disastrous results. Ten Hurricanes had taken off at 1655 with instructions to ground strafe along the Acroma-Capuzzo road, and were followed a few minutes later by a section from 73 Squadron's C Flight, again led by Flg Off Sowrey, as escort to a 6 Squadron Hurricane on a reconnaissance. Along the specified road some 20 to 25 M/T were located and attacked by 274 Squadron, while an escorting Hs126 of 2(H)/14 was encountered by Flg Off Joe Hobbs (W9268) and shot down about 15 miles south-west of El Adem. The Henschel's pilot, Fw Herbert Schädlich, was killed but his observer, Oblt Karl Münch, although wounded, managed to bale out. The Messerschmitts then struck, shooting down Sgt Michael Daniels (V7371), who had only joined the Squadron with the 229 Squadron detachment three days earlier; he was killed, as was veteran Frenchman Wt Off Charles Coudray, his aircraft (Z2643) last seen being pursued 15 miles west of Sidi Barrani. Two other French pilots were more fortunate, Flg Off Antoine Péronne being seen to force-land V7827 inside enemy territory (and was subsequently taken prisoner), while Flt Sgt Marcel Lebois force-landed Z4612 near the Trigh Capuzzo road[4]. 73 Squadron's C Flight section was also engaged by the Messerschmitts, both Flg Off Sowrey (Z4471) and Plt Off S.J. Leach RAAF (V7822) claiming probables but losing Plt Off John Logan whose aircraft (Z4788) was seen to go down with smoke pouring from its engine; the Rhodesian pilot baled out but apparently his parachute failed to open and he was killed. SAAF Hurricanes were also in the area at this time and, during the course of 16 sorties flown by the 2SAAF Squadron detachment, three Hurricanes encountered eight Ju88s about to attack troops west of Capuzzo. A beam attack was carried out but, before any damage could be inflicted, three Bf109s dived on them from out of the sun and shot down Lt B. Guest's aircraft. The damaged Hurricane force-landed and the SAAF pilot was able to reach safety with the help of an army unit. Victories were claimed in this action by Oblt Franzisket and Lt Friedrich Hoffmann of 3 Staffel, both south-east of Gambut, another by Lt Willi Kothmann of 2 Staffel north-west of Fort Capuzzo, and a fourth by Oblt Redlich of 1 Staffel, west of Fort Capuzzo, while Hptm Neumann, the Gruppenkommandeur, claimed a probable south of the fort. One Messerschmitt (WkNr4123) was damaged in a fight near Sollum but the pilot was able to return to base safely. The reconnaissance Hurricane (V7769) was also shot down and its pilot, Flt Lt John McFall, recipient of two DFCs, was critically wounded. He had been chased back to Sidi Barrani but was forced down before he

---

[4] During the course of the following three nights and two days, Flt Sgt Lebois walked some 50 miles before being picked up by an army patrol near Sofafi, having suffered severely lacerated feet.

reached the landing ground, and was wounded when his aircraft was strafed as he climbed out, dying shortly afterwards. It seems probable that his victor was Uffz Karl-Heinz Ehlen of 7/JG26, who opened the Staffel's North African account when he reported shooting down a Hurricane near Sidi Barrani during the evening.

73 Squadron scrambled two sections just before dusk when further enemy air activity was reported over the battle area, Flt Lt Green (Z4697) and Plt Off G.R.A.McG. Johnston (V7802) – one of the new arrivals and a future CO – encountering a Bf110, presumably a reconnaissance machine from 2(H)/14. Both reported seeing their opening bursts hitting the aircraft as it dived away towards German lines, the Hurricanes then meeting considerable AA fire which damaged Green's aircraft. Air Commodore Collishaw's small fighter force had thus suffered severely during the day's fighting, with the loss of ten Hurricanes and seven pilots, of whom two were prisoners of war; a further two pilots had been wounded and put out of action. Blenheim fighters were also active against ground targets during the day, four strafing an M/T convoy in the Barce area with crews reporting five vehicles hit and one overturned. Four others attacked a convoy on the Maruara-Slonte road, claiming two or three vehicles damaged together with an Italian tank, while four more attacked a convoy of ten vehicles in the el Brega-Jedabya area. From these operations all returned safely.

Dawn on 16 June at Sidi Haneish witnessed six Hurricanes from 274 Squadron take to the air, the pilots briefed to patrol the forward area, returning two hours later without having encountered any enemy aircraft. At the same time a single Hurricane patrolled over naval craft just offshore, also without incident, but a patrol led by Plt Off D.F.K. Edghill (V7492) of the 229 Squadron detachment encountered Bf109s of 3/JG27, Edghill (an experienced pilot with three victories to his credit) claiming one shot down at about 0900, Lt Hoffmann in turn claiming a Hurricane probably destroyed eight miles south-west of Buq-Buq. Apparently neither side suffered a loss in this combat. A lack of enemy aerial activity greeted subsequent patrols put up by 274 Squadron throughout the day, Flt Lt Woodward having led seven Hurricanes over the forward area at 1230, followed by Flg Off Hobbs and Flt Sgt Tom Morris carrying out reconnaissance flights to locate enemy lines of communication, which they successfully fulfilled, while three more patrolled as far as Sidi Barrani, and later over the forward area, again without meeting any opposition. Finally, during the evening, the Squadron despatched five Hurricanes led by Flg Off E.J. Woods of the 33 Squadron detachment to patrol over Sollum, Capuzzo and Sidi Aziez, all returning safely. 73 Squadron was similarly unsuccessful in meeting enemy aircraft during the course of two squadron-strength patrols carried out during the day. The CO, Sqn Ldr Wykeham-Barnes, had gained permission from Group to use his aircraft in this manner rather than each squadron providing piecemeal patrols which were invariably outnumbered and consequently overwhelmed by the Messerschmitts. The pilots, many of whom were inexperienced, welcomed the new instructions which generally allowed them a greater sense of security. But, in the event, not so for the South Africans who were able only to muster seven Hurricanes from the two squadrons for a patrol planned for the late morning.

Maj Ross-Theron, CO of 1SAAF, led the composite patrol which was to cover the Sollum-Capuzzo-Bardia triangle, with Capt J.A. Kok at the head of the three Hurricanes from 2SAAF. Suddenly, from out of the sun, a Bf109 dived on Kok's tail. Within seconds the Hurricane was on fire, but Kok was able to glide the crippled aircraft to a crash-landing about five miles east of Sollum. Maj Ross-Theron dived after the Messerschmitt and reported that it crashed "in a cloud of flames, smoke and dust". As he climbed to rejoin his patrol, Ross-Theron sighted a formation of six G50bis approaching and these attempted to manoeuvre onto his tail but were unable to hold the tight turns necessary, allowing the South African an opportunity to attack one as it fell away. Opening fire, he reported that it also went down in flames but his own aircraft was then hit by what he believed was 'friendly' fire, when east of Sollum:

> "I gave a violent kick to the joystick to force myself out of the smoke-filled cockpit and fell headfirst from 7,000 feet and, as the chute opened, felt myself fall through the loose harness. My legs caught. I slipped further. I hung by my ankles. My left arm was broken and swinging loose past my head. As the earth rushed up I hunched and hit the ground with my right thigh. Wind filled the canopy and dragged me across the stoney desert with a dislocated hip until soldiers fell on the canopy."

The G50bis were from 358^Squadriglia and were escorting six Ju87s of 239^Squadriglia attacking M/T and tanks south-east of Sollum harbour. Four of the Italian Stuka pilots – Ten Giacomo Ragazzini, Ten Ettore Amisano, Serg Magg Ennio Tarantola, Serg Dino Fabbri – each reported being engaged by Hurricanes but before any damage could be inflicted they witnessed the leader of the escort, Cap Sterzi, shoot down one of the attackers near Sidi Omar, which may have been Ross-Theron's aircraft. German Stukas from I/StG1 were also involved in the assault on the Commonwealth forces, and it was these that were sighted by Capt Quirk and Lt Archie Tatham attacking troops between Capuzzo and Ruweibit. Diving after them, Quirk claimed two shot down in rapid succession while narrowly avoiding collision with a third. As he pulled away a Messerschmitt closed on his tail and a cannon shell exploded in the Hurricane's cockpit, slightly wounding him and setting the aircraft on fire. He baled out over enemy lines but his parachute drifted him away from capture and he came down south of Capuzzo, where soldiers helped him to a casualty clearing station for treatment of his wounds. At least one of the Stukas attacked by Quirk crashed, Uffz Karl Steinmann of 3 Staffel and his gunner Gfr Erwin Helmrich being captured west of Sollum. On his return to Sidi Haneish following this action, Lt Burger reported seeing a Hurricane on the ground near Capuzzo which appeared to have landed wheels down but had a large hole in its starboard wing. The hood was closed. No occupant could be seen. Both the downed Hurricanes (believed to have been Z4090 and Z4422) were credited to pilots of I/JG27, Fw Elles of 2 Staffel reporting victory over one Hurricane south of Bardia, while Lt Hoffmann of 3 Staffel claimed a probable in the same general area.

17 June was to prove to be another bad day for 204 Group's fighters, when a further ten Hurricanes were lost, mainly victims of the Messerschmitts of I/JG27. It was the South Africans who were first to suffer when a formation of seven Hurricanes from the two squadrons, led by Lt Burger, were jumped at about 1100 south-east of Sidi Omar by seven Bf109s which were escorting Ju87s. Two of the Hurricanes fell in flames, both pilots baling out but Lt Smith died from his wounds

in captivity, while Lt K.K. Mitchell was taken prisoner but was later able to escape. A third Hurricane, flown by Lt J.B. White, also failed to return, his demise unnoticed by his colleagues. Two of the Hurricanes fell to Lt Heinz Schmidt of 3/JG27 and the third to Lt Klaus Mietusch of the attached 7/JG26, while Uffz Melchior Kestler of the same Staffel claimed another which was not confirmed. As the survivors of the SAAF flight attempted to make good their escape Lt Durose's aircraft was hit by AA fire over Sidi Omar, necessitating a crash-landing at Sidi Barrani. He was flown back to Sidi Haneish in a Lysander. It was a bad start to the day. Worse was to follow.

At 1150, six Hurricanes of 73/274 Squadron carried out a patrol over the forward area, also meeting a number of Ju87s engaged in dive-bombing troop concentrations. Flg Off Bary (V7828) led the Hurricanes into the attack and claimed one damaged, as did Plt Off T.L.W. Officer (Z4533) and Plt Off Johns (W9268), but Sgt Gordon Wooller (P3977) failed to return and was later reported to have been killed. The Squadron was then called upon to provide three Hurricanes to escort General Wavell's Proctor to the forward area, as noted by Air Marshal Tedder:

> "Wavell very naturally became worried about the unsatisfactory progress of the offensive and flew up to the Desert. On the morning of 17 June, he and [Lt Gen Sir Noel] Beresford-Pierse [OC Western Desert Force] were foolish enough to go up in a Proctor and land in the forward area where 7th Armoured Division was on the move. No one quite knew where the two Generals were, and it was only thanks to much good luck and a very heavy fighter escort that Wavell escaped. That evening, when he got back to Cairo, I told him politely that this had been an act of criminal lunacy. It was not merely a question of his personal value, but the effect that the loss of the GOC would have from the point of view of prestige. We had lost enough Generals already."

During the mid-afternoon, at 1645, 204 Group ordered the despatch of a dozen Hurricanes to carry out ground strafing sorties along enemy lines of communication and to attack dumps, camps and M/T in the Sidi Omar area. Six of the aircraft were drawn from the 33 Squadron detachment led by Flt Lt Woodward, and two from 229 Squadron detachment, plus one from 73 Squadron, with Flt Lt Honor leading the 274 Squadron section. Shortly into the flight a large number of enemy aircraft were sighted – Ju87s from II/StG2 and 239^Squadriglia, with escort provided by Bf109s of 3/JG27 and G50bis from 150^Squadriglia. Three of the pilots managed to successfully engage the Stukas, of which 229 Squadron's Plt Off Edghill (Z4366) claimed two shot down and Plt Off R.R. Mitchell (Z4630) one, while Flg Off D.T. Moir (W9298) of 33 Squadron also claimed one. At least one aircraft of II/StG2 was totally lost in which Lt Franz Lauberger and Uffz Thomas Mantsch were killed. Meanwhile, the other Hurricanes soon became embroiled in a series of dogfights with the escort, Flt Lt Vernon Woodward (Z4377) shooting down the G50bis flown by Ten Serafino Molinari, who was killed, before he engaged and damaged a second; Sgt George Genders (Z4174), also of 33 Squadron (with five victories from the fighting in Greece, who had earlier served briefly with 73 Squadron), damaged two more. Flt Lt Honor (Z4614) claimed a Messerschmitt damaged and Lt D. Dove SAAF (Z4175, attached to 33 Squadron) reported that he had shot down another, but four Hurricanes failed to return including one (Z4509) flown by 33 Squadron's Flg Off Eric Woods (with at least four victories to his credit), who was killed. The 274 Squadron section lost two pilots, Frenchman Sous-Lt Robert Grasset (Z4510) and Plt Off Terrence Officer (Z4533), both of whom survived to be taken prisoner, Montpellier-born Grasset's aircraft crashing in the Hasbardia area of Tobruk. The fourth missing Hurricane (W9198) was flown by the sole 73 Squadron representative, Plt Off Bert Reynolds, though he returned next day and reported that he had been shot down by AA fire. The Messerschmitt pilots reported four victories, Uffz Schmidt again claiming two, while Fw Karl Mentnich claimed one and Obfhr Marseille a probable. The G50bis pilots also submitted claims for three Hurricanes shot down, Sottoten Agostino Celentano, M.llo Olindo Simionato and Serg Magg Patriarca being the claimants.

At 1830, Lt Bester led six SAAF Hurricanes to patrol the Sofafi-Halfaya area at 10,000 feet, where they were to cover retreating troops moving south-east along the escarpment. An hour into the patrol nine Ju88s were observed and some minutes later two further formations of twin-engined aircraft were seen. Bester delivered attacks on five of the first formation of bombers, without observed results. During this engagement a Bf109 dived on him from out of the sun, but this was chased away by Lt Tennant. Although then engaged by three Bf110s of the escort, Bester managed to evade and attack two Ju88s from above and below but was again intercepted by Bf110s, with which he exchanged fire, believing he had silenced two rear gunners and disabled the port engine of another:

> "The 110 reared up, stalled and fell over towards the ground ... its pilot could never gain control at that altitude."

Unable to confirm its destruction owing to the attention of a Bf109, Bester returned to Sidi Haneish convinced of a victory nonetheless. Meanwhile, Lt Taylor found himself in the centre of a defensive circle framed by four Bf110s. Despite heavy fire from the rear gunners he turned inside the circle and fired four long bursts into the rear aircraft although with unobserved results. Another formation of four Bf110s was engaged by Lt Johannes Conradie, who, despite having been wounded in the head by return fire, reported gaining strikes on two of the Zerstörer, one of which fell away with smoke pouring from both engines. Conradie was then engaged by another Bf110 and again wounded but succeeded in flying his damaged aircraft back to Sidi Barrani. His courage and determination in this action was later recognized by the award of the DFC. Both Maj Kaschka, Gruppenkommandeur of III/ZG26, and Oblt Schulze-Dickow, the Staffelkapitän of 8 Staffel, claimed Hurricanes, one south of Sulieman and the other south-east of Sollum. Two of the Bf109 pilots also made claims, Obfhr Marseille of 3 Staffel reporting a Hurricane probably destroyed about 10 miles east of Sidi Omar, while Obfw Hermann Förster of 2 Staffel identified his victim as a 'Brewster'. This latter aircraft was in fact a Brewster Buffalo (AX813) of 805 Squadron FAA piloted by Lt Lloyd Keith DSC[5],

---

[5] Lt Lloyd Keith, a Canadian former RAF officer, had participated in successful combats against SM79s while flying Sea Gladiators with Cdr Keighly-Peach from *Eagle* in July and August 1940, in addition to his normal duties as a Swordfish pilot, and, more recently Buffaloes with 805 Squadron.

who was flying a convoy escort patrol from Mersa Matruh. He was seriously injured when his aircraft crashed north-west of Sidi Barrani and although recovered by a German patrol, he succumbed to his injuries ten days later.

Keith was a member of an ad hoc RN unit comprising a mixture of Buffaloes, Fulmars, Sea Gladiators and borrowed RAF Hurricanes with pilots drawn from 803, 805 and 806 Squadrons, which was based at Dekheila near Alexandria, tasked mainly with escorting convoys between Mersa Matruh and Tobruk. Most of the sorties were uneventful. During the morning of 18 June, six Hurricanes arrived at Sidi Haneish from Ma'aten Bagush flown by more pilots from the FAA unit led by Lt J.M. Bruen RN DSC of 803 Squadron who had been flying Fulmars from the carrier *Formidable*. They were to operate with 73 Squadron and amongst their number was Sub Lt Duncan Richards who had flown off *Furious* to Takoradi with 73 Squadron the previous November. The others were Lt D.C. Gibson and Sub Lts B. Sinclair, R.I.M. Scott and A.C. Wallace. The following day a seventh FAA pilot arrived, Lt A.J. Wright, a Royal Marine. Lts Bruen and Gibson, in particular, were combat experienced, the former having shared in the destruction of four enemy aircraft, while Donald Gibson had survived crashing over the side of the carrier in his damaged Fulmar following a combat with Italian torpedo-bombers during which he had been wounded, an incident in which his observer was killed. Of the attachment to 73 Squadron, he later wrote:

> "... we were ordered to Amiriya where the RAF would give us some desert-modified Hurricanes to replace our old Fulmars. On arrival we jumped out of our Fulmars, Bill [Bruen] signed a piece of paper and we got into desert Hurricanes fitted with special air filters. The same afternoon we flew our new aircraft to Ma'aten Bagush where our long-suffering maintenance men awaited us. Neither we, nor the ratings, had any chance to find out anything about these aircraft but I must say we found them delightful and very easy to fly."

A duststorm started to blow at midday just as 73 Squadron was instructed to carry out a strafe of Gambut aerodrome, preventing the operation from being undertaken until 1450 when Flg Off Sowrey (Z4270) led eight Hurricanes into the air, three flown by FAA pilots (Richards W9327, Scott Z4177, and Wallace W9354), and were followed 50 minutes later by a further five led by Plt Off W.C. Russell (a new pilot) which included the remaining three FAA Hurricanes (Bruen V7816, Gibson W9343, and Sinclair Z4236) which were to strafe M/T in the Sidi Omar area but, in the event, they returned without firing their guns, the only sightings being a couple of derelict lorries. Meanwhile, the first formation encountered bad visibility and strong winds and was subsequently blown off course. The leader had headed northwards from Sidi Barrani and then turned westwards for a time over the sea before finally turning south, but when landfall was made he found he was over friendly territory. Realising the error, Sowrey called up the section, telling them to refuel at Sidi Barrani before making another attempt. The message was not received by the RN pilots and, thinking they were over enemy territory, they dived down to strafe the aerodrome in view below – which *was* in fact Sidi Barrani! Lt Gibson recalled:

"... while refuelling at Sidi Barrani we were strafed by our colleagues.
Fortunately they concentrated their fire on a wrecked Maryland in the centre
of the airfield, but they also set fire to a Hurricane near me and caused me to
dive into a slit trench. This party was led by a junior pilot who got his
navigation fouled up. Bill Bruen broke our party away and tried to call them
off whereupon, realising their error, they landed and asked for fuel. Whatever
disciplinary action was taken I never heard about it. I had sympathy for the
perpetrator of this boob, as the desert has few features and a strong wind from
the west led him astray."

Apart from the Hurricane set on fire on the aerodrome, a number of M/T were
damaged during the strafe but fortunately no casualties were inflicted upon ground
personnel. As a direct result of the unfortunate incident the navy pilots were
immediately withdrawn from operations and ordered to proceed to Palestine
forthwith – an inauspicious start for the FAA detachment which was later expanded
to become the Royal Naval Fighter Squadron (RNFS), a unit which distinguished
itself in later air battles over the desert.

204 Group suffered a further blow during the day when eight Tomahawks of 250
Squadron, strafing along the Bardia-Tobruk road shortly after dawn, were bounced
by Bf109s of 1/JG27. Three were promptly shot down by the Messerschmitts and
all three pilots killed, while a fourth fell to AA fire, the pilot returning to the
Squadron some two weeks later. Fortunately for 204 Group's squadrons the
operation to relieve Tobruk was now cancelled owing to the disastrous ground
battle which had seen Wavell's tanks knocked out by German anti-tank units.

Meanwhile, the wounded CO of 1SAAF, Maj Ross-Theron, arrived at Sidi
Haneish on board an ambulance to enquire after the welfare of his pilots, and was
saddened and shocked to learn of the latest casualties. The Squadron was now under
the temporary command of Capt Le Mesurier pending the arrival of a replacement
CO since Ross-Theron's injuries – a broken femur, a fractured hand and the loss of
two fingers – would take some time to heal. Air Commodore Collishaw sent him a
personal message:

"I much regret that you were wounded in action with the enemy. The Squadron
you prepared and trained has done excellent work against the enemy. We all
wish you a speedy recovery and the best of luck. Your ME109 was some
compensation for your wound."

The ground fighting had gone badly for the Commonwealth forces. As predicted by
General Wavell, the British light tanks had proved too slow for desert warfare and
were vulnerable to German anti-tank guns, while the faster cruiser tanks had
suffered numerous breakdowns; of the 190 British tanks committed to the battle, 91
were lost to enemy action or breakdowns. The German 5th and 8th Panzer
Regiments lost only a dozen tanks. Wavell ordered a withdrawal. Operation
Battleaxe was over. Tobruk remained under siege. During the course of the five-day
battle 204 Group had lost 33 fighters, of which 29 were Hurricanes, and three
bombers. Sixteen fighter pilots had been killed, four taken prisoner and a further six
wounded. In return the Hurricanes had claimed 17 air victories plus four probables.

Air Commodore Collishaw concluded that the high fighter attrition was mainly due to inexperienced pilots being thrown into action. Nevertheless, the AOC sent a signal to Collishaw at the conclusion of *Battleaxe*:

> "Please express to all your fighter squadrons the deep admiration I feel for their magnificent work during the recent operations. During the initial stages ... they had to operate under conditions which exposed them to attack by superior numbers whenever the enemy chose to concentrate. Only in this way could continuous cover be ensured for the army. It was a hard job but it was done and the cover was completely successful ... relentless low attacks before the land operation ... and the final stages ... were a potent factor in preventing the enemy from concentrating or maintaining large forces in battle ..."

The Prime Minister's reaction when he received the news was predictable:

> "... its failure was to me a most bitter blow. Success in the Desert would have meant the destruction of Rommel's audacious force. Tobruk would have been relieved, and the enemy's retreat might well have carried him back beyond Benghazi as fast as he had come."

With a lull in ground fighting and, as a consequence, a reduction in air operations, the Hurricane units were able to fly many of their aircraft back to the Delta for servicing and several pilots were able to catch up on leave. Among those operationally tour-expired was 73 Squadron's Sous-Lt Denis[6]:

> "During this first tour of operations I got six confirmed victories, a CR42, three ME109s and two Ju87s. We didn't keep a precise count of the missions we flew during the siege [of Tobruk]. Most of them just happened over the airfield [El Gubbi] and didn't last more than 15 minutes – time for take-off, interception and landing when the chargers were empty. In such conditions there was no problem to confirm victories. Great Britain awarded me the DFC."

Following the failure of *Battleaxe* and the consequential failure to relieve Tobruk, the Germans returned to a form of psychological warfare by dropping leaflets over the garrison:

---

[6] Promoted Capitaine, James Denis was posted to Beirut following the successful conclusion to the fighting in Syria and Lebanon, and later he briefly commanded a flight in Groupe de Chasse III/2 *Alsace*, a Free French Hurricane unit formed in Syria at the end of 1941. Of the remaining pilots of *Escadrille Denis*, both Albert Littolf and Noël Castelain later joined *Normandie-Niémen*, the French volunteer fighter group under the command of Cmdt Jean Tulasne, formerly of 274 Squadron, which served on the Eastern Front with the Soviets, losing their lives in the same air battle on 16 July 1943. By then both had increased their individual scores, Littolf having been credited with seven destroyed plus eight shared (of which five were claimed while attached to 73 Squadron), while Castelain was credited with a further six in Russia. Cmdt Tulasne was killed in action next day.

Aussies

After Crete disaster Anzac troops are now being ruthlessly sacrificed by England in Tobruk and Syria. Turkey has concluded pact of friendship with Germany. England will shortly be driven out of the Mediterranean. Offensive from Egypt to relieve you totally smashed.

You Cannot Escape

Our dive-bombers are waiting to sink your transports. Think of your future and your people at home. Come forward. Show white flags and you will be out of danger!

Surrender!

But there was to be no surrender. The stalemate continued. This second phase of the war in the Western Desert had come to an end and British feathers had been ruffled but there was tremendous activity behind the lines, where re-grouping and re-equipping was taking place. However, there was a price to be paid for the failure of *Battleaxe* and General Wavell was relieved of his command, General Sir Claude Auchinleck, until recently C-in-C India, arriving to take his place, which led to an immediate improvement in the co-operation between army and air force. Although Air Marshal Tedder admired Wavell, he had distrusted many of his staff: with Auchinleck he was to form a strong partnership. Air Commodore Collishaw was also relieved of his command, Air Vice-Marshal Sir Arthur Coningham DSO MC DFC, another WWI ace, taking over 204 Group the following month.

With the European coastline of the Mediterranean now completely in Axis hands or under its influence, and the North African coastline from Algeria to Libya as far as the Egyptian border similarly controlled, there remained only the tiny rocky outpost at Gibraltar, besieged Malta – a mere speck in the central Mediterranean, though a vitally important one – and the isolated Tobruk garrison still in British hands. There was also a German-inspired uprising in Iraq for the British to contend with, a strong Vichy resistance to the British invasion of Syria, and a wavering Turkey to consider; while the newly arrived armoured force had been severely mauled and had proved unreliable, and Hurricane stocks had been badly depleted. British Middle East Command needed breathing space, a lifeline. It came in an unexpected if not totally unanticipated manner when Hitler invaded Russia on 22 June. The pressure was relieved, even if the Tobruk garrison had not been so fortunate.

TOBRUK RELIEVED, LOST, RECAPTURED

July 1941 – November 1942

"The enemy, who has fought with the utmost stubbornness and enterprise, had paid the price for his valour ..."
>Prime Minister Churchill on the raising of the siege, November 1941

"Tobruk glared upon us, and, as in the previous year, we had no doubt that it should be held."
>Prime Minister Churchill with Tobruk again threatened, June 1942

"Tobruk was a symbol of British resistance, and we were now going to finish it for good."
>General Rommel, June 1942

"[The loss of Tobruk was] one of the heaviest blows I can recall during the war."
>Prime Minister Churchill on reflection on the fall of Tobruk in June 1942

Tobruk was finally recaptured on 13 November 1942 following the success of the Eighth Army at El Alamein

With the failure of Operation *Battleaxe*, the new British Command drew up plans for the next offensive while front-line troops consolidated their positions. Rommel and his Afrika Korps similarly desperately needed time to build up supplies since its lines of communication were strainfully overstretched. The Axis failure to take Tobruk and thereby gain its harbour placed added burden on the overland supply routes, all of Rommel's armour and other fighting vehicles, his ammunition and supplies, fuel, food and water having to be transported hundreds of miles along the tortuous and often treacherous coastal road – and vulnerable to air strike. Although *Battleaxe* was a defeat for the British, under the circumstances it could be considered nothing much more than a Pyrrhic victory for the Germans. Tobruk remained a thorn in Rommel's side.

There were changes within the garrison at this time, the Australian government demanding the withdrawal of its forces which had suffered some 3,000 casualties

in April alone. This seemingly impossible task was achieved surprisingly easily –
under cover of darkness and the very noses of the German and Italian besiegers, fast
naval vessels audaciously evacuated the majority of the Australian troops and
replaced them with Indians, South Africans, Poles and British. There followed,
therefore, a period of relative little offensive activity on the ground and in the air,
the summer months of 1941 witnessing the occasional escorted sweep by RAF and
SAAF light bombers, with the odd skirmish between opposing fighters, in which
the Messerschmitts of I/JG27 continued to dominate, while the Axis concentrated
mainly on attacking Allied shipping plying the coastal route, with the occasional
fighter sweep over the forward areas and in protection of their bombers.

After three months of this relative calm, German attacks began to intensify as
Rommel regained confidence with the build up of supplies and equipment. The
Tobruk garrison was on the receiving end of a 100-plus Stuka raid at the beginning
of September, followed by continuous German tank assaults during October, but
still the troops held firm. Hitler had recently promoted Rommel to full general and
placed him in command of the newly created Panzergruppe Afrika (later renamed
Panzerarmee Afrika). With the arrival of the 21st Panzer Division, the Afrika Korps
had a paper force of some 272 Mark II and Mark III tanks, although almost one-
third were temporarily unfit for battle, to which could be added those of the Italian
Ariete Division, but the Allies had numerical superiority in this department,
Auchinleck having amassed almost 600 cruiser tanks although these were inferior
in fire-power and armour-plating compared to the panzers. And it was the Allies
who took the initiative, launching Operation *Crusader* at dawn on the morning of
18 November 1941. The ambitious plan called for a wide sweeping move by the
massed armour to the area of Gabr Saleh, 40 miles south-east of Sidi Rezegh, where
it was hoped to lure Axis forces into a decisive tank action, while infantry were to
attack Sollum and Sidi Omar. Once achieved, the British force would advance to
relieve Tobruk. To provide air cover for the offensive, RAFME had amassed a
strong fighter force: 258 Wing comprising 1SAAF, 94, 238 and 274 Squadrons with
Hurricanes, and 2SAAF and 3RAAF Squadrons with Tomahawks; 262 Wing
comprising 229 and 260 Squadrons with Hurricanes, 4SAAF, 112 and 250
Squadrons with Tomahawks, plus 80 Squadron with Hurricane fighter-bombers;
269 Wing comprising 30 Squadron with Hurricanes, and RN Fighter Squadron with
Hurricanes and Martlets; 253 Wing comprising 208, 237 and 451RAAF with TacR
Hurricanes, and a detachment of newly arrived Beaufighters (from 272 Squadron)
was also available. There were two wings of light bombers equipped with
Blenheims (seven squadrons), Marylands (two squadrons), plus one squadron with
Bostons.

Fliegerführer Afrika now possessed four Staffeln of the new Bf109Fs (from I and
II/JG27), a Staffel of Bf109E fighter-bombers (Jabo Staffel 10/JG27), three Staffeln
of Bf110s (III/ZG26), and a Staffel of Ju88C nightfighters (2/NJG2). Ju87s and
Ju88s provided the bomber force together with a Staffel of He111s for night
operations. There were also at least 19 Italian fighter squadrons equipped with
MC202s (seven squadrons) from 6°, 9°· and 17°Gruppi, MC200s (seven squadrons)
from 153° and 157°Gruppi plus 374^Squadriglia, G50bis (three squadrons) from
20°Gruppo, and CR42s (two squadrons) from 9°Gruppo; in addition there were
several other CR42 units available in reserve.

After some of the fiercest ground fighting of the whole Desert War which saw heavy casualties on both sides, Axis forces were compelled to retreat westwards, pursued and harried by RAF fighters and bombers, and by 10 December advanced British troops entered the garrison at Tobruk, more than seven months after the siege had begun. The relief of Tobruk was triumphantly announced next day in the House of Commons by the Prime Minister in his typical eloquent fashion:

> "The enemy, who has fought with the utmost stubbornness and enterprise, had paid the price for his valour, and it may well be that the second phase of the Battle of Libya will gather more easily the fruits of the first that has been our experience so far ...[adding] I will go so far on this occasion as to say that all the danger of the Army of the Nile not being able to celebrate Christmas and the New Year has been decisively removed."

In the air the fighting had also been fierce and furious with the Messerschmitts of I and II/JG27 taking a heavy toll of British fighters and bombers, but superior numbers of RAF aircraft finally won the day as Axis ground forces retreated and continued to do so throughout the whole of December. By the beginning of 1942 Derna, Barce and Benghazi were again in Allied hands. But it was now the British lines of communication that were overstretched. This, together with the Japanese entry into the war which meant some of the British and Commonwealth forces currently in, or destined for, the Middle East being diverted to the Far East to counter this new threat, gave Rommel the encouragement to strike back within the near future. Obviously the capture of Tobruk remained a priority.

For the first five months of 1942 there remained a lull in major offensive operations as both sides again consolidated in readiness for the next major clash. This time Rommel took the initiative, striking just before dawn on 26 May against the British forward positions at the Gazala Line, defensive positions running southwards from Gazala and including the fortress village of Bir Hacheim held by the Free French Brigade. Making use of its large Stuka force to batter the defences, a breakthrough was soon achieved by the Germans and many forward positions were overwhelmed. A British withdrawal began but not without much bitter close quarter fighting, the French at Bir Hacheim holding out until 10 June when the majority of the garrison escaped into the desert where they were later retrieved by British motorised forces. The Axis forces pushed on towards Tobruk where, unknown to Rommel, the defences had been badly neglected during the preceding months since the raising of the siege. Many of the minefields had been removed and the main anti-tank ditch had progressively become ineffective. However, there remained a garrison of some 35,000 troops, mainly South Africans of the 2nd South African Division under Maj Gen Henry Klopper. By 15 June Axis forces were closing in on the port, the South Africans expecting an assault from the south-west and strengthening that area appropriately, but Rommel struck from the south-east. By 18 June Tobruk was surrounded and the noose was tightened. Massed artillery and air attacks blasted a way through the outer defences on 20 June and the garrison fell next day. General Klopper personally surrendered his troops to General Rommel. Tobruk had finally fallen.

Rommel was immediately promoted to Feldmarschall and was acclaimed by the

German press. Prime Minister Churchill was saddened and shocked. General Neil Ritchie, Western Desert Force commander was sacked by General Auchinleck, who was in turn soon to be sacked by the Prime Minister but not before he had orchestrated a halt to Rommel's push eastwards by the end of July, both sides taking up defensive positions west of El Alamein. A crucial factor in favour of the Allies was air power; hundreds of aircraft continued to pour into RAFME's coffers – Spitfires were now arriving which could at least fight on equal terms with the Bf109s, while scores of Hurricanes and Kittyhawks swelled the numbers of fighters and fighter-bombers available to harass the enemy and to escort ever increasing numbers of medium bombers striking at Rommel's forces and lines of communication, the vulnerability of which would lead ultimately to the destruction of the Deutsches Afrika Korps. New generals arrived to take the war to Rommel – General Sir Harold Alexander having succeeded Auchinleck as Middle East commander, while Lt General Bernard Montgomery was appointed to command the Eighth Army, as the Western Desert Force had now become.

In October 1942 the decisive Battle of El Alamein was fought and won. Rommel and the Afrika Korps was finally and utterly defeated by Montgomery and the Eighth Army. Egypt was saved. Libya was reoccupied and Tobruk relieved once again (on 13 November 1942), this time permanently, but it was now of little importance to the Allied cause. The war had passed it by. Tobruk was now history. Meanwhile, the Germans and Italians were forced to retreat into Tunisia where they eventually surrendered in May 1943. North Africa was free of Axis forces. The Battle for Europe was about to begin.

FREE FRENCH FIGHTER FLIGHT 1

Free French Fighter Flight 1 was formed at RAF Odiham at the end of August 1940 by escapees from France following the armistice at the end of June. The unit was under the command of Lt André Feuillerat who had escaped from Toulouse-Francazal on 22 June in a Dewoitine D520 of GCIII/7, in company with two others flown by Sous-Lt Albert Littolf, an experienced fighter pilot with six shared victories under his belt from the recent fighting, and Sgt-Chef Adonis Moulenes. They landed at an airfield near Southampton. Among the other French pilots and aircrew then assembling in England were Sous-Lts James Denis and Louis Ferrant, both of whom had reached England aboard a four-engine Farman 222.2 on 20 June with 17 others. Denis and Ferrant had taken turns in flying the aircraft which landed at St Eval in Cornwall at 0945, having departed from St Jean-d'Angély training airfield at 0500. Another of the group was Sous-Lt Noël Castelain who, disguised as a Polish aviator, embarked upon a Polish collier at St Jean de Luz on 20 June and reached England two days later.

The pilots of the Flight did not see action during the Battle of Britain, nor were their aircraft used in that desperate struggle; instead, eight pilots – Feuillerat, Denis, Littolf, Ferrant, Castelain and Sgt-Chefs Moulenes, René Guédon and Xavier de Scitivaux de Greische[1] – were selected to participate in Général de Gaulle's ill-fated attempt to land French forces at Dakar on the West Coast of Africa in late September 1940, in an effort to gain the French garrison's support (codenamed Operation *Menace*). More than 1,000 of de Gaulle's followers were on board various craft which comprised the task force, protected by a strong RN escort including the aircraft carrier HMS *Ark Royal*. Three of the Fighter Flight's D520s (Nos 127,139, and 409) were stowed on the deck of the Dutch liner *Pennland*, as were six disassembled Blenheims, a dozen crated Lysanders, and a twin-engined Goeland, while two Luciole light aircraft travelled aboard the cruiser HMAS *Australia* although these were later transferred to *Ark Royal*. These aircraft, with the exception of the Lucioles, were to be offloaded at Freetown for onward flight to the Middle East for use by French air force units currently being assembled.

---

[1] Xavier de Scitivaux's brother Philippe, a pilot in the Aéronavale, also escaped to England and retrained as a fighter pilot. He later commanded 340 Squadron and was awarded a DFC before being shot down in April 1942, becoming a PoW. The brothers used the abbreviated surname de Scitivaux while serving with the RAF.

Embarked on the carrier were two squadrons of FAA Skuas (800 and 803) and three of Swordfish (810, 818 and 824), but the appearance of British aircraft patrolling off Dakar only served to antagonise the French on shore who scrambled Hawk 75A fighters of GCI/4 to investigate. As a result of ensuing skirmishes between the British patrols and the openly hostile French aircraft, a Swordfish strike was launched against the French battleship *Richelieu* in harbour and patrolling cruisers and destroyers. The battleship was damaged, a French destroyer and two submarines were sunk, but six Swordfish were shot down by fighters and AA fire, as were two Walrus amphibians (from HMS *Barham* and HMAS *Australia*), against French losses of one Hawk (which crashed into the sea while attacking a Swordfish), one Martin 167F (severely damaged by three Skuas and subsequently written off) and a Loire 130 seaplane (shot down by a Swordfish). In addition, Free French Flight 1 suffered a loss when Sgt-Chef Moulenes was arrested having flown one of the Lucioles from the deck of *Ark Royal* to Ouakam airfield in a futile attempt to convince French aviators to join de Gaulle.

Following the abject failure of the operation, the Allied task force retired to Freetown to lick its wounds, from where the pilots of Free French Flight 1 were assigned, with their D520s, to the French airbase at Douala in the Cameroun, while the French Blenheims and Lysanders were assembled and flown to Fort-Lamy in French Equatorial Africa. Général de Gaulle also set out for Fort-Lamy, but very nearly did not make it as he later recalled:

> "The career of the leader of Free France and of these accompanying him nearly came to an end in the course of this journey. For the Potez 540 which was taking us to Fort-Lamy had engine trouble, and it was a marvel that it managed to land, without too much trouble, in the middle of a swamp."

On arrival at Douala, 35-year-old Sous Lt Denis, a former fighter pilot and most senior member of the Flight, was appointed station commander. However, tragedy struck in November when Lt Feuillerat was killed performing aerobatics in one of the Dewoitines. With the death of the CO, Denis was appointed to command the Flight in his place. After biding their time, awaiting developments, the six remaining pilots were eventually ordered to Egypt, scrounging lifts on aircraft staging through, and all had arrived at Ismailia by 17 January 1941. The Flight was now officially accorded the title 1ere Escadrille de Chasse (EC1, or 1st Fighter Squadron) but it became known locally as *Escadrille Denis* after its commander. Following their arrival at Ismailia all six pilots were posted to 70 OTU where they converted to the Hurricane and soon after were flown to Athens aboard a Sunderland flying boat where they flew patrols in the defence of the Greek capital, although without sighting any enemy aircraft. On their return to Egypt, Denis was ordered to take his unit to Tobruk, arriving on the morning of 10 April 1941.

APPENDIX II

Plt Off Jean Pompéï of 274 Squadron, who had been shot down by a Bf109 on 21 May 1941, later related an account of his adventures:

"Shortly after [the crash-landing], I saw a group of eight to ten people marching towards me. A few metres away their presumed chief made a Fascist salute. I didn't respond. He asked me 'Germani?' I still didn't respond. 'Inglese?' As I had been flying an English plane, with English markings, and spoke no Arabic, I answered 'Si'. To my amazement they rushed towards me and gave me big slaps on the shoulders and shouted 'Quiès englis, quiès englis' (Englishmen are nice). They were a group of Senussi, violently anti-Italian, dressed in Italian clothes and armed with Italian weapons. They took me to their camp, five canvas tents. There, the wiseman looked at my leg. Then, quietly, he took a long curved needle usually used to sew tents and started to remove shrapnel. I counted almost 90 pieces.

I spent a few days with them at their camp, waiting for my wound to cauterize. Then, one day, one of them said he would try to cross the lines and take a message to an English camp. I saw him coming back five days later. He had become lost and almost died of thirst but had been rescued by an Italian armoured car. When I felt better, ten days later, my hosts proposed that I cross the lines far to the south. I agreed, and one night we left: the one I called the 'Poet', the only man in the tribe who could read and write, who always carried a bottle of China ink and a feather, and the guide, a man of 75 years of age who had seen half of Africa on foot, and myself. We walked towards the south-west to get far from the lines. At 9pm we crossed the road from Bardia to Tobruk and, at 5am, we arrived at a place from where we could see Gambut airfield. We spent the day in caverns, and departed at 6pm, heading due south. But this time I was riding a mule. After an hour we saw shadows on the horizon, like a caravan of camels, and we joined this caravan of 104 camels. They knew of our imminent arrival and were waiting for us, but without stopping to avoid suspicion. We continued south. I was now dressed in Arab clothes and headwear. At 10pm we crossed the Trigh Capuzzo road from Sollum to El Adem. Two German armoured cars on guard switched on their lights. We crossed without problems. And then we walked without stopping until 7pm next day. The desert was flat and rocky. Our guide lived there. He received me in his tent and I spent the night there. When the sun came up I was taken to a cave, via a three feet wide hole. It was a tomb, but was also used by shepherds. I found there a water bag and a woollen bag in which to sleep. They gave me a few cakes and, before they left, the guide asked me to write a note for the

British. I wrote a message:

'I'm Plt Off Pompéï, Free French officer of 274 Squadron. I was shot down on 21 May, found and rescued by Bedouins. The bearer will tell you the place where I am. The ground is flat and an aircraft can land very easily.'

The guide tore his collar off, folded the message and sewed it in his collar and sewed his collar back onto his garment. I learned later that he walked 140km in two days, walking at night, resting by day. On the third day he met a British armoured car and delivered the message. He was taken to the unit's HQ from where they phoned Marsa Matruh, and was then driven there to repeat the story. He was asked where I was and answered 'Bir Bdehi'. They looked in vain on the map: no Bir Bdehi. They asked him where it was: 'When the sun comes up in the morning, you pray, then you walk with your back to the sun. Two days later, maybe three, you arrive at Bir Bdehi.' Supplied with this information, the Long Range Desert Group at Siwa Oasis was contacted to carry out a search. Two trucks were sent to search for me.

On the morning of the seventh day the Poet arrived in my tomb. He brought water and flour. Early in the afternoon we heard an engine. The Poet warned me not to move, and climbed out. I heard him say 'Maffich Inglese, andato, andato ...' (There's no Englishman here, he's gone). I glanced between two rocks and saw a magnificent young man in shorts, with naked chest, his skin darkened by the sun, an astounding beard, and on his head the yellow veil and black ring of the Transjordan Frontier Force. He was driving a Ford truck. I understood the confusion and got out of my hole. I asked him 'Are you British?'. 'Yes!' he replied, 'Are you the bloody Free French officer?' I nodded and he added 'We came here to pick you up. Is your kit ready?' It was, I had nothing. I got into the first truck after having ceremoniously thanked and said goodbye to the Poet but, at the last moment, he expressed the desire to come with us. He got in the second truck. I was given the task to operate the front gun. At around 4.30pm, in a flat area, the truck stopped suddenly. I jumped on the gun, believing we were about to be attacked by planes. Then the smiling Lieutenant asked me if I would like some tea! We made some tea on a gas can, and then drove again, due south. It was around 7pm when we stopped, as we navigated by the sun. The sun being too low made reading the compass imprecise. We raised a tent and cooked tins of beef with peas: I don't think I had appreciated a meal more after having been fed flour [bread] without salt for a month. At dusk we moved on, towards the east. At 11pm we crossed the barbed wire marking the border south of Fort Maddelena, then drove south again. Two hours later we arrived at Siwa Oasis. I stayed the night in a modest hotel. Next day a message arrived for me. I was to fly a Lysander to Mersa Matruh, and was accompanied on the flight by the Poet. I was then flown to Cairo, arriving on 21 June, exactly one month after having been shot down, and reported to Air Marshal Tedder, to whom I gave my report."

It was then that Plt Off Pompéï learned that he had been presumed killed when shot down. His belongings had been sold or otherwise dispersed, and a memorial service had been held in his honour. He did not return to operational flying.

APPENDIX III

DIRECTIVE BY THE PRIME MINISTER AND MINISTER OF DEFENCE

The War in the Mediterranean

14 April 1941

1. If the Germans can continue to nourish their invasion of Cyrenaica and Egypt through the port of Tripoli and along the coastal road they can certainly bring superior armoured forces to bear upon us, with consequences of the most serious character. If, on the other hand, their communications from Italy and Sicily with Tripoli are cut, and those along the coastal road between Tripoli and Agheila constantly harassed, there is no reason why they should not themselves sustain a major defeat.

2. It becomes the prime duty of the British Mediterranean Fleet under Admiral Cunningham to stop all sea-borne traffic between Italy and Africa by the fullest use of surface craft, aided so far as possible by aircraft and submarines. For this all-important objective heavy losses in battleships, cruisers and destroyers must if necessary be accepted. The harbour of Tripoli must be rendered unusable by recurrent bombardment, and/or by blocking and mining, care being taken that the mining does not impede the blocking or bombardments. Enemy convoys passing to and from Africa must be attacked by our cruisers, destroyers, and submarines, aided by the Fleet Air Arm and the Royal Air Force. Every convoy which gets through must be considered a serious naval failure. The reputation of the Royal Navy is engaged in stopping this traffic.

3. Admiral Cunningham's fleet must be strengthened for the above purposes to whatever extent is necessary. The *Nelson* and the *Rodney*, with their heavily armoured decks, are especially suitable for resisting attacks from the German dive-bombers, of which undue fears must not be entertained. Other reinforcements of cruisers, minelayers, and destroyers must be sent from the west as opportunity serves. The use of the *Centurion* as a blockship should be studied, but the effectual blocking of Tripoli harbour would be well worth a battleship upon the active list.

4. When Admiral Cunningham's fleet has been reinforced he should be able to form two bombarding squadrons, which may in turn at intervals bombard the port of Tripoli, especially when shipping or convoys are known to be in the harbour.

5. In order to control the sea communications across the Mediterranean sufficient suitable naval forces must be based on Malta, and protection must be afforded to these naval forces by the Air Force at Malta, which must be kept at the highest strength in fighters of the latest and best quality that the Malta aerodromes can contain. The duty of affording fighter protection to the naval forces holding Malta should have priority over the use of the aerodromes by bombers engaged in attacking Tripoli.

6. Every endeavour should be made to defend Malta harbour by the U.P. weapon [rockets] in its various developments, especially by the F.A.M. [fast aerial mine], fired by the improved naval method.

7. Next in importance after the port at Tripoli comes the 400-mile coastal road between Tripoli and Agheila. This road should be subjected to continuous harassing attacks by forces landed from the Glen ships in the special landing-craft. The Commandoes and other forces gathered in Egypt should be freely used for this purpose. The seizure of particular points from the sea should be studied, and the best ones chosen for prompt action. Here again losses must be faced, but small forces may be used in this harassing warfare, being withdrawn, if possible, after a while. If even a few light or medium tanks could be landed these could rip along the road, destroying very quickly convoys far exceeding their own value. Every feasible method of harassing constantly this section of the route is to be attempted, the necessary losses being faced.

8. In all the above paragraphs the urgency is extreme, because the enemy will grow continually stronger in the air than he is now, especially should his attack on Greece and Yugoslavia be successful, as my be apprehended. Admiral Cunningham should not therefore await the arrival of battleship reinforcements, nor should the use of the Glen ships be withheld for the sake of Rhodes.

9. It has been decided that Tobruk is to be defended with all possible strength. But [holding] Tobruk must not be regarded as a defensive operation, but rather as an invaluable bridgehead or sally-port on the communications of the enemy. It should be reinforced as may be necessary both with infantry and by armoured fighting vehicles, to enable active and continuous raiding of the enemy's flanks and rear. If part of the defences of the perimeter can be taken over by troops unprovided with transport, this should permit the organisation of a mobile force both for the fortress reserve and for striking at the enemy. It would be a great advantage should the enemy be drawn into anything like a siege of Tobruk and compelled to transport and feed the heavy artillery forces for that purpose.

10. It is above all necessary that General Wavell should regain unit ascendancy over the enemy and destroy his small raiding parties, instead of our being harassed and hunted by them. Enemy patrols must be attacked on every occasion, and our own patrols should be used with audacity. Small British parties in armoured cars, or mounted on motor-cycles, or, if occasion offers, infantry, should not hesitate to attack individual tanks with bombs and bombards, as is planned for the defence of Britain. It is important to engage the enemy even in small affairs in order to make him fire off his gun ammunition, of which supply must be very difficult.

11. The use of the Royal Air Force against the enemy's communications, or concentration of fighting vehicles, is sufficiently obvious not to require mention.

*   *   *

The Prime Minister added an appropriate note in his memoirs – "All this was easier to say than do."

APPENDIX IV

REPRODUCTION OF A PAGE FROM THE LOGBOOK OF SGT A.E. MARSHALL DFM[1], 73 SQUADRON

YEAR 1941 MONTH / DATE		AIRCRAFT Type	No.	PILOT, OR 1ST PILOT	2ND PILOT, PUPIL OR PASSENGER	DUTY (INCLUDING RESULTS AND REMARKS)
—	—	—	—	—	—	TOTALS BROUGHT FORWARD
APRIL	11	HURRICANE	A.	SELF	SOLO.	SCRAMBLE - PATROL TOBRUCH
APRIL	11	"	F	SELF	SOLO.	SCRAMBLE FOR DIVE BOMBERS
APRIL	12	"	J	SELF	SOLO.	PATROL TOBRUCH HARBOUR.
APRIL	12	"	J	SELF	SOLO.	SCRAMBLE LOST IN VERY BAD SANDSTORM. LANDED GASSABA
APRIL	13	"	J	SELF	SOLO.	GASSABA TO TOBRUCH (GUBBI)
APRIL	13	"	H	SELF	SOLO.	PATROL, SEARCHING FOR ENEMY LANDING GROUNDS, STRAFFING
APRIL	14	"	A	SELF	SOLO.	TOBRUCH TO ABOUKIR FOR NEW ENGINE AND INSPECTION.
APRIL	21	"	H	SELF	SOLO.	ABOUKIR TO SIDI HENISH
APRIL	21	"	Q V	SELF	SOLO.	SIDI HENISH TO TOBRUCH.
APRIL	22	"	M.	SELF	SOLO.	SCRAMBLE - TOBRUCH DEFENCES.
APRIL	22	"	H	SELF	SOLO.	COVERING PATROL FOR SPOTTING LYSANDER OVER LINES,
APRIL	22	"	H	SELF	SOLO.	SCRAMBLE PATROL 15000
APRIL	23	"	A	SELF	SOLO.	SCRAMBLE FOR DIVE BOMBERS. BOMBING HARBOUR AND DROME - BOB
			SQUADRON EVACUATED TOBRUCH			
APRIL	25	BLENHIEM	O84	F/o BLANK.	SELF	TOBRUCH TO SIDI HENISH
APRIL	27	WELLINGTON	T2826	H/T RODEN	SELF	FUKA TO GABRIT (CANAL ZONE)

GRAND TOTAL [Cols. (1) to (10)]

[1] Later Flt Lt A.E. Marshall DFC DFM, killed in a flying accident 27/11/44.

SINGLE ENGINE AIRCRAFT				MULTI ENGINE AIRCRAFT						PASS-ENGER	INSTR/CLOUD FLYING [Incl. in cols. (1) to (10)]	
DAY		NIGHT		DAY			NIGHT					
DUAL	PILOT	DUAL	PILOT	DUAL	1ST PILOT	2ND PILOT	DUAL	1ST PILOT	2ND PILOT		DUAL	PILOT
(1)	(2)	(3)	(4)	(5)	(6)	(7)	(8)	(9)	(10)	(11)	(12)	(13)
6·05	448·30	2·90	13·10							19·15	9·25	3·05
	·35											
	·20		DESTROYED 1 6.50 CRASHED ON BEACH W. OF TOBRUCH, THIS									
	1·35		E/A WAS ONE OF 4 WHICH ATTACKED ME. CONFIRMED BY									
	2·05		R.A. GUN BATTERY IN VICINITY,									
			F/LT BALL. D.F.C. MISSING (SINCE PRISONER OF WAR)									
	1·36		SGT. WILLS AND A FREE FRENCHMAN MISSING BELIEVED KILLED									
			(SINCE CONFIRMED " KILLED IN ACTION) - WILLS DOWN IN FLAMES									
	·55		STRAFFING TROOP CONCENTRATIONS - SUCCESSFULL -									
	2·28		DIVE BOMBED AT DAWN BY 50-60 J.U.87's- SQUADRON ONLY HAS 5									
	,		SERVICEABLE AIRCRAFT - DESTROYED 9 ENEMY - LOST									
	2·05		P/O LAMB - F/LT SMITH AND SGT WEBSTER.-									
	1·35		· DIVE BOMBED AT DUSK BY 40 E.A. VERY FRIGHTENING									
	·20		DESTROYED 1 6.50. CRASHED OUTSIDE TOBRUCH DEFENCES. E/A									
			WAS AT 200' ESCORTING J.U.87 WITH M.E. 109's, HEAVY MACHINE GUN FIRE									
	1·00		FROM GERMAN TROOPS. —— CONFIRMED BY FREE FRENCH PILOT- LT LITTOLF									
	·90											
	·45		DESTROYED 1 J.U.87 CRASHED 15MILES W OF TOBRUCH — ON LANDING I WAS									
			STRAFFED, IN COCKPIT BY A ME.109 - WOUNDED IN HEAD AND SHOULDER.									
			(SINCE 0480) CPL WEBSTER AND ANOTHER SERIOUSLY INJURED AT WING TIPS. LOST									
			P/O HOLDENBY.— THE C.O AND F/O MARTIN BALED OUT									
										1·35		
										2·15		
	,											
62·05	464·15	2·40	13·10							23·05	9·25	3·05
(1)	(2)	(3)	(4)	(5)	(6)	(7)	(8)	(9)	(10)	(11)	(12)	(13)

HURRICANE PILOTS' CLAIMS & ROLL OF HONOUR
258 FIGHTER WING/204 GROUP RAF

January – June 1941

Claims

3/1/41:	Sgt A.E. Marshall	V7299	73 Sqn	3 SM79s, SM79 damaged
4/1/41:	Plt Off S. Godden	V7558	274 Sqn	2 CR42s
	Flt Sgt T.C. Morris	V7293	274 Sqn	CR42
	Unknown pilot		33 Sqn	CR42
	Flt Lt M.L.ff. Beytagh	V7561	73 Sqn	CR42 (ground)
5/1/41:	Flg Off E.M. Mason	P3722	274 Sqn	2 CR42, SM79, (plus 3 CR42 damaged, ground)
	2/Lt R.H. Talbot	P3721	274 Sqn	CR42, SM79
	Sqn Ldr P.H. Dunn	P3723	274 Sqn	CR42
	Plt Off Wilson	N2624	274 Sqn	CR42 damaged
	Flt Lt P.G. Wykeham-Barnes	V7558	274 Sqn	SM79, SM79 damaged
	Sgt A.E. Marshall	V7562	73 Sqn	SM79
	Sgt H.G. Webster	V7551	73 Sqn	CR42, CR42 damaged
	Plt Off R.L. Goord	TP-M	73 Sqn	CR42
	Flt Lt M.L.ff. Beytagh	V7561	73 Sqn	CR42
6/1/41:	Flg Off J.E. Storrar	V7562	73 Sqn	CR42
	Sgt R.I. Laing	V7553	73 Sqn	CR42 damaged
	Wt Off H.J. Goodchild		33 Sqn	CR42, CR42 damaged
8/1/41:	Sqn Ldr P.H. Dunn	P3723	274 Sqn	2 SM79 (ground)
	Flg Off E.M. Mason	P3722	274 Sqn	2 SM79 (ground)
9/1/41:	Flg Off E.M. Mason	P3722	274 Sqn	CR42
	2/Lt R.H. Talbot	V7484	274 Sqn	CR42
10/1/41:	Flg Off E.M. Mason	P3722	274 Sqn	2 SM79, G50 damaged (plus CR32 ground)
	2/Lt R.H. Talbot	V7484	274 Sqn	SM79, G50, G50 damaged
14/1/41:	Plt Off Wilson	N2646	274 Sqn	5 SM79 strafed
17/1/41:	Flt Lt P.G. Wykeham-Barnes	P2641	274 Sqn	SM81
21/1/41:	Sqn Ldr A.D. Murray	V7560	73 Sqn	G50
	Plt Off B.P. Legge	TP-M	73 Sqn	G50 damaged
25/1/41:	Flg Off P.B. Turnbull	(Gladiator)	3RAAF Sqn	G50 damaged

26/1/41	Flg Off T.L. Patterson	P3823	274 Sqn	2 G50, G50 damaged
	Flg Off E.M. Mason	P3722	274 Sqn	3 CR42s
29/1/41	Flg Off L.T. Benson[1]	N2611	208 Sqn	SM79
30/1/41	Flg Off E.M. Mason	P3722	274 Sqn	CR42
1/2/41	Sqn Ldr A.D. Murray	V7560	73 Sqn ⎫	Ghibli (ground)
	Flg Off J.E. Storrar	V7544	73 Sqn ⎭	2 Ghibli, Ca310 (ground)
	Plt Off M.P. Wareham	V7299	73 Sqn	
	Sgt W.C. Wills	V7544	73 Sqn	CR42
4/2/41	Plt Off J.B. McColl	V7372	73 Sqn	Ca133
	Flg Off G.E. Goodman	V7716	73 Sqn	CR42
5/2/41	Sqn Ldr A.D. Murray	V7560	73 Sqn ⎫	8 or 9 SM79s
	Flg Off J.E. Storrar	V7544	73 Sqn ⎬	damaged (ground)
	Sgt A.E. Marshall	V7553	73 Sqn ⎭	
15/2/41	Flg Off J.H.W. Saunders	P5176	3RAAF Sqn	Ju88
18/2/41	Flg Off J.H. Jackson	P5176	3RAAF Sqn	Ju87, 2 Ju87 damaged
	Flt Lt G.H. Steege	V6737	3RAAF Sqn	Ju87 probable, 2 Ju87 damaged
	Flg Off J.H.W. Saunders	V7770	3RAAF Sqn	Ju87 probable, Ju87 damaged
19/2/41	Flt Lt J.R. Perrin	V7557	3RAAF Sqn	Ju87, Bf110
	Flg Off J.E. Storrar	V7553	73 Sqn	Bf110 damaged
	Plt Off O.E. Lamb	V7371	73 Sqn	Ju88 damaged
22/2/41	Sqn Ldr A.D. Murray	V7551	73 Sqn	Ju88
28/2/41	Sqn Ldr D. Campbell	P3980	3RAAF Sqn	Ju88
31/3/41	Sqn Ldr D. Campbell	P3980	3RAAF Sqn	Bf110
	Flg Off J.H.W. Saunders	V6737	3RAAF Sqn	BR20 damaged
	Flg Off L.E.S. Knowles	V7566	3RAAF Sqn	2 BR20 damaged
2/4/41	Flg Off M.D. Ellerton	V7353	3RAAF Sqn ⎫	SM79 probable
	Flg Off A.M. Edwards	V7566	3RAAF Sqn ⎭	
3/4/41	Flt Lt G.H. Steege	P3967	3RAAF Sqn	Bf110, 3 Bf110 damaged
	Flt Lt P.B. Turnbull	V7492	3RAAF Sqn	Bf110 probable, 3 Bf110 damaged
	Flt Lt A.C. Rawlinson	V7772	3RAAF Sqn	2 Ju87
	Flg Off J. Davidson	V7566	3RAAF Sqn	Ju87
	Lt G.K. Smith	P3980	3RAAF Sqn	Ju87
	Flg Off J.H.W. Saunders	V6737	3RAAF Sqn	Ju87 damaged
5/4/41	Flt Lt M.L.ff. Beytagh	V7810	73 Sqn	Ju87, Ju87 damaged
	Plt Off W.T. Eiby	V7550	73 Sqn	Ju87, Ju87 damaged
	Plt Off K.M. Millist	V7766	73 Sqn	Ju87, Ju87 damaged
	Sgt G.W. Garton	V7716	73 Sqn	Ju87
	Flt Lt J.R. Perrin	P3967	3RAAF Sqn	3 Ju87
	Flg Off W.E. Jewell	P3818	3RAAF Sqn	3 Ju87
	Flg Off M.D. Ellerton	V7353	3RAAF Sqn	2 Ju87
	Flg Off J.H. Jackson	V7772	3RAAF Sqn	Ju87, 2 Ju87 probables

---

[1] Flg Off Benson is believed to have shot down this aircraft but failed to return from this sortie; see text.

Flg Off W. Kloster	P5176	3RAAF Sqn	Ju87
7/4/41: Sgt K. Souter	V7553	73 Sqn	Ju88 damaged
Sgt A.E. Marshall	V7560	73 Sqn	⎫
Flt Lt A.C. Rawlinson		3RAAF Sqn	⎬ 2 Ju52 (ground)
Flg Off L.E.S. Knowles	P3980	3RAAF Sqn	⎭
9/4/41: Flg Off J.E. Storrar	P3818	73 Sqn	Ju87
Sgt A.E. Marshall	V7562	73 Sqn ⎫	G50 probable
Plt Off W.T. Eiby	V7810	73 Sqn ⎭	
Flg Off G.E. Goodman	V7546	73 Sqn	Bf110
Flg Off R.F. Martin	V7553	73 Sqn ⎫	
Sgt G.W. Garton	V7766	73 Sqn ⎬	Hs126
Sgt H.G. Webster	V7716	73 Sqn ⎭	
Sgt A.E. Marshall	V7562	73 Sqn	Ju52
Flt Lt J.D. Smith	V7371	73 Sqn	⎫
Plt Off R. McDougall	V7560	73 Sqn	⎬
Sgt R.I. Laing	P2646	73 Sqn	6 Bf110s, SM79, plus one
Sgt J.E. Elsworth	V7552	73 Sqn	u/i aircraft (ground)
Sgt W.C. Wills		73 Sqn	
Flg Off R.F. Martin	V7553	73 Sqn	
Sgt A.E. Marshall	V7562	73 Sqn	⎭
10/4/41: Sous-Lt J. Denis	V7716	73 Sqn	CR42
11/4/41: Sous-Lt N. Castelain	V7853	73 Sqn ⎫	Bf110
Sgt-Chef R. Guédon	V7859	73 Sqn ⎭	
Sgt A.E. Marshall	V7560	73 Sqn	G50
Sgt R.I. Laing	V7371	73 Sqn	Ju87 damaged
14/4/41: Flg Off G.E. Goodman	V7673	73 Sqn ⎫	Hs126
Sgt H.G. Webster	V7553	73 Sqn ⎭	
Sgt R.V. Ellis	⎧ V7299	73 Sqn	2 Ju87s
	⎩ V7810	73 Sqn	Ju87
Flt Lt J.D. Smith	P2652	73 Sqn	2 G50, G50 damaged
Sous-Lt A. Littolf	⎧ V7856	73 Sqn	Ju87, 2 Ju87 probables
	⎩ W9198	73 Sqn	Ju87
Sous-Lt J. Denis	W9198	73 Sqn	Ju87
Flg Off R.F. Martin	V7299	73 Sqn	Bf110 damaged
Flg Off W.S. Arthur	V7728	3RAAF Sqn	Bf110) plus Ju52 damaged
Lt A.A. Tennant	P3725	3RAAF Sqn	Bf110)　(ground)
15/4/41: Sqn Ldr P. Jeffrey	V7770	3RAAF Sqn	Ju52 (plus 2 Ju52 & Ju52
			damaged, ground)
Flg Off L.E.S. Knowles		3RAAF Sqn ⎫	Ju52 (ground)
Flg Off R.F. Donati		3RAAF Sqn ⎭	
19/4/41: Flg Off A.A.P. Weller	P3977	274 Sqn	SM79, 6 CR42 damaged
			(ground)
Flg Off D.J. Spence	V7354	274 Sqn	Ju88, Bf109
21/4/41: Flg Off D.J. Spence	V7354	274 Sqn	Bf109
Sgt G.W. Garton	V7673	73 Sqn	Ju87
Flg Off G.E. Goodman	AS990	73 Sqn	Ju87
Sous-Lt J. Denis	V7834	73 Sqn	Ju87, Bf109

22/4/41:	Plt Off M.P. Wareham	V7837	73 Sqn	Ju87, Ju87 damaged
	Plt Off R.M. Chatfield	V7492	73 Sqn	Ju87 probable
	Flg Off R.F. Martin	V7372	73 Sqn	Bf109
	Sous-Lt A. Littolf	V7353	73 Sqn	Bf109
	Sgt A.E. Marshall	W9299	73 Sqn	G50
23/4/41:	Sqn Ldr P.G.Wykeham-Barnes	V7837	73 Sqn	Ju87, Bf109
	Sgt A.E. Marshall	V7353	73 Sqn	Ju87
	Plt Off R.M. Chatfield	W9299	73 Sqn	Ju87
	Sous-Lt A. Littolf	V7728	73 Sqn	Ju87, Bf109
	Sous-Lt J. Denis	AS990	73 Sqn	Bf109, Bf109 probable
26/4/41:	Flg Off T.L. Patterson[2]	V7763	274 Sqn	2 Bf110s
27/4/41:	Plt Off S. Godden	V7780	274 Sqn	Bf110
	Flg Off A.A.P. Weller	P3971	274 Sqn	Ju52, 7 Ju52 damaged (ground)
30/4/41:	Plt Off J. Pompéï		73 Sqn	Hs126
	Plt Off S. Godden	V7825	274 Sqn	Bf110, Bf110 damaged
1/5/41:	Flg Off D.G.S. Honor	W9269	274 Sqn	Bf109
	Flg Off N.leC. Agazarian	V7829	274 Sqn	Bf109
	Plt Off P.H.V. Hutt	V7755	274 Sqn	Bf109 probable
10/5/41:	Sgt C.R. Glover	P3469	274 Sqn	Bf109 (plus 4 or 5 Bf109s strafed)
11/5/41:	Plt Off R.A. Griffiths	V7753	6 Sqn	Bf109
12/5/41:	Maj T Ross-Theron		1SAAF Sqn	Ca310 possibly damaged
	Capt K.A. Quirk		1SAAF Sqn	
15/5/41:	Flt Lt D.G.S. Honor	W9269	274 Sqn	Bf109, Bf109 probable
	Plt Off P.H.V. Hutt	V7831	274 Sqn	Bf109 probable
	Flg Off R.J. Hardiman	V7710	6 Sqn	Hs126 damaged
16/5/41:	Lt R.H. Talbot		1SAAF Sqn	Ju87
	Sgt C.R. Glover	P3469	274 Sqn	Bf109
18/5/41:	Plt Off A.J.C. Hamilton	P3469	274 Sqn	Bf109 strafed
20/5/41:	Flt Lt D.G.S. Honor	P3977	274 Sqn	Bf110 (plus Ju52 ground)
21/5/41:	Sous-Lt J. Denis	V7859	73 Sqn	Bf109
	Plt Off J. Pompéï	V7813	73 Sqn	Bf109
22/5/41:	Lt A.J. Botha		1SAAF Sqn	2 Ju87
23/5/41:	Flg Off G.E. Goodman	W9198	73 Sqn	Ju88 damaged
	Plt Off J.H. Ward	V7816	73 Sqn	Ju88 damaged
25/5/41:	Plt Off A.J.C. Hamilton	V7562	274 Sqn	Ju88
	Flt Lt D.G.S. Honor	W9266	274 Sqn	SM79, Ju52
	Sqn Ldr P.G.Wykeham-Barnes	V7012	73 Sqn	Ju88 damaged
26/5/41:	Flg Off O.V. Tracey	Z4511	274 Sqn	Ju52, Bf109
	Sgt G. Kerr	Z4312	274 Sqn	Ju52
	Flt Sgt M. Lebois	Z4250	274 Sqn	Ju52
	Flg Off A.M.D. Péronne	Z4538	274 Sqn	Ju52
	Flt Lt P.J.F. Jacquier[3]	Z4632	274 Sqn	2 Ju52

[2] Flg Off Patterson FTR (killed) from this sortie and details of the action are retrospective.
[3] Flt Lt Jacquier FTR (PoW) from this sortie and details of the action are retrospective.

27/5/41:	Flg Off A.A.P. Weller	Z4250	274 Sqn	Ju88
	Sgt P.B. Nicolson	Z4536	274 Sqn	Ju88
29/5/41:	Flg Off O.V. Tracey	V7830	274 Sqn	Ju88
		Maryland	24SAAF Sqn	
	Plt Off A. Sumner	V7855	274 Sqn	Do17 damaged
30/5/41	Flg Off A.D.M. Péronne	Z4536	274 Sqn	He111
	Wt Off A. Ballatore	W9303	274 Sqn	
	Plt Off A. Sumner	V7855	274 Sqn	Ju88
	Plt Off G.A. Tovey	W9329	73 Sqn	He111
31/5/41	Lt R.H. Talbot	Z4510	274 Sqn	Ju88
			(attached)	
		Maryland	24SAAF Sqn	
	Capt K.W. Driver	Z4614	274 Sqn	Ju88
			(attached)	
	Sous-Lt A. Littolf	W9329	73 Sqn	Ju88, Z1007 damaged
	Lt R.H. Talbot	W9322	274 Sqn	Z1007
			(attached)	
1/6/41	Lt A.J. Botha		1SAAF Sqn	Hs126
2/6/41	Capt K.A. Quirk		1SAAF Sqn	
	Capt G.J. Le Mesurier		1SAAF Sqn	
	Lt R.H. Talbot		1SAAF Sqn	3 Ju87, Bf110, plus 10 u/i
	Lt M.S. Uys		1SAAF Sqn	aircraft damaged (ground)
	Lt R.A. Durose		1SAAF Sqn	
	Lt A.A.L. Tatham		1SAAF Sqn	
3/6/41	Flg Off R.E. Bary	Z4510	274/229 Sqn	Bf109
9/6/41	Flt Lt P.O.V. Green		73 Sqn	
	Plt Off G.A. Tovey	Z4118	73 Sqn	6 Bf109s/G50s strafed, plus
	Sgt R.I. Laing	Z4429	73 Sqn	Storch destroyed (ground)
	Flt Lt D.L. Gould		274 Sqn	
	Sgt W.E. Marsh		274 Sqn	
	Flg Off A.D.M. Péronne		274 Sqn	8 Ju87s strafed
	Flg Off A.A.P. Weller		274 Sqn	
	Wt Off C.G.M. Coudray		274 Sqn	
14/6/41:	Flg Off G.E. Goodman	Z4507	73 Sqn	
	Plt Off R.M. Chatfield	Z4384	73 Sqn	
	Plt Off F.M. Moss		73 Sqn	7 u/i aircraft strafed
	Plt Off J.H. Ward		73 Sqn	
	Plt Off J.S. Logan		73 Sqn	
	Sgt J. White	V7389	73 Sqn	
	Lt A.J. Botha		1SAAF Sqn	Ju87, Hs126
	Capt D.H. Loftus		2SAAF Sqn	Bf110
	Lt J.R.R. Wells		2SAAF Sqn	
	Lt L.A. Stone		2SAAF Sqn	
15/6/41:	Plt Off J.L. Briggs	Z4612	274 Sqn	CR42
	Flg Off J.B. Hobbs	W9268	274 Sqn	Hs126
	Flg Off J.A. Sowrey	Z4471	73/213 Sqn	Bf109, Bf109 probable
	Flg Off C.B. Temlett	Z4323	73/213 Sqn	Bf109

Sgt P.P. Wilson	V7673	73/213 Sqn	Bf109
Plt Off S.J. Leach	V7822	73/213 Sqn	Bf109 probable
Flt Lt P.O.V. Green	Z4697	73 Sqn ⎤	Bf110 damaged
Plt Off G.R.A.McG. Johnston	V7802	73 Sqn ⎦	

16/6/41:

Plt Off D.F.K. Edghill	V7492	274/229 Sqn	Bf109
Maj T. Ross-Theron		1SAAF Sqn	Bf109, G50
Capt K.A. Quirk		1SAAF Sqn	2 Ju87

17/6/41:

Flg Off R.E. Bary	V7828	274/229 Sqn	Ju87 damaged
Plt Off T.L.W. Officer	Z4533	274/229 Sqn	Ju87 damaged
Plt Off G.B. Johns	W9268	274/229 Sqn	Ju87 damaged
Plt Off D.F.K. Edghill	Z4366	274/229 Sqn	2 Ju87
Plt Off R.R. Mitchell	Z4630	274/229 Sqn	Ju87
Flg Off D.T. Moir	W9298	33 Sqn	Ju87
Flt Lt V.C. Woodward	Z4377	33 Sqn	G50, G50 damaged
Sgt G.E.C. Genders	Z4174	33 Sqn	2 G50 damaged
Lt D. Dove	Z4175	33 Sqn	Bf109
Flt Lt D.G.S. Honor	Z4614	274 Sqn	Bf109 damaged
Lt A.J.B. Bester		1SAAF Sqn	Bf110 probable, 2 Bf110 damaged
Lt J.J. Conradie		1SAAF Sqn	Bf110 probable

Fighter Pilot Roll of Honour

4/1/41:	Flt Sgt J.C. Hulbert	N2625	274 Sqn
21/1/41:	Plt Off A.G. Wainwright	P2639	73 Sqn
29/1/41:	Flg Off L.T. Benson	N2611	208 Sqn
19/2/41:	Flg Off A.A. Gatward		3RAAF Sqn
5/4/41:	Sqn Ldr D. Campbell	V7567	3RAAF Sqn
7/4/41:	Flg Off K.M. Millist DFC	V7550	73 Sqn
9/4/41:	Sgt J.P. Elsworth	V7552	73 Sqn
12/4/41:	Sgt W.C. Wills	V7560	73 Sqn
14/4/41:	Sgt H.G. Webster	V7553	73 Sqn
	Flt Lt J.D. Smith	P2652	73 Sqn
	Plt Off O.E. Lamb	V7766	73 Sqn
19/4/41:	Sqn Ldr R.E. Weld		6 Sqn
23/4/41:	Plt Off P. Haldenby	V7834	73 Sqn
26/4/41:	Flg Off T.L. Patterson	V7763	274 Sqn
30/4/41:	Flg Off C.H. Greenhill	V7734	274 Sqn
	Flg Off D.J. Spence	V7555	274 Sqn
1/5/41:	Plt Off S. Godden	V7825	274 Sqn
12/5/41:	Flg Off K.P. English	V7820	274 Sqn
	Sgt J.T. Berridge		73 Sqn (accident)
15/5/41:	Sgt F.H. Dean	V7829	274 Sqn
16//5/41:	Flg Off N.leC. Agazarian	V6633	274 Sqn
	Flg Off D.H.J. Clostre	W9302	274 Sqn
21/5/41:	Flg Off A.M. Ross		274 Sqn ⎤ accident -Magister
	Plt Off P.H.V. Hutt		274 Sqn ⎦

23/5/41:	Plt Off R.L. Goord	V7736	73 Sqn
	Plt Off R.H. Likeman	V7764	73 Sqn
25/5/41:	Flt Lt H.C. Down	P3469	274 Sqn
26/5/41:	Sgt C.R. Glover	Z4606	274 Sqn
29/5/41:	Sgt P.B. Nicolson	Z4634	274 Sqn
31/5/41:	Sgt A.J.P. Guillou	W9273	274 Sqn
2/6/41:	Lt R.H. Talbot		1SAAF Sqn
3/6/41:	Sgt P.W. Crump	Z4369	274/229 Sqn
9/6/41:	Plt Off G.A. Tovey	Z4118	73 Sqn
14/6/41:	Flg Off G.E. Goodman DFC	Z4507	73 Sqn
	Sgt J. White DFM	V7389	73 Sqn (died of injuries)
	Lt A.J. Botha		1SAAF Sqn
	Lt R.V. Christie		1SAAF Sqn
15/6/41:	Plt Off A. Sumner	V7348	274 Sqn
	Sgt M.K. Daniels	V7371	274/229 Sqn
	Wt Off C.G.M. Coudray	Z2643	274 Sqn
	Plt Off J.S. Logan	Z4788	73 Sqn
	Flt Lt J.E. McFall DFC	V7769	6 Sqn
17/6/41:	Lt G.K. Smith		1SAAF Sqn (died of wounds, PoW)
	Lt J.B. White		1SAAF Sqn
	Sgt G. Wooller	P3977	274/229 Sqn
	Flg Off E.J. Woods	Z4509	33 Sqn
	Lt K.L. Keith DSC	Buffalo AX813	805 Sqn FAA (died of wounds 27/6/41, PoW)
18/6/41:	Plt Off D.A.R. Munro	Tomahawk AK383	250 Sqn
	Sgt J.A.A. Morton	Tomahawk AK399	250 Sqn
	Sgt C.M. Sumner	Tomahawk AK403	250 Sqn

APPENDIX VI

FIGHTER CLAIMS & FIGHTER PILOT ROLL OF HONOUR
5^SQUADRA AEREA

January – June 1941

Claims

1/1/41:	Serg Magg Fiorenzo Milella	366^Sqd	Blenheim, Blenheim probable
3/1/41:	Serg Mario Veronesi	84^Sqd	Blenheim
4/1/41:	TenCol Carlo Romagnoli	91^Sqd	Hurricane
	M.llo Leonardo Ferrulli	91^Sqd	Hurricane
	Cap Pietro Calistri	75^Sqd	Hurricane
	Ten Claudio Solaro	70^Sqd	Blenheim probable
5/1/41:	Cap Mario Pinna	74^Sqd	Hurricane
	TenCol Giuseppe Baylon	150^Sqd	Hurricane damaged
10/1/41:	Ser Magg Albino Fabbri	152^Sqd	Hurricane
21/1/41:	Serg Magg Antonio Patriarca	358^Sqd	Hurricane
23/1/41:	Serg Magg Ezio Masenti	368^Sqd	Blenheim
25/1/41:	M.llo Giovanni Accorsi	368^Sqd	Blenheim probable
	Cap Annibale Sterzi	358^Sqd	Gladiator
	M.llo Marco Aicardi	358^Sqd	Gladiator
	Ten Bruno Mondini	358^Sqd	2 Gladiators
	Ten Giuseppe Vitali	75^Sqd	Blenheim probable
26/1/41:	Serg Magg Annibale Ricotti	368^Sqd	Hurricane
	Ten Giuseppe Zuffi	368^Sqd	Hurricane probable
29/1/41:	Serg Giuseppe Sanguettoli	74^Sqd	Hurricane
30/1/41:	Serg Mario Turchi	368^Sqd	Hurricane
1/2/41:	Cap Bernardino Serafini	366^Sqd	Hurricane
2/2/41:	Ten Mario Ferrero	366^Sqd ⎫	Hurricane probable
	Serg Magg Fiorenzo Milella	366^Sqd ⎬	
4/2/41:	Ten Furio Lauri	368^Sqd	Blenheim
	Serg Antonio Camerini	368^Sqd	Hurricane probable
10/3/41:	M.llo Felice Longhi	95^Sqd ⎫	Blenheim
	Sottoten Franco Bordoni Bisleri	95^Sqd ⎬	
1/4/41:	Ten Italo Larese	152^Sqd ⎫	Blenheim probable
	Serg Elio Cesaro	152^Sqd ⎬	

9/4/41:	Ten Carlo Cugnasca	351^Sqd	Hurricane
11/4/41:	Cap Bruno Tattanelli	378^Sqd	Hurricane
	M.llo Lorenzo Serafino	378^Sqd	Hurricane probable
14/4/41:	Sottoten Franco Bordoni Bisleri	95^Sqd	Hurricane
	M.llo Guido Fibbia	95^Sqd	Hurricane
	Cap Angelo Fanello	351^Sqd	Hurricane
	Ten Carlo Cugnasca	351^Sqd ⎱	Hurricane
	M.llo Angelo Marinelli	351^Sqd ⎰	
17/4/41:	Sottoten Franco Bordoni Bisleri	95^Sqd	Blenheim
22/4/41:	Cap Annibale Sterzi	358^Sqd	Blenheim
	Cap Salvatore Teja	358^Sqd	Hurricane
2/5/41:	Serg Arturo Imberti	366^Sqd	Blenheim
	Ten Amedeo Guidi	366^Sqd	Blenheim damaged
16/5/41:	Serg Magg Mario Lingura	95^Sqd	Blenheim
29/5/41:	Serg Spartaco Petrignani	85^Sqd	Blenheim
	Serg Luigi Gorrini	85^Sqd	Blenheim
2/6/41:	Sottoten Franco Bordoni Bisleri	95^Sqd	2 Blenheims
16/6/41:	Cap Annibale Sterzi	358^Sqd	Hurricane
17/6/41:	Sottoten Agostino Celentaro	150^Sqd	Hurricane
	M.llo Olindo Simionato	150^Sqd	Hurricane
	Serg Magg Antonio Patriarca	150^Sqd	Hurricane

Fighter Pilot Roll of Honour

4/1/41:	Sottoten Ennio Grifoni	91^Sqd
5/1/41:	Sottoten Oscar Abello	70^Sqd
	Serg Pardino Pardini	70^Sqd
	Sottoten Sante Schiroli	74^Sqd
	Sottoten Leopoldo Marangoni	75^Sqd (died of wounds as PoW, 6/1/41)
26/1/41:	Sottoten Alfonso Nuti	368^Sqd
	M.llo Guido Papparato	368^Sqd
	M.llo Ottorino Muscinelli	358^Sqd
31/1/41:	Cap Bruno Locatelli	368^Sqd
1/2/41:	Ten Carlo Dentis	75^Sqd (accident)
4/2/41:	Cap Guglielmo Chiarini	368^Sqd
	M.llo Giovanni Accorsi	368^Sqd
14/4/41:	Ten Carlo Cugnasca	351^Sqd
	M.llo Angelo Marinelli	351^Sqd
22/4/41:	Serg Enzo Falcinelli	358^Sqd

APPENDIX VII

FIGHTER CLAIMS &
FIGHTER PILOT ROLL OF HONOUR

FLIEGERFÜHRER AFRIKA

January – June 1941

Claims

19/2/41:	Lt Alfred Wehmeyer	8/ZG26	Hurricane
	Uffz Max Hohmann	8/ZG26	Hurricane
	Fw Richard Heller	8/ZG26	Hurricane
	Oblt Prang	8/ZG26	Hurricane
31/3/41:	Hptm Thomas Steinberger	9/ZG26	Hurricane
3/4/41:	Hptm Georg Christl	7/ZG26	Hurricane
	Obfw Franz Sander	7/ZG26	Hurricane
5/4/41:	Staffel victory	7/ZG26	Blenheim
8/4/41:	Uffz Schwerzel	7/ZG26	Blenheim
9/4/41:	Hptm Georg Christl	7/ZG26	Hurricane
10/4/41:	Lt Alfred Wehmeyer	8/ZG26	Hurricane
14/4/41:	Lt Karl-Heinz Bittner	7/ZG26	Hurricane
	Fw Werner Reiner	7/ZG26	Hurricane
18/4/41:	Lt Glanz	7/ZG26	Blenheim
19/4/41:	Oblt Karl-Wolfgang Redlich	1/JG27	2 Hurricanes
	Lt Werner Schroer	1/JG27	Hurricane probable
	Uffz Hans Sippel	1/JG27	Hurricane
20/4/41:	Uffz Hans Sippel	1/JG27	Wellington
21/4/41:	Obfw Albert Espenlaub	1/JG27	Hurricane probable
23/4/41:	Oblt Ludwig Franzisket	St/JG27	2 Hurricanes
	Lt Eugen von Moller	1/JG27	Hurricane, plus Hurricane on ground
	Obfhr Hans-Joachim Marseille	3/JG27	Hurricane probable
	Oblt Karl-Wolfgang Redlich	1/JG27	Blenheim
28/4/41:	Obfhr Hans-Joachim Marseille	3/JG27	Blenheim
30/4/41:	Oblt Karl-Wolfgang Redlich	1/JG27	Hurricane
1/5/41:	Oblt Gerhard Homuth	3/JG27	2 Hurricanes
	Obfhr Hans-Joachim Marseille	3/JG27	Hurricane, Hurricane probable

5/5/41:	Oblt Gerhard Homuth	3/JG27	Maryland
8/5/41:	Oblt Gerhard Homuth	3/JG27	Blenheim probable
15/5/41:	Oblt Gerhard Homuth	3/JG27	Hurricane
16/5/41:	Fw Franz Elles	2/JG27	Hurricane
	Oblt Karl-Wolfgang Redlich	1/JG27	Blenheim
18/5/41:	Obfw Franz Sander	7/ZG26	Blenheim
21/5/41:	Oblt Gerhard Homuth	3/JG27	2 Blenheims
	Obfw Herbert Kowalski	3/JG27	2 Blenheims
	Lt Heinz Schmidt	3/JG27	Blenheim
26/5/41:	Oblt Ernst Maack	2/JG27	Lysander
3/6/41:	Fw Franz Elles	2/JG27	Hurricane
9/6/41:	Oblt Karl-Wolfgang Redlich	1/JG27	Hurricane
	Uffz Günther Steinhausen	1/JG27	Hurricane
14/6/41:	Oblt Ludwig Franzisket	3/JG27	Hurricane, Maryland
	Lt Friedrich Hoffmann	3/JG27	Maryland
	Oblt Karl-Wolfgang Redlich	1/JG27	Hurricane
	Oblt Hugo Schneider	1/JG27	Hurricane
	Uffz Karl-Heinz Ehlen	7/JG26	Hurricane
15/6/41:	Uffz Rudolf Stöckler	2/JG27	Hurricane
	Fw Franz Elles	2/JG27	Hurricane
	Oblt Karl-Wolfgang Redlich	1/JG27	2 Hurricanes
	Obfhr Hans-Arnold Stahlschmidt	2/JG27	Hurricane
	Lt Friedrich Hoffmann	3/JG27	Maryland, Hurricane
	Lt Willi Kothmann	2/JG27	Hurricane
	Oblt Ludwig Franzisket	3/JG27	Hurricane
	Hptm Eduard Neumann	St/JG27	Hurricane probable
16/6/41:	Lt Friedrich Hoffmann	3/JG27	2 Hurricane probables
	Fw Franz Elles	2/JG27	Hurricane
17/6/41:	Lt Heinz Schmidt	3/JG27	4 Hurricanes
	Obfhr Hans-Joachim Marseille	3/JG27	Hurricane, Hurricane probable
	Fw Karl Mentnich	3/JG27	Hurricane
	Obfw Hermann Förster	2/JG27	Brewster [Buffalo]
	Lt Klaus Mietusch	7/JG26	Hurricane
	Uffz Melchior Kestler	7/JG26	Hurricane probable
	Maj Karl Kaschka	StabIII/ZG26	Hurricane
	Oblt Fritz Schulze-Dickow	8/ZG26	Hurricane
18/6/41:	Lt Hans Remmer	1/JG27	Brewster [Tomahawk]
	Oblt Karl-Wolfgang Redlich	1/JG27	Brewster [Tomahawk]
	Uffz Günther Steinhausen	1/JG27	Brewster [Tomahawk]

Fighter Pilot/Air Gunner Roll of Honour

16/2/41:	Lt Hesterkamp Ogfr Bracht (AG)	7/ZG26	Bf110E WkNr3896 3U+FS
31/3/41:	Obfw Josef Bracun Uffz Werner Kasper (AG)	9/ZG26	Bf110E WkNr3948 3U+PR
9/4/41:	Fw Helmut Jaculi	7/ZG26	Bf110E WkNr 3U+

Lt Heinrich Schultz	7/ZG26	Bf110E WkNr3874 3U+OR
Gfr Pia (AG)		
21/4/41: Uffz Hans Sippel	1/JG27	Bf109E WkNr3777
22/4/41: Obfhr Heinrich Pompsch	1/JG27	Bf109E WkNr4112
23/4/41: Fw Werner Lange	1/JG27	Bf109E WkNr4163
26/4/41: Lt Oskar Lempke	8/ZG26	Bf110E WkNr3870 3U+
Uffz Rudi Petters (AG)		
15/6/41: Uffz Rudolf Stöckler	2/JG27	Bf109E WkNr4123
Uffz Heinz Greuel	2/JG27	Bf109E WkNr2943

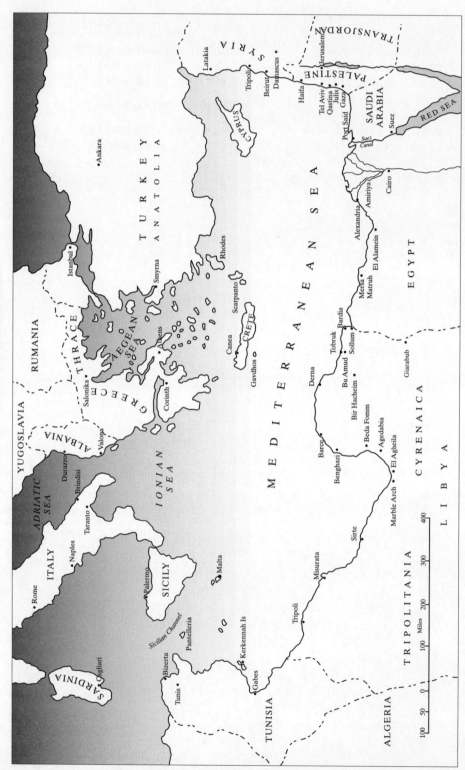

THE EASTERN MEDITERRANEAN

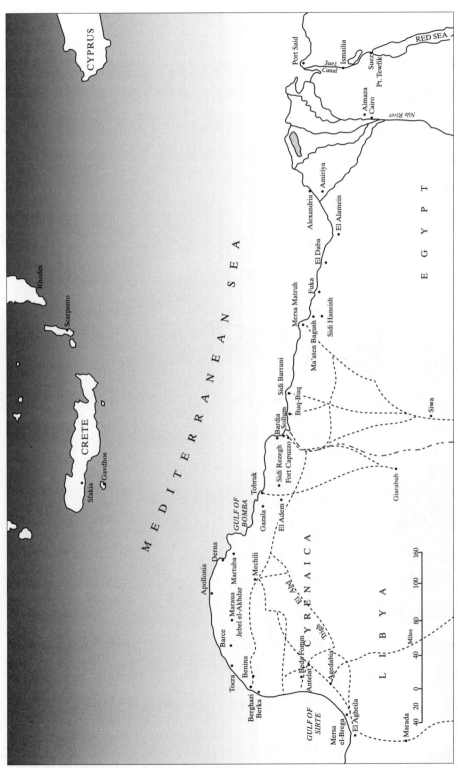

THE WESTERN DESERT

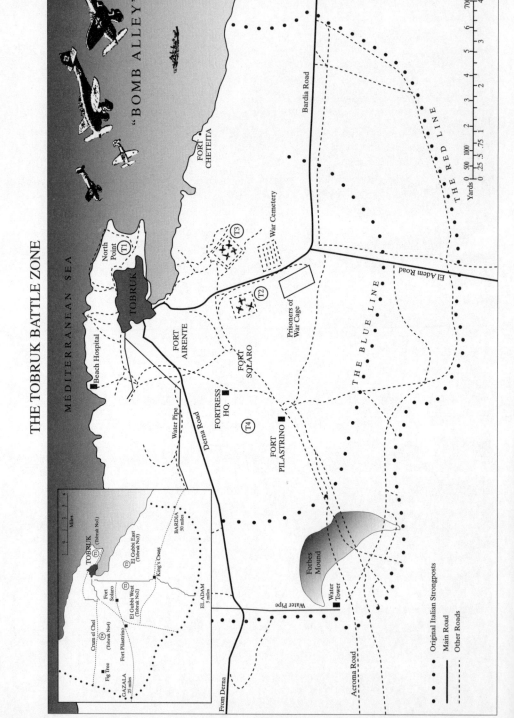

THE TOBRUK BATTLE ZONE

SELECT BIBLIOGRAPHY

Primary Sources: PRO Air 27 series (RAF squadron records), Air 26/362 (258 Wing ORB), Air 20/2096 (War Diary Middle East) plus correspondence/logbooks/diaries, and interviews with veterans.

Published material:
Air War for Yugoslavia, Greece and Crete 1940-41: Christopher Shores and Brian Cull with Nicola Malizia
Eagle's Wings: Hajo Herrmann
Eagles Strike: J.A. Brown
Fighters over the Desert: Christopher Shores and Hans Ring
Fortress on Sand: Eric Rosenthal
Fortress Tobruk: Jan Yindrich
From Sea to Sky: Air Chief Marshal Sir Arthur Longmore GCB DSO
Haul, Taut and Belay: Vice-Admiral Sir Donald Gibson KCB DSC JP
Hurricane at War 2: Norman Franks
Impact: Peter C. Smith
Imshi: Alys Myers
Malta: The Hurricane Years 1940-41: Christopher Shores and Brian Cull with Nicola Malizia
Mediterranean Front: Alan Moorehead
Rommel: In His Own Words: (Ed) Dr John Pimlott
Shoulder the Sky: Gil Thomas
Six Squadron: Peter Moulding
The Call to Honour 1940-42: Général Charles de Gaulle
The History of 73 Squadron, Part 2: Don Minterne
The Luftwaffe War Diaries: Cajus Bekker
The Mediterranean and Middle East, Volume II: Maj General I.S.O. Playfair CB DSO MC
The Pirate of Tobruk: Alfred Palmer with Mary E. Curtis
The Rats of Tobruk: John Devine
The Rats Remain: John Cumpston
The Second World War, Volume III: The Grand Alliance: Winston S. Churchill
The Trail of the Fox: David Irving
They Flew Through Sand: Sqn Ldr G.W. Houghton
Tobruk: The Story of a Siege: Anthony Heckstall-Smith
Tobruk 1941: Chester Wilmot
Top Hats in Tobruk: Kenneth Rankin
With Prejudice: Lord Tedder
3 Squadron at War: Wg Cdr John Watson and Louis Jones

Other sources: the excellent *Icare* series, in particular Nos 128 and 136; *Air-Britain* RAF Aircraft Serial Registers; various issues of *RAF Flying Review*; plus an Italian article by Cesare Gori entitled *Tullio De Prato, un pilota contadino*.

PERSONNEL INDEX

Höckner, Oblt Walter 6/JG77 160
Hoffmann, Lt Friedrich 3/JG27 180-182, 212
Hohmann, Uffz Max 8/ZG26 67, 139, 211
Homuth, Oblt Gerhard 3/JG27 140, 142, 147, 150, 174, 211, 212
Hovel, Uffz Heinz I/KG2 163
Hozzel, Hptm Paul-Werner I/StG1 39
Hummel, Lt Erich 4/StG2 116

Ihlefeld, Hptm Herbert I(J)/LG2 160

Jaculi, Fw Helmut 7/ZG26 103, 212

Kaschka, Maj Karl StabIII/ZG26 39, 147, 174, 184, 212
Kasper, Uffz Werner 9/ZG26 85, 212
Kaupisch, Lt II/KG26 38, 39
Keil, Hptm Anton II/StG1 147
Kestler, Uffz Melchoir 7/JG26 183, 212
Kirchheim, GenMaj Heinrich OC 5th Light Div 108
Kleselhorst, Fw Heinrich 4/StG2 93
Klinkhardt, Uffz Alfred 9/KG30 124
Köhler, Fw Otto 4/JG77 159
Köhne, Gfr Hermann I/JG27 142
Kothmann, Lt Willi 2/JG27 180, 212
Kowaleski, Hptm Robert II/KG26 38
Kowalski, Obfw Herbert 3/JG27 212
Kraft, Uffz Kurt 8/KG30 124
Kratz, Lt Dr Fritz 7/LG1 72
Kroll, Uffz Heinrich 4/StG2 116

Lange, Fw Werner 1/JG27 133, 134, 213
Lauberger, Lt Franz II/StG2 183
Lempke, Lt Oskar 8/ZG26 139, 213
Loos, Obgfr Kurt 6/StG2 92

Maack, Oblt Ernst 2/JG27 212
Mantsch, Uffz Thomas II/StG2 183
Marseille, Obfhr Hans-Joachim 3/JG27 133-135, 140, 142, 153, 184, 211, 212
Marschhausen, FjGfr Günther 5/JG77 159
Martinez, Lt Hans StabIII/StG1 116
Matthes, Oblt Wilhelm 7/ZG26 39
Mentnich, Fw Karl 3/JG27 184, 212
Mietusch, Lt Klaus 7/JG26 183, 212
Milch, Feldmarschall Erhard Inspector-General Luftwaffe 165, 166
Morgenstern, Fw Erich I/StG1 66
Müller, Uffz Peter 7/LG1 72
Münch, Oblt Karl 2(H)/14 180
Müncheberg, Oblt Joachim 7/JG26 174, 179

Nentwig, Uff Walter 5/StG2 67
Neumann, Hptm Alfred 8/KG30 124
Neumann, Hptm Eduard I/JG27 80, 126, 147, 174, 180, 212
Nowack, Gfr Rudolf 1(F)/121 56

Olbrich, Oberst OC 5th Panzer Regt 102
Orlowski, Gfr Heinz 6/StG2 92
Ott, Uffz Peter 5/StG2 89

Pech, Fw Rudolf 8/KG30 124
Peters, Obfw Hermann 1(F)/121 37
Petters, Uffz Rudi 8/ZG26 139, 213
Pfeil, Uffz Gerhart 8/LG1 130
Pia, Gfr 7/ZG26 213
Pohl, Uffz Helmet StabIII/StG1 116
Pompsch, Obfhr Heinrich 2/JG27 129, 130, 213
Popp, Uffz Eugen 8/KG30 124
Prang, Oblt 8/ZG26 39, 67, 211

Rauer, Ogfr Walter 4/StG2 94
Rass, Fw Heinrich 4/StG2 116
Redlich, Oblt Karl-Wolfgang 1/JG27 123, 142, 147, 173, 174, 178, 186, 211, 212
Reichstein, Uffz 2/JG27 172
Reiner, Fw Werner 7/ZG26 118, 211
Reinicke, Obfw Werner 2(F)/123 97
Remmer, Lt Hans 1/JG27 212
Riedinger, Oblt Peter 6/StG2 92
Rink, Fw Erwin 7/LG1 65

Rommel, General Erwin GOC Deutsches Afrika Korps 60, 63, 70, 71, 79, 81, 83, 86, 94, 98, 99, 101, 112, 122, 126, 142, 150, 151, 167, 170, 171, 187, 189-192

Sander, Obfw Franz 7/ZG26 89, 211, 212
Schädlich, Fw Herbert 2(H)/14 180
Schafer, Uffz Wolfgang I/StG1 65
Schauer, Uffz Karl 7/LG1 65
Schmidt, Uffz Heinz 3/JG27 183, 184, 212
Schmidt, Uffz Rudolf 5/JG77 159
Schneider, Oblt Hugo 1/JG27 178, 180, 212
Schneider, Fw III/KGrzbV.1 105
Schneuder, Uffz Heinz KGrzbV.9 58
Scholten, Uffz Georg 2(H)/14 170
Schorm, Lt Joachim 5th Panzer Regt 115, 122, 125, 129, 145
Schröder, Lt Erich I/JG27 159
Schroer, Lt Werner 1/JG27 123, 124, 128, 129, 211
Schultz, Lt Heinrich 7/ZG26 213
Schulze-Dickow, Oblt Fritz 8/ZG26 147, 174, 184, 212
Schwarz-Tramper, Oblt Franz 4(F)/121 164
Schwerzel, Uffz 7/ZG26 211
Seigner, Obfw Otto III/LG1 68
Sippel, Uffz Hans 1/JG27 125, 128, 129, 211, 213
Sonntag, Oblt Hans 4/StG2 93
Stahlschmidt, Obfhr Hans-Arnold 2/JG27 180, 212
Steinberger, Hptm Thomas 9/ZG26 83, 85, 211
Steinhausen, Uffz Günther 1/JG27 173, 212
Steinmann, Uffz Karl 3/StG1 182
Sterzel, Uffz Wolfgang 8/KG30 124
Steuber, Uffz Kurt 5/StG2 67
Stirnweiss, Uffz Georg 7/ZG26 89
Stöckler, Uffz Rudolf 2/JG27 179, 180, 212, 213
Straeten, Uffz Heinz 2(H)/14 104
Stulken, Fw Günther 4/StG2 94

Tiede, Uffz Walter 7/LG1 65

Unger, Fw Otto 2(H)/14 178

von Moller, Lt Eugen 1/JG27 133, 211

Wala, Uffz Johann 7/ZG26 103
Wanek, Uffz Wenzel 8/KG30 124
Weber, Uffz Fritz 4/StG2 116
Wehmeyer, Lt Alfred 8/ZG26 67, 108, 211
Weith, Oblt Kurt 2(H)/14 104
Wilke, Gfr Heinz 6/StG2 92
Wünsche, Uffz 8/ZG26 139
Wust, Ogfr Wilhelm 8/ZG26 67

MILITARY UNITS & OPERATIONS

BRITISH & COMMONWEALTH
Air
202 Group 9-11, 14, 15, 17, 25, 36, 40, 42, 47, 60, 63
204 Group 99, 117, 154, 156, 160-162, 166, 169, 174, 182, 183, 186, 188, 202
253 (F) Wing 190
258 (F) Wing 29, 40, 42, 45, 63, 75, 136, 140, 190, 202
262 (F) Wing 190
269 (F) Wing 190
70 OTU 17, 22, 36, 106, 152, 169, 194
103 MU 39
6 Squadron 17, 39, 53, 60, 73, 75, 77, 78, 83, 86, 90, 94-97, 99, 100, 105, 121, 125, 131, 137, 139, 143-146, 149-151, 154, 170, 174, 178-180, 205, 207, 208
14 Squadron 152
30 Squadron 190
33 Squadron 9, 11-14, 16, 17, 23-30, 34, 36, 55, 154, 174, 179, 181, 183, 184, 202, 207, 208
39 Squadron 139
45 Squadron 60, 140, 151
73 Squadron 17, Chapter I-Chapter VIII, 195, 196, 202-208
80 Squadron 9, 12, 14, 17, 36, 190
94 Squadron 190
112 Squadron 9, 14, 16, 17, 36, 170, 190
113 Squadron 40
208 Squadron 9, 17, 29, 31, 40, 43, 47, 51, 59, 60, 64, 73, 83, 150, 190, 203, 207
213 Squadron 154, 159, 169, 170, 174, 178, 206